FRENCH SOCIETY IN THE
EIGHTEENTH CENTURY

FRENCH SOCIETY
IN THE
EIGHTEENTH CENTURY

BY

LOUIS DUCROS

DOYEN HONORAIRE DE LA FACULTÉ DES LETTRES D'AIX

Translated from the French by W. DE GEIJER.
With a Foreword by J. A. HIGGS-WALKER, M.A.

Illustrated

WAYNE, NEBR.
STATE TEACHERS COLLEGE
LIBRARY

G. P. PUTNAM'S SONS
NEW YORK—LONDON
1927

Copyright, 1927
by
G. P. Putnam's Sons

NOTE

La Société Française au Dix-huitième Siècle, of which this work is a translation, is published by A. Hatier, 8 Rue d'Assas, Paris.

Made in the United States of America

AUTHOR'S PREFACE

"It is perhaps rather absurd that, while we are so well acquainted with French Society in the Middle Ages, with that of Rome, and even with Society in Ancient Egypt, we should be so ignorant of Seventeenth-Century Society in France."[1] This absurdity becomes still more striking when we remember that we are equally ignorant of French Eighteenth-Century Society which, in so many respects, carried on and developed the main features of that which had preceded it.

This curious gap in our knowledge is due to many causes, and it is obviously impossible that I should even venture to fill it. Still I shall endeavour, in this little work, to provide students and all lovers of France with some definite knowledge as to the manner in which our ancestors lived. With this end in view, then, rather than with any intention of writing an elaborate dissertation, I have gathered from contemporary authors such details and instructive passages as bear on the customs of the age, and have strung them together with some brief comments of my own.

But the extracts which I have chosen are not intended either to extol those who figure in these pages, nor yet to hide their shortcomings or their misfortunes. These people were French, but they were also human; for, unlike the Germans, the French are not a nation of supermen, nor does our patriotism take the same form as theirs. It is

---

[1] Lavisse, *Histoire de France*, vol. vii. Part II. p. 323.

rather our curious and even annoying habit to lower ourselves in the eyes of others than to boast before all the world. In this book I have tried to show the Eighteenth Century as it really was.

Again, this slight contribution to history is not an apology for the age of Louis xv., nor is it a book of scandal. Many people regard this century merely as a chronicle of the immorality of the Regency, of suppers and the cafés, and of doubtful anecdotes. But this was only one side, and, in my humble opinion, one of the least interesting; and I have, therefore, not written a History of the Regency, and have purposely omitted the lampoons of Maurepas and his tribe.

Under Louis xv. people differed widely as regards their manner of life and their way of thinking, according as to whether they lived at Versailles, in Paris, or in the Provinces, and we must therefore visit, as indeed we shall do, each of these three " environments." We shall not confine ourselves, as is so often the case, to the courtiers and the world of fashion, but we shall, as far as possible, endeavour to give a picture of French Society as a whole.

In dealing with the Court, I have chosen authors who actually lived there: the Duc de Luynes, the Count de Cheverny, the Duc de Croÿ, and various others; while, in describing Paris, I have had recourse to Parisians who were keen observers, and who, in many cases, expressed themselves vividly—such as Buvat, Marais, Barbier, Mercier, Voltaire, Mme du Deffand, etc. But where the Provinces are concerned, I have found greater difficulty, for contemporary authors did not trouble about them, and I have had to augment their scanty details with extracts from such documents as have been found in archives and published by authors of monographs. As regards the clergy of all degrees I have chiefly consulted ecclesiastical authors, and military men and writers on military subjects have helped me in the chapter on the Army.

Perhaps I ought to apologise for quoting Montesquieu, Chamfort, and others who have left no *Mémoires*, but I have only borrowed from them where they seem to confirm or illustrate what I have already extracted from my usual sources, the contemporary writers of my period. I need not say that I have deliberately omitted all that essentially belongs to the spheres of politics, religion, and literature.

In the Preface to his *Chronique du temps de Charles IX.*, Merimée notes that, "only such *mémoires* as take the form of familiar conversation between author and reader give us a picture of 'Man' at the various stages in history," and he adds, "if we wish to acquire some idea of sixteenth-century Frenchmen we must not go to Mézerai, but to Montluc, Brantôme, and d'Aubigné." May the authors of *Mémoires* whom I have quoted in this work give my readers as interesting and as accurate a portrait of the eighteenth-century Frenchman.

So as not to burden these pages with too many references I have, as a rule, merely given the author's name and the page from which I have quoted, and have relegated the full titles of the works and their dates to a List of Authors, where more detailed information may be found.

L. D.

FOREWORD

EVERY institution bears the seeds of its own decay. Gibbon, writing of the decline and fall of a great empire fourteen hundred years away from him, was quite blind to the decline and imminent fall of the greatest monarchy of his day. It is certain that he never foresaw the French Revolution, and indeed he praised the social and political institutions of his age as the best that civilisation had yet produced. Yet within a few years most of these institutions had collapsed into ruin. Their collapse was sudden and complete enough to surprise and startle the best intelligences of that day. Louis XVI. was not alone in mistaking a revolution for a riot. This fact is, perhaps, the more remarkable in that, as M. Ducros points out, educated France was keenly self-critical in the years preceding the Revolution. But its introspection was merely an intellectual game. It enjoyed hearing and preaching in its salons social and political sermons which it had no intention of putting into practice. It did not understand how rotten, politically and socially, the fabric of French society was. But M. Ducros' book leaves us no room for any such misunderstanding.

The seventeenth century is known as "the century of Louis XIV." And it is well named so, for Louis XIV. was France at a time when France swayed the destinies of Europe. The work begun by Cardinals Richelieu and Mazarin, the makers of the French monarchy, seemed, by the end of the seventeenth century, to be complete and unshakable. In France the power of the monarchy was, in fact as well as in name, absolute: in Europe it threatened to extend its sway over what had once been the empire of Spain. William of Orange hindered, but did not stop, the French flow through Flanders and Burgundy toward the Rhine. Marlborough, indeed, won at Blenheim, but the Bourbon remained at Madrid. When Louis XIV. was dying in 1715 he might still have muttered " L'État c'est moi " and " Les Pyrenées n'existent plus."

In importance, though not in time, the French Revolution is the central fact of the eighteenth century. Up till 1789 everything in European history moves towards it ; and for the last eleven years of the century everything radiates from it. Socially and politically, the Revolution is as pregnant as the Reformation—and it is far more dramatic. As past history (and, one may say, as "present politics"), as drama, and even as fiction, the French Revolution holds the interest of English people little less to-day than it did when it flung its refugees exhausted on our shores, and threatened to fling its red-capped legions after them.

Some modern writers, repeating and paraphrasing opinions which had a certain popularity in the heated atmosphere of revolutionary Europe, have tried to show that the great upheaval of 1789 and the succeeding years was produced by the operations of malicious foreigners smuggling into France Prussian propaganda, international anarchism, or even English gold. Such a thesis is as foolishly superficial as would be an attempt to prove that a volcanic eruption could be produced by doctoring an inoffensive mountain with chemicals. The interaction of certain long-established geological formations produces a volcanic eruption; and the interaction of certain long-established sociological formations produced the eruption of 1789 in France. These French social strata are laid bare for us by M. Ducros, as the strata of an extinct volcano can be laid bare by the hammer of a skilled geologist.

The eighteenth century might be called "the century of Louis xv." That inept monarch might, with quite as much truth as Napoleon, have said, "I am the Revolution"; for while without Napoleon the Revolution might not have been completed, without Louis xv. it might never have been begun. Thus, if we speak of the "century of the Revolution" we shall do no historical injustice to Louis xv.

It may be that, as some think, a king more able would have averted the Revolution in France—by forestalling it. For the Revolution was anti-aristocratic rather than anti-monarchic in origin. But such a king, confronted with a task far more difficult than Napoleon's, would have had to initiate and enforce a programme of reform which socially, politically, and economically would have been tantamount to a revolution; for, to succeed at all, it would have had to change the structure of French society from top to bottom. No reader of M. Ducros' book can doubt this. For the author shows us a complex organism which was moribund for more than half a century before the Revolution broke out; he describes a complicated machine which had run down and was too worn out to be started-up again. When we read his account of eighteenth-century French life in all grades of society, we realise how inadequate must be most attempts to tabulate simply the causes of that Revolution which overthrew *l'Ancien Régime*.

In theory, it was the King who controlled the machinery of French political and social life and supplied its driving power. Indeed, such a king was demanded by facts as well as by theories. Richelieu and Mazarin had destroyed the castles of a turbulent nobility that even Henry of Navarre had failed to tame: the cardinals turned the would-be king-makers into courtiers; and by the time Louis XIV. took up the reins of government into his own hands in 1660, the administrative duties of the nobles had passed into the hands of a bureaucracy of "Intendants" appointed by, and responsible to, the central government. The activities of these Intendants were directed by the King himself in consultation with his Council of State. The individual power of these Intendants, the good work done by many of them in their provinces, and the hatred felt for them by the haughty *noblesse*, which nevertheless dared not defy them, is well illustrated in this book. It was said by Cardinal Fleury, the easy-going ruler of France in the last years of Louis XV.'s minority, that France was governed by thirty Intendants. Unfortunately for France, however, it soon appeared that there was no one to govern the Intendants.

It has been asserted that the Revolution came about because in eighteenth-century France there was a monarchy, but no monarch. The character of Louis XV., as revealed in this book, supports this theory. The callous viciousness of his private life might be ignored by the historian if the extravagant futility of his public career did not emphasise it. The Council of State was the driving-wheel of the machine that had done the work of Louis XIV. But his decadent great-grandson took so little interest in its operations that he was always ready to save himself the trouble of thought and decision by signing quite contradictory orders concerning matters of the most serious national importance. We learn too that La Pompadour might almost have said that she was the State; for she virtually appointed its generals, and, as in the case of the inglorious Soubise of Rosbach infamy, maintained them in the face of well-informed criticism until they had achieved some startling catastrophe.

Nor could any minister, however patriotic, hope to succeed in any policy, however wisely designed, in the face of the Pompadour's hostility. Indeed, no minister of Louis the Well-Beloved could consider his tenure of office secure for twenty-four hours ahead: his master (as a well-chosen story in this book shows us) was quite likely to invite him to dinner at night, only to dismiss him into exile by a curt note in the morning.

The first and main assault of the Revolution was to be directed not against the monarchy but against "privilege." We meet first those "privileged" persons who surrounded the King himself—the most important of "the nobility of the sword." But we find that, by the eighteenth century, they had beaten their swords into shoe-horns and button-hooks: the great nobles, who had once honestly earned their privileges by doing their feudal duty as local governors or leaders in war, now competed for royal favour in the performance of intimate domestic services which were menial or trivial: the bearers of names that had once sounded like a trumpet-call in battle now justified their existence, their estates, and their honours by warming the royal nightshirt or removing the royal boots. Yet this privileged class was still exempt from all the more burdensome taxes, and for it, exclusively, were reserved the attractive posts in Church and Army alike, those profitable abbeys and regiments that went respectively to abbots who had but recently been trousered, and to colonels who were still in bibs. "Privileged" also in their exemptions and monopolies of office were those more recently ennobled members of the magistracies or councils, those promoted lawyers of *bourgeois* origin and terrific professional pride from among whom were largely recruited the members of those pugnacious **Parlements** which so infuriated the King and the old nobility. Here, half a century before the

Revolution, it is possible to detect both that obstinate spirit which was to inspire the last of the *Parlements* in its refusal to tax the exempt, and also the envy that was to induce so many middle-class advocates and attorneys to join the ranks against privilege.

For, if one fact stands out more emphatically than another in these pages, it is the growing importance of the middle class. "The eighteenth century is," says M. Ducros, "the century of the middle class." This is true; but no one who was born, or had risen, above that class was willing to recognise the fact: hence that bitterness which eventually was to create the middle-class Republican represented by such diverse types as Maximilien Robespierre and Madame Roland. And as the middle class grew in wealth (so that even the nobility of the sword deigned to go to it for rich husbands and wives), it suffered more and more from a fiscal system under which it bore the bulk of the burden of taxation, and from a financial disorder which threatened to engulf its investments and its loans. For it is indubitably true, however strange it may appear, that the beginnings of the French Revolution were initiated and directed not by the proverbial "have-nots" but by the "haves"—all those who were sick of a state of affairs in which there was neither security for their possessions nor outlet for their financial ability. "The Revolution was brought about by vanity," cynically said Napoleon; in the case of the middle class, it was a vanity for which their hard-won wealth provided some excuse, mixed with an envy of those privileged persons who simultaneously spurned and exploited them. The middle class made the *Tiers État* what it was said to be in the first year of the Revolution—"Everything."

"This bankruptcy," said Mirabeau, "will be the salvation of France." But the bankruptcy to which he referred may be seen almost naked and unashamed in the earlier years of the century. If the nobles, deserting their châteaux for an existence as insanitary and uncomfortable as it was useless, at far-famed Versailles, had spent their substance in riotous living, so had the Government: no one who reads M. Ducros' description of the Farmers-General—the pick of the new plutocracy of the period—can feel any hesitation in applying to eighteenth-century France the words which the dying John of Gaunt applied to fourteenth-century England: "This land . . . is now leased out . . . like to a tenement or pelting farm." Nor could Louis xv. have claimed to be more than landlord of France—not King.

Financial stability rested then, in a sense, with the peasantry of France, as it does now; for the peasantry, in some manner that still seems almost miraculous, managed to save, and steadily invested their savings in land. The fiction that the peasantry of France were revolutionary in any but that purely local sense which led them to rise against all that caused them personal inconvenience in their own district, has long been exploded. What we read in this book of conditions among them throughout the country is wisely qualified by the author's warning to us to remember that these conditions varied between the provinces, and even between one village and another; and that everywhere the peasant very sensibly tried to appear as penurious as possible to deceive fiscal assessors whose calculations were mainly based upon outward appearances. But here and there we get an intimate picture of the working-out and satisfaction of that landhunger which drove the peasant to acquire more and more land right up till 1789—and together with the satisfaction of this hunger, the creation of a still more urgent one, that desire to hold his land free from all

b

vexatious feudal exactions, which the Revolution was to satisfy and on which Napoleon was to rest his power.

But though it may be true that the peasantry of some parts were, even if secretly, prospering in the eighteenth century, yet each of the many periods of famine in that century drove a fresh army of starving unemployed into the towns to howl for bread, and to form the early beginnings of those revolutionary mobs which eventually were almost to master their middle-class revolutionary leaders. In 1749 there were thirty thousand beggars in Paris, and many of them showed some of that sadistic taste for cruelty and blood which led to such appalling scenes in the Revolution—we hear of men, women, and children rushing to see a highwayman hanged. Another premonitory shadow of one of the most sensational of coming events is seen in a custom that grew throughout the century among the fishwives of Paris—the habit these herring-sellers (or *harengères*) contracted of airing their grievances at Versailles in "harangues" delivered to the Queen herself. Thus there was no novelty in that dramatic procession of 5th October 1789—the novelty was in its horrible ending.

To the English reader, perhaps because his own country is so much smaller, one of the most remarkable features of French life is the gulf which exists between the Parisian and the provincial Frenchman. This gulf was apparently much wider in the eighteenth century than it is to-day. Certainly Paris occupied a position with regard to the rest of France which London has never occupied with regard to the rest of England. Indeed, Paris was to play a much more important part in the French Revolution than London played in the English Civil War. The driving force on the Parliament side in England was a man—Cromwell; but the driving force

FOREWORD

(which was itself never controlled till Napoleon appeared) in the French Revolution was Paris itself; for the capital imposed its will on the less resolute provincial towns, and hurled defiance at the whole might of counter-revolutionary Europe. This is a fact to be remembered by any reader who may be tempted to think that M. Ducros has given Paris too much prominence in this book. And such scornful remarks as that of the character in Gresset's *Le Méchant*, who said that "one lives only in Paris; elsewhere one vegetates," must have gone a long way to build up that provincial attitude of embittered suspicion towards the capital upon which the counter-revolutionary party were to base most of their plans. The dominance of Paris over the rest of France was not to pass away until railway and telegraph had made possible that combination of the Provinces which humbled the pride of the capital in 1871.

The picture drawn by M. Ducros of French provincial life in the eighteenth century is in some things reminiscent of that depicted by Addison in his *Tory Foxhunter*. There is the same invasion of the countryside by new, and therefore suspect, commercial interests in France as in England. There is the same bucolic zest in field-sports, though no Englishman suffered under the much-abused Game Laws a tithe of what thousands of Frenchman suffered under the laws of the *Capitaineries* or royal hunting districts. There are the same out-of-date views based largely upon out-of-date news; there is the same sense of isolation from intellectual interests that Addison deplored in remote English country districts; and there is the resultant narrowness of opinion and servility to local convention which must, for young or original minds, have so much increased that temptation to go to Paris which seems to have been the undoing of so many families. The few French nobles who remained, either from pride, penury, or a love of country life which enabled them to resist the lures of the Court, provide us with pictures of Gallic Coverleys, Westerns, or Allworthys—a varied squirearchy from which a French Addison or Fielding might have been glad to draw his characters. We have the splendid and sincere generosity and goodness of a Norman Harcourt or of the Breton noble described in the *Mémoires* of Rochejaquelin, who treated the peasants living round his castle "like a father, visiting them in their farms, talking with them about their daily life and their cattle, and sharing their accidents and misfortunes, which necessarily affected him also." But we also have Ysoré, Lord of Pleumartin and La Rocheposey, the noble ruffian who in his own smithy nailed horseshoes to a peasant's feet. Harcourt and his like help to explain the loyalty of whole districts to the lords they loved, and through them to the King they never saw; Ysoré helps to excuse the brutalities of the *Jacquerie* of the late summer of 1789.

An introduction to one book should not, even by implication, serve also as an introduction to another. But one cannot but hope that the reader of this book will go on to read the late J. E. Bodley's *France*, for the latter contains descriptions of nineteenth-century provincial life which form a natural sequel to the account given by M. Ducros: both writers, for example, emphasise that curiously primitive petty noble, the *hobereau*, who, if he existed in eighteenth-century, had the grace to disappear in nineteenth-century England. Moreover, provincial town life in France apparently changed little between the time of which M. Ducros has written and that which Bodley described. The same cliques, jealousies, and swarms of municipal officials are rampant in both periods even the smouldering discord between the *bourgeoisie* and the aristocracy is still there—the difference being that while in the one case the aristocracy is only decaying, in the other it has nominally disappeared.

M. Ducros is as fair as the tenderest consciences could wish in his treatment of the eighteenth-century Church in France. He disguises neither the faults of the higher clergy nor the virtues of the lower—and when virtue is to be found in high places he gives it its due. But he leaves no doubt in the reader's mind that the higher clergy, resident or absentee, virtuous or not, idle or industrious, belong necessarily to "privilege" and all that the Revolution has to destroy; and after reading of them one is prepared for the fact that, when the Revolution comes, twelve bishops only, but nearly all the lower clergy, will join the Third Estate in forming a National Assembly. One is prepared by this book for that devotion of the peasantry to their parish priests against which the fierce but short-lived anti-clericalism of the Revolution beat in vain, and which (as Vandal graphically showed in his *Avènement de Bonaparte*) Napoleon had to recognise as early as 1800—that love of the old religion which gave the Counter-Revolution in Brittany something of the character of a Crusade.

In the chapter devoted to the pre-revolution army, which one could have wished was longer than it is, the picture of inefficiency before the rout of Rosbach, and of demoralisation afterwards, is so arresting that one wonders where and how the steady improvement of the old French army (which begot the new one and made possible the victories of the Revolution) began. Between 1763, when the Seven Years War ended, and 1792, when France faced the rest of Europe at the beginning of a twenty-three years' fight, new methods and new men seem to have taken the places of Louis xv.'s travelling theatres and his "colonels in bibs." Some at least of these drastic reforms, to the success of which the skill of Bonaparte and a score of young officers trained in the old army bears witness, were due to the ill-treated but patriotic and energetic Choiseul. We are not told in this book of the steady growth of Freemasonry in France, which, though its influence in civilian life has been much exaggerated, undoubtedly played a large part in spreading egalitarian doctrines in the army, even making it possible for a private to take precedence of his colonel at a lodge meeting.

We learn from the chapters on " Public Opinion in the Eighteenth Century " that this nebulous but very real political and social force did exist, that it operated at times with marked effect, and that the Court certainly did not dare to leave it out of account. This "public opinion" in its higher form was manufactured in the *salons* of great ladies like Madame Geoffrin, just as in its lower forms it originated in the arguments of the fishwives.

The part played by these *salons* cannot be exaggerated. It is estimated that they provided a regular intellectual occupation for at least three thousand people, and an intellectual stimulus to ten times that number, and it is certainly safe to assume that many of those who frequented the *salons* retailed the opinions voiced there in less select circles. In this way the views of the *intelligentsia* were gradually spread and popularised till they became, though in garbled form perhaps, the views first of Paris, then of the rest of France. Thus it is that Voltaire and Rousseau eventually came to capture the heads and hearts respectively of thousands of Frenchmen: so that, in a sense, the *salons* helped to destroy that Eighteenth-Century French Society of which they were the finest flower.

J. A. HIGGS-WALKER.

CONTENTS

BOOK I.—VERSAILLES

CHAPTER I

THE COURT

                                                                                                      PAGE

The King—The Queen and the Royal Family—The Palace of Versailles and the King's daily Life: The Honours of the Court and the Honours of the Louvre—Presentation at Court—The *Entrées*—The King's *Lever*—The *Grand Couvert*—The *Petit* and *Grand Coucher*—The King's Hounds—Etiquette . . 1

CHAPTER II

THE NOBILITY OF THE SWORD

The Court Nobility—The King's Pensions and Bounty—The *Tabouret*—The *Cordon Bleu*—The Extravagance of the great Nobles: Food, Clothes, Gambling—Marriage among the Nobility—The Morals of the Nobility—The Frivolity, Ignorance, and Wit of the Courtiers—Their Bad Manners and Habits—The Men of Fashion: Richelieu—Good Men and True . . . 48

BOOK II.—PARIS

CHAPTER I

PARIS UNDER LOUIS XV.

How Paris came to absorb the Provinces—The Capital supplants the Court—The Traffic Problem in Paris—Paris at Night—The Post—The Latest Improvements in Paris—New Houses and Small Apartments—Meals—Amusements and Promenades—The New Boulevards—Paris the "Hub of Society" . 95

CHAPTER II

THE LAWYERS

The Nobility's Disdain of the Legal Profession—The Great, the Middle, and the Small Lawyers—The Pride of the Bar—Offices Bought and Sold, and Hereditary in Certain Families—Perquisites—Never-ending Lawsuits—Youthful Judges—The Barristers—Procurators and Registrars—The Clerks—At the Palais: The Great Hall—The Magistrate in Private Life—The Case of Monnerat—Mirabeau and the *Lettres de Cachet*—The Members of the Parliaments the Champions of the People . 122

CONTENTS

CHAPTER III

THE FINANCIERS

The Farmers-General — How they were Taxed and Plundered—Dislike of the Financiers as a Class—Their Power and Luxury—The Concerts at La Poplinière—The Theatre of La Chevrette—A Financier who was a Spendthrift: M. d'Epinay—How Mlle de Bellegarde became Mme d'Houdetot 152

CHAPTER IV

THE DOCTORS

Physicians now Men of Fashion and no longer the Pedants of Molière—The Quarrels of Two Physicians: Bordeu v. Boudart—Influenza the prevailing Scourge—Remedies: Bleeding: The Dislike of Inoculation—The Great Doctors of Paris . . 172

CHAPTER V

THE BOURGEOIS OF PARIS

What a *Bourgeois* was in the Eighteenth Century—His Character—How he spent his Sundays: at Versailles and at Meudon . 185

CHAPTER VI

THE POPULACE OF PARIS

How the Lower Classes Lived and Dressed: Provincials in Paris and their Different Trades—Popular Risings: "Give us Bread!"—The Faubourgs—La Courtille and Ramponeau—The Sellers of Elixirs and Strong Waters, and the *Regrats*—Beggars—The Sick of the Hôtel Dieu—The Sisters of Charity . . . 193

BOOK III.—THE PROVINCES

CHAPTER I

PROVINCIAL LIFE IN THE EIGHTEENTH CENTURY

The Governor: The Intendants: Activities of the Latter—How they protected Travellers on the High Roads: The Lyons Mail: They create a Network of Roads—They clean out the Towns: How Towns were lit in the Eighteenth Century—Provincial Society: The Magistrates—The *Bourgeoisie* at Home—Quarrels on Precedence—Disdain of Trade—Provincial Amusements: Travelling Players, Fairs, etc.: Processions: That of King René—Fashionable Society at Autun in the Eighteenth Century—Good Old Days in a Little Town of the Limousin—The Rise of the *Bourgeoisie* in the Eighteenth Century . . . 201

CONTENTS

CHAPTER II

THE HIGHER CLERGY

Rich and Poor Bishops—The Vocation of the Younger Son—Absentee Bishops—The Vicars-General—The Luxury of Prelates who were great Nobles: M. de Thémines—Abbots *in commendam:* The Chevalier de Boufflers—Worldly Obligations incumbent on Eighteenth-Century Bishops—Bishops as Administrators: M. de Narbonne—Building Bishops: M. de Dillon—Spendthrift Bishops: The Cardinal de Rohan and his Castle of Saverne—The Philosopher Bishops: The Cardinal de Brienne—The Heroic Devotion of Some Bishops: M. de la Ferronais, M. d'Apchon, M. Belsunce—"The Father of the Poor": Massillon—How a Good Bishop died: M. de Croissy . 226

CHAPTER III

THE COUNTRY GENTRY

The Gentry and the Intendants—The Castle of Combourg—The Meeting of the Estates of Brittany—The Manor—How the Provincial Nobles ruined themselves—Poverty and Vanity of the Hunting Squires—The *Hobereau's* Sad Plight—The Abuse of Hunting Rights and the *Capitaineries*—Bad Lords: The Devil of Coulonche, Ysoré—Good Lords: The Castle of Harcourt—The Gentlemen of Brittany and Poitou—A Great Lady's Charity 242

CHAPTER IV

THE VILLAGE

Condition of the French Peasant in the Eighteenth Century—The Taxes he paid: The Land Tax—The "Cocks" of The Village—The "Collectors"—The *Rats de Cave*—La Bruyère's "Wild Animals"—How the People of Auvergne wintered in their Stables—The *Gabelous* and the *Faux-saulniers*—Manorial Rights—Vintage Time in Champagne—The Parish Priest—The Schoolmaster—Insecurity in the Country: Rogues and Vagabonds—The Beast of the Gévaudan—The *Porteballes*—Character of the French Peasant in the Eighteenth Century—How he rose to be a Farmer—The Justices of the Village 265

CHAPTER V

THE ARMY

The Recruiting Officers—The Militia: Recruiting by Lot—Halts on the March and Winter Quarters—The Nobles of the Court and the Provincial Nobles and the Army—"Colonels in Bibs"—The Luxury of Officers on a Campaign—Retired Officers—The Knights of St. Louis—The Weakening of Discipline—The Disasters of Minden and Rosbach—The Feudal Reaction in the Army: the Ordinance of 1781—Bravery of the Officers—A Great Leader: the Count de Gisors—French Courage and Gaiety: Philipsburg and Fontenoy 291

CONTENTS

BOOK IV.—PUBLIC OPINION IN THE EIGHTEENTH CENTURY

CHAPTER I

PUBLIC OPINION: A NEW FORCE

The Birth of Public Opinion at the Beginning of the Eighteenth Century—Its growing Power—It chastises incompetent Generals and consoles Ministers dismissed by the King—Public Opinion exalts Authors who have been sent to the Bastille and whose Works have been Burned—The Expression of Public Opinion: "The Mistress of the Realm" at the Opera Ball—Popular Songs—Demonstrations at the Theatre—The *Harengères*—The Newsmongers—Famous Cafés of the Eighteenth Century 313

CHAPTER II

THE SALONS

The Part they played in Eighteenth-Century Society—The Great Minister of Society: Mme Geoffrin—Growing Prestige of Men of Letters—Intellectual Pleasures due to the Spirit of Equality now reigning in Social Relations—Why the Privileged Classes welcomed the Authors who attacked their Order . . 322

CHAPTER III

FRENCH MANNERS

The "Arbiter of Good Manners": Mme de Luxemburg—The Gifts necessary to an Eighteenth-Century Hostess—The Art of Bowing and Entering a Drawing-Room—The Art of Conversation—Topics of Conversation during the Century—Politeness and Gallantry of the French at this Time 331

LIST OF PRINCIPAL AUTHORS CITED . . . 343

INDEX 349

LIST OF ILLUSTRATIONS

PLATE		FACING PAGE

   I. LOUIS XV. 4
       From an engraving by Pierre Drevet, after Hyacinthe Rigaud.

  II. MARIE LECZINSKA 16
       From an engraving by Jacques Chevau, after Carle Van Loo.

* III. "LA GRANDE TOILETTE" 34
       From an engraving by Antoine Louis Romanet, after J. M. Moreau le Jeune.

  IV. "LES ADIEUX" 78
       From an engraving by De Launay le Jeune, after J. M. Moreau le Jeune.

*V. THE CARD PARTY 86
       From an engraving by Jean Dambrun, after J. M. Moreau le Jeune.

  VI. LEAVING THE OPERA HOUSE 106
       From an engraving by G. Malbeste, after J. M. Moreau le Jeune.

  VII. CARNIVAL IN THE STREETS OF PARIS . . 114
       From an engraving by C. Le Vasseur, after Etienne Jaureat.

  VIII. SAMUEL BERNARD 160
       From an engraving by Pierre Drevet, after Hyacinthe Rigaud.

  IX. THE CONCERT 167
       From an engraving by A. J. Duclos, after Augustin de St. Aubin.

  X. (a) "NEW BROOMS! NEW BROOMS!" . . . 194
    (b) "BELLOWS TO MEND! BELLOWS TO MEND!" . 194
       From "The Cries of Paris." Engraved by E. Bouchardon.

  XI. JEAN CHARLES PHILIBERT TRUDAINE . . 206
       From an engraving by Louis Carmontelle.

LIST OF ILLUSTRATIONS

PLATE	FACING PAGE
*XII. "WHAT DOES THE ABBÉ SAY?"	234

From an engraving by Nicholas de Launay, after J. M. Moreau le Jeune.

XIII. THE SQUIRE AND HIS TENANT FARMER . . 246

From an engraving by J. L. Delignon, after J. M. Moreau le Jeune.

XIV. THE PROFESSIONAL LETTER WRITER . . 272

From an engraving after J. J. de Boissieu.

*XV. AN ASSEMBLY IN A SALON 323

From an engraving by François Dequevaullier, after Nicholas Lavreince.

*XVI. PRECAUTIONS 334

From an engraving by Pietro Martini, after J. M. Moreau le Jeune.

NOTE.—*The Illustrations marked with an asterisk are reproduced from engravings in the possession of Mr. Basil Dighton; the remainder from examples in the British Museum.*

FRENCH SOCIETY IN THE EIGHTEENTH CENTURY

BOOK I.—VERSAILLES

CHAPTER I

THE COURT

COURT Life in the Eighteenth Century cannot be said to have come into being until the year 1722. For seven years during the Regency, from 1715 to 1722, a Court, as such, did not really exist, for the young King resided at the Tuileries, the Regent at the Palais Royal, and the great nobles lived either in Paris or upon their estates, and it was not until the latter year that the King took up his residence at Versailles, whither the courtiers followed, and thus a Court was once again established in France. A year later, on the 16th February 1723, Mathieu Marais, the lawyer, wrote in his journal: "The King having been born on the 16th February 1710, on this day entered upon his fourteenth year. *Attigit annum quatuordecimum*, in accordance with the edict of Charles v., of August 1374. He is thus of age, and there is no longer a Regent nor a Regency. God grant it be for his glory and for our happiness."

What kind of a man was this new monarch, who was destined to rule France for fifty-one years, from 1723 to 1774?

He was very good-looking, and in later years was considered to be the most handsome man in all the Court.

The Duke de Lévis, writing of him in his *Souvenirs*, says: "He had the most beautiful eyes in the world, and his glance gave the impression of exceptional dignity, and this deeply affected me, although I was but a child when I saw him. His look and the coat of cloth of gold which he was wearing that day combined to form, in my imagination, the ideal of a great king."

But it is on the moral rather than on the physical attributes of the young King on which it is important to dwell, for in a country with a form of absolute government such as France then had, the personal character of the King was of vital importance. As d'Argenson shrewdly wrote in his journal: "It is always necessary to define the monarch in order to judge events in a monarchy such as ours." What, then, was the character of Louis xv.?

While yet a child he displayed an annoying tendency to tell home truths of a disagreeable nature to those who approached him. This trait might pass as a mere piece of childishness if, later on, it had not come to be recognised as definitely characteristic. When M. de Coislin, Bishop of Metz, whose features were not very prepossessing, was presented to the young King, the latter exclaimed: "Oh, my God, how ugly he is!" On this occasion the Bishop himself pointed the moral, saying, as he withdrew: "That little boy has been very badly brought up." That criticism could be applied only too often to the children of the greatest families, and the judgment passed by Mme Cornuel on a sprig of the Rohan-Chabot family: "He is well enough born, but has been insufficiently whipped"— was no less true of them than of the young King.

Louis xv. had been brought up as badly as possible, both by Mme de Ventadour, his governess, who yielded to all his whims; by his tutor, the Bishop of Fréjus, who encouraged his idleness and only sought to please him in order to rule him more effectively later on; and by his governor, the old and frivolous Villeroy, whose only thought was to flatter him. Saint-Simon relates an incident which shows us the kind of "lesson" which Villeroy used to give his royal pupil: "On the Feast of St. Louis, the band of the opera gave a free concert for the public's amusement in the Tuileries garden. The King being in residence, this attracted more people than usual in the hope of seeing him appear occasionally on the terraces, which are on a level with his apartments. An increase in enthusiasm was very marked this year (1717); an enormous crowd invaded not only the garden, but the courtyard and square on the other side, filling every space, and even occupying the windows and roofs of the houses overlooking the Tuileries. The Maréchal de Villeroy with great difficulty persuaded the King to show himself, first on the garden side and then on the side overlooking the courts, and as soon as he appeared, cries of 'Long live the King' broke out again and again. The Maréchal de Villeroy pointed to this immense concourse, and sententiously remarked to the King: 'Look, my master, upon all these people, this concourse, this huge crowd—they are all yours, and you are their master'—and he repeated this lesson over and over again in order to drive it home. He seemed to be afraid that Louis was unaware of his power." [1] There is a curious commentary in Montesquieu on this oft-quoted passage of Saint-Simon: "That princes usually have a very false impression of their grandeur is due to the fact that the people who educate them are themselves dazzled by it; the latter are the first dupes, and the princes only become dupes later." The Maréchal de Villeroy always spoke to the King of his "subjects," but never of his "people."

In Barbier's *Journal* we read: "He had a white hind which he had reared and which would eat only out of his hand; she was very much attached to the King, who one day had her brought to La Muette and said he was going to kill her. Having sent her some distance off, he shot at and wounded her, but the hind ran back to the King, who fondled her and then sent her from him again. He shot a second time and killed her." [2]

After he had attained his majority, his chief delight was "to indulge in malicious tricks on all kinds of people,

[1] Saint-Simon, xiv. 101.   [2] Barbier's *Journal*, April 1722.

cutting their cravats and their clothes, tearing off their wigs and pulling away their canes. One day, as he was taking his shirt from the hands of M. de la Trémouille, the First Lord of the Bedchamber, he soundly smacked the face of Bontemps, the First Valet of the Bedchamber, who happened to be near him. Bontemps seems to have been his chief victim, for when he was younger, Marais reports in September 1715: "M. Bontemps having knocked at the door of the Mirror Cabinet and entered, the King maliciously spat in his face." On another occasion he amused himself by shooting at the Grand Provost. "Seeing the Grand Provost de Sourches in the Garden of Diana, he exclaimed: 'I will give the Grand Provost a good fright,' whereupon he loosed his arrow and hit the Grand Provost in the stomach, but was upset at having been so skilful. The Grand Provost is in a bad way."

He was timid and taciturn, and people said there was a spell on his tongue. Baron de Chambrier, the Prussian representative at Paris, and an experienced politician, has given us a portrait of Louis xv., which is valuable because it was drawn from observation extending over thirty years: "The King of France, according to the testimony of all who know him, lacks neither intelligence nor knowledge. He has a general acquaintance with all topics of ordinary conversation among educated people and in intellectual circles; he knows a fair amount about the history of all countries; he is exceptionally conversant with the genealogies of all the great families of Europe; he speaks sensibly of military operations, both of those which he has seen himself and of the campaigns of his generals; finally, he expresses himself with facility when he is at his ease, that is to say, when he is with those people who are accustomed to associate with him." [1]

Like all shy people, he had a horror of new faces. In 1768, the young King of Denmark, Christian vII., came to France, and "when he met Louis xv. for the first time, the latter, who never knew what to say to a stranger, embraced

[1] Rélation générale sur la Cour de France, dans les *Nouvelles archives des Missions scientifiques et littéraires*, viii. 25.

LOUIS XV

From an engraving (1723) by Pierre Drevet, after Hyacinthe Rigaud

the King of Denmark without saying a word to him, and then turned to Count Bernstorff and talked with him, as he had known him formerly during his Embassy in France. The King of Denmark, feeling the awkwardness of this reception, immediately turned about on his heel to the Duke de Choiseul, who stood beside him, and the latter quickly drew the attention of his master to the conversation which had been broken off with the young monarch."

He was abrupt in manner and had violent fits of anger. "Meuse," he said to one of his intimates, "I have just created a Duke and a Peer of my own accord."—"And who is that, sire?"—"M. de Taillebourg."—"I hope that on the occasion of bestowing this favour, Your Majesty will graciously deign to remember that he has promised me a similar one."—"That is not true," said the King, and repeated the words twice.—"But, at least, sire, Your Majesty has given me grounds for hope."—"Never," replied the King, and went off very red in the face and evidently extremely angry. That, however, did not last long, for he approached M. de Meuse again at dinner and joked with him as usual.[1]

Some of the subjects which he took most pleasure in discussing were of an embarrassing nature. "The details of illnesses and operations and questions as to the place of one's prospective burial are, unfortunately, his usual queries."[2] It should be added that it amused him to address these to the sick and old, which enhanced their politeness. He was often cruel in his talk, and, apparently, without suspecting it. At the Lever du Roi, M. de Fontanieu's nose had bled, upon which the King said to him: "Take care; at your age that is the forerunner of an apoplectic stroke." Another day, when dining in public, "the King having asked for news of one of his intimates, was informed that he was dead. 'Well, I warned him of it,' said he, and then, turning to the courtiers who surrounded him, and fixing the Abbé de Broglie with his eye, he addressed him with these words: 'Your turn next!' This gentleman, hardly able to contain himself, replied: 'Sire, Your Majesty went hunt-

---

[1] Luynes, x. 22. [2] *Ibid.* v. 94.

ing yesterday, and when the storm broke, Your Majesty was drenched like the rest,' and thereupon left the room, boiling with rage. 'That is just like the Abbé de Broglie; he always gets annoyed,' said the King." [1]

Nor was he more amiable towards ladies. "Mme de Vintimille always has a little fever in the evenings and is always in a very bad temper. Some days ago at Choisy, the King put several questions to her as to the origin of this bad temper; he asked her if she felt ill, or if she had any worry, but elicited no other reply than that she did not feel herself to be in her normal health; at length she would not answer his questions any more. Upon this the King said: 'Madame, I know full well what remedy should be employed in order to cure you—your head ought to be cut off; that indeed would suit you rather well, for, anyhow, your neck is too long; all your blood would be let out, and sheep's blood should be infused instead, which would be a good thing, for you are sour and bad-tempered.' This speech was made before ten or twelve persons, and it can well be imagined that Mme de Vintimille made no reply." [2]

But the dominant traits of his character, and they appear in all the descriptions which have come down to us from his contemporaries, were an overmastering apathy and an astonishing indifference to the affairs of his realm. As Chambrier says: "The education which he received from Cardinal de Fleury conformed to the ambitious designs of that prelate, and left him with an insuperable aversion for work and an extreme mistrust of his own powers, especially in matters connected with the government of the realm. He leaves his ministers in absolute control of their respective departments and divests himself of his sovereign authority in their favour to the extent of not even taking the trouble to co-ordinate their measures when they take them independently or in opposition to those of their colleagues. These measures inevitably prove harmful to the State owing to their contradictory nature."

Chambrier was right. Thus on 30th September 1743,

[1] Mouffle, iv. 185.   [2] Luynes, iii. 458.

the celebrated Mme de Tencin, sister of Cardinal de Tencin, who was Minister of State from 25th August 1742, and therefore fully informed by her brother of all that passed in the King's Council, wrote to the Duke de Richelieu: "Each minister is absolute master in his own department, and as they never meet together and as none of them ever reports what he does or what he wishes to do, it is, in the nature of things, inevitable that the State will collapse. I cannot help feeling a great contempt for the man who thus leaves everything to the individual will of his subordinates, and signs everything that is laid before him with the same indifference. I can best compare the King's Council to your son, who hastens to finish his task in class so as to be rid of it the quicker. The Council is really laughable. Scarcely anything is said which concerns the State. Those who wish to occupy themselves seriously with such affairs are obliged to give up any such desire owing to the lack of interest which the King seems to take in them and the silence he keeps. One would think that it was anything but his affairs which were under discussion. He has been accustomed to look upon the affairs of his realm as being quite foreign to him personally." [1]

He was born lazy, and we have seen why Fleury did nothing to overcome his sloth. During the first years of his married life, and while still under the guardianship of his over-indulgent tutor, his surgeon, Le Peyronnie, found him "so idle that when he is in his room he amuses himself by killing flies." Later, the King's indifference was such that he would sign completely contradictory decisions laid before him by his ministers, by writing at the bottom the formula "Vu bon"—and this came to be called "un bon du Roi."

What, then, did he do? He amused himself by walking on the roofs. "For some time he has been in the habit of climbing out on to the roofs of the Château after supper, and of walking there with those who have had the honour of supping with him, to the end of the new wing and thence to the Prince's wing. He has several times been to converse

[1] *Lettres de Mmes de Villars, de La Fayette et de Tencin*, 1823.

with Mme de Chalais through a window which opens on to the roof, and with Mme de Tallard down a chimney." These suppers, after which he indulged in such aerial walks, sometimes lasted all night. Passages like the following are frequent in the *Mémoires* of Luynes: "The King drank champagne and remained at table till five o'clock in the morning [at Mademoiselle's, Louise Anne de Bourbon-Condé]. Then he returned to his own apartments with the gentlemen who had been at supper. His Majesty played at backgammon till six, then went to Mass, and on his return retired to bed and did not get up till five in the evening."

But, above all, he hunted—and hunted tirelessly. "Sunday, 13th October 1748: The King has hunted or shot every day this last week. To-day he hunts the stag at Fontainebleau, to-morrow he is going to kill partridges in the plain of St. Denis, and thence goes to La Meutte [which later came to be written, though in error, La Muette], where it is already estimated that three thousand head of game have been killed or wounded by the King or those who had the honour of accompanying him with their guns." [1] Mme Campan also writes: "The King thought of nothing but the pleasures of the chase; one might have thought that the courtiers were permitting themselves an epigram when, on days when the Louis xv. was not hunting, they were heard to say quite seriously: 'The King is doing nothing to-day.'"

He devoted himself far more to his packs of hounds, of which he had a large number, as well as being fully conversant with all kennel matters, than to the affairs of his kingdom. "The King really leads a dog's life where his dogs are concerned, for at the beginning of every year he arranges what all these animals are to do up to the end of that year. He has five or six packs of hounds. It is necessary to divide them for purposes of hunting, resting, and exercise, and I am speaking not only of the drafting and care of old and young hounds, of their names and qualities, which the King knows better than any of his huntsmen, but of the arrangements for all their moves according to

[1] Luynes, ix. 79.

the journeys which have been, or may be, arranged for. These are made on a special calendar, and it is said that the King disposes of matters affecting finance and the course of the war with a great deal less labour than the above." [1]

He had, however, other more important hobbies, for, unknown to his own ministers, he corresponded with his personal agents abroad. This was "The King's Secret." He had secret first-hand information about foreign governments, but was quite content merely to be well informed, and allowed his ministers to perpetrate blunders which he himself could have avoided. What interested him as much as the affairs of the realm was information about the intrigues of Paris and the Court, which was supplied him by his Secret Service agents, by whom private letters were opened for his amusement. "The method was a very simple one. Six or seven post-office officials sorted the letters, which they had been ordered to open, and took an impression of the wafer with a drop of mercury. They then laid the letter with the wafer downward on a glass of hot water, which melted the wax without doing any other damage; whereupon the letter was opened, extracts were made, and it was then sealed up again with the aid of the impression already taken. That is the method which was told me. The Postmaster-General carried the extracts to the King on Sundays, and, when employed on this arduous mission, he came and went like a Minister of State. Doctor Quesnay often flew into a rage in my presence at the thought of this infamous Department, as he called it, and so violent would he become that he foamed at the mouth. He used to say, 'I would as soon dine with the executioner as with the Postmaster-General.'"

He was secretive as the grave. Chambrier writes of him: "Except with the one person who possesses his confidence, he is very reserved. He is impenetrable where his own secrets are concerned, and he has shown that he can carry dissimulation to extremes when he deems it necessary."

[1] D'Argenson, ii. 261.

D'Argenson, in speaking of the King, used the same expression as Chambrier and calls him "impenetrable" or even "inexplicable." He tries, however, in various passages of his journal to describe this secret and enigmatic character. "The King," he says, "has two qualities which are essential to the sovereign power: one is dissimulation, which he can use when he wishes and even carries to great lengths, and in the second place he can be severe on most unexpected occasions." [1] We shall see farther on how these two "qualities," as d'Argenson calls them, came into play.

In 1757, Louis xv. dismissed his two ministers, Machault and d'Argenson, the former because he had been too hasty to pay court to the Dauphine in the belief that, after Damiens' attempt on the King's life, Mme de Pompadour would fall; and the Pompadour did not condone his "treason." When he received the King's letter decreeing his exile, M. de Machault was carried away by his feelings, and cried aloud: "Is this the reward of so many services?" D'Argenson, on the other hand, fell into disgrace because he continued to see Mme d'Estrades after she had ceased to be the friend of Mme de Pompadour. "The hostility which Mme de Pompadour feels toward Mme d'Estrades has fallen on M. d'Argenson also." [2] On 1st February 1757, he received from his Master the following letter, which Collé rightly considers "curt and harsh": "M. d'Argenson, as I no longer require your services, I order you to surrender to me your office as Secretary of State for War and your other posts, and to retire to your property at des Ormes. Signed: Louis."

On the occasions when the King parted with his ministers, he added dissimulation to harshness. On 23rd April 1749, at the King's levee, M. de Maurepas, his minister and intimate friend, had, as usual, given full rein to his sparkling wit, and the King had laughed loud and long at his brilliant sallies. As M. de Maurepas was attending the wedding of Mlle de Maupeou that evening, the King in dismissing him said: "I command you to amuse yourself." On the next day—24th April—at

[1] D'Argenson, v. 454. [2] Luynes, xvi. 285.

eight o'clock in the morning, M. de Maurepas received from M. d'Argenson in person a note from the King, written as follows: "Fulfilling the promise I made you that I would myself inform you if the occasion should arise that I no longer required your services, I herewith order you to place your resignation in the hands of M. d'Argenson and to depart within the week. As Pontchartrain is too near Versailles, you will proceed to Bourges. You will only see your family, and you will make no reply to this letter." Maurepas' exile was to last until the King's death, that is, for twenty-five years. Thus did Louis xv. sacrifice to the resentment of his favourite, whom Maurepas was accused of having lampooned, a man who had been the friend of his youth and his minister since 1723, *i.e.* for twenty-six years.

Even in his amusements the King could be brutal. Thus, when present *incognito* at a ball at the Opera, "His Majesty remained for an hour and a half without being recognised. On two separate occasions he struck Mademoiselle [Louise Anne de Bourbon-Condé] with his fist, and she was vastly astonished to be treated thus by a masked stranger."[1]

An elderly friend of Mme de Pompadour, Darboulin, was made Administrator of the Post Office, and later Secretary to the Cabinet, a post which was a sinecure, but gave admission to the "entrées." In his old age he was seized with violent paroxysms of gout which prevented his frequenting Versailles as often as formerly. "At length, feeling better, he decided to visit Mme de Pompadour, who did not wish to let him go before he had seen the King. The King, on descending to her apartments and seeing Darboulin, went up and asked him how he was. Darboulin replied that he had had an attack of gout in both his great toes and had but just recovered. The King spoke of other matters and joked with some of his friends; then, approaching Darboulin, he turned his back on him, and pressing with his heel on each of Darboulin's feet he asked him if that was where he had the gout. The attack was

[1] Luynes, i. 198.

barely over, and the old man suffered agonies. Mme de Pompadour saw him change colour, and asking the King to come and speak to her, made the latter move.

"The King never put himself in any one else's place. He had never had the gout, and did not think of the pain he might cause. He only thought of making a joke, like a child who inflicts pain while at play until, by treating it in the same way, one makes it realise the consequences." [1]

He was, however, not quite as callous as has been made out. When Mme de Vintimille, the second of the four de Nesle sisters, died, he was seen in tears, and on the day of Mme de Pompadour's funeral, it is unlikely that he displayed the attitude ascribed to him by historians. Thus, Campardon, the historian of Mme de Pompadour, assures us that Louis xv. "in his withered heart had not a single tear for the woman who for twenty years had shared his existence. He coldly drew out his watch and calculated the time it would take for the procession to reach Paris." But there is no reason to doubt the following account given by the Count de Cheverny, who is usually so well informed and who was much at Court:

"Champlost, the First Valet of the Bedchamber, was then in waiting, and slept in the same room as the King. A bell-rope was fixed to his arm from the King's bed, and gave the signal in case the King needed him in the night. The King slept but little, and rose as soon as he was awakened, in order to withdraw even from his intimates, and retired to his closet. At last the day of the Marquise's funeral dawned. The King knew the hour as fixed by his orders regulating the ceremony. It was six o'clock of a winter's evening, and an appalling storm was raging. In her will the Marquise had expressed a wish to be buried at the Capucines in the Place Vendôme, where she had occupied a splendid apartment. The King took Champlost by the arm, and, at the glass door of the Privy Closet which opens on to the balcony facing the avenue of the Court, he made him close the entrance door and stepped out with him on to the balcony. He remained motionless

[1] Cheverny, i. 322.

and in silence, watching the procession pass down the avenue, and in spite of the bad weather and the biting air, of which he seemed unconscious, his eyes followed it until it was out of sight. Re-entering his apartments, two large tears rolled down his cheeks, and his only words to Champlost were: 'These are the only respects I can pay her.'"[1]

When he took the trouble he could undoubtedly be witty. During a visit he once made to the War Office, he found a pair of spectacles on a desk and tried them on to see if they were better than those he used. A paper which had been purposely placed there containing a fulsome eulogy of the King and M. de Choiseul was then submitted to him. " 'These spectacles are no better than mine,' said the King; 'they magnify things too much.' "[2]

The Family of Kinsale had, in England, obtained the privilege of covering themselves before the King. A member of this family having been made prisoner at the Battle of Laufeld, appeared before Louis xv. with his head covered. "The King was pleased not to be offended that he exercised this privilege in his presence, and even asked him to dine with him. 'Sire, I am not hungry,' replied Lord Kinsale rudely. 'I did not ask you whether you were hungry,' said the Monarch, 'but merely whether you wished to have the honour of dining with the King of France.' "[3]

Finally, Louis xv. had, and this should be said to his honour, one great quality: he was not only brave in battle, but brave with that gaiety which is typically French. At the Siege of Menin in 1744, he faced the enemy's fire like any other soldier and dined in the trenches. At Fontenoy he remained calm in the midst of the general confusion, and retained his sang-froid in the face of danger.

His Queen was, essentially, a pious woman. Luynes says on the 16th November 1747: "The Queen's high character and her genuine and fervent piety place her above all criticism. One day at Compiègne, on her way to Mass, she

---

[1] Cheverny, i. 324.
[2] Hippeau, *Gouvernement de Normandie*, Part II. i. 4.
[3] Dugast de St. Just, i. 253.

saw Voltaire's *La Religion Naturelle* displayed in a shop, and was very grieved. On her return she took the book and tore it into pieces, saying to the shopkeeper that if she continued to sell such books, her shop would be closed. The shopkeeper was quite dumbfounded, for she had been deceived by the word 'religion' on the cover." The good woman thought it was a work dealing with her own religion.

What did the public think of the Queen, and what feelings did she inspire in the people ? "The Queen," says Talleyrand, "was venerated, but her virtues were of rather a gloomy nature and never stirred any enthusiasm on her behalf. She lacked the beauty which made the nation so proud of Louis xv.'s good looks." [1] This summary and severe verdict needs amplifying and correcting.

"Thémire has a good deal of intelligence, a warm heart, a gentle temper, and an attractive figure. Her education has stamped on her soul a piety so real that it has impressed itself upon her consciousness, and she appeals to it to direct all her feelings. Her discernment leads her to appreciate all idiosyncrasies and all that is ridiculous, but her goodness and her charity enable her to bear them all with patience and rarely permit her to laugh at them. On seeing Thémire, one forgets that there may be a grandeur and attributes higher even than those she derives from her disposition. One might well delude oneself that there is no gulf between her and us save her greater excellence, but a fatal awakening would reveal to us that this Thémire, so perfect and so amiable, is none other than—the Queen." [2]

It should, however, be noted that this very flattering portrait was drawn for the purpose of being seen—and perhaps even rewarded. It was sent to Mme de Luynes by her niece, Mme du Deffand, in December 1748. Thus in December 1752 we find Luynes recording that the Queen "had accorded Mme du Deffand the privilege of dining with her privately, although the latter had never been presented," and later Mme du Deffand herself writes to the Abbé Terray : "In 1763 the King, at the Queen's re-

---

[1] *Mémoires*, i. 4. [2] Mme du Deffand, *Correspondance*, ii. 761.

quest, granted Mme du Deffand an annual pension of six thousand livres. This princess honoured her with her protection out of regard for her late aunt, the Duchess de Luynes." Moreover, Mme du Deffand is speaking of the Queen from hearsay, so it is as well to consult those who saw Marie Leczinska at closer quarters and knew her intimately. President Hénault, the Queen's Comptroller, has left us the following portrait of his sovereign: "She spends the morning in prayer and pious reading, pays a visit to the King, and then indulges in some relaxation, usually in painting. The hour of her toilet is at half-past twelve, followed by Mass and dinner, after which I follow her to her closet. But here there is quite a different atmosphere. I find no longer a Queen but a private individual. All sorts of articles are gathered here—tapestries, handicrafts of all kinds, and so forth"—(Luynes writes: "She can read the works of Pere Malebranche and reads them with pleasure, but some think she can hardly understand them")—"and while she works she is gracious enough to recount what she has read. Her favourite books are histories, which she reads in their original language—French, Polish, German, Italian, etc.—for she knows them all. The Court assembles in her apartments to play cavagnole; she sups in private, and then proceeds to visit Mme de Luynes about eleven. The persons admitted do not exceed five or six in number, and at half-past twelve she retires.

"Conversations in which there are certainly no scandal and in which Court intrigues (and, still less, political ones) never have any part would seem difficult to carry on, nevertheless they could not be more lively. No one appreciates a jest better than the Queen, and she laughs readily. Her irony is gentle, for no one in the world appreciates the ridiculous more than she, and it is as well for those who lay themselves open to it that her charity restrains her, otherwise they would never hold up their heads again."

The Duke de Luynes tells us of the liveliness of the Queen's sallies, of which the following are examples: On the death of the Maréchal de Saxe, who was a Protestant, the Queen made a remark which in itself was a funeral oration: "It is sad that we cannot say a *De Profundis* for a man who so often has caused us to sing a *Te Deum*." And she said of the courtiers: "If they asked the favours of Heaven as they solicit those of the Court they would be great saints."

Kind and amiable, yet possessed of a sense of humour, Marie Leczinska appears to have been at heart, and so indeed we see her in some extracts from letters which are here quoted. Her lady-in-waiting, Mme de Luynes, was ill, and it was feared that her malady was the dreaded smallpox which spread such terror in the eighteenth century. Sure enough the smallpox was diagnosed, and we read in the letters of the Queen to the Duke de Luynes how great was her anxiety while the danger lasted, how touching her joy and her tender solicitude when it was over. On the 12th December 1750 she writes to the Duke: "I know that the night has been far from good. I thank you for writing so regularly, and I would still ask you to send me three more letters—to-day, to-morrow, and after, at noon, six, and nine. They will reassure me."

To Mme de Luynes she writes, after writing to the Duke de Luynes on the same day, 22nd December: "Your letter moved me to tears. All I ask is that you should not feel indebted to me for my friendship, for it is you yourself who have earned it. When I wrote to M. de Luynes I said, ' I embrace Mme de Luynes,' but as this is to you and the message for him, I think it more honest if I ask you to do it for me." The next day the Queen writes: "I did not want to write any more but I cannot help it, for my heart has overcome my reason. In twenty-four hours I shall have the pleasure of seeing and embracing you. By the way, I do not think any one has ever said prayers for a nose, but that happens to be the object of mine." (It was the nose of Mme de Luynes which had been particularly affected by the smallpox.)

On 1st January 1751, the Duke had sent a casket containing some small gifts to the Queen, who thanks him on the same day, and on the next writes: "I shall be happy

MARIE LECZINSKA
PRINCESS OF POLAND AND QUEEN OF FRANCE
From an engraving by Jacques Chevau, after Carle Van Loo

all day now that I have heard that Mme de Luynes has had a good night. Do you know what I was doing when I got Monseigneur's letter?" (Monseigneur was the Bishop of Bayeux, the Duke's brother.) "I was—can you guess?— ogling my casket." (There was a pair of spectacles in the casket which the Duke had sent.) " 'L'Avare' " (Molière's) "never loved his more."

In order to render Marie Leczinska full justice and to understand the real merit there was in her keeping up her pleasant manner and her good humour, one must look in the *Mémoires* of de Luynes for passages like the following. On 2nd May 1741 he writes: "It has been noticed that when the King arrives in the Drawing-room, he does not go near the table where the Queen is playing at cavagnole, and also that, more significant still, for several days the Queen has remained standing for a long while without being asked to be seated by the King, and this while he was talking to Mme de Mailly."

When the King had recovered from his illness at Metz and was preparing to leave Paris in order to proceed to Strasbourg, where he was to rejoin the army of Maréchal de Noailles, "the Queen said to him that she hoped he would permit her to follow him. The King replied coldly: 'It is not worth it,' and not appearing to wish to discuss the matter further he moved on and conversed with others who were present" (24th September 1744).

The Queen had to suffer these affronts in the presence of the whole Court, for she never saw the King except on the visits required by etiquette—in the morning at his "Petit Lever," with all the others who had the privilege of the "entrée": in the evening, at supper, when it was in public—that is, when the King supped with all the doors open: and on rare occasions when the King would visit her after supper "for the conversation," and honour her with his presence for a few brief moments.

The affection of her daughters was all that was left to her, but in 1738 she saw them all, with the exception of the third, Mme Adelaide, leave her for the Abbey of Fontevrault, thirteen days' journey from Versailles. This step was decided upon by the parsimonious Fleury for reasons of economy and without any regard for the distress of their mother, for whom he had little love. Barbier relates in his Diary for April 1738: "The Cardinal has discovered a new source of economy in our princesses, who, now seven in number, encumber the Palace of Versailles and cause expense. This has taken the form of sending five to the Abbey of Fontevrault, where the Abbess, Mme de Mortemart, will supervise their education. Their attendants will be few, and this will dispense with a large number of women and servants. The third princess is seven years old, and is much loved by the Queen, who was deeply affected at her departure. They say she is the most attractive of them. She was well instructed in pleading to remain here. Every day the two eldest daughters go to wait upon the King on his return from Mass. One day the third also presented herself before him, kissed his hand, and, throwing herself at his feet, burst into tears. The King was moved by this scene, shed a few tears, as did all the Court, and promised her she should not go. All preparations are being made for the departure of the other four." The little Ladies, as they were called at Court, were placed under the tutelage of Mme de Fontevrault; one of them, Madame Sixième, died at the convent without seeing her mother again. Mme Victoire was called home ten years later, in 1748, and Mesdames Sophie and Louise in 1750, after twelve years' absence. In her solitude the Queen worked at her tapestry, painted, and played at her everlasting cavagnole. She went to sup with her lady-in-waiting, the Duchess de Luynes, at first regularly twice a week, without being announced, while in 1747 she supped 198 times, according to de Luynes, who was very proud of the fact. Let us attend one of these suppers in company with the Duke de Croÿ:

"I went to Mme de Luynes', where the Queen was supping, as indeed she was very often wont to do. I stayed to watch. She was greedy and ate heartily. There were, of course, only ladies at table, usually only those who formed part of her cavagnole parties. M. de Luynes waited upon the Queen and obviously took great pains, whereas Mme de Luynes, who had the most perfect manners of any one at Court, was less embarrassed. All who usually supped with Mme de Luynes were allowed to enter. The gentlemen paid their homage, standing during supper, another meal being served for them and M. de Luynes, who joined them for the second course, in a different room. The Queen withdrew after supper to another apartment, where there was music. She herself played the viol very badly, the rest of the party consisting of musicians and some young courtiers, MM. d'Antin, Turpin, etc. Finally, she returned to Mme de Luynes' drawing-room and played her dreary cavagnole till late into the night." [1]

The last sentence recalls Voltaire's:

> "We think that games of chance distract,
> But boredom comes with measured steps
> To sit between two Majesties
> At Cavagnole."

If one is curious to know what exactly was this game of cavagnole, de Luynes explains it thus:

"*June* 1737: For some time a game called cavayole (or cavagnole) seems to have been growing in popularity. It is said to come from Italy, and is a kind of ' biribi.' The table is divided into six, eight, or even ten parts of twelve squares each, and there are as many balls as there are numbers. One is not allowed to stake more than twenty-two counters at one throw. When the number on which the twenty-two counters have been placed turns up, each of the other players pays twenty-two counters and one besides. If only part of twenty-two have been placed on a number and the remainder on others, one pays the number of counters on the winning number and one besides. Finally, if a number turns up on which there are no counters, every one has to pay one counter. Each table spins six balls. Besides this, bets are made from table to table, at the corners, in the centre, etc. This game causes amusement without being especially exciting, and it entertains a lot of people at the same time, as some can play

[1] Croÿ, i. 82.

low and others higher by side bets. The King played very high at Rambouillet, and people are beginning to play it here." [1]

On Monday, 22nd September 1749, Luynes notes the following event: "The Queen has not played cavagnole for two or three days," and he adds that "although losing with good humour, it would be more pleasant if she did not show quite so marked a desire to win." [2]

She amused herself by taking a great interest in unimportant details of etiquette, as, for instance, one evening at the Dauphin's "there were only two violins, and a dozen ladies and gentlemen dancing. The Queen wished to eat a small cake, and a napkin was brought, which was presented by the Duke de Châtillon. But the Queen did not take it, and yesterday told M. de Luynes that she was surprised at M. de Châtillon, for although, when she dined at private houses, it was customary for the host and hostess to present the napkin and wait upon her, when she was with the Dauphin it was as if she were in her own home. The napkin ought therefore to have been handed by Mme de Luynes, who would have presented it to the Dauphin to give to the Queen." [3]

On their return to Court, Mesdames, the King's daughters, exercised no influence and confined themselves to looking askance at the favourite and supporting to the best of their ability "the devout party" which grouped itself about the Queen, "because, in spite of herself, the Queen has a party. Her rank is a standard to which all those who deplore the scandal rally, attaching themselves to her in order to annoy the King and the favourite. Their murmurs are in proportion to the royal patience." [4]

Louis XV. had, as is well known, ten children, of whom seven survived—the Dauphin, Louis, and six daughters, Mesdames de France: Mesdames Elisabeth and Henrietta who were twins, Mesdames Adelaide, Victoire, and Madame Sophie, and, last of all, Madame Louise or "Madame Dernière." Mme Adelaide had a high-pitched voice, and

---

[1] Luynes, i. 272. [2] Ibid. x. 168.
[3] Ibid. iii. 302. [4] D'Argenson, iv. 169.

ruled the family. The King—"Papa-Roi"—called her "the duster." They were all devout. Louise, the youngest, died a Carmelite, having become one in the pious hope of atoning for the sins of her father. But for all that, the King loved them, visited them of an evening on his return from hunting, brought them dainties prepared with his own hand, and in this connection there is an amusing letter from Mme du Deffand to Walpole of 27th October 1767:

"After supper the King went to Madame Victoire, called a page, and gave him a letter, saying: 'James, take this letter to the Duke de Choiseul and tell him to give it to the Bishop of Orleans at once.' James went in search of M. de Choiseul, and eventually found him with M. de Penthièvre. M. de Choiseul was informed and, taking the letter, handed it to his wife's first footman, Cadet, who was close at hand, with instructions to search everywhere for the Bishop and to return immediately with the information as to where he could be found. After an hour and a half Cadet came back, saying he had been first to his Lordship's apartment, but that no one had answered to his vigorous knocking, and that he had then searched the whole town without finding the Bishop or hearing any news of him. The Duke thereupon decided to go to the Bishop's apartment himself, climbed up a hundred and twenty-eight steps, and knocked at the door so violently that one or two servants were awakened and came in their shirts to open the door. 'Where is the Bishop?' 'He has been in bed since ten.' 'Open his door.' The Bishop wakes up. 'Who is there?' 'It is I, with a letter from the King.' 'A letter from the King! Good heavens! what is the time?' 'Two o'clock.' Taking the letter, he exclaimed: 'I can't read without my spectacles.' 'Where are they?' 'In my breeches.' The minister went to look for them, and during his search they said to one another: 'What can there be in this letter? Has the Archbishop of Paris died suddenly? Has a Bishop hung himself?' Both felt considerable anxiety. The Bishop took the letter and the minister offered to read it, but the former thought it wiser to read it first himself. He did not read it to the end, but handed it to the minister, who read these words:

"'MY LORD BISHOP OF ORLEANS,—My daughters are anxious to have some cotignac' (a marmalade made of quinces for which Orleans was noted). 'They want some quite small jars. Please send for some, if you have none by you. I beg of you' (here a sedan-chair was drawn on the paper, under which the letter continued as follows:) 'to send immediately to your episcopal city to procure some, and let them be very small jars. May God have you, my Lord Bishop of Orleans, in His holy keeping. Signed: LOUIS.'

"But lower down there was a postscript: 'The sedan-chair means nothing; it was drawn by my daughters on this piece of paper which I happened to pick up.'

"The astonishment of the two ministers can be imagined! A courier was dispatched immediately, the cotignac arrived the next day, but no one troubled about it any more. The King himself told the story, which the ministers themselves were not anxious to repeat."[1]

The Dauphin was well educated, very pious, and bitterly opposed to the party of the Encyclopedists. "Extremely short, disliking movement and any form of exercise, passionless and even without taste," is d'Argenson's description of him, and this is borne out by de Luynes: "Last Sunday the King asked the Dauphin how he intended to amuse himself during the Carnival. 'By going to bed at ten instead of at my usual hour of eleven,' was the reply." It is difficult to imagine any one of the Dauphin's age behaving in this way, he being then nineteen.

He was devout to a degree which was generally deemed exaggerated. During Lent he indulged in excessive asceticism, which injured his health. "He lives like a hermit. His dinner consists only of the heart of a lettuce eaten with salt but without oil or vinegar, and with it he drinks four or five glasses of water."[2]

But he could speak cheerily of his frugal tastes. "The Queen sent M. de la Motte this morning to ask for news of

[1] Lescure, *Correspondance*, i. 448.   [2] Stryenski, p. 341.

him and to inquire whether he was hungry, to which he replied in majestic tones: 'A prince such as I am cannot regard food as a necessity but merely as a pleasure, and I only eat so as not to wound the susceptibilities of ordinary mortals.' " [1]

In 1765, during a visit to Compiègne, when the King reviewed his regiments of cavalry and where the Dauphin lived a camp life, the latter, whose health had been very bad during the last year and who had over-exerted himself during the manœuvres, fell seriously ill. His malady was diagnosed as consumption, and the anxiety of the Court spread to Paris and the provinces. It was then apparent how much he was beloved, for the churches were crowded, and it was a not uncommon sight to see large numbers of all sorts and conditions of people kneeling in the middle of the Place Ste Geneviève.

Mme de Sevigné writes: "The fat St. Géran had to be killed before he could be properly appreciated." It was during this illness that those real qualities, which until then had not been suspected, showed themselves. Many touching utterances of the dying prince have been recorded, and here is one demonstrating his simple, kind, and familiar manner. To the Queen's first physician who had watched by his bedside, he said: "Ah, my poor Lassone, I am so sorry that I have made you spend such a restless night. Go and lie down; you must be very tired."

Diderot only echoed public opinion when he wrote to Mlle Volland on 20th December 1765: "This day, Thursday, the eve of St. Thomas, we have lost M. le Dauphin after a protracted and cruel illness, and sufferings which he bore with truly heroic fortitude. A number of touching anecdotes are told such as that some time ago he cut off his hair and distributed it among his sisters as the only gift he could make them. There is in this act something so affecting and akin to the ancients that it delights me. Throughout his illness he has had the good taste to display to those around him a confidence as to his health and life which he cannot have felt. He never gave any sign of regret at the thought

[1] Luynes, xii. 105.

of death save when his father showed him some tenderness which deeply moved him.

"It is certain that the Dauphin had read much and reflected deeply, and that there were few matters of importance on which he was not well informed. It is said that, quite lately, when he learned that the Genevese Rousseau had not been allowed to settle at Strasbourg, he disapproved of such severity, and that he considered him a man to be pitied rather than persecuted. That certainly is not a sign of intolerance."

The Philosophers, seizing on a remark of his which has been often quoted, "Let us not persecute," have represented him as favourable to their cause; but it appears certain that the Dauphin in preaching forbearance was not thinking of them, but only of the Jesuits, who were about to be expelled and who were his friends.

"This is how the King announced to Mme la Dauphine the death of her husband. Sending for the Duke de Berry, and making a short discourse to him suitable to the occasion, he led him to Mme la Dauphine, and upon entering her apartments he said to the Gentleman Usher: 'Announce the King and M. le Dauphin.' The princess understood what was meant, and threw herself weeping at His Majesty's knees."[1]

D'Argenson said that, "All the realm is in Paris and all Paris is at Versailles. Thus all the talents of the Kingdom are concentrated at Court."

But why was the Court at Versailles? Saint-Simon explains it in his *Parallèle des trois derniers Bourbons*: "The wars of Paris [that is, those of the Fronde] in his youth were never forgotten by Louis XIV., and he determined never to live in that town and to visit it only on very rare occasions, and then without sleeping there. To do so would only be as a kind of favour."

Louis XV. followed his example, and it became more and more repugnant to him, as we shall see, to honour Paris with his short visits. He resided, therefore, at Ver-

[1] Hippeau, Part II. i. 15.

sailles, surrounded by his Court, and we may now see how access was gained to him, and picture to ourselves what the Palace of Versailles was like at that time.

The approach to the King's apartments was by the Marble Staircase, on the landing of which the Guard-room of the King's Guards was on one side, that of the Queen's on the other. Beyond the King's Guard-room was the first anteroom, where the King dined in public, and then came the anteroom known as the Œil-de-Bœuf, which opened direct into the King's apartments. These consisted of two rooms—la Chambre (where the ceremonies of the Lever and Coucher took place) and the Cabinet de Conseil, or Council Chamber, (where the King held his councils with his ministers).

This chamber was also the King's Closet, where private audiences were given, the petitions of the Parliament presented, and marriage-contracts signed. Louis XV. spent most of the day here. The King's Closet, also called the Mirror Closet, was a very fine room which was enlarged in 1756 by the removal of the Wig Closet (where the King was powdered). It was then decorated with magnificent carving by Antoine Rousseau, "the king's sculptor."

Louis XV.'s Petits Cabinets, or private apartments, were situated above these rooms on the first floor, and occupied the next three stories. Here Louis XV. had his library, his observatory, and his aviaries, and here took place the intimate supper parties called the "soupers des petits cabinets," of which the *Mémoires* of the time are so full.

But not only did the King and Royal Family inhabit the Palace, but the great nobles also had apartments there. They were very badly lodged, as will be seen from this description of Mme Roland: "We journeyed to Versailles, the only object being to show me the Court, and to amuse ourselves at the show. We lodge at the Palace. Mme Legrand, one of the Dauphine's ladies, was known to the Abbé Bimont, he having been a friend of her son, and as she was not in waiting she lent us her apartments. It was under the tiles, opening on to the same corridor as those of the Archbishop of Paris, and so close to his that the Prelate had to be careful lest we should hear him talking, and the same applied to us. There were two rooms meanly furnished, in one of which they had managed to fix up a sleeping-place for a man-servant, with an approach rendered horrible by the darkness of the passage and the smell of the latrines. Such was the habitation in which a Duke and Peer of France took pride." [1]

Why did the prelates and great nobles put up with such lodgings in a Palace crowded with people, rather than remain peacefully and comfortably in their own homes, and why did they endure, even cheerfully, to be chilled for hours, uncomfortably seated or standing in the Œil-de-Bœuf, waiting for the King to pass, and hoping for a word from him? It was in order to enjoy there "les honneurs," and we will now see all that these two words signified.

"Les honneurs de la Cour" for ladies meant that they were admitted to the Queen's balls and receptions, and for gentlemen that they could ride in the coaches and take part in the King's hunts. In order to be admitted to these, one had to be of noble birth and "prove" one's descent back to 1400, before which no nobility was created.

"Les honneurs" merely, or "Les honneurs du Louvre," belonged only to titled ladies, that is to say, to duchesses, the wives of Grandees of Spain, and those who were called the King's cousins, and lastly to some other ladies who were otherwise qualified by their title, and whose family possessed the hereditary "honneurs" of the Louvre. These ladies had the right to the "tabouret" or stool: their coaches were upholstered in red velvet, and had a gilt edging, while in their own homes they were entitled to a dais and a dais-chamber. They drove into the Palace courtyard with four horses, and when the King "draped" (covered his coaches with black cloth) they had the right to do the same. When they were presented, the King embraced them.[2]

By an order dated 17th April 1760, Louis XV. defined the etiquette prescribed for ladies on presentation at

[1] *Mémoires*, p. 95.   [2] Mme d'Oberkirch, ii. 92.

Court: "Desiring, like his predecessors, to extend the privilege of being presented only to the wives of such as are noble by race," the King required that the title-deeds showing the husband's pedigree back to 1400 should be submitted to the College of Arms, "provided there is no subsequent ennoblement or any one belonging to the judicial profession. We reserve the right to exempt from this rule those who may hold offices under the Crown or in our household."

Petitions for the wives of officers or of nobles with ancient titles endorsed by a minister can be found among the archives of the Royal Household, at the foot of which is written in the King's own handwriting a pitiless "No," or, what must have been even more wounding to the pride of many, the cruel sentence, "I wish to hear no more of this."

There were different forms of this ceremony, and d'Argenson describes that of "Mme de Verneuil [a family related to the Chassepoux], the wife of the Marshal of the Diplomatic Corps, who was presented to the King in his apartments, but as she was not a lady of quality she was not embraced. She had not been told of this, and when she presented her cheek, the King drew back blushing."[1]

Mme d'Oberkirch also gives an amusing description of the preliminaries and of the actual ceremony.

"*13th June.*—My hair was dressed immediately after dinner, as high as possible in accordance with the fashion, together with my diamonds and a bunch of feathers.

"The Duchess de la Vallière having been good enough to undertake my presentation to their Majesties, I went to her house at half-past four in company with Baroness Mackau, and we drove to the Palace together. I was first presented to the King—a very solemn moment with so many people staring at me! I had to remember my lessons, to walk backwards, to kick my train away so as not to get it caught in my shoes and be in danger of falling, which would have been the height of insolence and the depth of desolation!

[1] D'Argenson, iv. 175.

"We then went to the Queen, where I made my three curtseys—one at the door, the second in the middle of the room, and the third close to the Queen, who rose and bowed. I removed my right glove and made as if to kiss the hem of her dress, but the Queen withdrew her skirt with a graceful move of her fan so as to prevent my doing so. 'I am charmed to see you,' said the Queen, 'but this presentation is only a formality, for we are old acquaintances.' I bowed respectfully, and after a few words more the Queen inclined her head and we withdrew backwards with the three farewell curtseys. Stools had been placed for us, but I was careful not to sit down, as I do not possess 'les honneurs.' The Duchess de la Vallière sat down, but graciously rose again instantly.

"I was then presented to all the Royal Family with the same ceremonial. The King said nothing, but smiled at me graciously. The Queen speaks little to ladies who are presented, and they say she is very shy with women. The King did not embrace me, as indeed was right, as he only kisses the Duchesses and the wives of the King's cousins.

"I then went to see the Queen at play. All ladies who have been presented, without distinction of title, sit on stools, forming a circle round the room while the gentlemen stand, but those who wish to play seat themselves at the round table in the centre at which the Queen is seated. After the game Her Majesty walks round the room and says a few words to each one. To me she said: 'I hope I shall see you often, Mme d'Oberkirch, so don't hurry your return to Alsace.' I curtseyed and went to wait upon the Princess de Lamballe, the Queen's Mistress of the Robes, and to make a second visit, as required by etiquette, to 'les honneurs.' "[1]

But when an ambassadress was to be presented, the ceremonial was minutely prescribed. When Mme de Castropignano, Ambassadress of Spain and the Two Sicilies, was presented to the Queen:

"At half-past twelve M. de Verneuil returned to the room and informed the Ambassadress that her audience

[1] Mme d'Oberkirch, ii. 94.

with the Queen was about to take place, and giving her his hand as far as the closet leading to the Queen's Chamber, remained there with her, while a groom of the chambers informed Mme de Luynes that she was waiting. The Queen was in her arm-chair with her back to the fireplace, her own ladies sitting on either hand and the other ladies standing, also to right and left. Mme de Luynes rose and, after curtseying to the Queen, went to the outer room, greeted the Ambassadress, and kissed her. She then preceded Mme de Castropignano, who was escorted by M. de Verneuil, and the Ambassadress then made three curtseys, and removing her glove, which was very long, approached the Queen and kissed the hem of her dress. A folding chair was then placed for Mme de Castropignano facing the Queen, and another at her left side. The King was in Council, but had told M. de Verneuil to fetch him even there, so the latter informed M. de la Trémoille of the King's orders. As soon as M. de Verneuil had delivered his message, His Majesty proceeded to the Queen's Chamber, by way of the gallery and the drawing-room. Every one rose, and then the Ambassadress approached the King, who greeted and kissed her. She thought that it was customary to be kissed on both cheeks, but the King only kissed her on one. The conversation was not very lively, as she hardly knew a word of French. She seemed very nervous, and even burst out laughing two or three times, which caused great surprise, but this was due to her nervousness. When the King retired, Mme de Luynes did not follow him, as she usually does, but I have already noted that on occasions such as this the lady-in-waiting does not leave the Ambassadress. The Queen seated herself again, as did all the others.

"Meanwhile M. de Verneuil had gone to inform the Dauphin, who came through the anteroom and the Queen's great closet. As he entered the Queen's Chamber, the Queen rose, but he first greeted the Ambassadress and then kissed the Queen. This visit did not last long, nor did Mme de Luynes accompany him on leaving, for the same reason as in the case of the King. The Queen remained standing, and the Ambassadress withdrew, making her three curtseys and escorted by Mme de Luynes as far as the outer cabinet."[1]

Let us now enter the King's apartments in company with those who enjoy the privilege of the *entrée*, which was so highly coveted, and assist with them first at the "Petit Lever" and then at the King's dinner in public. But we must first know who possess these *entrées* and distinguish between their various categories, which are of great importance. The *entrées* to the King's apartments are, firstly, his intimates, then the *grandes entrées*, the *premières entrées*, and the *entrées de la chambre*.

The first enter when the King is awakened and is still in bed. They are the Princes of the Blood (except the Prince de Conty), the Cardinal, the Duke de Charost, Mme de Ventadour, and his nurse, Mme Mercier. These are the only individuals who enjoy this privilege.

The *grandes entrées* include the chief gentlemen of the Bedchamber, who are admitted when the King is about to rise.

The *premières entrées* enter when he has risen and is still in his dressing-gown. This privilege is bestowed by Royal Warrant and is enjoyed by those whose duty it is to read aloud to the King, the Keeper of the Privy Purse, the barbers, clockmakers, doctors, surgeons and apothecaries, the Princes de Rohan and Soubise, the Dukes de Villeroy, Luxembourg, etc.

The *entrée de la chambre* takes place when the King is seated in his arm-chair opposite his dressing-table, and de Luynes states that the officers of the household and other persons to whom the King has accorded this privilege are very numerous.

The following is an exact account of the complicated ceremonial attending the Lever—or Rising—of the King, drawn up by the Benedictines of St. Maur in *L'État de la France de 1712*:

"The King rises at the hour he has indicated before retiring on the previous night, and if he does not wake at

[1] Luynes, iii. 114.

the hour named, the First Valet of the Bedchamber awakens him. In the morning the First Valet-in-waiting, who has slept in His Majesty's room, usually rises an hour before the King, quietly leaves the bedroom, and goes out to dress in the anteroom. A quarter of an hour before the King is called, usually about half-past eight, the First Valet as quietly returns, and a servant lights a fire or, if it be winter, adds some logs of wood. At the same time the pages gently open the shutters, and remove the night-light and candle, which have remained alight throughout the night. They also remove the refreshments which are nightly placed at the King's bedside. When this has been done, the First Valet alone remains in the room until the hour at which the King has ordered that he is to be awakened. As soon as this has struck, the First Valet approaches the King and says: 'Sir, the hour has struck,' and then goes and admits the pages, one of whom has, a few minutes earlier, proceeded to notify the Lord Chamberlain and the First Lord of the Bedchamber-in-waiting for the year; another has been to warn the *Gobelet* and the *Bouche* to bring breakfast, while another takes charge of the door and only admits those whose rank or office permits them to enter when His Majesty has been called and is still in bed, and the First Valet, holding a small ewer of scent in his right hand, pours it over His Majesty's hands, under which he holds a gilt basin. The Lord Chamberlain or the First Lord of the Bedchamber then presents the stoup, and His Majesty makes the sign of the Cross with holy water. If any of the above-mentioned princes or nobles have anything to say to the King, they may speak to him now. His Majesty then recites the Office of the Holy Ghost and prays in bed for the space of a quarter of an hour.

"Before the King rises, M. Quentin, his barber, who has charge of the wigs, approaches him with two or more wigs of different sizes, and the King chooses the one he wishes to wear, in accordance with the plans for the day.

"At the moment when the King leaves his bed, he puts on his slippers, which are presented to him by the First

Valet. The Lord Chamberlain hands him his dressing-gown, and the King, again taking Holy Water, goes to the armchair, which is placed ready for him. As soon as he has left the rail which surrounds his bed, a Valet of the Wardrobe enters within and removes the breeches and sword from the arm-chair next to the bed. At this moment the 'Petit Lever' begins.

"The Lord Chamberlain or the First Lord of the Bedchamber removes the King's nightcap, and one of the barbers combs the King's hair, at which point commences the *première entrée*, that is to say, the page admits those who have the right to enter in virtue of their office or of a Royal Warrant. When the King's hair has been sufficiently combed, M. Quentin hands him the wig he uses while dressing, which is shorter than the one he usually wears for the rest of the day, and when he has put it on, the Officers of the Wardrobe advance to dress him, and at the same time the King asks for his Court.

"The Gentlemen Ushers enter and take charge of the door of the King's room, and one of them whispers to the First Lord of the Bedchamber the names of all who are without (such as Cardinals, Archbishops, Bishops, the Nuncio, Dukes and Peers, the Marshals of France, Governors of provinces, Lieutenant-Governors, the Presidents of the Parlements, and others), the latter repeating them to the King, who is pleased to order their admittance. The usher who holds the door then lets in, as soon as he sees them, certain persons for whom a special order has been given, such as the Duke de Vendôme, etc. He also admits, as they arrive, the chief officers of His Majesty's Household, for whom he does not ask permission. Then he allows to enter all the nobles and the remainder of the officers at his discretion, according to their qualifications and the importance of their duties, and such as occupy the higher posts. It is his duty to ask the name and rank of those unknown to him, and these must not take it amiss, for it is his business to know all whom he allows to enter. Meanwhile the King is dressing, and begins with his shoes. First a Page of the Wardrobe hands his socks and garters to the First Valet, who presents them one after the other to the King, who puts them on himself. Then a Valet of the Wardrobe hands him his breeches, to which his silk stockings are attached, and finally another page puts on his shoes, which usually have diamond buckles. The King then asks for his breakfast, and if he desires broth it is brought to him first, or else he takes a cup of sage water, which is brought by the Chief Cellarer.

"After his breakfast the King takes off his dressing-gown and the Master of the Wardrobe pulls the right arm of his nightshirt and the First Valet the left, and they then hand this garment to their subordinates. Before discarding his nightshirt, the King removes the relics which he wears day and night and gives them to the First Valet, who carries them to the King's closet and, together with the King's watch, places them in a little bag which lies on the table, and keeps them till the King enters his closet. Meanwhile a Valet of the Wardrobe brings the King's shirt, which has been warmed if it has been necessary to do so. If the Dauphin is attending the ceremony, at this juncture the Lord Chamberlain takes the shirt from the valet and gives it to the Dauphin, who, in turn, presents it to His Majesty. But in his absence a Prince of the Blood takes it from the valet, to whom he hands his hat, gloves, and stick, or, if none such be in attendance, the Lord Chamberlain, a First Lord of the Bedchamber, the Grand Master of the Wardrobe, or one of the other officers of the Wardrobe, in order of rank, present his shirt to the King. The First Valet of the Bedchamber now holds the right sleeve and the First Valet of the Wardrobe holds the left, the King rises, and the Master of the Wardrobe assists him to pull up his breeches.

"The Valets of the Wardrobe bring him his sword, his waistcoat, and the blue riband. The Grand Master of the Wardrobe fastens the sword to his side, slips his waistcoat over his arms, and passes over his shoulder the blue riband to which the diamond cross of the Order of the Holy Ghost is attached, together with the Order of St. Louis on its red riband. These hang with the sword on the left side. Finally, one of the valets presents the coat, which has also been warmed if necessary, to the Grand Master of the Wardrobe, who assists the King into it. The Master of the Wardrobe offers him his hat, gloves, and stick, and if it be a great Feast Day, the Grand Master of the Wardrobe hangs his mantle on his shoulders and gives him the collar of the Order, which the officers of the Wardrobe fasten to the mantle. But if the King was going hunting, he would wear an overcoat and a muff, if the weather warranted it.

"Should the King rise before daylight, a candle is lit and the King having indicated to the First Lord of the Bedchamber to whom he wished it to be given, the First Valet hands it to the person thus honoured to hold during His Majesty's toilet.

"While the King is dressing, the clockmaker winds the clocks in the room and in the other apartments, and even the watch which the King wears, and this he places on the table in the Closet.

"A valet always holds a mirror before the King while he is being dressed. The King being fully dressed advances to the bedside, an usher making way before His Majesty, and kneeling down on two cushions placed before the arm-chair by the bed, sprinkles himself with Holy Water and prays, while the valet remains within the railing. When the King has finished his orisons, the Grand Almoner says in a low voice the prayer beginning, *Quæsumus omnipotens Deus*, and the King then gives his orders as to where and when he will hear Mass, and gives directions to his First Steward as to the hour of dinner, and whether he will eat in public or in private.

"When the King dines in public it is called *Le Grand Couvert*, and dinner is then served in the King's anteroom, called *La Salle*. On these days the Usher of the Salle proceeds to the Guard-room, knocks at the door with his wand, crying: 'Gentlemen, to the King's dinner.' The Captain of the Guard on duty thereupon takes command of the salle and orders fourteen guards to form up in line with sloped arms, seven on each side, in front of His Majesty's table. Another guard precedes the Gentleman

"LA GRANDE TOILETTE"
From an engraving by Antoine Louis Romanet, after J. M. Moreau le Jeune

THE COURT

Waiter each time he brings the King anything to drink. These gentlemen stand close to the table and present the dishes to the Officers of the King's Table, who taste each dish before placing it before the King. There are six Gentlemen Waiters. The one who acts as cup-bearer cries, 'The King desires to drink,' every time the King requires it, and then, bowing to His Majesty, goes to the sideboard and receives from the Chief Cellarer the gold cup with a glass cover and two crystal flagons—one of wine and one of water. When it pleases His Majesty to dine privately, it is called *Le Petit Couvert*."

The menu of the *Grand Couvert* was always the same, and de Luynes records it in detail:

"The King's dinner always consists of the same number of courses: two soups, or one soup with a plate of bread to crumble in the broth, then two roasts, mutton or beef on alternate days, and always veal, of which the King eats most, and also an entrée of veal or mutton, which he rarely touches. Next, three dishes, all of which are larded and roasted, one of chicken, one of partridge or hare, and one of pigeon or some river bird, but he usually eats but little of these. Finally, fruit is served, together with two dishes of preserves and two of dried fruits, always including a little citron."[1]

At the *Grand Couvert*, the King's and the Queen's caskets were placed on the table, these being pieces of silver plate in the shape of a dismasted ship, containing their Majesties' napkins lying on perfumed cushions, and they were guarded by two armed guards. Luynes tells us that: "I used to see the ladies of the former Court making a deep curtsey to these caskets whenever they passed them on their way to the King's supper, but this is no longer customary."[2]

But how and where did the Gentlemen dine who served the King's table? The *Serd'eau*, or Gentlemen Waiters, received all the dessert of the King's table, which was carried to their room, and the dishes were handed to them and to all who ate with them, and their servants then re-

[1] Luynes, ii. 80.   [2] *Ibid.* ii. 290.

ceived what they left. The daily expenditure of Louis xv.'s table amounted to 399 livres, 18 sols, and 11 deniers.

A special ceremonial was prescribed for the taking off of His Majesty's boots, called *Le débotté*. When the King returned from hunting or a walk, he found in his room the officers of his household ready to change such clothes as might be necessary. A Valet of the Bedchamber took off his right boot and a Valet of the Wardrobe the left, and at this ceremony such persons might be present who had the *entrée* to His Majesty's Lever. Thus Voltaire writes in his *Épître à Mme Denis* (1748):

"Happy is he who may approach his Master! For him there is naught more to seek, but Jupiter, in the Empyrean deep, hides his adored presence from the eyes of humans, and only a few demigods may at night enter the Holy of Holies."

Let us now follow the "demigods" to see Jupiter go to bed.

"All the entrées of the Lever are on an equal footing when the King retires to bed: the intimates, the grandes, and petites entrées remain until the *Petit Coucher*, that is to say, until the King is in bed. The others leave when the King's arm-chair is brought to his dressing-table, and this is called the *Grand Coucher*. The *entrées de la chambre* and the courtiers who have no *entrée* withdraw when they are told, 'Pass, Gentlemen,' that is, when the King has removed his shoes and stockings, and his arm-chair is placed before his dressing-table. In the evening, when the King leaves his Closet, he goes to his *prie-Dieu* within the rails and close to his bed, and there removes his blue riband and his coat, and then indicates to the First Valet to whom the candlestick is to be given. The King puts on his night-shirt, which is handed to him by a Prince of the Blood or by one of the great officers of the household, according to rank, and then his dressing-gown, after which he seats himself, takes off his shoes, and when the pages of the Bedchamber have put on his slippers, the arm-chair is carried to his dressing-table, and all leave except those mentioned above.

THE COURT

"In the evening, two officers of the cellar bring a tray with refreshments for the night, of which the King partakes in case of need. These consist of three pieces of bread, two bottles of wine, a flagon of water and a glass, seven or eight napkins, and three plates. The pages pour out water and wine as the King may desire, hand him a napkin, and light a night-light in a corner of the room and a candle, both of which burn all night." [1]

And so, at long last, the King may sleep.

We see to what lengths the division of work was pushed at Court. The servants themselves had their duties regulated and defined down to the smallest detail, and as none of them dreamed of doing anything outside their own particular functions—a real "ca-canny" policy—none were more badly served than the King and Queen of France. Thus Luynes writes:

"The day before yesterday, the Queen, rising from table and walking in her room, found dust on the bedspread of her state bed, and informed Mme de Luynes, who sent for the Queen's upholsterer on duty. The latter, who is also the King's upholsterer, pretended that this was no concern of the upholsterers, who were not allowed to touch the furniture although they made the Queen's bed, and that this matter was for the Keeper of the King's Furniture. According to this argument, not only the Queen's bed, but the chairs and sofas which always have covers upon them, might be covered with dust, as indeed they are, but this would not be the fault of the upholsterers! Mme de Luynes told him that, at any rate, it was his business to notify the Keeper of the Furniture. This was done, and then the dust was removed." [2]

The Queen of France found that the more servants she had the less work was done. Her household was about the same as that of Maria Theresa, wife of Louis xiv., which numbered 572 officials and servants. Maria Leczinska herself had fourteen maids. The King's establishment was quite as numerous, and equally inefficient, as we can gather from another extract from Luynes: "About a week

[1] Lüynes, i. 263.   [2] *Ibid.* viii. 264.

ago, the King was dining in private and had reached the dessert stage when, wishing to put sugar in his cream, he found that the sugar-bowl was empty. He showed no impatience, and only said jokingly: 'There certainly was some yesterday,' and waited till a supply was brought. Three days ago, having retired earlier than usual, and having undressed, he found no night-shirt put out. 'Ah,' said he, 'my night-shirt has not come yet,' and going to the fire he put on his dressing-gown and waited. I was present on both occasions. I have also heard it said that one day, while hunting and being ready to mount, they brought him two boots for the same foot, whereupon he sat down to wait, saying: 'The man who forgot is probably more annoyed than I.' " [1]

But the King was even worse guarded than served, in spite of all his guards. Any one might enter the King's apartments. Thus, on the Feast of St. Louis, while the King was dining in public, a man dressed in black actually went right up to His Majesty and threw himself at his feet. He was a deserter who had been told that on this particular day the King would grant free pardons. He was handed over to the Guard which had protected the King so well! At the end of September 1757 the *Petites Affiches* announced that the King's watch had actually been stolen from his room, and du Hausset relates that: "One day as the King was on his way from his dressing-room to his bedroom, he suddenly met a stranger. It was a cook from outside, who had come to visit a friend in the Palace and, having mistaken the staircase, and finding all the doors open, had penetrated into the King's own apartments. Mme de Pompadour raised a great outcry that such a thing should be possible, but the King spoke quite calmly of this strange apparition, though he was obviously put out and had, not unnaturally, been rather frightened." [2]

When Damiens made an attempt on his life, the writers of the time were amazed that the assassin had found it so easy to approach and strike the King, and Mouffle notes: "On the eve of the Epiphany, Louis xv. was stabbed in

[1] Luynes, iii. 188.   [2] Du Hausset, p. 173.

his own Palace, in the midst of his guards, surrounded by the great officers of the Crown and in the presence of his son."¹

This incident is recorded in great detail by Luynes, writing on 6th January 1757: "The King had given orders to return to the Trianon at half-past five, and the coaches were waiting at the entrance to the new Guard-room. At six o'clock he came down, preceded by M. de Montmirail, with M. de Brionne and M. le Premier, and with M. de Baudreville immediately before him, while the Dauphin was on his left and the Duke d'Ayen followed.

"There are several steps leading down from the Guard-room, and it was on the bottom one that he felt himself struck, and cried out: 'I have been elbowed.'

"A man was seen, of about forty-five years of age, dressed in a brown overcoat, wearing his hat on his head, and the Dauphin said to him: 'Do you not see the King?' and a guardsman knocked off his hat. M. Didreville, King's equerry in attendance on the Dauphin, had already seized the man by the shoulders, but was just going to let him go (he is indeed my informant), believing him to be a country bumpkin, when the King, pressing his hand to his side and finding it covered with blood, exclaimed: 'I am wounded. That is the man who struck me'; adding, when he saw him being arrested: 'Seize him, but do not kill him.' About six seconds elapsed between the time the blow was struck and when the equerry seized the miscreant, and he might easily have escaped among the men and horses; but when it was found that the King was wounded, he was consigned to the Guard and kept there until he was removed to prison."²

When, some time later, the King met the Duke d'Ayen, who was then Captain of the Guard-in-waiting, he said to him: "You must admit, sir, that I am indeed well guarded."

The King, as we have seen, spent most of his time hunting, and Chateaubriand, who had then just been presented at Court, gives a graphic account of a day with

¹ Mouffle, iii. 128.   ² Luynes, xv. 356.

His Majesty's hounds, though this was in the succeeding reign:

"The Duke de Coigny informed me that I would hunt with the King in the Forest of St. Germain. I set out early for my ordeal, in the uniform of a 'novice'—grey coat, red waistcoat and breeches, riding-boots with tops, my hunting-knife at my side, and a small hat with gold braid. There were four of us—novices at the Palace of Versailles—the two St. Marsault brothers, the Count d'Hautefeuille, and myself. The Duke de Coigny gave us our instructions, and warned us not to override hounds, hinting that the King was furious if any one came between him and the quarry. Drums beat, arms rattled, orders were shouted. There were cries of 'The King!' and he came out, entered his coach, and away we rolled after him. What a difference between this ride and this hunt with the King of France and those on my own plains in Brittany! We arrived at the meet, where a great number of horses, already saddled and evidently impatient, were awaiting us under the trees. The coaches remained with the Guards in the forest. The crowd of ladies and gentlemen, the hounds straining at the leash, the whippers-in, all this formed a very animated picture, while horns blew, horses whinnied, and hounds bayed all around.

"On leaving my coach I handed my card to a whipper-in and was assigned my mount, a mare called 'Happy,' very speedy, but with no mouth, shy, and full of tricks. The King mounted and rode off, and was followed by the rest of the hunt, all taking different paths. I remained behind wrestling with 'Happy,' who had no idea of letting her new master bestride her; but, at last, I managed to jump on her back, though by then the hunt was already far away.

"At first I managed to control 'Happy' fairly well, but when I pulled her up she put her head down, shook her bit all covered with foam, and sidled down the glade, till, finally, when we got near the scene of action, nothing would hold her. She bolted, I slid on to her neck, and we galloped full tilt into a group of huntsmen, swept every one from our path, and did not stop till we collided with the horse of a lady which almost fell, amid roars of laughter from some and cries of terror from others.

"But I was not at the end of my misfortunes. About half an hour after my discomfiture, I was riding down a long glade in a part of the forest which appeared quite deserted, and saw a lodge at the end which set me thinking of the palaces raised here and there in the Crown forests in memory of kings of long ago and their clandestine pleasures. A shot rang out, 'Happy' swung round, bolted into the wood, and carried me straight to where the buck had fallen—and then—the King rode up! All too late I remembered the Duke de Coigny's instructions—that infernal mount of mine had spoiled everything. I jumped off, holding my mare with one hand and my hat in the other. The King gave me a look and perceived a novice who had arrived at the kill before him. He felt he ought to say something, but instead of flying into a rage, he remarked in a kindly tone and with a loud laugh: 'He did not last long.' And those were the only words that Louis XVI. ever addressed to me."[1]

Louis XVI. was, indeed, as silent as his predecessor, for Mallet du Pan describes how one day, while hunting in the forests of Verrières, the King and his attendants were obliged to dismount owing to the rain and seek shelter under some trees where du Pan and some friends had also taken refuge. During a whole half-hour the King never opened his mouth.

Sometimes strange scenes were witnessed. "One day," de Croÿ tells us, "the meet was a long way away, near Argentan. The hunt was long and tiring, and, losing my way, I joined the coaches, together with the Marshal d'Harcourt, when a second stag passed close to us. I followed and witnessed a fine ending to the day's sport, for the stag came right up to the castle, and would have entered the kennels if the gate had been open. Instead, he jumped into the mall, and when the two packs of hounds were unleashed, dashed into the garden and jumped into

[1] *Mémoires d'Outre-Tombe*, i. 206.

the great pond which is opposite the Fountain Court, a thing which has never happened before. All the Court and the whole town of Fontainebleau rushed to the waterside, and this, together with the many hounds both in and out of the water, and all the horns blowing, formed a very fine spectacle, and was one of the prettiest kills it was possible to witness."[1]

But stag-hunting was not without its dangers, for the Dauphine Marie-Josèphe wrote to her brother, Prince Xavier, that the stag passed so close to her that she could almost have touched him, but she had not the slightest desire to do so, for the danger was so great that, coward that she was, she was terrified.

These incidents were unforeseen, but at the Palace every other contingency was provided for—the etiquette for the whole day, the actions and even the gestures of the King and his gentlemen being minutely prescribed. It was a real science, and it was extremely difficult to remember exactly the rank and privileges which, in certain ceremonies, were assumed by this or that gentleman or lady of the Court. One man was completely familiar with the procedure—the Duke de Gesvres et de Tresmes, First Lord of the Bedchamber and Governor of Paris—as his father and grandfather had been before him. The following is the tribute paid by de Luynes to the memory of one who had been the reigning arbiter of the Court on all matters touching its etiquette:

"He is deeply regretted, and certainly deserves to be. He was brought up at Court, and no one knew its usages so well as he. His memory was amazing, for he never devoted himself to science or to letters, but was fully acquainted with the doings of the last Court, and with the details of the ancestry and genealogy of all who lived at Court or in the town. He was infinitely kind to his friends, and just as kind to others with whom he was less well acquainted. There was no one at the Court or in the town, not even the Princes of the Blood, who did not bow before him, for they themselves submitted to him all the disputes

[1] Croÿ, i. 90.

which often arose among them. He conducted himself with such tact that he always retained the friendship and confidence of both parties, and he was able, upon occasion, to speak quite plainly to them. Every one was only too glad to follow his advice." [1]

His father, on the contrary, was not a faultless judge of etiquette if Saint-Simon can be believed:

"The Marquis de Gesvres (First Lord of the Bedchamber), afterwards Duke de Tresmes, asserted that, once dinner had begun, M. de Bouillon (Lord Chamberlain) could not supersede him in his duties, but he was proved wrong. I have seen M. de Bouillon appear behind the King's chair in the middle of dinner, and M. de Beauvilliers, who was waiting upon His Majesty, offer to retire in his favour, but this he politely refused, saying he coughed too much and had a bad cold. Thus he remained behind the King, and M. de Beauvilliers continued to perform his duties, but only after M. de Bouillon had publicly refused to assume them. The Marquis de Gesvres was wrong: the First Lord of the Bedchamber only has charge of the Bedchamber, but no functions, whereas the Lord Chamberlain has the performance of the functions but no charge, and it is only in his absence that they fall to the former. But should the First Lord of the Bedchamber be absent, and there be no other there, his place is taken, not by the Lord Chamberlain, but by the First Valet of the Bedchamber." [2]

These grave debates on the respective functions and prerogatives of these great officers make us smile, but they can be understood when we reflect that the courtier of that time had no other occupation during the whole of his life but to carry out his duties as such, and had no thought but to be at his post. As Montesquieu says: "We have come to regard as all-important the tasks which constitute our duty and which people like ourselves perform every day. Our vanity ranks these very high among the functions of the Universe. A Master of Ceremonies at Rome burst into tears when the Cardinal d'Estrées made a bow at the

[1] Luynes, xvi. 186.   [2] Saint-Simon, xii. 175.

wrong moment. To this man a bow was of far greater import than was a battle to Prince Eugène." [1]

Thus innumerable disputes of the most futile description would often arise among the King's household touching some point of etiquette, and Saint-Simon tells of one when "the First Lords of the Bedchamber had an argument with the Stewards of the Household as to who should inform the King that his dinner was served, but in the days of the late King I always saw the Steward inform the First Lord of the Bedchamber, who then went into the King's closet alone and announced that dinner was served, and in the evening, even when the King was with Mme de Maintenon, the Steward informed the Captain of the Guard, who then went in alone and announced His Majesty's supper." [2]

But it was at Court Balls that the most delicate questions arose as to the honours to be shown to guests of distinction whose presence had not been foreseen. Mouffle, writing of the festivities at Versailles on the occasion of the Dauphin's wedding in 1770, says:

"The State Ball, which was the most boring of all because it is always most hedged in by etiquette, gave rise to much bickering. His Majesty had previously approved the ceremonial to be followed, and had consented, at the request of the Ambassador of the Emperor and the Empress-Queen, to show some mark of distinction to Mlle de Lorraine, who was related to the Imperial House, inasmuch as she would dance before all the Duchesses and immediately after the Princesses of the Blood, in the same way as the Prince de Lambesc took the floor immediately after the Princes. This was a grave decision. The Dukes and Peers assembled at the house of M. de Broglie, Bishop and Count of Noyon, as the senior Peer then in Paris, and, in spite of the Church's horror of dancing, a memorandum was drawn up and revised after much discussion, and this the Bishop was charged to carry to the King." [3]

Sometimes it was found convenient to retire to bed in

---

[1] *Mélanges inédits*, p. 147.   [2] Saint-Simon, xiv. 191.
[3] Mouffle, iv. 218.

order to avoid the countless difficulties which the rules of etiquette created. Thus Voltaire describes how, when Cardinal de Richelieu was treating with the English Ambassadors with regard to the marriage of Henrietta Maria and Charles I., the negotiations were all but broken off because the English demanded that the Cardinal should take two or three more steps at a certain door. To avoid the difficulty, the Cardinal went to bed. Similarly, when Peter the Great visited Mme de Maintenon at St. Cyr, Marmontel records that she took to her bed as soon as she heard of his arrival, so as to avoid all ceremony.

In short, the King was the greatest slave, and, one might add, the greatest victim, of this rigorous etiquette which condemned him to the misery of never being alone for a single moment. Gleichen illustrates this: "In negotiating with M. de Choiseul on the manner in which the King of Denmark was to be received, it was impressed on me to secure a private interview between the two monarchs on the occasion of their first meeting, that the King of France should address the Danish King as Majesty, and that the latter should then assume the strictest incognito. M. de Choiseul told me that, though his master had ordered him to grant me all I wished as far as etiquette was concerned, I ought to realise that this request was impossible to grant, because the King of France never remained alone for one moment of his life, not even in his dressing-room, and that he could not dismiss from his apartments those whose privileges and office gave them the right to remain. The first interview, therefore, took place in the presence of all the chief personages of the Court."[1]

Boileau remarks how Louis XIV. complained at the crossing of the Rhine "that his greatness chained him to the bank"—but how much more cause to complain had Louis XV. who was chained the live-long day to an etiquette which foresaw, and regulated accordingly, his every action. As Montesquieu says: "Kings, in spite of all the machinery with which they have surrounded themselves—their

[1] Gleichen, xxxv.

guards, their officials, and their household—are reduced to being the slaves of circumstance and etiquette. A King's sole merit is to be punctual, and his life is identified with his duties. What are the advantages a Louis xiv. has over a Henry iv.? The former has lost his liberty, and the properties attached to his Kingship are fitted to him like his own skin." [1]

This etiquette, however, should not be derided and condemned too much. It had its uses at Court and even elsewhere. One fine day the Count de Clermont, great-grandson of the great Condé, thought he would like to belong to the Academy. On the day of the election, those Academicians who were of noble birth proposed that he should be admitted by acclamation, but Duclos firmly insisted on carrying out the regulations, and Clermont was elected only by a majority. Then came the day for admitting him. As Luynes says: "It was a difficult position for the Count de Clermont, who was a Prince of the Blood, a title of respect and deserving of honour, but, in a way, not comparable to a body whose distinction was that it was based on Liberty and Equality."

Now when a new Academician was admitted, it was customary for his colleagues to be seated round a table in order of seniority, the last elected occupying the lowest place. The Household of M. de Clermont submitted a memorandum demanding a higher place for their master and requesting an immediate reply. Duclos, who was well up in questions of etiquette, very courteously refused the demand, "leaving the rise or fall, in short the Academy's ultimate fate, entirely in the Count's hands." But he preferred to forgo the public reception, thus, as Collé says, "avoiding having to make a speech which, if it had been a good one, would have been attributed not to him but to his 'teinturier'." (a name given to those who were paid to write other people's speeches).

" One day when the Academy was sitting, he decided to visit it incognito, so as to surprise that august body, but, unfortunately, he opened the wrong door at the Louvre

[1] *Pensées et fragments inédits,* ii. 335.

and found himself in the Academy of Sciences, so he withdrew and eventually arrived in the Academy. On that day, 26th March 1754, M. de Mirabeau was presiding, but he did not rise and offer him his seat, so the Count sat down in the first vacant chair, made himself very affable, called them all his friends and dear colleagues, took his badge when they were distributed, and with great amiability expressed himself so highly honoured that he would like to have it pierced in order to wear it in his buttonhole." [1]

Etiquette had saved Equality, or, rather, in this case the dignity of the Academy.

[1] Collé, i. 409.

CHAPTER II

THE NOBILITY OF THE SWORD

MONTESQUIEU once said: "In France there are three professions which confer nobility—the Church, the Sword, and the Bar—and each feels the utmost disdain for the other two." This was a true saying, for we read in Saint-Simon how the nobility "of the sword" triumphed with glee over the pretensions of the nobles of the Bar who were humiliated at the Lit de Justice of 1718, while, on the other hand, it is well known how bitter was the feud between the Bar and the Clergy during the eighteenth century, when the clergy refused burial to all lawyers suspected of Jansenism, and the Parliament decreed the arrest of the intolerant priests, while the Bishops wrote Pastoral Letters and the clergy thundered from their pulpits against the proud magistrates.

This definition of Montesquieu has to be amplified, for not only were there three distinct and hostile classes in eighteenth-century society, but in each of them there were still further divisions, each suspicious and jealous of the others. We will, therefore, first confine ourselves to the Nobles, of whom there were three kinds.

Montlosier, quoting Chérin, who was an authority on the history of France as conceived in his day, said that, "as the first known titles of nobility dated from the fourteenth century, and adopting the generally held theory of a conquering and a vanquished race, all who could submit 'proof' by title-deeds anterior to this century must belong to the conquering race—that is, to the Franks.

"There was therefore a *noblesse présentée*—that is to say, a nobility which could prove its descent back to the

THE NOBILITY OF THE SWORD

fourteenth century, and there was also another *non presentée*, which, for one reason or another, could not produce such ancestry. Though unable to show title-deeds dating back as far as this, the second class, provided it had sufficient title to be admitted to the Order of Malta or to be pages in Noble Colleges, claimed, like the first class, to belong to the original nobility. In virtue of this claim it separated itself as much as possible from yet another class, namely, the 'ennobled' (*les anoblis*).

"Thus, as one section was excluded from Court owing to lack of title-deeds, and another—the merely ennobled—was denied office and the dignities attached thereto, there arose three distinct factions within the class of the nobility, and these divisions were sorely wounding to self-esteem."[1]

In the provinces also these distinctions were found, and were even accentuated, and quarrels as to precedence would blaze up in the same town, and even in the same family. Thus in Lorraine, the four chief families were called "les grands chevaux," while the second "chevalerie" consisted of those families which were descended from the first in the female line, and were called "les petits chevaux," and naturally tried to emulate "les grands."

Talleyrand has collected and summarised all these pretensions and conflicting claims in the following passage of his *Mémoires*: "In the noble class there was no definite hierarchy, since the titles which ought to distinguish the various ranks had no constant value. In place of one class, there were seven or eight—one of the Sword and one of the Bar, one of the Court and one of the Provinces, one old and one new, one large and one small. One pretended to be superior to the other, which, in turn, claimed to be equal to the former."[2]

The State, as we know, raised money by creating offices the purchase of which conferred nobility, and at the side of, or rather below the nobles, arose the ennobled. The *bourgeois*, or middle class, hastened to buy these *savonettes à vilains*, as they were called, as, for instance, the

[1] Montlosier, i. 151.   [2] *Mémoires*, i. 116.

young Caron who, in 1757, had just married the widow Francquet, an Aubertin by birth, and assumed the name of Beaumarchais, from a tiny fief belonging to his wife. In the course of his famous quarrel with Goëzman, the judge, the latter wrote, not without malice: "M. Caron borrowed from one of his wives the name of Beaumarchais, which he has now lent to one of his sisters," whereupon Beaumarchais in his *Mémoires* replied with his usual assurance: "Take note that I can already prove twenty years of nobility, that this nobility is mine own, recorded in black and white and sealed with a big seal of yellow wax; further, that, unlike that of many people, there is no doubt about it, nor is it dependent on word of mouth alone, and no one dare dispute it, for I hold a receipt for it."

It was only the new nobility which was regarded with suspicion by the old, and this because of the receipts aforesaid, "for if it is assumed that every ennobled person is noble, then the dignity of 'gentleman' must be reserved for him who cannot show his ennoblement and who, consequently, can claim nobility by his acts alone"—writes the Marquis de Mirabeau on 26th March 1780.

An aristocracy is essentially a body of citizens which governs or takes part in government, whereas a caste is a closed corporation, and the distinctive mark of its members is birth. Now in France, in the eighteenth century, the nobility had ceased to be an aristocracy and had become a caste, so that Tocqueville could write: "While the nobility is losing its political power, the noble extends his privileges and enlarges them. One might say that the members were enriching themselves at the expense of the class. The nobility can less and less claim to direct affairs, but the nobles are more and more assuming the exclusive prerogative of being the first among the prince's servants," and Montesquieu says: "A great noble is a man who sees the King, speaks with his ministers, and who possesses ancestors, debts, and pensions." Of all the privileges which the nobility enjoyed, the most splendid, as well as the most lucrative, was that of seeing the King and of living in his shadow, for it was at Versailles that the rain of pensions, offices, and posts was poured forth, and Versailles, in fact, was inhabited, not only by the courtiers who thronged with outstretched hands, but also by ladies who disputed with one another for the privilege of approaching the Queen and the supreme honour of sitting on a 'tabouret.'"

According to Loyseau, the days had gone when "the nobility was now so exalted that even a poor younger son almost dead of hunger in his cottage would think it dishonourable to serve in the King's Household." [1] That was in the reign of Louis XIII. In that of Louis XV. the nobility hastened—in the phrase of Saint-Simon—"to exchange liberty for slavery."

The King's absolute power had bent all heads beneath its yoke, and at the approach of the eighteenth century the anonymous author of an eloquent pamphlet, entitled *The Moans of Enslaved France sighing for Liberty* (1689), wrote, without exaggeration: "In the present government all are mere scum. To such a height has the Monarch raised himself, that all poor humans are but dust beneath his feet." All were equal in this slavery, and Chamfort ironically and bitterly affirmed that "all are courtiers at Court, whether they be a Prince of the Blood, the chaplain-in-waiting, the surgeon on duty, or the apothecary," and he lays stress on the moral consequences of this abasement of the nobility: "I do not know how a Frenchman who has been in the King's Anteroom or the *Œil-de-Bœuf* can say of any one there: 'Behold a great noble.' Practically all of them were great beggars, and the highest in the land of both sexes thronged the minister's waiting-room; for is not Influence the Goddess of the French? . . . and the minister is the High Priest who sacrifices many a victim to her." [2]

It was not, however, merely favours and pensions which were expected from the King's generosity and the minister's complaisance—the courtiers hoped also to fill their pockets, for which various Court customs, as expensive as they were ridiculous, afforded innumerable

---

[1] Loyseau, ch. v. (*Des Ordres*).   [2] 88th *Lettre persane*.

opportunities. Thus in 1717 the Duke de Tresmes, as Saint-Simon tells us, received 80,000 livres in compensation for mourning which had been due to him but had not been paid at the King's death, he being First Lord of the Bedchamber-in-waiting that year.

Besides these fees, chargeable to the Treasury and assigned to the gentlemen who held any office, the adroit courtier could also rake in other perquisites, if one may so call them, and Duclos alludes to the Prince d'Auvergne who received a pension of 6000 livres for his *droit d'avis*, a sort of " counsel's opinion," when he devised balls at the Opera House, which took the place of private balls at which disorder often occurred necessitating a military guard. Even the greatest of ladies did not disdain what may be called the petty perquisites to be obtained at Court. According to Buvat: "When the King reached his seventh year on 15th January 1717, the Regent, with the Princes and Princesses, proceeded to the Palace of the Tuileries to perform the ceremony of stripping the King of his clothes and verifying 'that he had no wound and was well nourished,' after which he was withdrawn from the ladies and entrusted to the Duke du Maine, the Maréchal de Villeroy, and those who were to take charge of his education. Mme de Ventadour, his governess, received all the garments of which he had been divested, all his linen, as well as all the furniture and plate, whether of silver or other metal, which had been used by His Majesty." [1]

The ladies of the Court did not hesitate to quarrel with their subordinates over what they considered the perquisites of their office. When the Dauphine was on her way from Spain to France, the town of Bayonne offered, as part of its homage, some large hams, which were not eaten, and Mme de Brancas declared that they belonged to her, while the Queen's head maid claimed them as her right, but eventually the matter was amicably settled. The incident was, however, reported to the King for his ruling, and he ordered that the arrangement was to stand, but that, as a matter of fact, the head maid was right.

[1] Buvat, i. 248.

Anyhow, Mme de Brancas was able to keep her share of the hams.

But let us return to Versailles and examine the usual methods of making a fortune at Court—at the expense of the Treasury. The Treasury seemed inexhaustible, such was the King's generosity. When a Master of the Ceremonies died, it was reckoned that he had an income of at least 84,000 livres from the King's bounty. Fortunate was the man who obtained the Governorship of the Bourbonnais, since it was worth 35,000 livres per annum. It is true that it was charged with an annuity of 8000 livres, but this was for the Duchess de la Vallière d'Uzès.

The ministers themselves, indeed, were among the worst " pluralists." Choiseul was created Duke and Peer, Minister of War as well as of Marine, Colonel-in-Chief of the Swiss Guards, Governor of Touraine, and High Bailiff of Haguenau, offices which brought him an annual income of 700,000 livres, besides some two millions which, according to Sénac de Meilhan, were given to him by the King to meet his stupendous expenditure, so that he could, with truth, write to the King in October 1763: "Through you and your goodness, sire, I have acquired the largest fortune that has been made during your reign."

Nor should the "amphibies" be forgotten—those who, as La Bruyère describes them, "lived both by the sword and by the Church," occupying secular posts in addition to their ecclesiastical benefices. Both he and Saint-Simon define the acquisition of fortunes at Court by the verb *cheminer*. The King aided and abetted this state of things, for he could refuse his courtiers nothing, and France was bled white for the benefit of about five hundred families, which led the Neapolitan Ambassador, Caraccioli, to coin the facetious aphorism: "In France nine-tenths of the population die of hunger and one-tenth of indigestion."

At the end of the century, Necker, auditing the pensions given by the King, expressed himself as follows in the memorandum he submitted in January 1781: "Even Your Majesty will be surprised to learn that these various bounties actually constitute a charge amounting to some

28 millions on the revenue of the State. I doubt if all the Sovereigns of Europe combined pay more than half this sum in pensions." It was to such privileged persons—"flies round a honeycomb," as d'Argenson called them—that all the great offices of the State were assigned, and Chamfort writes with his usual sarcasm: "In France merit and good repute are no more qualifications for office than is the rose wreath of a virtuous village maiden for her presentation at Court. The impossibility for any one except a nobleman to rise to any post of consequence leads to a most unhappy state of things throughout the country. To me it is as if donkeys had superseded horses in all jousts and tournaments. Nature does not consult Cherin before making a man virtuous or creating a genius."

The highest of all honours was the "tabouret" for ladies and the "cordon bleu" for men. "The divine tabouret," as Mme de Sévigné called it, was "a small stool in use at Court and much sought after; great alliances failed to mature because a wife might not have had the satisfaction of sitting on one." That is Coyer's definition. A warrant creating a Duchess carried this privilege with it. On 12th October 1752, the King, wishing "to bestow some mark of his very special consideration on Mme the Marquise de Pompadour, and to show his esteem for her person, His Majesty was graciously pleased to direct that she should enjoy all the honours, rank, and privileges appertaining to Duchesses," and, as a result, the meticulous de Luynes notes: "On the 17th October at Fontainebleau the new Duchess took her seat on her tabouret at a quarter past six, the Princess of Conty introducing and Mme d'Estrades and M. de Choiseul supporting her."[1]

The knights of the Royal Order of the Holy Ghost were generally known as "cordons bleus" because they wore the cross of the Order suspended from a riband of blue watered silk. Appointments to this Order were usually made on the 1st of January, the Feast of the Order, and one of the great Court festivals. The dress was magnificent: in the procession on the 1st of January, the Knights wore

[1] Luynes, xii. 170.

a long mantle of black velvet embroidered with *fleurs-de-lis* and tassels of gold, and sown with cyphers in silver and flames of gold. On the left, the eight-pointed cross with the dove in the centre was embroidered in silver; the collar was formed of *fleurs-de-lis* and golden cyphers alternately, linked with knots, and from this the Cross with its dove was suspended.

It was a very ancient Order, for Henry III. had instituted it in the sixteenth century, and it was limited to one hundred knights, which in itself added great lustre to the Order, for, as in the case of the tabouret to which only duchesses could aspire, both "distinguished" the recipients of these honours from the common herd of courtiers. "I wish to be distinguished above all others," cried Alceste, and this ambition, though from very different motives, inspired every noble and great lady. Voltaire in the article on ceremonies in his *Dictionnaire Philosophique* may have referred to this incident. A Grandee of Portugal spoke to a Grandee of Spain and kept addressing him as "Your Excellency." The Grandee of Spain, in reply, addressed him "Your Courtesy," a title given to such people as have not any. The Portuguese felt hurt and, in turn, called the Spaniard "Your Courtesy," who immediately countered with "Your Excellence." At last the Portuguese wearied of it and said to him: "Why do you call me 'Your Courtesy' when I address you as 'Your Excellence,' and 'Your Excellence' when I give you the title of 'Your Courtesy'?" "Because," answered the Spaniard humbly, "all my titles are equal provided that there be no equality as between you and me."

In order to play a part in high places and to hold offices of great dignity, the nobility squandered their fortunes without a thought and ruined themselves gaily. D'Argenson notes that "the more impoverished nobles become, the more do they increase the magnificence of their clothes, table, and houses," and here is one example among thousands told by Barbier: "The Prince de Soubise had built a charming cottage at Saint-Ouen. The King promised to come and sup there as soon as it was finished—a favour which, although costly, no courtier would seek to evade. There were illuminations and supper for all the King's suite, and it was said that this fête and this honour cost the Prince de Soubise about 200,000 livres."[1] This is no exaggeration, for another author tells of a single omelette which Soubise set before the King and what it cost him. "Maréchal de Soubise had 500,000 livres per annum, but that was not enough for him. Among his expenses was one item which is worth recording, and which recurred annually, whenever the King came to rest at the Maréchal's house at Saint-Ouen after his shoot. This was an omelette which was prepared for His Majesty, made of pheasants' and partridges' eggs and other ingredients so costly that this omelette cost twenty-five louis. This was an agreed price, and the rest was in proportion."[2] (The louis then was equal to twenty-four francs, so that at a pre-war valuation the omelette would have cost 600 francs—truly a royal omelette!)

Enormous numbers of servants of all kinds were required to wait on the numerous guests invited to a gentleman's table, and for the upkeep of his establishment; in fact, a large staff of retainers was indispensable to any one who wished to live up to his rank—the Duchess de Berry, for example, according to Buvat, kept no less than eight hundred.

The Court itself gave the most noticeable example of waste by creating, or maintaining, offices which were both useless and expensive, such as the one mentioned by Luynes: "One of the posts in the Queen's household is a strange one, because it is of considerable value and yet has practically no duties attached to it. This is the Keepership of the Wardrobe, which M. de Triel has just sold to M. de la Morlière for 24,000 livres. The holder has to superintend the transport of the Queen's trunks when she travels, but has few opportunities of so doing, and, in fact, does not do so. It is worth 2800 livres a year."[3]

These absurd extravagances naturally went hand and

[1] Barbier, iv. 459. [2] Lévis, *Souvenirs*, p. 157.
[3] Luynes, x. 240,

THE NOBILITY OF THE SWORD

hand with poverty, and the latter reared its head even at Versailles. "The contractors declare they can no longer supply His Majesty's table, and hide themselves so that others have to be found. The King's grooms beg for alms, while the expenses of the King's household increase daily. Each progress to one of the King's country seats costs 100,000 livres. The Crown Equerry makes money in his department, and the ladies-in-waiting on the Princesses make a profit of eighty per cent. It is said that their coffee and little piece of bread costs two thousand francs a year for each lady, and so on in proportion. No one has sufficient authority to reform the household, which is a bottomless pit as far as the nation is concerned." [1]

In April 1752 pensions to the amount of 120,000 livres were distributed among the ladies of the Court, "and these, moreover, were among the wealthiest." Later, a lady said to Necker: "What is a pension of a thousand crowns to the King?" "A thousand crowns!" cried Necker. "Why, that is what a whole village pays in taxes!"

D'Argenson remarked truly, if somewhat bitterly as was his wont: "The Court is the Nation's grave."

A most dangerous practice which afforded the King every facility for wasteful extravagance had gradually grown up at Court. This was the use of *les acquits du comptant*, which were sums paid into the Royal Treasury on the King's signature alone, but for unspecified objects. Under Louis XIV. such sums reached ten million, while under Louis XV. the Parliament in its Remonstrances placed them at over a hundred million. Under the heading of extraordinary expenditure the King was, as if to justify it, made to pay prices which certainly were extraordinary. Luynes records that he had to give ten livres for two pears, and disbursed no less than 2000 crowns for a dinner of fifteen covers at La Meutte. Besenval relates the following anecdote: "M. de Choiseul told me that one day, when accompanying Louis XV. to the meet, the latter asked him how much he thought the coach they were riding in had cost. M. de Choiseul said that he thought five or six

[1] D'Argenson, vii. 408.

thousand francs would have been a fair price, but as His Majesty had to pay like a King it would more probably have been nearer eight. 'You are very wide of the mark,' said Louis; 'this carriage, just as it is, cost me thirty thousand.' "[1]

The three principal objects which absorbed the fortunes of the great nobles were their clothes, their table, and gaming. The money lavished on clothes was prodigious, and had become customary since the days of Louis XIV., who, as Saint-Simon says, was passionately fond of every sort of sumptuous display at Court, and on ceremonial occasions wore his blue ribbon with pearls valued at eight to ten millions, and praised the courtiers whose dress he considered to be the richest and most magnificent. The same held good under Louis XV., and what Mme de Sévigné said of her son was true of all courtiers: "Their hand is a crucible in which all money melts." They were often unable to buy clothes and jewels for the Court entertainments, and were therefore forced to hire them, although even this was ruinous. Barbier, writing of the Dauphin's arrival in February 1745, says: "These fêtes will seriously inconvenience both gentlemen and ladies of the Court as regards clothes. They say that the gentlemen's suits will cost anything up to fifteen thousand livres, and three suits are needed for the three days. The Marquis de Mirepoix, who, it is said, will be our Ambassador on the occasion of the Emperor's election [that of Francis I., husband of Maria Theresa], has hired three at six thousand apiece from a tailor to whom he returns them after only wearing them for one day. The Marquis de Stainville, the Grand Duke of Tuscany's envoy, whose son is a Colonel in our army, has a suit of cloth of silver embroidered with gold and lined with marten's fur. The lining alone is said to cost twenty-five thousand livres. One lady is reported to have hired diamonds for fifteen thousand livres to wear at the Court Ball at Versailles."[2]

Let us now see how a newly married couple set up house, from a description given by the Count de Cheverny:

[1] Besenval, *Mémoires*, i. 425.   [2] Barbier, iv. 13.

"My establishment consisted of a Swiss porter, a *maître d'hôtel*, or steward, Mlle Gentil as housekeeper, a maid, a cook and his assistant, and two magnificent footmen for my own use. My wife also had two, a small one given her by Mme le Gendre and another called Lapierre, lately promoted to be my private courier. I had six carriage horses—two for my wife and four for myself—two coachmen, a postillion, three saddle-horses, and one groom. I kept my faithful Boissy, called Saint-Jean, who had been my father's coachman, and was considered one of the best coachmen in Paris, as indeed he was." [1]

But this luxury was nothing to the magnificence of a Choiseul in his splendid exile at Chanteloup. According to Cheverny: "It is impossible to imagine the pomp that surrounds him. On arriving at night one would think one was at Versailles, so magnificent is the illumination without and within this enormous mass of buildings. It took me twenty minutes to traverse the passages from the room allotted to me to the apartments of the Abbé Barthelemy. On the return from hunting, if the ceremony of breaking up the quarry took place in one of the courtyards, this was immediately filled by women and men and whole families, all attached to his service. He had six musicians besides a young man who played the clavecin extremely well. He or the Duchess would play the pianoforte, and in a room next to the drawing-room, and set apart for music, the best and latest symphonies were played daily for one hour, from noon to one. This superb residence was thrown open to all who were respectably dressed, and orders had been given that everything was to be shown. A magnificent library in a vaulted gallery was full of the most exquisitely bound books and of the most beautiful editions. The collections of prints and coins were worthy of a prince with real taste.

"His table was excellent without being too lavish. Three tables were served after that of the Duke, and at these even Knights of St. Louis did not disdain to sit." [2]

Such expenditure inevitably entailed debts which were

---

[1] Cheverny, *Mémoires*, i. 164.   [2] *Ibid.* i. 417.

often appalling. It is not surprising, after the above, to read in Sénac de Meilhan that Choiseul had to have recourse to the King in order to pay his debts, though he and his wife, between them, had a million a year.

One of his creditors once asked the Marquis de Louvois when he thought he would pay him. "You are very inquisitive," was his sharp reply. But the Marquises themselves were less so, for they pretended ignorance of their debts until the moment of bankruptcy approached. The Countess de Coislin wrote to the Duke d'Harcourt: "The bankruptcy of the Prince de Guéménée is for debts of from 25 to 30 millions, and there are 3000 creditors. The whole Rohan family is in despair, especially the Prince de Soubise, who neither sleeps nor eats since this fatal event took place. A crowd of wretched people have been reduced to beggary. The wits—and they were not among the creditors—called the Prince's bankruptcy 'the most serene bankruptcy.' "

But it must be said that even the greatest fools lost their fortunes without losing their good humour. Among these was the eccentric Count de Lauraguais, whose mad extravagance had reduced him to poverty. "He had long been the most luxurious, the most splendid, and the most gallant of great nobles, but for even longer now he has been seen about, badly dressed, ill-combed, and affecting the simple ways of a Danubian peasant.

"I remember one morning he called on me thus carelessly dressed but with a beaming face. 'Oh,' said I, 'wherefore this unusually joyful countenance?' 'My friend,' he replied, 'I am the happiest of mortals. I am completely ruined.' 'Good heavens! that is a strange piece of good fortune. I should have thought it more a cause for suicide.' 'You are quite wrong, my dear fellow,' replied he. 'Whilst I was but embarrassed, I was overwhelmed with business, pestered, alternating between hope and fear; but now that I am ruined, I am independent, calm, free from all worries and anxiety.' "[1]

But gambling—"that hellish pastime"—was the chief

[1] Ségur, i. 138.

cause of ruin to all the great houses. On every page of de Luynes, the historian of the Court, we find passages such as the following: "Play was very high until eight or nine in the morning," and it is, therefore, not surprising to read in d'Argenson: "M. de Livry is ruined by gambling, and his estate at Livry is about to be sold."

To repair one's fortune "and cleverly restore the ravages of one's youth," as Don Juan has it, there was a convenient remedy—a good marriage. As de la Bruyère wrote: "The need of money has reconciled the nobility to the plebeians, and the necessary qualification of four quarterings has been thrown overboard." By the middle of the eighteenth century this "reconciliation" of the classes had become a necessity for the French nobility, which, as d'Argenson said with a sigh, "is so ruined that it can only exist by marrying beneath them."

Marriages of this kind were, in fact, very common in the fashionable world. The Duchess de Chaulnes said to her son who was unwilling to marry the daughter of the enormously rich M. Bonnier, that, "to marry advantageously beneath oneself is merely taking dung to manure one's acres." And, heaven knows, the acres of the nobility needed manure!

Sometimes it even occurred that a girl was kidnapped in order to obtain her marriage portion. Luynes describes how "Mlle de Moras, daughter of the late Director of the India Company, who has been dead two or three years, was kidnapped a week ago. She is extremely rich, and thirteen or fourteen years of age. She was in a convent in Paris whilst her mother was in the country, and a letter purporting to be from Mme de Moras was brought to the governess ordering her to bring the girl to her, and informing her that a two-horsed carriage had been sent for the purpose. Mme de Moras was quite unaware of this, and only heard of it by chance a week later. No one knows who is the perpetrator or where the girl is." [1]

But such abductions became less frequent in the course of the eighteenth century. Among the nobility it was

[1] Luynes, i. 389.

customary not only to ask the family's consent, but also the King's permission for a marriage. "Last Friday I asked the King's leave for my son's marriage with Mlle d'Egmont," writes Luynes. Sometimes the future husband and wife were amazingly young. Luynes writes: *Sunday, 1748.*—The Duke de Randan and the Prince de Talmond came to ask the King's consent to the marriage of Mlle de Randan, aged 13, to the Duke de la Trémoille, aged 11. They cannot marry for three years."

The Countess de Coislin announces to the Duke d'Harcourt on 16th May 1779 that "her niece Montbarrey is to wed the only son of the Prince de Nassau. The disparity in their ages is, if possible, even greater than that of their fortunes. He is eleven, she is seventeen." Though the idea of marriage where such children were concerned may cause us to smile, it was, in those days, dictated by the following considerations. In society, such as it then was, social expediency was of greater weight than mutual affection between the parties concerned, and the union of two families was considered more important than the wishes of individuals. They married to obtain position in society or at Court, the essential thing being that the race should not die out, and that the family property should not be dispersed through division among many heirs. That would be ensured by the birth of a son, and, if there should be two, the eldest of the family received the fortune and entered the army: the younger was usually destined for the Church. Coyer, commenting on this, writes: "So as to bestow all on one, the others are immured for life in prisons, where they periodically fast and scourge themselves, and over and above these penalties they are forced to sing, while the adored child for whom all the others have been sacrificed is sent to the wars to get killed."

But the younger son did not always "immure himself in a lifelong prison," though he often permitted his elder brother to decide what the honour and interest of the family might dictate. A younger son of a family of Provence, Mirabeau, Governor of Guadeloupe, replies to his elder brother on the subject of a marriage which the latter has broached: "I leave the settlement of such big questions to you. I have enough of my own here. If you think it is for the good of the family that I raise up heirs, you will approach a certain young lady as you may deem fit."[1]

Sometimes they married, not their wives, but, if one may say so, their fathers-in-law—that is, if they were rich. The Duke de Luynes, that very polished and trustworthy gentleman, tells us that: "The daughter of the Duke de Saint-Simon was so small, deformed, and ugly, that far from wishing to marry her off, her parents did their utmost to keep her in the background." The poor girl's father himself says quite frankly: "There are some women who are far happier as spinsters, living on the income of the marriage portion which would be theirs. Madame de Saint-Simon and I were of opinion that our daughter belonged to this class, and we intended to act by her accordingly. My mother thought otherwise"—and so did the Prince de Chimay. He was, as Saint-Simon noted, "very well made, with a pleasant face and the manners of a great gentleman." But, alas! the affairs of this Prince Charming were seriously embarrassed, and the Duke de Saint-Simon was the Regent's counsellor and intimate friend. And so Mlle de Saint-Simon became Princess de Chimay, and the upshot can be imagined from the following brief comment written by her father: "The Duchess Sforza (a friend of the Prince's) predicted to me all that I eventually witnessed."

A marriage in high society was a simple affair which was arranged in a business-like way, often through a third party, and settled in a week or two. Let us hear what the Duke de Croÿ has to say: "30*th June* 1741.—Mme de Solre, my aunt, arrived with M. Cordier, who had been called in about my marriage to Mlle d'Harcourt, which had been under discussion for just two months. I had already seen the young lady twice, at the house of Mme d'Ursins, who was managing the business. On Saturday, 4th February, we repaired to her father's house, where all the relations were assembled, to ask for her hand. An hour later the marriage-contract, the terms of which had been

[1] De Loménie, *Les Mirabeau*, i. 178.

agreed upon the evening before, was read and signed. The next day, the 5th, the Duke d'Harcourt took me to Versailles to obtain the Royal assent. On 18th February, after midnight, the Abbé d'Harcourt betrothed and married us in the Chapel of the Hôtel de Belle-Isle." [1]

In view of the haste in which such lifelong contracts were entered upon, the rather severe criticism of de Chamfort can, perhaps, be understood: "Marriage, as practised by the great, is merely a legalised act of indecency." Certainly disagreeable surprises were not uncommon. Here is an instance of one, reported by d'Argenson to his aunt, the Marquise de Balleroy, on 31st October 1718:

"I have just come from the country. During my absence my hand has been disposed of, and I found the contract signed on my return. I am about to become related to a most respectable family, from which one fine day, without exaggeration, millions are to be expected. The daughter is well brought up, can dance and sing and play the spinet. Moreover, she is fair. . . . I forgot to tell you who she is. She is Mlle Méliand." The first interview between the betrothed couple took place on 19th November at the Convent of the Filles Ste. Marie, where the young lady was living, she being fifteen and having been told on the 18th that she was marrying d'Argenson on the 22nd.

Now the father of the Marquis d'Argenson was Minister of Finance and Keeper of the Seals. Let us refer to the diary of his son, the writer of the letter quoted above, for September 1742: "I don't know how they could have married me off (without even consulting me) and made me the most unhappy man in the world. My father gave me a property which brought me in 5000 francs a year, and an annuity of 4000. And that was all. They said they were repairing my fortunes when they made me marry Mlle Méliand in preference to a financier's daughter, but with my rank I should have been as honoured with either. The Méliands at that time were insignificant middle-class folk of Mantes, and their daughter to whom my father desired

[1] Croÿ, i. 30.

to affiance me only had, on her marriage, the office of a *maître des requêtes*, with which I was invested, and a mortgage on the town of 40,000 crowns at twenty-five per cent.—nothing more. Thus my marriage was but a union of hunger and thirst." "The millions which were to be expected" would have been for the children. But d'Argenson was divorced when he penned these lines.

In the middle of the century—in 1751, to be exact—the wise Turgot wrote to Mme de Graffigny, the author of *Lettres péruviennes*: "I have long been thinking that our nation requires instruction on happy marriages." People were no longer marrying, with such unhappy examples before their eyes. Bourdaloue had denounced these marriages from his pulpit, calling them "mercenary traffic," and foretelling what such traffic might, in the end, become; and the eighteenth century, with its scandals in the homes of the highest society, seemed to prove how true his prophecy had been, when, in his sermon "On the Married State," he thundered: "Marriages contracted without mutual attachment are criminal attachments without marriage."

. . . .

We have now seen the courtier at the *Lever* and at the *Grand Couvert* and, in a manner of speaking, been guests at his wedding. That was all on the outside, but let us try to penetrate underneath and study his character, his morals, and his mental outlook. Voltaire warns us to be cautious when we embark on this task:

> "à la Cour, mon fils, l'art le plus nécessaire
> N'est pas de bien parler, mais de savoir se taire.
> Depuis deux mois au plus vous êtes a la cour,
> Vous ne connaissez pas ce dangereux séjour,
> Sur un nouveau venu le courtisan perfide
> Avec malignité jette un regard avide,
> Pénètre ses defauts, et, des le premier jour,
> Sans pitié le condamne, et même sans retour.
> Craignez de ces Messieurs la malice profonde."
>
> *L'Indiscret*, i. 1.

"Savoir se taire"—to know how to keep silent, and to feign what he does not feel, has always been the courtier's habit and practice. This led Chamfort to say: "The rarity of any really genuine emotion makes me sometimes stop in the street and watch a dog gnawing a bone. It is after a visit to Versailles that this especially excites my curiosity." Versailles, in fact, was the home of dissimulation, but it was, also, an amusing home for an acute observer like the author of the following letter.

Piron had gone to Fontainebleau in October 1732. He hoped to produce his *Gustave Vasa* there, and wrote to the Abbé le Gendre: "The days come and go, and all are identical. Every day there is a hunt, and there are more kennels than houses. The baying of hounds, the blowing of horns, rain, wind, mud, that is our daily bread. Our weekly portion is as follows: Monday, a concert; Tuesday, a tragedy; Wednesday, a concert; Thursday, the Comédie française; Friday, Benediction; Saturday, the Comédie italienne; Sunday, High Mass.

"I should be awfully bored at Court were it not for a window niche where I stand for some hours, eyeglass in hand, and God alone knows the pleasure I have in watching the crowd! What masqueraders they are! To see how edifying the members of your profession look, and how important the courtiers! How some alternate between fear and hope, and, above all, how false are their airs and graces for the most part, when one looks at them closely. It really is extraordinary! One sees nothing honest save the faces of the Swiss guard, who are the only philosophers at Court. With their halberds on their shoulder, their big moustaches and their tranquil bearing, one would think that they regarded all these dupes of fortune as people who were running after something which these poor Swiss had captured long ago. In this respect I imitated them, and yesterday was looking around me much at my ease when Voltaire, rolling about among the crowd like a little green pea, saw me and cried: 'Ah, my dear Piron, what are you doing at Court? I have been here three weeks and they played *Mariamne* the other day. They are going to put on *Zaïre*, and when shall we see *Gustave*? How are you? Oh, Your Grace, just a word. I was just looking for you.'

THE NOBILITY OF THE SWORD

All this was said quite incoherently while I stood and began to feel quite young again."

The one obsession of the courtier was to be ever on the watch for any job that might fall vacant. Saint-Simon writes: "Mornay died very suddenly. He was a Lieutenant-General and also Governor and Constable of St. Germain. The Duke de Noailles, on the alert for anything of this kind, heard the news on waking and hurried off at once to the Duke d'Orleans. He applied for, and was immediately given, the post. My father had held it, but I did not know of Mornay's death and Noailles' haste until after dinner. It was not easy to get up as early as he did."[1]

To rise before the other rivals for a coveted post, attend the King's daily Mass, wait upon the Minister and on the Favourite, to keep one's eyes open and then to court the man who might, to-morrow, be the new Minister or Favourite, such was the anxious and fatiguing existence which the inmates of Versailles were content to undergo. Nivernais said of them that they were "more unfortunate than their servants."

Let us try, however, to lift the mask and to see what sort of people they were, without calumniating these intimates of the Prince nor yet permitting ourselves to be dazzled by the splendour which surrounded them.

The first characteristic which strikes us is their frivolity. Etiquette was their passion and their whole interest was absorbed by trifles. Luynes would note that the Queen had taken medicine as a precaution, or that she, or the Dauphin, had had a tooth pulled; or again he could write in 1746: "The King and Mme de Pompadour were weighed to-day. She only weighs 111 pounds, and the King, who weighed 165 pounds in 1736, now turns the scale at 185." Was that so very interesting and important? Let Montesquieu answer: "When I see the Great Mogul, great fool that he is, go annually to be weighed like a bull in the scales, and when I see his people rejoice that their prince has become more corpulent, that is to say, even less capable of govern-

[1] Saint-Simon, xiv. 187.

ing them, then indeed, Ibben, I pity the folly of the human mind."[1]

Trifles such as these, together with the thousand details of etiquette, were usually the daily occupation of a courtier. But in troublous times, such as during the war of 1744, what was then the chief topic at Versailles? "Would Mme de la Tournelle have four or six horses to her coach?" In 1753 Mme de Luynes writes to her husband from Compiègne, where the Court then was: "Playing ombre, I was told that the affair of the Princes is becoming more critical, but an unsuccessful robbery makes much more stir, I assure you. This must be the Golden Age in this country, and you would not believe that there had ever been a Parliament in France! [At this time there was serious trouble in the Parliament of Paris.] The Chancellor and Ministers are keeping great state. Something will have to be done."

In the same year the Parliament was exiled to Pontoise. Paris had cried: "Long live the Parliament!" had clamoured for bread and railed at the Ministers and at the Favourite, and had not even spared the King. At this juncture d'Argenson writes in his diary: "In the midst of this universal distress, Marly is quite blind to any shortcomings on the part of the Government. Never has the Court been more brilliant, play is ruinous, and the King has won very large sums."

The 5th November 1757 was one of the saddest dates in French history—the day of the disastrous defeat at Rossbach, when the French, badly led by Soubise, lost three thousand dead and seven thousand prisoners. On that day the Army of France was disgraced; for the generals could not sufficiently denounce the soldiers for their cowardice, while the latter's contempt for the generals, whom they knew to be incapable, was deep and lasting. In Paris "the public could not accustom itself to the shame of the defeat." But what was said at Versailles? "The Court was very interested in the lost battle in *as far as it affected M. de Soubise*, but ignored its effects upon the State." It is Bernis,

[1] Montesquieu, 40th *Lettre persane*.

THE NOBILITY OF THE SWORD

the Minister, himself who thus sadly notes the feeling of the Court in his patriotic letter to Choiseul on 22nd November 1757. The Court thought only of comforting poor Soubise for his annoying reverse, and Bernis continued: "Mme de Pompadour has given him proof of her undying friendship, as has the King also."

Still, "the King seemed to pray with great devotion, and Mme de Pompadour continued to hear Mass every day," and Luynes was edified by such scrupulous piety, though it is strange that this honest man was not nauseated by what the Cardinal de Retz termed "this stew of devotion and sin." Mme de Sévigné wrote that "she belonged neither to God nor devil," and thought this "the most natural thing in the world"; but to belong to both and to worship first the one and then the other on the very same day was a compromise which only a courtier could possibly regard as being natural! At the beginning of the century, the Regent, that great debauchee, never missed his devotions at St. Eustache on feast days, but Saint-Simon, friend though he was, rightly judged "that less devotion to the calendar and less licentiousness at night would have rendered his life more worthy and more decent."

Luynes, at least, even if he does not openly blame the conduct of his King, sometimes judges him as his conscience bids him, for his real thoughts are not always concealed from the eye of one who can read between the lines of his diary. If his indulgence as a courtier is often to be regretted, he cannot, at any rate, be accused of cowardice or servility—vices which were so openly displayed by others of whom Bernis paints the following picture: "I must here record an incident which faithfully reflects the mentality of the courtiers. M. de Villeneuve, formerly Ambassador at the Porte, had been appointed Minister of Foreign Affairs. The King on his return from Fribourg was lodged at the Tuileries, and so great was the crowd at his levee that we could hardly move. M. de Villeneuve had not yet seen the King, but came to thank him, as all believed, for the post conferred upon him. His appearance was not imposing, but all this vast crowd made way before him, and the expression of all showed the deepest respect as he passed through. He went in to the King, and in a few minutes the news spread that M. de Villeneuve had told the King that his very moderate abilities and poor health did not permit him to assume so heavy a burden. This was the act of a very wise and virtuous citizen. The King yielded to his entreaties, and this was already known in the anteroom as he came out. But now not one of that crowd would make room for a man before whom it had prostrated itself a quarter of an hour previously." The Duke d'Orléans, the Regent, once said of a courtier: "He is the perfect courtier; he is without honour and without humour." This definition would perhaps be more complete if we add: "and without shame." [1]

Montesquieu, who for a moment dreamed of being an Ambassador, but was unable to make good at Court, writes, doubtless with a touch of bitterness: "At first I had a childish awe for most of the great ones, but when I came to know them, I passed almost at once to the other extreme, and now I despise them. I say to a man: 'Fie, you have ideas as degraded as those of a gentleman of quality.'"

As a whole, the Court was a demoralising place in which to live, and even the best were corrupted and sank in the mire. Mme de Maintenon herself had written at the end of the previous century to the Archbishop of Paris: "The Court transforms even the best." D'Argenson puts it thus: "Its two idols are wealth and fashion, and the fashion is to intrigue in order to gain wealth." The Duke de Croÿ, dining with M. de Boynes, writes: "His wife talked well, and, except for intrigue, which is inevitable, they seem honest folk," a description which recalls Frontin's line in *Le Méchant*: "My master is very nearly an honest man."

Bourdaloue has a pithy phrase in one of his sermons dealing with the dangers to which an honest man was exposed if he frequented Versailles too often. "By living

[1] Bernis, i. 90.

at Court one gives in to one's weaknesses. Even if one goes there with high ideals, the fact of breathing the air of the Court and listening to its language accustoms one to vice, which one no longer dreads, until one suffers it, then begins to excuse it, and eventually, without knowing it, one forms a new standard of ideals." [1]

Towards the end of the reign of Louis xv. some great nobles had been implicated in frauds and swindles, and Bourdaloue again found occasion to say: "When ambition has set up ideals of its own in order to attain its ends, what duties does it not outrage, what feelings of humanity does it not stifle? What laws of honesty, equity, and fidelity does it not subvert? A conscience may remain, but, corrupted as it now is by ambition, what damnable intrigues will it not hatch, what trickery, what treason, will it not resort to, to obtain its object?"

The Court was incredibly ignorant. The courtiers arrived with but little education, and dissipations of all kinds afforded but little time for reading: even if they knew the names of the great writers of the time, they knew little or nothing of their works. Montesquieu died in February 1755, and Luynes writes: "He had two poor carriage horses and never dined at home, which would go to show that he was miserly. He was a man of much wit, and was a member of the Academy here and of that of Berlin. His treatise on *The Spirit of the Laws*, a work very highly thought of" (Luynes obviously speaks from hearsay only), "gave rise to a suspicion that his religious views were not altogether sound," and he goes on to explain at length that Montesquieu "made this clear during his last illness," and then quotes a very insignificant and silly anecdote about a hobby of Montesquieu, adding that "his character can be judged from these details." This quotation reveals the intellectual poverty of a courtier who can find nothing better to say of a Montesquieu. Dangeau, recording La Fontaine's death in his diary, merely noted that "he was known for his Fables."

In November 1749 the tragedy *Venice Preserved* was

[1] *Sermon sur 'la fausse conscience.'*

performed at Fontainebleau, and Luynes writes in his diary: "It is translated from the English original, which is by Shakespeare." But it was Otway, not Shakespeare, who was the author, and Luynes probably confused it with *The Merchant of Venice.*

The following is even more illuminating, and Saint-Simon vouches for it: "One day the Marquis de Gesvres was admiring the fine pictures which hung in the King's apartments, evidently considering himself a connoisseur. Among them were several of the Crucifixion by various great artists, but he believed them to be by the same hand. Every one laughed at him, and told him the different painters and how they could be distinguished. 'Nonsense,' cried the Marquis; 'the man who painted all these was called INRI. Can't you see his name on every picture?' "[1]

We can now understand Montesquieu's condemnation: "No one can compete with the ignorance of those who frequent the Court of France."

Some did, however, atone for their ignorance by their wit. Whereas in Paris wit walked the streets, the bons mots of Versailles passed from mouth to mouth in the anterooms. They were, of course, at the expense of others, and were generally malicious. A malicious wit, indeed, well became a courtier at a time when Gresset was producing his *Méchant* (1747), a play admired and applauded for its truthfulness, and in which occur the following lines (Act IV. 5):

> "J'ai l'esprit de mon siècle et je suis comme un autre.
> Tout le monde est méchant et je serais partout,
> Ou dupe ou ridicule avec un autre goût."

Cléon is the hero of this play, and is as malicious as the taste of the age required. But just because it was the eighteenth century he was witty also. Duclos says that the Duke de Choiseul, whom he had known well before the latter became a Minister, "was small and disagreeable to look at, but he had worth, wit, and, what was more, audacity. His ambition was to achieve a reputation for

[1] Saint-Simon, ii. 146.

THE NOBILITY OF THE SWORD

malice, for which he had a very great talent, and of this he was very proud," so that Sénac de Meilhan could write of him that: "His gift for idle talk and the quarrels he had stirred up in various circles gave rise to the belief that Gresset had drawn the character of his *Méchant* from the Duke." [1]

Thus Choiseul with his mocking airs was, like Cléon, notorious for his impertinence and malice, but like Cléon he possessed great wit, of which Frénilly gives a good example: "La Fayette, for all his great qualities, is considered to be too conceited, and has, moreover, a rather silly expression. Choiseul on one occasion, after listening to his conversation for some time, turned to the ladies with the words: 'Why, this is Cæsar turned buffoon.'" And here is another anecdote, which, if less cruel, is not without its sting. In 1760 the times were evil, for the Seven Years War was raging, and Louis xv. one day asked the Duke d'Ayen whether he was sending his plate to the Mint. "No," was the answer. "But I have sent mine," said the King. "Ah, sire," replied the Duke, "when Jesus Christ died on Good Friday, He knew He would rise again on Sunday."

Voltaire often inveighs against puns, though he perpetrated so many himself; but if some puns are bad, others are good. M. de Bièvre was the "chief punster" at the Court of Louis xv., and had written a comedy called *The Seducer*. On the eve of its production, the comedian Molé told him that he was afraid he could not play the part of the seducer because he was too *enroué* (hoarse). "But it is precisely *en roué* (as a rake) that the part should be played," was the quick reply.

Louis xv. one day asked him to make a pun. "On what subject, sire?" "It does not matter. On me if you like." "Your Majesty is not a subject," was de Bièvre's prompt reply.

Mercier wrote that puns were going out of fashion, and that the people preferred the language of Vadé, the inventor of the Parisian "Billingsgate." But if they were no longer

[1] *Portraits*, p. 29.

cracked in Paris, they were still popular at Court. Mme Roland wrote to her friend, Sophie Cannet, in 1776: "The Queen wore shoes of *vert noir* (dark green), and remarked to M. de St. Germain, Minister of War, that she was aiding the cause of economy by wearing such plain shoes, hardly worthy of a Queen. Whereupon he replied: 'Surely not! Those shoes are entirely worthy of Your Majesty, for it is surely natural that the *uni-vert* (universe) should be at your feet.' "

But besides jokes both witty and artless, others of a stupid kind must also, unfortunately, be recorded. Barbier tells how the young Duke de Crussol handed sweets filled with bitter aloes to various gentlemen. Count Rantzau was annoyed and called him a nasty brat, whereupon a duel followed and Rantzau was killed.

Even in the Royal Family this kind of humour was not unknown, and Luynes records the following incident: "Mme de Duras entered the King's Little Gallery while waiting for the Opera to begin. The Dauphin and Mme Adelaide sat down on her train, and the former, who was then twenty, tried to upset Mme Adelaide by pulling her skirt. The result was that Mme Adelaide fell, but did not hurt herself, whereas Mme de Duras, who also fell, broke her ankle. Luckily she lay still, as the bone might have pierced the skin and the fracture would then have been very difficult to mend. Mme de Duras suffered great pain in the night, and has been thrice bled." [1]

Such were the amusements of Princes.

"Blows are the jokes of uneducated folk," says an old French proverb, and the latter were certainly to be found at Court, for they often struck one another. Mouffle narrates that the Duke de Maine, having tacitly acquiesced in the decision of the Parliament which upset the will of Louis XIV. to his own detriment, was badly received at Sceaux, where his wife, in her fury, boxed his ears.

Having seen how bad manners could be, we must, if the picture is to be a true one, take notice of yet another bad habit which was very prevalent—namely, overeating.

[1] Luynes, ix. 327.

Hippeau tells us that when the Duke de Bourbon separated from his wife, the Prince de Condé stipulated that "she should have for supper every day one roast, six entrées, two courses of game, and five kinds of sweet."

Luynes, a very meticulous historian, often records the Queen's indigestion, and she herself, writing to Mme de Luynes on 28th October 1750, says: "I would have answered before, but I gave myself indigestion and was ill all yesterday." Her dinners were lavish, consisting of twenty-nine courses, not counting fruit, and the Marquis de Flammarens, whose appetite was notorious, was said to enjoy attending these banquets. The King also liked a good table, and if we except the Dauphin, whose abstemiousness was adversely criticised, we might well say that gluttony was the Royal Family's venial sin. D'Argenson says: "The Princesses" (Louis xv.'s daughters) "always keep their cupboards full of hams, Bologna sausages, pies, Spanish wines, etc. They lock themselves in and eat all day long." Mercy-Argenteau wrote to Maria Theresa that the Dauphin (afterwards Louis xvi.) made himself ill from eating pastry, and Marie Antoinette was obliged to banish this dish from the table.

Like master, like man. The Duke d'Humières was very fond of his food and always ate heartily. He died of indigestion, and many others went to their graves owing to the same cause. Thus Saint-Simon notes: "The Carthusians, who sometimes give great banquets, the other day entertained several distinguished courtiers. I was invited, as was Puysieux" (the Marquis de Puysieux was a Lieutenant-General), "who was very popular. The repast was copious and excellent. Puysieux, a man of nearly eighty, and short and stout at that, ate so heartily that he was seized with indigestion and fever that very night, and was dead in a few days."[1]

Even the clergy sometimes succumbed to the pleasures of the table, as, for example, Rastignac, Archbishop of Tours, who, as Luynes tells us, bathed after rising from dinner at which he had eaten largely, because he thought

---

[1] Saint-Simon, xvi. 209.

a bath would give him an appetite for supper, which indeed it did, but the result was such a violent attack of indigestion that he died. Nor was a simple priest more frugal than an Archbishop, for Saint-Simon writes in 1722: "The Abbé de Verteuil died shortly after my return from Spain. I was accused of having killed him with a surfeit of sturgeon on which he had, as a matter of fact, overeaten himself at my table."

Drunkenness was also widespread, and was the complementary vice to greed. Thus we hear from Saint-Simon of a Princess of the Blood dying literally from alcoholic poisoning. "Mme de Vendôme died at Paris on 11th April 1718, without making a will or receiving the Sacraments, from the effects of strong waters, of which her room was full"; and if such a case was rare it was not exceptional, for Buvat records the death of "the Duchess d'Albret, who died on 28th February 1717, aged thirty-six. Her demise is attributed to her habit of drinking very potent liqueurs with the Duchess de Berry."

Here is the pretty invitation to supper which Voltaire sent to the Duchess de Luxembourg, entitled "An impromptu to Her Grace the Duchess of Luxembourg on her supping with His Grace the Duke de Richelieu":

"Un dindon tout à l'ail, un seigneur tout à l'ambre
  A souper vous sont destinés:
On doit quand Richelieu parait dans une chambre
Bien deferdre son cœur et bien boucher son nez." [1]

Why hold her nose? Because Richelieu used musk to excess, and, on this ground alone, could well be called the first of the *muscadins* (a name given in 1793 to Royalists of fashion). And why beware of her heart? Because this was the man who, if Soulavie, his biographer, can be believed, said of himself: "At fourteen I was an expert in every department of gallantry."

Louis François Armand de Vignerot du Plessis, born in Paris in 1696, was the son of Armand Jules II. de

[1] "A turkey full of garlic and a gentleman scented with ambergris await you at supper. When Richelieu enters the room, ah, then, beware of your heart and forget not to hold your nose."

THE NOBILITY OF THE SWORD 77

Vignerot du Plessis, Duke de Richelieu, who was grand-nephew of the great Cardinal. The Princess Palatine, who detested him, wrote in 1719: "He is small and beautifully made, graceful, and not lacking in wit. But his insolence is unequalled, and he is the worst of all spoiled children."

At fifteen he made his bow at Court, and Dangeau notes in his diary that "the King talked to the little Duke de Fronsac, who is very much the rage and extremely witty." A year later Saint-Simon writes of him: "This little Duke de Fronsac, when but sixteen, was, both in mind and body, the most delightful little person imaginable. His father had presented him at Court, where Mme de Maintenon, an old friend of M. de Richelieu, adopted him as a son, and, consequently, every one from the King and the Duchess de Bourgogne downward spoiled him. He knew how to display such elegance and to comport himself with so much wit, freedom, and politeness that he soon became the idol of the Court."

He was already versed in the rudiments of seduction, "and," writes Saint-Simon again, "learned to fly under the wing of de la Feuillade, whom the fashion of the day had made his oracle."

He also became acquainted with the Bastille, which he honoured three times for certain escapades, one being for having compromised the reputation of the Duchess de Bourgogne. He was to compromise many others, but this is not the place to recount the unedifying and not very creditable history of his successful gallantries. At this period, however, he was *le prince de la jeunesse,* the acknowledged leader of the young courtiers, and was to be, for many a year, the glass of fashion, and he is, therefore, worthy of our notice, as being the most brilliant representative of the generation which grew up and scintillated at the Court of Louis xv.

Chamfort writes in his criticism of Soulavie's *Mémoires de Richelieu*: "Let us not dwell on the morality of that age, licentious and futile as it was, for it was not deficient in either grace or wit, and often displayed considerable aptitude for business, qualities which had come to be regarded as the perfection of French character. The debauchery in which Richelieu passed his youth was the usual education of all the nobility of France. But he surpassed all his rivals in the art, which was then so assiduously practised, of gilding vice, adorning it with the charm of polite manners, and lending to seduction an amusing levity which turned its evils into a pastime and cast a glamour over its scandals. These were talents which the descendants of the ancient chivalry thoroughly appreciated, and all strove to imitate Richelieu, who was their ideal. On his return to Paris from his Embassy to Vienna, he again became the hero of numerous amorous adventures. It was during this period that he acquired the fame, with which posterity has always credited him, of having carried corrupt morals to their perfection. The nobility regarded him as their model, and his imitators were found even among the lower orders, often with ridiculous results."

Duclos, in his *Considérations sur les mœurs*, remarks: "The most dangerous man in the moral sense is he who cloaks his viciousness with gaiety and grace; there is nothing which these gifts will not excuse or render less odious." That was exactly the case with Richelieu. That compound of fine qualities, for which he is rightly admired, with faults and vices which are perhaps too indulgently regarded, have earned him the title of the Alcibiades of his age, and Voltaire, who was his friend, writes of him: "He is the Alcibiades of France, so full of wit and audacity and every attraction."

In turn, courtier, governor of a province, and general, we see him now at Court, now in Languedoc, now in Guyenne or at the head of his armies, but, since this is not a biography, we can only study him in these three capacities and estimate those characteristics which make him so typical of his times. Let us then first consider him as a courtier. On 12th December 1744, he took the oath as a First Lord of the Bedchamber, and thenceforth served the King at his *Lever* and *Coucher* until his last hour—that is to say, for forty-four years, and whenever he was at Court he performed his duties (and we know that these

"LES ADIEUX"

From an engraving by De Launay le Jeune, after J. M. Moreau le Jeune

were not regarded as servile, but as a great honour) with the utmost punctuality, and, moreover, with a care for the most rigorous etiquette. He was jealous to excess of even the slightest infringement of the smallest prerogatives attached to his office, as, for instance, when at the wedding festivities of the Dauphin in 1745, he raised the grave question as to whether he or the Duke d'Ayen should seat the guests at the Court Ball, and it was Richelieu who received the great honour of being deputed to invite the ladies. Mme de Luynes received the following note:

"MADAME,—His Grace the Duke de Richelieu has received His Majesty's commands to inform you, on his behalf, that a Ball will take place at Versailles, at 5 p.m. on Wednesday, 24th February 1745. His Majesty counts upon your presence. Ladies who dance will wear their hair in curls."

Such notes must have titillated his pride, for he was very vain. His disdain for people of inferior birth amounted, indeed, to insolence. Chamfort says: "M. de Richelieu was never able to utter the name of a bourgeois without mispronouncing it. Any one who was not a gentleman was, in his eyes, a person whom it was merely sufficient to designate as necessity might require, but to remember his name appeared to him an absurdity from which he ever refrained. There are twenty witnesses to this trait, including the Abbé Arnaud, whom Richelieu, though a brother Academician, always called l'Abbé Renaud. As a matter of fact, great noble though he was, he did not disdain to belong to the Academy, but in order to take his seat he was obliged to deliver, if not to compose, a speech. The Duke ordered his from three different *teinturiers*, professional speech-writers whose aid was sought by all who could not write well, an accomplishment which Richelieu had never troubled to learn. He did not write as a man of letters, for that would have been derogatory to himself as a gentleman, but, on the other hand, he prided himself on writing "like a man of quality"—a saying which has become famous. He could not boast of his orthography, and his ignorance of spelling surpassed even that of the other fine gentlemen of that time. He would write *Crétien* for *Chrétien, reigne* for *règne*, and, what was even more strange for a courtier, *Court* for *Cour*. The authentic, but unfortunately mutilated, text of his *Mémoires* has been found in his splendid library, and has recently been published. These curious lines, written in his own hand, may amuse the reader (the Duke always wrote of himself in the third person):

"The second occasion of his being sent to the Bastille was a duel with M. de Matignon, Sieur de Gacé, in 1716. This had been strictly forbidden, and the most stringent orders had been issued to prevent such duels. Although M. de Richelieu was wounded, he went to the Opera in order to hush up the affair, but the Regent, informed by the young Duke's enemies, ordered him to be committed to the Bastille. A commissioner and a surgeon were appointed to examine his wounds, but he concealed them so well that the surgeons overlooked them, and their report being wholly in his favour, no further action was taken." [1]

But his ancestral pride did upon one occasion extricate him from a difficulty in a manner redounding both to his wit and to his honour. In October 1751 the King suggested that he should marry his son, the Duke de Fronsac, to Mlle Alexandrine, daughter and sole heiress of Mme de Pompadour. M. de Richelieu replied that, as his son's mother had belonged to the house of Lorraine, he must first obtain the Emperor's views on such a marriage. The result was an open rupture, and Richelieu did not reappear at Court till 1752. He was not always so proud, and he is a sad example of the degradation and servility to which, as we have already seen with regret, even the greatest in the land could stoop. He gladly put himself in the position of a Mercury to the Jupiter who ruled with so little dignity at Versailles, and when Mme de Pompadour had gone her way he adroitly prepared the reign of her

[1] Boislisle, *Mémoires du Maréchal Richelieu*, p. 169.

successor and did not hesitate to become the mentor of a Dubarry.

As governor, he shows to more advantage than as courtier, and if we were writing his biography we should note, to do him justice, that he did take his duties seriously, which most governors certainly did not. When we come to study the Provinces we shall see that most governors were but governors in name and never resided in their provinces. But we must confine ourselves here to what is purely personal, and merely point out what he had in common with his contemporaries, for whom he serves us as a model. We must mention his toleration of the Protestants of Languedoc, whom he protected, in spite of the bishops, and whose exodus to foreign lands he wished to prevent in the interests of the State. "This honest tolerance," as d'Argenson calls it, was, moreover, not unnatural in Richelieu, who, like other great nobles in this philosophic age, professed a certain indifference to religion, and who, though a friend of the King, was also the patron of Voltaire—truly a sign of the times. The latter was a frequent guest at his table, and, if Longchamp can be believed, it was Richelieu who once, after supper, suggested the idea of *La Pucelle* to Voltaire. That play was worthy of a sponsor such as Richelieu.

One more anecdote must be quoted before we leave Richelieu the governor, and it illustrates effectively his incredible self-esteem. Piron writes to the Count de Livry in 1741: "It is said that in Languedoc, M. de Richelieu exacts all the honours which the ambition of the Cardinal of that name claimed in his day—salutes, deputations, speeches, *Te Deums*—these are all he lives for."

An elderly canon who waited upon him at the head of his Chapter and had been ordered to deliver an oration, asked the Duke how the King was. The Duke, surprised at so intimate a question, remained silent, and somewhat confused. The priest again inquired. "Your Grace, I asked how the King's health is," and received the very terse reply: "Oh, very well." Whereupon the Canon, turning to his Chapter, cried: "You hear the good news which the

Duke has given us of the King's health. Let us go and thank God with a *Te Deum,* and His Grace will doubtless honour us with his presence." And so he did, but he had intended the *Te Deum* for himself.

Lastly, let us consider Richelieu as a warrior. Duclos is wrong in calling him an "arm-chair general." On the battlefield he was, like all gentlemen of his time, brave even to foolhardiness, and d'Argenson says of him: "He scorned death as a gambler scorns ruin, loving risks and trusting to his luck."

After a successful campaign in Italy during the War of the Austrian Succession he was created a Marshal of France in 1748. But during the Seven Years War his campaign in Westphalia in 1757, with its rapine and plunder, earned him the less honourable title of *Père la Maraude*—the Old Marauder—and Duclos writes: "Far from deprecating or even trying to conceal, his brigandage, he displayed the greatest pomp on his return to Paris. He built that pavilion which the public in derision called 'The Pavilion of Hanover,' which name it still bears."

Happily the army commander had a long and distinguished service behind him, and Chamfort, who disliked him, has recorded it in the passage following: "Let us revert to M. de Richelieu, whom one meets everywhere, as brilliant as ever. He was particularly so at Fontenoy, and whatever his enemies and those of Voltaire may say (for the latter is accused of sacrificing the fame of the Marshal de Saxe to that of his idol), it seems impossible to deny him the honour of having given the advice which determined the success of the battle. The idea of sweeping the English ranks with artillery fire seems so obvious that we are led to think that only de Saxe's illness prevented his giving an order to that effect. Richelieu's courage and coolness placed him in the van of those who charged the shattered columns, and this was one of the great moments of his life. Again, all must agree that in the Minorca expedition, M. de Richelieu displayed the talent and resource of a true general. He arrived at Toulon and found no preparations made, but this did not surprise him, for he knew that the opposition of the Ministers was being secretly abetted by Mme de Pompadour. He did not draw back, but accelerating the fitting out of the expedition and aided by the enthusiasm of the citizens of Marseilles, eventually set sail, landed at Mahon, and laid siege to the citadel. He supervised every detail and exposed himself like any private. His method of putting an end to drunkenness in his camp will long be remembered. 'I hereby decree,' said he, 'that any one among you who in future is found to be drunk will not have the honour of taking part in the assault.' He knew his French troops."

One last characteristic which it would be wrong to omit, demonstrates how he could give a bad as well as a good example to his companions in arms. In 1733 he was merely colonel of the regiment bearing his name, and Barbier notes that "he already has 72 mules, 30 horses, a host of servants, and his tents are copied from the King's. Generals who are rich keep such a staff of kitchen and other servants that one would think they were celebrating some great occasion, while those who are poorer ruin themselves and are unable to take part in any more campaigns."

We have already noticed the extravagant expenditure of the courtiers, but Richelieu's was quite fantastic. Thus, when he was appointed Ambassador to Austria in 1725, his entry into Vienna on 7th November was almost fairy-like. There were running footmen, lackeys in splendid livery, some being attired in Hungarian costumes, as well as pages: and in the midst of this retinue the Ambassador, resplendent in his robes as a Peer of Parliament, reclined in a coach decorated with symbolical figures and drawn by horses sumptuously caparisoned. Their shoes were of silver, and so loosely attached that the people were able to pick them up as the dazzling Ambassador passed on his way. But his fate was that of other courtiers, and Voltaire, while calling him "the Alcibiades of France" and "endowed with every attractive quality," adds: "He was blessed with virtue, honours—and debts!"

Voltaire knew something about it, for he was his creditor, and one who now and again was obliged to recall the fact. On 26th November 1736 he wrote to his man of business, l'Abbé Moussinot: "M. de Richelieu has paid me my 50,000 livres," and in April 1738: "I am owed 12,000 livres extending over three years." He had suggested an arrangement which he says "should henceforth assure me a certain and regular income of that 4000 livres which is my largest source of revenue. Life is short, and, as Solomon says, we must enjoy it." It was just because his life was to be a short one—he hinted to Richelieu that he was very ill—that he lent the latter 40,000 livres for life at a very high interest.

In his relations with Voltaire, who called him his "hero," let us note, finally, a resemblance between them which greatly struck their contemporaries, and which Sénac de Meilhan has summed up as follows:

"There was a great resemblance between Voltaire and the Marshal de Richelieu both in gesture and voice, and this was so remarkable that one could hardly believe that they were not imitating one another. The writer doubtless copied the mannerisms of the man who enjoyed the greatest renown and success in the world of fashion, and the courtier had seized upon some of the expressive gestures of the celebrated author, who combined a highly cultivated mind and knowledge of the world with the very greatest talents."

Before taking leave of Richelieu, let us say a word on his marriage, or rather on his first marriage. We have seen that a nobleman married very young, sometimes, even, when barely out of infancy. In 1711 Richelieu married Mlle de Sansac, daughter of the Marquise de Noailles, when he was not yet fifteen, and, on the wedding-day, Mme de Maintenon wrote that she "had very nearly chucked Fronsac under the chin." Fronsac did not love his wife, boasted of it, and even in this respect created a host of imitators. Luynes tells us: "On Wednesday, 28th January 1750, La Chaussée's *Le Préjugé à la Mode* was acted in Mme de Pompadour's apartments. It is the story of a young married man who is in love with his wife but dare not show it, as it would be regarded as ridiculous by the world of fashion. M. de Richelieu, who in his youth was the hero of so many gallant adventures, might really be called the author of this comedy. His first wife, Mlle de Sansac, was very pretty and devoted to him, but he could not abide her, and thus it became the fashion among the gilded youth that it was absurd to love your wife." In this play, which La Chaussée wrote in 1735, these words occur:

"I note it is no longer fashionable to love one's spouse, a custom now found only among the middle classes."

M. de la Trémoille, who "loved his wife passionately," is mentioned by Luynes, along with M. de Melun, as one of those followers of Richelieu who never dared see his wife except at night.

Richelieu lived this life until extreme old age, for even at eighty he did not abdicate, and Duclos describes him as being "still the mirror of fashion and its oldest exponent." D'Argenson, when peevish, calls him "an old butterfly," and even Voltaire, when he could not pay the interest on his loan, describes him as "an old doll." But he remained to the end—and that is why we have taken him as a type of the eighteenth-century courtier. "A nation volatile, easy-going, and changeable, where a man who shines one day is obscured the next, seemed to have been enslaved by Richelieu, and owned his unquestioned sway as the arbiter of taste and the model of youth. He had survived every change of fashion." Such was the tribute of Sénac de Meilhan.

But this does not mean that all the gentlemen of France resembled Richelieu. Far from it, for, though there may have been worse characters at Versailles, there were also many of greater worth. Let us take the former first. Many of the courtiers were quite shameless and battened on the losses of others by keeping gaming-houses, like the Duke de Gesvres et de Tresmes, and by this means encouraged the evil. The Duke derived a considerable income from his establishment, but was suddenly ordered to close it, whereupon, according to Luynes, the Duke d'Orleans, doubtless to console him, "gave him, in his

capacity as Governor of Paris, an annuity of 20,000 livres";
but this did not make up for the 40,000 crowns he used to
obtain from his den. Such a transaction was not under-
hand, even if it was not very honourable, but as much,
unfortunately, cannot be said of the behaviour of some
other great gentlemen who were little better than sharpers
at the gaming-table. Even in the reign of Louis xiv.,
gambling with all its evils had been very prevalent at
Court, and Saint-Simon records that the King himself was
passionately devoted to it, and "liked to play high and
often," as did Maria Theresa, for Mme de Sévigné com-
placently notes in her diary for 24th November 1675: "The
other day the Queen lost both her Mass and 20,000 crowns
before midday."

Many, however, lost not only their money but their
honour at the tables. In his sermon " On Penance,"
Bourdaloue declared: "Gambling is a vice which entails
yet another, for it engenders those unworthy stratagems
or, if I may use a stronger term, those frauds to which the
thirst for gain drives its victims." The term was certainly
strong, but it was true, and Saint-Simon employs it in
speaking of the Count de Grammont, the author of the
famous *Mémoires*. "At play he was a notorious cheat."

Those Viscounts de la Case, who are to be found in
Regnard's comedies, are not absent from the Court of
Louis xv.:

"They know, when necessary, how to repair the malice
of an evil fortune by some slight artifice."

Even the Royal table was not above suspicion. The
adventure of Voltaire and Mme du Châtelet at Fontainebleau in 1747 is well known. They were playing at the
Queen's table, and Mme du Châtelet insisted on continuing
to play, although losing persistently, and at the end of
the evening owed 84,000 francs. Voltaire was a sympathetic
witness of this disaster, and whispered to the Marquise
that she had been too engrossed to realise that she was
playing with rogues. But though he said it in English, he
was understood, and wisely retired with the Marquise.

Finally, while refraining from those generalities in

THE CARD PARTY

From an engraving by Jean Dambrun, after J. M. Moreau le Jeune

THE NOBILITY OF THE SWORD

which some authors indulge, exaggerating at will the corruption of the eighteenth century, we must admit that it is often surprising to meet in the *Mémoires* of the time instances where we would have thought that the position and education of these thieves of both sexes would have prevented them from falling so low. Bourdaloue, preaching on "Restitution," did not hesitate to quote Seneca's vigorous saying: *Multi furto non erubescunt*, and he had in mind some of the greatest personages of the Court. Thus a distinguished member of the judicature, M. de G——, whose name is not given, being invited to dine with M. de Miromesnil, Keeper of the Seals, was caught in the act of carrying off a silver spoon and fork. He tried to escape from his embarrassment with a foolish joke, explaining that, as the Keeper of the Seals had told him that there was always a place for him at table, he was under the impression that he could remove these articles with impunity.[1]

Here is another impudent attempt at theft which occurred in the highest circles and was reported to Walpole by his friend, Mme du Deffand, on 3rd June 1766:

"M. de—— and Mme de—— had gone to sup with Mme de Beuvron, but, not wishing to go in to supper, instead of remaining in the drawing-room or cabinet, withdrew to a small and remote boudoir. After supper Mme de —— accosted Mme de Beuvron in great agitation and distress, and told her hostess that she had been the victim of a great misfortune. 'If you have broken my china, there is no great harm done.' 'No, Madame, it is far worse than that.' 'You have spoiled my ottoman?' 'Oh no, it is something much worse.' 'But what has happened? What could you possibly have done?' 'Oh, I saw such a pretty writing-table, and we wanted to see what it was like inside, so we used our keys to try and open it, and one of them broke in the lock.' 'Can that really be true? I confess I could not have believed such a thing had you not told me yourself.' A servant whom they suspected of having witnessed their efforts was besought with prayers and promises to fetch a

[1] Dugast, ii. 132.

locksmith to repair the damage, but he refused, saying he would certainly not touch anything belonging to his mistress. Thus the fear, or rather the certainty, of being denounced by this man decided them to forestall him by making a full confession. Would you like to be in the shoes of M. de ——? Personally, I would rather have been caught picking pockets, for that would have entailed more skill and less ignominy. It is a horrible story! How can they stay in a place where they have covered themselves with such shame!" [1]

We have had to blame these courtiers for many weaknesses and faults, and it must be admitted that, shorn of its outward trappings, the Court does not appear to great advantage. Should we therefore conclude that it was given up to profligacy and hypocrisy to an extent which would warrant d'Argenson's biting verdict: "There is not a single good man in all the Court"? We must not, however, forget that d'Argenson was banished from Court and revenged himself by speaking ill of it, and that he sought a bitter solace, like many another disgraced courtier, in exaggerating and denouncing the failings and vices of the King, Mme de Pompadour, and of those who had, unlike himself, the good fortune of making their bow to the King and his favourite. D'Argenson, when speaking of Versailles, which he only visited on rare occasions, and with which he was, therefore, ill acquainted, is doubtless an interesting witness, for he had a penetrating eye and was independent in his views, but he is not reliable, because he was also passionate and vindictive. Without doing him a wrong, we may say that his view of people and things was so jaundiced, and that his criticisms and accusations were so sweeping, that they led him to slander the Court. Bourdaloue, who knew it so well and who so boldly denounced its vices, says in the very same sermon in which he thunders against the hypocrites: "We can still see men who live up to their religion and whose exemplary lives may serve as our models. They

[1] *Correspondance* (Ed. Lescure), i. 364.

THE NOBILITY OF THE SWORD 89

exist in all circles, even at Court." They existed, without going far afield, even among those whom we have mentioned so often—a Saint-Simon, for instance, whose candour and dignity none could gainsay; a Duke de Luynes, both honest and conscientious; a Duke de Croÿ, who, like the other two, lived what Bourdaloue called "an exemplary life."

The main interest of the Court chroniclers centred in scandals, and those were their principal theme. They dwelt on all the dishonest folk and their unpleasant histories because such stories caused a stir and a sensation, while honest people, who had no histories, found no place in the memoirs of the time. The same applies to family life. We have spoken of unhappy homes and we could discuss them indefinitely if we took the trouble to ransack all the doubtful anecdotes which were so assiduously circulated in the eighteenth century. But we must remember that the French, descended as they are from the Gauls, have always had a taste for stories of a somewhat questionable type, and that, unlike other nations, they do not hide their faults, but at times even enlarge on them in order to laugh at themselves the more. Let us add, also, that these newsmongers and pamphleteers, who, as a rule, were but frequenters of gaming-houses, judged the world by their own standards In this connection there is an anecdote about the Regent, who only lived among rakes—his *roués*. "One day he said to Fontenelle: 'I don't believe in virtue.' And the discreet Fontenelle had the courage to reply: 'Sir, there are honest folk, but they would not come into your ken.'"

Rousseau's Emile, seeking the loving and virtuous Sophie, did not find her in Paris, where Rousseau "was sure that she would not be," and, shaking its dust off his feet, cried: "Farewell, Paris, marvellous and noisy city, full of smoke and mud, where women do not believe in honour nor men in virtue. Farewell, Paris, for we go to seek love, happiness, and innocence. We shall never be far enough removed from you." Without leaving Paris or even Versailles, we shall, perhaps, find what Rousseau was so certain that he would not meet with there.

We have seen how, in the first half of the century, fashionable people, under the influence of Richelieu, their model, were careful not to incur ridicule by loving their wives, a "bourgeois" affectation in their eyes. But even so there were many good bourgeois in Paris, and even at Versailles. There were great nobles who loved their wives devotedly and who did not echo le Durval in *Le Préjugé à la Mode*:

"I know full well the ridicule to which this love exposes me."

And there were women deeply attached and faithful to their husbands, but the chroniclers do not mention them because they had nothing to say about them, for about good women there was no gossip.

The Duke de Chevreuse had married the eldest, and the Duke de Beauvilliers the third, of Colbert's daughters, and Saint-Simon is almost lyrical in describing their union: "The Dukes de Chevreuse and de Beauvilliers and their respective wives were so perfectly united that they formed but one heart and soul, and had but one thought and one passion all their life long. Their mutual friendship, consideration, satisfaction, and confidence never varied. These ties had united the two sisters and soon extended to the two brothers-in-law, living, as they both did, at Court, to which they were attached by their offices, and their wives by their appointments as ladies-in-waiting. They saw one another daily, and dined with each other in alternate weeks. It was rare that any one was to any appreciable extent the friend of one without also being the friend of the other, and of the two wives."[1]

M. de Brezé was Grand Master of the Ceremonies and a Lieutenant-General of the King's Armies. "Mme de Brezé, whose conduct has always been exemplary, was rendered very happy by her husband's attentions, and he is a very worthy gentleman."

When the Prince de Conti married Mlle de Blois, Mme de Sévigné wrote in raptures to her daughter: "They love each other like people do in novels." The same could be

[1] Saint-Simon, x. 279.

said of the Pontchartrains. "The Chancellor, de Pontchartrain, had the happiness to find a wife who possessed all one could wish for as regards wit, conduct, and compatability, and so they were happy together."

Saint-Simon had no need to envy Pontchartrain "the happiness" of finding the wife he wished for, and in his *Mémoires* he dwells continually on the virtues of the Duchess de Saint-Simon. She was the daughter of Mme de Lorges, "who lived only for her husband and family"; and Saint-Simon, who had not only lived among the orgies of the Regency but had been the intimate friend of the most debauched of Regents, wrote of his wife in the following delicate and moving terms, praising "the perfection of her exquisite and unerring taste, and her mild and tranquil temper, which not only subdued her own inclinations but led her to efface herself all her life with unvarying modesty, charm, and virtue." There is another example in Mme de Belle-Isle, who died of smallpox, aged forty-six, mourned by her husband and regretted by all, a perfect friend and wife. Luynes describes her thus: "No one was ever more dutiful or pious, and she never spared her health. I cannot describe all the care and devotion and eagerness to further his interests which she displayed during the vicissitudes of M. de Belle-Isle's career. She went everywhere and saw everybody whom it was necessary to see, although naturally shy, and she was the same with her friends, being deeply interested in their affairs, and when she lost one she would be so affected as to fall ill of grief. M. de Bernstorff, the Danish Envoy, who was much in her company, said of her that her body was but a veil covering her soul."

She had a son worthy of her, the heroic and charming Count de Gisors. Nearer the throne we see the Count de Toulouse, the legitimised son of Louis XIV. and Mme de Montespan, who lived with his wife at Rambouillet, where it pleased the King often to visit the Countess. "Never was so happy a marriage seen in France. During their thirteen years of married life there was never a shadow between them, and their life at Rambouillet and the principles which were to be found there were so exemplary that they gave a new tone to a society which the Regency had depraved. It was at this Court that Louis xv. came to learn the habits of the world."

We might mention yet another lady in this connection, and she also, it will be well to note, belongs to the Court. M. de Luynes has already made us acquainted with his wife through her letters, which he inserts in his *Mémoires*, and Mme du Deffand describes her more clearly still in this passage: "The Duchess de Luynes was born with an intelligence which others can only strive to attain. She is fond of pleasure and amusements, but never to excess and without any passion, and she is happy at Court without being too absorbed by it, being content with a post of distinction and seeking only entertainment and amusement. Her temper is equable and charming, her heart generous and full of sympathy. Busy with her duties and full of consideration and attentions for her friends, she makes happy all who come within her influence—father, children, husband, friends, servants. If there be anything which casts a shadow on the affection she inspires, it is the thought that she listens rather to the counsels of her reason than to those of her heart. Perhaps this reproach is unjust, but it would appear that no one is essential to her happiness, whereas she is essential to the felicity of all who, having lived in intimacy with her, cannot exist without it." [1]

When the Duke de Luynes died on 2nd November 1758, he merited Hénault's eulogy, which can be found in his *Mémoires*: "He is a great loss to the Court, to his friends, and to the poor: in fact, to all good people"; and Mme de Luynes receives this delicate compliment from the same pen: "She had all the virtues and all the qualities of the best of men."

Sometimes the husband was licentious like the King, or fickle like Choiseul, but the wife was none the less faithful or devoted, and never ceased to love her unworthy spouse; while the delightful Duchess de Choiseul deserved the following flattering portrait drawn by her friend, Baron

[1] *Correspondance* (Ed. Lescure), ii. 743.

THE NOBILITY OF THE SWORD

de Gleichen: "Morally, Mme de Choiseul was the most perfect being I have ever encountered. She was a wife without equal, a faithful and prudent friend, and a woman without reproach. She was a saint, though she held no belief save what virtue dictated; but her bad health, her sensitive nerves and melancholy disposition, together with her acute mind, made her serious, severe, fastidious, argumentative, and inclined her to metaphysics and even to prudery. This at least was how her sister-in-law and her gay friends described her to her husband; but he, in spite of this, was not lacking in esteem, gratitude, and respect for a wife who adored him, reconciled him with the enemies of his sister, and in whom he was, at heart, constrained to acknowledge as being a character more pure, more dependable, and more deserving than his own." [1]

Her courage was as great as her devotion. The Duke was disgraced, and hurried to Paris. "He found the Duchess sitting down to table. On seeing him she said: 'You look like a man who has been exiled, but sit down, our dinner won't be served any less well.'"

Having spoken of the wives, it is hardly necessary to dwell on the mothers, for the mothers of France were as incomparable then as they have always been, and foreigners who know France well will not dispute this. But, in conclusion, here is a picture which will give the reader some idea of what one of our old French families was like. When the Duke de Vaujours married in 1732, his wedding was presided over by Mme de Noailles, his grandmother, who was surrounded by a family consisting of exactly fifty-two members: sons, sons-in-law, daughters-in-law, grandchildren, and great-grandchildren. Who was this Mme de Noailles, wife of the Marshal of that name? Saint-Simon will tell us:

"She it was who governed husband, children, family, business, and Court affairs as gaily and as readily as if she had never done anything else in her life; a noble, splendid woman, liberal and full of solicitude for her children, her family, and her name. She made friends easily and

[1] Gleichen, p. 35.

made many, although she deserved even more. She was a woman who rarely said all that was in her mind, and never anything which she did not believe. She was kind by nature, gentle, and good-tempered, frank as far as it was prudent at a Court, though it was unwise to cross her, for she could speak plainly to the offender whoever it might be, though never spitefully. She is still alive, her senses as keen as ever, and full of health and humour; at the age of eighty-seven, the matriarch of a numerous family, very rich, and very generous, as pious as it is possible for her to be, still active, and the delight of her friends, of whom she still has many, and preserving that spirit of banter with which she has always treated even the most serious subjects." [1]

[1] Saint-Simon, vi. 167.

BOOK II.—PARIS

CHAPTER I

PARIS UNDER LOUIS XV.

It was during the eighteenth century that Paris was beginning to "swallow the provinces," as Montesquieu expresses it. What was happening was that the policy of successive sovereigns had centralised all the administrative functions at Paris, and had made the city the centre of the nation's life. But, although the whole history of the Revolution was to be the most conclusive witness to the supremacy of Paris over the rest of France, Arthur Young had, with no little surprise, already noted its dominant position as early as 15th July 1789, the morrow of the fall of the Bastille. He was then at Nancy, and we find him writing in his diary: "Letters from Paris, but the news is most disquieting. The Ministry has been replaced, and M. Necker has been ordered to leave the kingdom secretly. This news has had considerable effect on the people of Nancy. I was with M. Willemet when the letters arrived, and those who were present remained to discuss them. One and all agreed that they were ominous and presaged grave trouble. As to what might result in Nancy, all whom I questioned gave the same answer: 'We are provincial folk and must wait to see what Paris does. But the people there may have resort to any violence, for bread is dear, and as they are starving there is no outrage they may not commit.' Such is the general opinion, and though they are as much concerned in this matter as Paris, they dare not make a move; in fact, they dare not even express an opinion, until Paris has spoken."

Many eighteenth-century authors deplored and even endeavoured to check, as far as they could, the flow from the country districts to the capital. Rousseau painted it in the blackest colours in the second preface to his *Nouvelle Héloïse*, when he wrote: "The country gentlemen and their wives and daughters no longer wish to be farmers, and are growing discontented with their villages. So they allow their ancestral homes to fall into ruin and migrate to the capital, where the father with his Cross of St. Louis becomes a footman or an adventurer, the mother keeps a gaming-house, and the daughter is her decoy." Voltaire writes ironically:

"The son of my casual labourer, brought up to useful labour on my farm, is carried off, when only fifteen, to swell the army of page-boys in Paris. He gets a job as a tax-collector, and returns to his native village swelling with pride. He brings actions against his fellows, imprisons them, and plays the tyrant, all 'By Order of the King.' "

But there was nothing to be done, for the tendency of the day was too powerful; Paris alone was fashionable, so that by living in the provinces one became a target for ridicule and the subject of mockery. Mirabeau, "the Friend of Man," and his fellow-economists denounced it: "To be called a provincial is regarded as an insult, and fashionable people are offended if asked to what province their family belongs. As if a Dauphinois or Poitevin were not a Frenchman!" Even Mercier, though a Parisian to the core, lamented the fact, and complains: "Formerly the roads leading to the capital were not trodden, for every town retained its children within its walls, which protected them from the cradle to the grave. Now every young man sells his share of his inheritance and goes away to riot, for one brief hour, in the hotbed of vice. 'He comes from Paris! He is but just returned from Court!' is the cry, and all the young men hasten to obey the dictates of this general folly which hurls the youth of our provinces into the abyss of corruption."

The attractions, however, which Paris could offer a provincial were many. In Paris there was no official to molest, nor a judge nor bailiff to humiliate him, and if he was engaged in litigation, Paris was too large a city for any policeman to alarm or pick a quarrel with him. On the other hand, Paris was full of allurements, for even more than in Boileau's day it was "a country flowing with milk and honey for a rich man," as we shall see farther on, and there alone the soldier found promotion and the parson preferment. For these reasons, Paris was steadily augmented by new arrivals, and in the course of this century the city grew both in size and splendour. Under Louis xv., France numbered 15,000,000 inhabitants, and, in 1755, Expilly, if he can be trusted, allots no less than 600,000 to Paris alone. This figure can, however, be only approximate, as it is based on the number of "hearths" which paid capitation tax, and the "hearth" varied, some holding it to mean three persons, whereas others, such as Voltaire, regarded it as representing an average of four and a half. Mercier, who probably exaggerated (Buffon's figure of 700,000 is closer to Expilly), protests against this aggregate as being too low, and declares that in 1783, that is thirty years later, Paris contained no less than 900,000 inhabitants, if, as they ought to be, all foreigners living there be included.

In the seventeenth century the expression, *La Cour et la Ville*—the Court and the City—was famous, meaning, "Versailles and Paris"; but the Court, in La Bruyère's phrase, was "the hub of fashion," and the reputations made at Versailles were humbly accepted in the City. In the eighteenth century the situation was reversed, and that good Parisian, Sébastien Mercier, proclaims with pride: "The word 'Court' no longer deceives us as it did in the days of Louis xiv. We do not accept the dominant opinion of the Court, which can no longer make or unmake reputations of any kind, nor do we murmur with ridiculous humility as of yore, 'The Court has decided' this or that. The verdict of the Court is merely quashed, and we just say: 'They don't know anything about it at Versailles; they have no ideas on the subject; they could not have any; they have, in short, no conception about the matter at all.' The Court itself, as all can see, dare not pronounce any favourable verdict on a book, a play, or some other new masterpiece, nor on any event of remarkable or extraordinary nature without first awaiting the sentence of the capital. In fact, the Court takes the greatest trouble to obtain this information, lest it should have to revise its first opinion, which would then be dismissed with costs."

Rousseau, who in nearly all of his books heaped curses upon Paris and yet had no greater wish than to end his days within its walls, admits in *Emile* that "few books are published in Europe in respect of which the author has not been to Paris in order to educate himself. The spirit which pervades society in Paris develops clear thinking and broadens the mind as much as possible. If you have even a spark of genius, go and spend a year in Paris. Soon you will be all that you can ever be, or else you will never be anything at all." Moreover, Voltaire agrees with Rousseau—and this a very rare occurrence—when describing the capital of the Gauls in his *Princesse de Babylone* (1768): "Time, which changes all things, had made a city, of which one-half was very noble and pleasant and the other rather crude and contemptible, and this is, indeed, emblematic of its inhabitants. Within its walls there dwelt, at the lowest computation, some hundred thousand people who had nothing to do but to play and amuse themselves. These lazy folk criticised the Arts which others cultivated. They knew nothing of what happened at Court, and the four short miles which separated them from it might as well have been at least six hundred. . . . Amazan expressed to his host a desire to go to Court, but the sluggards, who happened to be of the company, told him it was no longer the fashion, that the times had changed, and that the only amusements were to be found in town. That same evening he was invited to supper by a lady (Mme Geoffrin) whose wit and talent were known beyond the confines of her country and who had travelled in lands (in Poland) which Amazan had also visited. He delighted in this lady's company and in the guests which frequented her house. There freedom was controlled by reason, gaiety was indulged in without excess, intellectual conversation was not discouraged, and wit preserved from affectation. He realised that the expression 'Good Company' was not an empty one, though it was much misused."

Let us then endeavour to glean from contemporary chroniclers a few details—some picturesque, others realistic —which will enable us to reconstruct Paris as it appeared in the eighteenth century.

The provincial or foreigner who had heard such marvellous tales of Paris would feel himself amazingly disillusioned on first entering the city. "Candide entered Paris by the faubourg St. Marceau and thought himself in the most wretched village of Westphalia." And Rousseau, who first visited Paris in May 1731, echoes Voltaire: "How the first impression of Paris belied my expectations! I had pictured a city as beautiful as it was large, of imposing aspect, where only splendid streets with palaces of marble and gold would meet the eye. On entering by the faubourg St. Marceau I found nothing but filthy and stinking streets, wretched and blackened houses, an air of meanness, crowds of beggars, carters, harlots, and sellers of nostrums and old hats."

If the first impression of Paris was unfortunate it was because this faubourg of St. Marceau (which, together with the Place Maubert, formed one of the twenty *quartiers*) was one of the poorest and most ill-planned in Paris, Mercier calling it "the abode of all secret misery," and adding, somewhat disdainfully: "The people who live there have no relations with the Parisians, who are very elegant and dwell on the banks of the Seine."

The mire of Lutetia has become proverbial, and Mascarille's aphorism is well known: "It is somewhat muddy, but we have our chairs." So let us also take a chair, "that marvellous defence against the insults of mud and bad weather," as Madelon calls it. But where shall we find one? "The chairs," Arthur Young assures us, "exist no more, for they would be upset every other moment" by the coaches, which drive too fast. But Young is a stranger, whereas Mercier is a Parisian and knows where, even in the eighteenth century, a sedan-chair may be found.

"It is not easy to carry a chair in the muddy and crowded streets of the capital. Nor can they ply except in the morning and in certain quiet districts. The dowagers use them to go to Mass, followed by their footmen carrying the prayer book in a red velvet bag. . . . Two strong hirelings, perspiring freely and bent double beneath their burden, their large shoes studded with iron, carry the man whose stomach and gout prevent his walking. Round a corner, perhaps, they come upon a herd of oxen, frightened and threatening. One butts the pole with his horns and upsets the whole contraption. The stout gentleman whose rotundity fills every crevice of it has to lie quiet till the herd has passed. The oxen bow to him at the door as they go by, he shrinks back, and eventually his box has to be turned over to open the door for him. The fury which this accident has roused in him has swollen his veins, and he can scarcely be extricated. He wants to beat the porters with his stick, but they have already fled, and in his rage he does not notice that he has lost his wig."

So let us leave the sedan-chair, and, in order to proceed with more speed and possibly with greater safety, take a cab. "My good friend," you say to the coachman, "do you imagine you will get there like that? Have you thought of the obstructions which your horses will meet with? Here you have the dustmen who spend two hours gathering up the garbage, and there a waggon laden with stones, so heavy that its horses cannot budge it . . . then come the water-carts, of which there are so many, blocking your way. They pull across the street so as to distribute water to the houses. A string of several covered carts are coming towards you, and they are even more dangerous than the chaises, because a blind and brutal rustic is leading them, while scaffolding poles and planks threaten to stave in the carriage panels and stake the horses.

"When will the crash come? It is an absolute maze which you have got to negotiate. Ah! there is a passage—but no, the heaps of stones which for months on end lie about the streets, narrow enough in all conscience, block your way once more. Meanwhile the coachmen crowd together as much as possible, but, clumsy and impatient, they prevent anything from passing, and whoever gains an inch is lucky. You want to pass in your carriage, and it is only by making himself as flat as he can that the unhappy pedestrian is lucky enough to escape the axle of the vehicle, which often projects more than a foot. A washerwoman's van, which she leaves standing for some three hours while she is in the house making out her bill, may well hold up some four hundred carriages. But there goes a chaise, taking advantage of a gap and just grazing the milestone; look—it has escaped from the hubbub. It is the lightning flash which cleaves the overcharged cloud, and a *sauve qui peut* ensues. The obstinate driver proposes to make up for lost time by driving over the bodies of his fellow-citizens. What is the madman doing?"

"Mad" is the very word which Arthur Young uses in describing the chaise-drivers who pass in a flash. He says: "Carriages are numerous, but, unfortunately, there is a large number of one-horse chaises driven by young men of fashion or their imitators, who are as mad as themselves, so furiously that they are a positive danger, and make the streets so insecure that one can only escape by unceasing watchfulness. A poor child has been run over and doubtless killed beneath our very eyes, and I have often been drenched from head to foot by water from the puddles. If our young noblemen in London, where the streets have no pavement, were to imitate their brothers in Paris, they would shortly, and with justice, find themselves soundly thrashed and rolled in the gutter. This makes it difficult for a foreigner to stay long, especially for families who have not the means of hiring a coach, a commodity as expensive as it is in London."

Here is an instance of how passers-by could be run over as if it were an everyday occurrence. The Duke de la

Meilleraye, driving his own chaise, ran over a poor woman who was selling fruit at the corner of a street. A priest of St. Sulpice ventured to remonstrate with the young coxcomb, who thereupon "proceeded to abuse him and struck him with his whip." He was sent to the Bastille, and "that was all the satisfaction that could be obtained, but it removed him out of the reach of the Law." Louis xv. is credited with the following saying, which shows his utter lack of interest in governing—and his lack of compunction for poor people being run over: "Were I a policeman, I would side with the carriages."

Let us then go on foot, and we shall find ourselves in good company, for Montesquieu writes to Mgr Cérati in 1740: "In Paris you will find a great number of honest folk on foot, whereas most of the coaches are full of scoundrels."

To help us in our wanderings about Paris we have the new street signs, which date from 1728—the names of the streets no longer being written on tin plates where any passing shower washed them off, but carved in stone. At the end of the century, houses began to be numbered, a system which, for purposes of visiting, "was more convenient than inquiring for Monsieur So-and-so at the sign of the Blue Riband or the Silver Beard, the fifth door on the right or left of such and such a street." Thanks to Sartine, these signs are now nailed to the walls of houses and shops, "whereas formerly they hung from long iron poles, so that in a strong wind both sign and post threatened to crush the passers-by. In a storm all these signs crashed and banged against each other, creaking as they swung, creating sounds so mournful and discordant that one could hardly believe them possible if one had not heard them. At night, moreover, they caused such deep shadows that they quite obscured the feeble gleam of the lanterns. These signs were of enormous size, and were carved in relief. They displayed before the eyes of the most stunted people in Europe imaginary paintings of some giant race with scabbards six feet long, boots as large as hogsheads, gloves which could have housed a three-year-old child comfortably in each finger, enormous heads, and hands holding sabres—all down the street."

Street lamps had taken the place of lanterns in 1745, but as these were only lit when the moon was not full, *falots* were introduced in order to augment what Mercier calls *l'invigilence du luminaire public*. These were "night watchmen carrying numbered lanterns, who roamed the streets at all hours of night, crying, 'Here is a lantern' (*falot*). These cries are to be heard after supper-time, and the porters are available up to any hour and are at the disposal of those who are out late at night, and they congregate wherever there is a ball or rout. Thus the *falot* is not only a convenience and a safeguard to those who go home late, but it lights you to your house and even to your room, be it on the seventh floor, and provides you with illumination should you have no footman or maid, nor matches, nor tinder, nor steel, as is often the case with young men who frequent the theatres and roam the streets. Moreover, these walking lanterns scare away thieves and protect the public almost as much as the police. These watchmen are attached to the police and see all that is going on, so that the burglar who wants to pick a lock in a side street no longer has the leisure required for such an operation, since a lantern may appear at any moment."

Among other novelties the chroniclers of this time extol the *petite poste* which began to function in 1760 and was of the greatest service to the people of Paris. Barbier notes: "The *petite poste* for the forwarding of letters has now been established for a year. Formerly, all who had no servants made use of the little Savoyards who hung about the streets, in order to communicate with each other. It was thought at first that this undertaking would fail, but it has been brought to such a pitch of perfection by its inventor, M. de Chamousset, a former civil servant, that it has become extremely popular, and is of great service to the rich as well as the poor. It only costs two *sols* to send a letter in Paris and three *sols* to any village in the neighbourhood which has no *grande poste*. The recipient is charged nothing, and one gets a reply either in the morning or afternoon. More than 200 men are employed in collecting and delivering letters, so that for two *sols* one is saved all the trouble of sending one's servant to the other end of Paris, and thus being deprived of his services. It is all extremely well organized."

Under Louis xv. the fashionable world changed its quarters. The austere quarter of the Marais with its old houses of the time of Louis xiv. was relegated to lawyers and old dowagers, who there perused their *Mercure de France*. The great nobles settled in the fine district about the Faubourg St. Germain, while the financiers took up their abode in the rue de Richelieu and the neighbourhood of the Palais Royal and the Tuileries. Rents had increased, and d'Argenson notes in this connection in January 1750: "House rents have everywhere risen to an excessive height, a proof of the growing popularity of residence in Paris and the desertion of the provinces, whereas all rich people ought to be sent back to the country in order to spend their money there, and alleviate the general distress."

The hub of Paris was the Pont Neuf, where Parisians and foreigners came and went in such numbers "that if one walked up and down there for an hour a day one would meet everybody that one wished to see. The police spies haunt it, and if they do not spot their man in a few days, they report that he has left Paris." In 1766 the temporary shops and stalls were removed as they obstructed the passers-by, and henceforth people bent on business or pleasure could enjoy the Pont Neuf at their ease. There one would meet women in high-heeled clogs carrying their huge hampers, and fine gentlemen with swords at their side and with their hat under their arm, long-haired lawyers in black, and priests with their bands and short cloaks. If one sent one's footman to the rue Dauphine and asked him to be back soon, he might well reply "that it all depends on the songs they are singing on the Pont Neuf." In the centre of the bridge stood the equestrian statue of Henry iv. by Dupré, completed in 1635, "one and a half times life size and generally admired more than the horse, which is thought too big for a charger." At the end, close to the Louvre, was La Samaritaine, "a very fine house of three stories, built on piles, like a small castle. In front of it is a fountain flanked by statues of Our Lord and the Samaritan Woman, as described in the Gospel. The water is pumped into a shell-shaped basin, whence it falls into the fountain, which represents Jacob's Well. Above is a clock surmounted by a little gilt turret, hung with bells which chime every hour and half-hour, bearing the inscription: *Fons hortorum puteus aquarum viventium.*"

In order to get a picture of all Paris and his wife going about their business or amusements, let us turn to the following picturesque and animated page of Mercier in which he describes, hour by hour, the life of Paris as it was in his day:

"At seven all the gardeners appear with their empty baskets, on their way to their gardens, astride their worn-out hacks. There are no coaches about, and one only meets clerks, already dressed and curled, at this early hour.

"At nine we see the wigmakers hurrying along, covered in powder from top to toe (whence they are called "whitings"), carrying their curling-tongs in one hand and a wig in the other, and now also appear the confectioners' boys in their linen jackets, bearing coffee and syrups to furnished apartments. Young men who are learning to ride may also be seen, followed by a groom, and careering about the streets, their inexperience often proving a menace to foot passengers.

"At ten o'clock a black host of minions of the Law swarms towards the Châtelet and the Palais, their clients running after them, so that one's view is obscured by bands, gowns, and brief-bags.

"At noon, stockbrokers and jobbers crowd to the Bourse, and the idlers to the Palais Royal, while the St. Honoré district, where the financiers and bankers live, is full of movement, and it is difficult to make one's way along the pavement. This is the hour for presenting petitions and requests of all kinds.

"At two o'clock appear those who are dining in town, with their hair all dressed and curled and powdered, walking on their toes for fear of soiling their white stockings, on their way to the remoter districts. All the cabs are on the streets by this hour, and none can be found on the stands, so that they are hotly disputed for, and it often happens that people open both doors simultaneously, and get in and sit down, and a policeman has to be appealed to, in order to decide who shall keep it.

"At three, few people are seen about, as every one is at dinner; it is a period of calm which, however, does not last long.

"At a quarter past five there is an appalling and infernal din. All the streets are packed; carriages rumble along in every sense of the word, hurrying to various entertainments or to the promenades, and the cafés begin to fill.

"At seven, peace falls once more—a peace which is both profound and universal. The horses stamp in vain, and the whole city lies silent, as if the tumult had been stilled by some invisible agency. In the middle of autumn this is the most dangerous time, as the watch has not yet come out, and many acts of violence are committed at dusk.

"Night begins to fall, and whilst the Opera is in full swing, the host of labourers, carpenters, and masons return in crowds to the faubourgs where they dwell. The plaster from their shoes whitens the pavement, and they can be recognised by the tracks they leave behind them. They are going to bed while the marchionesses and countesses sit down to their toilet.

"At nine o'clock the noise begins again, for at this hour the theatres empty, and houses tremble from the traffic in the streets, but it is soon over, as the world of fashion only pays short visits before going to supper.

"At eleven, silence once more. Supper is over, and the cafés vomit forth the idlers, the unemployed, and the poetasters, who retire to their attics.

"At one o'clock in the morning, six thousand peasants arrive with vegetables, fruit, and flowers, on their way to the markets, their horses jaded and tired out, for they may have come seven or eight leagues.

"Twice a week, at six o'clock, the bakers of Gonesse,

LEAVING THE OPERA HOUSE

From an engraving by G. Malbeste, after J. M. Moreau le Jeune

who supply all Paris, bring a huge quantity of bread, which they have to dispose of in the town, as they are prohibited from taking any back.

"Soon the workmen tear themselves from their pallet-beds, take up the tools of their trade, and make their way to their workshops. *Café au lait*—though it sounds incredible!—has found favour with these strong men. At the street corners, by the light of a flickering lantern, women, carrying tin urns of enormous size, dispense it in earthenware bowls at two *sous* apiece. There is not much sugar in it, but the workman considers it excellent."

Voltaire describes in *Le Mondain* what "a respectable man's life" was like in 1736. Voltaire's verses are, of course, well known, but the following, not so familiar, if less graceful, are certainly more accurate than his. The author is the humorous writer, Boissy, who describes a day in the life of a baron in his play, *L'Homme du jour*. The baron is being addressed by a provincial:

"Aller d'abord montrer aux yeux de tout Paris
  La dorure et l'éclat d'un nouveau vis à vis (carrosse);
Eclabousser vingt fois la pauvre infanterie (les piétons)
Qui se sauve, en jurant, de la cavalerie;
De toilette en toilette aller faire sa cour,
Puis *au Palais Royal* joindre un cercle agréable
Et lier pour le soir une partie aimable.
Ne boire à ton dinêr que de l'eau seulement
Pour *sabler le champagne* à souper largement.
Faire l'après-midi mille dépenses folles,
En deux *médiateurs* (jeu de quadrille) perdre deux cent pistoles;
Sur une tabatière ou bien sur des habits
Dire ton sentiment et ton sublime avis;
Conduire *à l'Opéra* la duchesse indolente
Médire ou bien broder avec la Présidente.
Avec le commandeur parler chasse ou chevaux,
Chez le petit marquis *découper* des oiseaux:
Voilà le plan exact de ta journée entière."
(Boissy, *Les Dehors trompeurs ou l'homme du jour* (1740), ii. 117.) [1]

---

[1] "First you display before the eyes of all Paris the gilded splendour of your new coach, splashing the wretched foot passengers a score of times and more, as they skip, swearing, out of the way of the riders. And so you flit from one lady's dressing-table to another, paying your respects,

On all sides magnificent houses had arisen, and Mercier counted no less than six hundred, either newly built or renovated, whose "interiors seemed to be the work of fairies." In fact, more care was lavished on the interior than on the outside, and the vast and chilly rooms of the preceding century were now abandoned, since people preferred convenient and comfortable apartments to imposing edifices. This was achieved by a "new distribution of buildings," which Patte, a contemporary author, describes in the following passage: "Nothing redounds more to our credit than to have discovered this new idea. Formerly it could be said with truth that our architecture was but a shell, displaying the feature we cherished most, namely, a magnificent exterior, to which everything else was sacrificed. Like the buildings of classical times, and of Italy, which we took as models, the interiors were huge and lacking the smallest comfort. The drawing-rooms were two stories high, the saloons vast, the ballrooms immense, the galleries so long that they ran out of sight, and the staircases gigantic, and all these rooms, adjoining one another, formed a long passage. In fact, we lived solely in order to entertain, and were entirely ignorant of the art of being housed in comfort and privacy. All the convenient arrangements which one admires in our modern houses, in which one room is so artfully separated from another, the staircases so cunningly hidden—all those carefully planned devices which save the servants so much labour and which make our houses such delightful and enchanting dwelling-places—none of them were invented till our day. It was at the Palais Bourbon in 1722 that they were first employed, and since then they have been copied in many

then join agreeable acquaintances at the Palais Royal and collect pleasant company for the evening. At dinner you only drink water in order to swill champagne at supper. You spend your money in a thousand silly ways in the course of the afternoon, and lose two hundred pistoles at the gaming-table. You deliver your opinion and exquisite judgment on some snuff-box or suit, then escort some languishing Duchess to the Opera, talk scandal with the judge's lady, and hunting or dogs with the commander, and then demolish a bird with the little Marquis—that is how you spend your day."

different ways. As regards interior decoration this change led to the substitution of delicate and light carving, at once tasteful and capable of a thousand variations, in the place of ornaments with which rooms had hitherto been overloaded. Beams have been abolished or concealed by these new ceilings which lend so much charm to our rooms and which are decorated with friezes and other pleasing features. Instead of adorning our mantelpieces with pictures or enormous bas-reliefs, we hang them with mirrors, and these, reflecting one another, show us moving pictures which enlarge and enliven the rooms with an air of gaiety and grandeur they certainly did not possess before. Foreigners are overcome with admiration when they see our houses so tastefully arranged and so charmingly decorated, and furnished, moreover, with such art and elegance. French architecture has earned a splendid reputation by these novelties, and nearly all sovereigns have hastened to attract our architects to their states in order to copy them. Wherever you may go—to Russia, Prussia, Denmark, Würtemberg, the Palatinate, Bavaria, Spain, Portugal, or Italy—there you will find French architects occupying the first place, not to mention our painters and sculptors. Paris is now to Europe what Greece was in the heyday of her artistic glory, and supplies artists for all the rest of the world." [1]

So let us enter one of these mansions, and a middle-class house as well, and endeavour to form some idea of the life that was lived in them. We will first turn our attention to the meals. At what hours were these served? Boileau in *Le Repas ridicule* lays emphasis on his eagerness to repair to his repast "as soon as midday strikes and Mass is over." But in the eighteenth century the dinner-hour became later and later. At the beginning people sat down to dine at one, but the ladies' toilette, which took a long time, and the convenience of business men, led to the dinner-hour being put off till two, while in 1782 it was the general custom, as Le Grand d'Aussy tells us, to dine about three, and in many places not until four. Supper was served

[1] Patte, v. 5.

correspondingly later. But there was another reason for this change. People dined later because they rose later. In 1756 the author of *L'Ami des Hommes* writes: "It was quite unusual for any one to get up at eight," and in the latter half of the century, when dinner was as late as three, Mercier asks: "Who would dare to arrive in a house for supper before half-past nine?"

Having answered the first question, we will consider what people ate and what their table cost. A passable dinner could be obtained at a *table d'hôte* for twenty sous. The *pot au feu* was, as ever, the national dish, and Mercier records the ordinary menu of a Parisian middle-class household: "For dinner, soup and boiled meat; in the evening, cold beef with parsley or *bœuf à la mode*. A leg or shoulder of mutton on Sundays, scarcely ever fish, and vegetables rarely, because they were so expensive to dress."

If you were somewhat of an epicure and wished to eat a fish stew, which so often figures as the stake in the bets of the day, you went to the Gros Caillou on the banks of the Seine above the Invalides: "A good fish stew costs a gold louis, but it is a delicious dish if well cooked. The most famous cooks dip their flag to the master mariner of the Gros Caillou, who has a famous recipe for mixing and preparing carp, eels, and gudgeon."

The potato, for which the French had a peculiar antipathy which Parmentier set himself to overcome, had a strange history during this century. "Gradually the potato came into favour in Paris. It appeared with distinction even on the tables of epicures. But this fleeting triumph, which was so little deserved, quickly passed. Its doughy and even insipid taste, and the unhealthy qualities of this food, led to its rejection by delicate eaters, and it was confined to the lower classes, whose coarser palates and stronger stomachs satisfy themselves with anything that can appease hunger."

The Venetian Ambassadors had reported in the sixteenth century that "in some parts of France lentils are sometimes eaten," and in the eighteenth they were still regarded with suspicion by country people. But in Paris they began to appear on Fast days even in the highest circles. Queen Marie Leczinska brought into fashion the little red lentils which hitherto had only been given to horses, and they came to be known as "the Queen's lentils."

The fruits of Montreuil provided dessert, and Montreuil's chief glory was the peach.

As we know, our ancestors were good trenchermen and liked good and plentiful meals, of which they ate, disregarding all consequences, rather more than mere hunger warranted. "Supper kills off half Paris, and dinner accounts for the other." Des Barreaux, that hero of the supper-table, one day replied to M. Delbène, who warned him that a particularly succulent morsel would make him ill: "Come, come; are you one of those fops who take pleasure in digesting their food?"

The use of tobacco spread gradually throughout Paris, thereby enriching the Treasury, but did not improve the ladies, to whom beautiful snuff-boxes were presented. Early in the century Le Sage, in his *Turcaret*, referred to a lady as being "so daubed with snuff that no one would take her for a country woman," but certainly for a Parisian; and in the 'fifties Voltaire wrote: "At the Court of Louis xiv. no one was allowed to put this acrid and dirty powder up his nose, as this was regarded as coarse; but to-day the State gets sixteen millions from farming tobacco."

But more interesting than the Paris which ate and took snuff was the Paris which amused itself; so let us examine it in a little more detail. The balls at the Opera were the great novelty after 1716. In this year they were thrown open to the public at six livres a head. All Paris thronged to them, and it was at one of these balls that the amusing scene occurred which eighteenth-century historians have so often described. The Regent attended one disguised, and in order still further to divert suspicion, the Abbé Dubois began to kick him. "Sir," said the Prince, turning round, "you really disguise me too much." But Dubois was perhaps having his revenge. While still only Archbishop of Cambrai and long a candidate for the Cardinal's hat, he one day chanced to irritate the **Regent**. The latter drove him into a corner and kicked him several times: once "for having been a Minister," and so on, until the fifth was bestowed "for his being an Archbishop." "Oh, I forgive you," said Dubois, laughing, "because I am waiting for a sixth for being a Cardinal."

At these balls, ladies of fashion appeared in black dominoes and masked to the eyes, and the disguise covered their feet, and, above all, their hair. They arrived in a sedan-chair, and went home in a wheel-chair. Gentlemen left their swords at the door, and it was considered bad form to address a mask as "Thou." Conversation was carried on in low tones, and as the men were not masked, half of the company knew the other half, but were themselves unknown; thus the ladies were able to mystify and "intrigue" the gentlemen.

The Parisians, who are inquisitive by nature, were sometimes privileged to see the King and his Court taking part in this amusement. "On Sunday, 8th March 1722, the King gave a ball in the theatre at the Tuileries, at which I was present. Admittance was by ticket only. The hall is magnificent at any time, but it had been extended as far as the King's box, and the illuminations turned it into a fairyland. The ball began at eight and finished about midnight. Fifteen gentlemen, including the King, and fifteen ladies of the Court, among whom were Mlle de Charolais, Mlle de Clermont, her sister, and Mlle de Roche-sur-Yon had been selected to dance, but none of the **Princes of the Blood**, who were sitting behind the King. His chair was placed at the lower end of the stage, the **Princesses of the Blood** occupying seats on his right, and the ladies who had been chosen to dance sitting on his left, thus forming an oval round the room. All the gentlemen and ladies who were not dancing were seated on benches behind them. It was a wonderful sight, as all the gentlemen wore cloth of gold or silver adorned with lace and shoulder-knots, and the rest of their apparel was in keeping. Those of lower rank wore velvet, trimmed with gold or silver lace, which, in my opinion, was even more effective. The **Regent** seems to have discovered the secret of obtaining further credit for the members of the Court, for the ladies were resplendent in their Court dresses, and blazed with diamonds. The clothes of the Marquis and Marquise de Nesle for these different festivities cost forty livres. The tailors were unwilling to give them any more credit, but they eventually accepted a bill of sale." [1]

It is unnecessary to give a list of all the theatres which flourished in Paris in the eighteenth century, or of all the popular plays and players of the time, and such details rightly belong to the history of the French Theatre, but among the singers we might mention the "incomparable" Jelyotte, so often mentioned in the *Mémoires* of the time, especially in those of Mme d'Epinay, and also "the great Dupré," who was the most famous dancer of his day, and whose successor was Vestris, *le Diou de la danse,* who once exclaimed: "I know of only three great men in *Ourope*: the King of *Proussia*, Voltaire, and myself."

The applause was unceasing whenever Dupré appeared and sang those lovely songs of Naïs, "les Indes galantes"; and the amazing fame which Vestris, Dupré, and their kind enjoyed in this century may possibly be explained by the prominent position given to dancing in the education of every woman, and even man, of the world.

In the various theatres, plays began between five and six and finished between eight and nine, when one went to sup, and after supper one conversed or played at "reversi," sometimes until two in the morning, and no one rose till the day was well advanced. Theatres were cheap: "For forty-eight sous you might enjoy Glück's sentimental melodies for an hour and a half, or la Guimard and la Théodore would charm your eye with their dancing," and for twenty sous you might hear a masterpiece by Corneille or Molière, while Mercier assures us that "Paris provides more public amusements than any other city in the world," and, as we have seen, more cheaply as well. For those of a studious rather than a merely curious disposition it was

[1] Barbier, i. 199.

possible, according to Mercier, to obtain admission to a reading-room for forty sous, and for a whole afternoon to read there the whole *Encyclopédie* in its ponderous tomes, including its fly-leaves.

From 1737 onwards the public exhibition of pictures in the great salon of the Louvre became an annual event, and this was the beginning of the Salon of to-day, and Diderot was the first of French art critics, his notices on the works exhibited there covering the period from 1751 to 1781.

There was no fête, at this time, at which fireworks did not play a prominent part, "and our artificers have invented rockets which can attain a height of 2000 toises." Fireworks were even indulged in at home, "for there is nothing more amusing than to let off small fireworks on one's table. Though they are only in miniature, yet they are almost as fine a sight and as enjoyable as the real ones."

Serious people who wished for more instructive pursuits might visit the King's Natural History Museum in the King's Garden, with its new collection of birds brought together by Réaumur, while those who only desired novelties were provided for by Vaucanson, who, in 1738, set up his "Automatic Flute-player," five and a half feet high, "a real flutist, playing on a real flute with his mouth, and moving his lips and rendering his variations with the utmost accuracy by the aid of his fingers," and in 1741 produced his "Automatic Duck," which "waddles, eats, drinks, dabbles in the water, and quacks and flaps its wings like a live duck."

The Parisians, like the provincial folk, as we shall see, indulged in an amusement which, in our day, is practically unknown. This was to spend their evenings at the Fair, walking up and down covered galleries, lined by two rows of illuminated stalls, and interspersed with booths which advertised puppet shows, giants, dwarfs, jugglers, and performing dogs, or in which they could refresh themselves with tartlets and pastries. These Fairs were very numerous, and each one provided its special curiosities and surprises. In March 1749 every one flocked

A CARNIVAL IN THE STREETS OF PARIS

From an engraving by C. Le Vasseur, after Etienne Jaureat

to the Fair at St. Germain to see "a rare and curious animal never before seen in France, namely, a rhinoceros, which had been brought from the Indies at great expense by a Dutch skipper. A ticket costs three livres and twelve sous. There are very few people who can resist this attraction, and the skipper must be coining money. . . . He has exhibited in various places, but first at Versailles, where all the Court went to see it. The animal is conveyed from place to place in a kind of cage on four wheels, drawn by six horses, and its daily ration is fifty pounds of hay, fifteen pounds of bread, and fifteen buckets of water. I have also seen it eat orange-peel, which one throws into its cavernous jaws."[1]

All Paris visited the Fair at St. Germain annually, and when in 1762 it was destroyed by fire with considerable loss of life, there was general consternation, as we can discover from the records of that time.

In the eighteenth century the fashionable promenade was no longer the Cours la Reine, or Cours, as it was called for short, of the reign of Louis XIII., nor the Tuileries Gardens which were so popular under the Great King, but at the beginning of the century the Palais Royal and, in later years, the boulevards became the centre of fashion. "On feast days and Sundays, after High Mass, my mother and stepfather would take me to walk in the Palais Royal. At this time the garden was far more extensive and beautiful than it is now, when it has been encroached upon and shut in by the surrounding houses. On the left there was a very broad and long avenue, shaded by enormous trees which formed a roof, impenetrable to the sun's rays. Here the fashionable world gathered in its smartest clothes. If the weather was bad we took shelter under the plantations. At that time the Opera adjoined the garden, being housed in the Palais. In summer the performances finished at half-past eight, and all the elegant folk came out to walk in the garden, and as it was the fashion for ladies to carry large bouquets, their fragrance, added to the scented powder which every one used on their hair, positively perfumed

[1] Barbier, iv. 356.

the air. Later on, but before the Revolution, I have known these evening parties continue until two in the morning, and there would be music by moonlight, while artists and even amateurs like Garat and Alzevédo would sing. Some played the harp and others the guitar, and when the celebrated Saint-Georges played his violin the crowd was enormous."[1]

When Voltaire's *Pauvre Diable* had come into his uncle's money, he went there to display his fine clothes:

"On summer evenings in this enchanted spot behind whose rampart love finds shelter and which Outrequin revives each day."

Outrequin was the contractor who was responsible for watering Paris. As for the "ramparts" (or boulevards), Barbier describes them as they were in 1753: "The Provost of the Merchants has arranged the boulevards very well, the sidewalks being sanded and stone benches set up, while the central avenue is watered every day to protect the neighbouring houses from dust. This summer, therefore, they have become the fashionable promenade of Paris. Chiefly on Sundays and feast days, there is an astonishing concourse of coaches, which form a block from the Porte St. Antoine to that of the Pont-aux-Choux. [The rue du Pont-aux-Choux abutted on a district occupied by market gardeners chiefly growing cabbages.] Towards the end of the century it became the custom to walk on the boulevards on Easter Monday and Tuesday, and an Englishwoman, Mrs. Cradock, describes the great crowds she saw there on these two days: 'I saw a crowd all dressed in springlike fashions, over two hundred carriages with footmen in superb liveries, and the horses decorated with tassels and ribands of various colours. On each side of the paved avenue, and beneath the sheltering trees, were tents in which refreshments were provided, and flowers and other objects for sale. Here and there people were dancing, and it was altogether a very gay picture.'"

But some further details must be added to the description of these boulevards which, in the eighteenth century,

[1] Mme Vigée Lebrun, i. 18.

rose so rapidly to fame. They consisted of three avenues planted with elms, and extended from the Bastille to the Porte St. Honoré. They were much frequented, especially on Thursdays, about five o'clock, and in the central avenue there was a chaotic procession of all sorts of vehicles, chariots, coaches, chaises, which crossed each other and collided, amidst the cries and oaths of their drivers, while, on the well-sanded sidewalks, vendors of oranges, nougat, and flowers mingled with the passers-by. People would stop in front of the guitar-players, among whom *Fanchon la vielleuse* was the queen; in front of the tight-rope walkers or at Nicolet's, the Puppets, or at Audinot's. In 1778, Curtius opened his famous show "where one only pays when leaving." "His wax figures on the boulevards are very famous and much visited. He has modelled kings, great writers, pretty women, and celebrated thieves. There may be seen Jeannot, Defruès, the Count d'Estaing, and Linguet, as well as the Royal Family seated at a banquet, with the Emperor (Joseph II.) next to the King. The showman cries himself hoarse at the door. 'Come in, gentlemen; come in and see the Grand Banquet exactly as at Versailles.' One pays two sous a head, and M. Curtius sometimes makes a hundred crowns a day by showing his mannikins all lit up."[1]

But Comus was the real King of the Boulevards—"that incomparable physician," as Mercier dubs him, "endowed with the most subtle and inventive genius." Diderot also mentions him in a curious and almost prophetic letter to Mme Volland, dated 20th July 1762: "So one of my letters has gone astray, and who knows what it contained, into whose hands it has fallen, or what use will be made of it? Would that Comus had perfected his secret! He is a quack of the boulevards who agitates all our doctors greatly. His secret consists in establishing communication between one room and another, or between two persons, without the visible assistance of any intermediary. If this man were to improve this, one day, so as to communicate between towns, or between one place and another, hundreds of

[1] Mercier, iii. 27.

miles distant, how delightful that would be! Each of us would only require a little box, like a miniature printing-press, and all that stamped itself on the one would suddenly print itself upon the other!"

In order that our picture of the amusements of Paris under Louis xv. may be complete, we must say a word or two about the Coliseum, "so called," says Dulaure, "because it resembled in some respects that of Vespasian." It was situated at the western end of the Champs Élysées, north of the Avenue de Neuilly, and was opened to the public on 22nd May 1771. "It was a very fashionable meeting-place, an immense circular building erected on one of the large plots in the Champs Élysées (they call it the Circus). In the centre was a lake full of clear water, in which aquatic sports took place, and one could walk around the avenues, which were sanded and provided with seats. At dusk every one repaired to an immense hall, where a large orchestra played excellent music every evening. Mlle Lemaure, then at the height of her fame, sang there several times, as did other famous singers. The large flight of steps, which gave access to this concert hall, was the meeting-place for all the gilded youth of Paris, who took their stand under the illuminated doorways, and allowed no woman to pass without making some smart remark about her."[1]

Before leaving the boulevards we ought to note that towards the end of the century the Bois de Boulogne became the fashionable resort during Holy Week. "On Wednesday, Thursday, and Friday of this week every one went out of Paris to hear the office of 'Ténèbres' at Longchamps, a small village about four miles from Paris, and all made a point of showing off their finest carriages, most spirited horses, and most sumptuous liveries."[2]

But Longchamp was not only a popular resort in Holy Week, but was also much frequented when reviews and races took place in that neighbourhood. So great were the crowds on these occasions, and the luxury of the clothes and carriages so dazzling, that they seem to have haunted

[1] Mme Vigée Lebrun, *Souvenirs*, i. 24.   [2] Mercier, ii. 45.

those who survived the agony of the Revolution. Frénilly writes: "I have seen Longchamps at the height of its splendour. Two lines of carriages started from the Place Louis xv., while two others were returning from the end of the Bois de Boulogne. Horsemen crowded the immense Avenue de Neuilly, and those on foot overflowed the sidewalks. Not a cab was to be seen, and a hackney carriage would have been greeted with hisses. Four-horsed carriages were regarded with contempt, for they betrayed the lower magistrates and small financiers, whose vanity prompted them to have more than two, though they could not rise to six. The high-water mark in good taste was to have either two or six horses at Longchamps, and this only on the Wednesday and Friday. . . . But no one except Parisians of my own age have ever seen anything to approach the undreamed-of luxury which reached its culmination on these two days. If you wished to be numbered with the elect, everything—horses, harness, carriages, liveries, clothes—had to be brand-new."[1]

The Paris of Louis xv. offered the foreigner theatres, promenades, luxury, and all the amenities of life, and those who appreciated such things could enjoy there all the delights of cultivated society once they had been admitted to those famous salons of the eighteenth century, of which we shall see more later, when we come to study the beginnings of "Public Opinion" at this period. Foreigners who frequented those salons and gladly lingered to talk with the men of letters and women of wit whom they met there, have been unanimous in proclaiming the superiority of Paris over all the other capitals of Europe, even if they, perhaps, were less flattering to its "airs and graces." They would undoubtedly have agreed with that dictum of Voltaire which they would have found in his *Siècle de Louis XIV.*, when it appeared in the middle of the century: "One can, to-day, perceive that politeness has spread to all classes and is to be met with even in a shop. The vanity of pomp and outward show is confined to those nations who only care to display themselves in public while wholly

[1] Frénilly, i. 28.

ignorant of the art of living. The spirit of freedom which has influenced social intercourse, the growth of courtesy, simplicity, and intellectual refinement have made Paris a city which probably far surpasses, in the amenities of life, both Rome and Athens at the zenith of their splendour.

"A great number of foreigners is drawn to visit or even to sojourn in this 'true home of Society' by the unequalled and unlimited facilities which it affords for the pursuit of the sciences and arts, and the satisfaction of their tastes and needs, offering, as it does, so many solid advantages as well as agreeable distractions—not least that freedom which is so typically Parisian."[1]

As early as the eighteenth century it was said that Paris was "hell for horses, purgatory for men, and paradise for women." But it was also the foreigner's "Paradise Lost" when, after enjoying its delights, he had to leave it for ever. Galiani, who called Paris "the Café of Europe," wrote to Mme d'Epinay on his return to Naples: "I am still inconsolable, even at Naples! at having left Paris . . . Paris my home; and even though I have been exiled, I shall return. . . . It is not merely a question of my pleasure but of my very existence. Every day, I feel and experience, more and more, that it is physically impossible for me to live away from Paris. Weep for me as for the dead if I do not return."

The Marquis Caraccioli, the Neapolitan Ambassador in Paris, was appointed Viceroy of Sicily. When he took his leave of the King, Louis XVI. said to him: "My Lord Ambassador, I must congratulate you on your going to live in one of the most delightful places in Europe." "Ah, sire," was the mournful reply, "the most delightful place in Europe is the one I am leaving, and that is the Place Vendôme."[2]

But we have no need of the evidence of foreigners when so many of our own countrymen have so worthily extolled our Paris of former days, beginning with Montaigne in the sixteenth century, who paid his homage "to the glory of France and one of the chief ornaments of the

[1] Voltaire, ch. xxix.   [2] Lévis, 181.

world," down to Voltaire, who, at the close of his life, as he was about to leave once more for his house at Ferney, paid his farewell to the Paris of the eighteenth century in these moving and very charming lines:

"Les Adieux du Vieillard

Mes yeux, après trente ans (d'absence) n'ont vu qu'un peuple aimable,
Instruit, mais indulgent, doux, vif et sociable.
Il est né pour aimer; l'élite des Français
Est l'exemple du monde. . . .
De la société les douceurs désirées
Dans vingt Etats puissants sont encore ignorées;
On les goûte à Paris; c'est le premier des arts:
Peuple heureux, il naquit, il règne en vos remparts.
Je m'arrache en pleurant à son charmant empire;
Je retourne à ces monts qui menacent les cieux,
A ces antres glacés où la nature expire:
Je vous regretterais à la table des dieux."

(*Au Marquis de la Villette*, 1778.)

CHAPTER II

THE LAWYERS

"I DO not understand," La Bruyère once remarked, "whence arises the mutual dislike between lawyers and nobles." The nobility of the sword disliked the lawyers just because they were noble, and, moreover, the only true nobility in France, whereas the lawyers, even though they might have been raised to this dignity and have assumed the most high-sounding titles, could never, in spite of their undoubted worth and great merits, contend against the old-fashioned prejudice that the sword alone conferred true nobility. "My mother," wrote the Abbé de Choisy, "who was a Hurault de l'Hôpital, often said to me : 'Listen, my son; never be vain or forget that you belong to the middle classes. I know quite well that your ancestors have held high office in the Civil Service and have been Counsellors of State, but, believe me, in France no nobility is generally acknowledged save that of the sword.' "

The lawyers, on the other hand, had their opportunities for revenging themselves for this slight, and reciprocating this disdain. The judges of the eighteenth century could have used the same words to their sons as Dandin used to his:

> "Qu'est ce qu'un gentilhomme? un pilier d'antichambre
> Combien en as-tu vus; je dis des plus huppés,
> A souffler dans leurs doigts dans ma cour occupés,
> Le manteau sous le nez ou la main dans la poche;
> Enfin, pour se chauffer, venir tourner ma broche." [1]

---

[1] "What is a gentleman? Just a loafer in anterooms. You have seen many, even of the highest rank, busy whistling through their fingers in my Court, muffled in their cloaks, with their hands in their pockets, forced, at length, to turn my spit in order to keep themselves warm."—*Les Plaideurs*, i. 4.

THE LAWYERS

The office of magistrate was very much sought after, and it was the dream of the common folk to arrange a wealthy marriage for their son in order to buy him some small post in the judiciary. The son in his turn, hoping to advance his family still further, married his daughter, who now had a rich dower, to some noble if impecunious magistrate, and the family could then claim relationship with the nobility of the Law. This gradual ascent of a middle-class or even a peasant family towards the highest rungs of the judicial ladder, and their consequent pride in being able, in their turn, to humiliate the haughty lord of the manor, was the brilliant prospect which the ambitious Mathurin set before the eyes of his children:

> "Je veux que tout se passe
> A mon plaisir, suivant mes volontés;
> Car je suis riche. Or, beau-père, écoutez:
> Pour honorer en moi mon mariage,
> Je me décrasse, et j'achète au bailliage
> L'emploi brillant de receveur royal
> Dans le grenier à sel; ça n'est pas mal.
> Mon fils sera conseiller, et ma fille
> Relèvera quelque noble famille.
> Mes petits-fils deviendront présidents:
> De Monseigneur un jour les descendants
> Feront la cour aux miens; et quand j'y pense,
> Je me rengorge et me carre d'avance."
> (Voltaire, *Le Droit du Seigneur*, i. 4.)[1]

It would indeed be something to be proud of if Mathurin's grandson were to rise to the dignity of a President of the Parliament, for that was the highest post in the judicature. But even Mathurin might aspire to higher things yet as far as his descendants were concerned, for

---

[1] "I desire everything to take its course according to my will and pleasure. I am a rich man, as you know, father-in-law, and this is what I have planned. I will rise in the world and I intend to purchase from the County Court the exalted post of Royal Collector of the Salt Tax—that will be a good beginning. My son shall be a Counsellor, my daughter shall repair the fortunes of a noble family, and my grandsons become Presidents of the Parliament. Then my lord's descendants will one day bow before mine, and the thought of that already makes me swell with pride and pleasure."

the daughter of the Marquis de Chatillôn had married a Bacqueville "who was rich but nothing more, his real name being Boyvin. His father, who called himself Bonnetot, was First President of the Court of Accounts at Rouen, and his father before him had, in his youth, been a farm labourer, and afterwards made a fortune from speculating in corn. This Bacqueville wished to be a noble. As a result of his marriage he obtained a regiment." [1] In this case the grandfather was a peasant who, having amassed a fortune, bought a judicial post for his son, and, finally, the grandson of Bonnetot the farm labourer and son-in-law of a Marquis took the name of de Bacqueville, and with his grandfather's money bought himself a regiment, and so, at length, behold him a Colonel!

Class distinctions, however, were so clearly defined in the society of those days, that a magistrate, even if a President, had to give place to a mere cornet of horse if the latter happened to be born "a gentleman." Thus "the most insignificant lieutenant of infantry may take precedence of a Chancellor, so that in this country, at any rate, we cannot say *cedant arma togæ*. None who are associated with the Law, even if they can be traced back to the Creation, can be admitted to the highest nobility; etiquette excludes them from eating with Princes of the Blood, and their wives can never be presented at Court." [2]

No one belonging to the *ancien régime* expressed with more vigour and, we may add, with more genius the antipathy and disdain which the higher nobility felt for the higher magistracy than did the Duke de Saint-Simon, Peer of France. At the *Lit de Justice* held at the Tuileries on 26th October 1718, the Parliament was obliged to listen to the reversal of the judgment it had delivered, relating to finance and currency, and of a declaration which deprived the legitimised princes of the honours bestowed on them by Louis XIV. This declaration was aimed, primarily, at the Duke de Maine, the protector of the First President, M. de Mesmes. The Keeper of the Seals, d'Argenson, read the preamble of the edict which reversed the Parliament's

---

[1] Saint-Simon, xvii. 11.   [2] *L'Espion anglais*, i. 172.

decision, and forbade that body to exceed its duties by meddling in affairs of State. Let us see how Saint-Simon describes the sitting and in what vivid terms his pen has immortalised a scene in which his soul delighted, just after d'Argenson had spoken. "This Parliament, which, even during the late King's lifetime, had so often summoned this same d'Argenson before it and given him its orders as if he were a mere Lieutenant of Police, standing uncovered at its bar—this Parliament, which, ever since the Regency, had expressed its dislike towards him in unmeasured terms, even going so far as to retain prisoners and papers in its custody in order to cause him annoyance; this First President (de Mesmes), who was so superior to him (d'Argenson), so full of vanity, so proud of his Duke de Maine, and so confident of obtaining the seals; this Lamoignon, who had boasted that he would hang him in his Court of Justice which he himself had so dishonoured—how completely were the tables turned! They saw d'Argenson in the robes of the highest office in the judicature, presiding at the session and completely overshadowing them, dismissing them, in virtue of his powers, to their duties, and thus, on the first occasion on which he appeared as their head, reading them a lesson which was as public as it was severe.

"These vainglorious presidents tried to ignore this man who in such strong terms lacerated their pride and demolished their arrogance in the very place whence they derived it. So confounded were they that they did not venture to meet his look.

"The First President wished to speak and submit the Remonstrance, in which the most subtle malice was conbined with impudence to the Regent and insolence to the King. The villain, however, trembled as he proceeded, and his hesitating speech, his shifty eyes, and the emotion and uneasiness which he displayed, betrayed the rancour which filled him and all his companions. On that day I experienced all the pleasure a man can possibly feel at seeing those proud lawyers, who dare to refuse us obeisance, grovelling on their knees and rendering at our feet a homage which was worthy of a throne. . . . My gaze was lowered and fixed on those proud bourgeois, and surveyed the bench where they stood or knelt, their furred robes swaying around them at each prolonged and repeated genuflection, which were only terminated at the King's command, voiced by the Keeper of the Seals. There they stood, uncovered, and as dust beneath our feet. When the Remonstrance was finished, the Keeper of the Seals mounted the steps of the throne, and then, without seeking the King's further orders, returned to his place, and addressed the First President with the words: 'The King desires to be obeyed, and that immediately.' This sentence was like a thunderclap, and had the most remarkable effect on presidents and counsellors alike. All bowed their heads, and most of them remained silent for a long time. While the edict was being recorded, I kept glancing here and there, and though I controlled my feelings, I was unable to resist the temptation of revenging myself upon the First President. On him, therefore, I fixed my gaze with burning intensity a hundred times during the sitting, and my eyes, as they raked him from top to toe, expressed all the hate, disdain, scorn, and triumph which filled me at the moment. Often his would fall when they met mine, though once or twice he met my stare, and I delighted in wounding him by scowling behind my hand, and at length covered him with confusion. I revelled in his mortification, and rejoiced in thus communicating my feelings to him. Occasionally I took pleasure in pointing him out to my neighbours, and we would smile just at the moment when he looked our way; in short, I emphasised without reserve and as openly as I could the gulf there was between us." [1]

The bitter delight which Saint-Simon displays in the above passage gives us some idea of the power of a magistracy which was able to inspire a Duke and Peer with such a fury of revenge.

As we have heard him describe the discomfiture of the President de Mesmes, so we will let him also narrate the sequel. Two years after that *Lit de Justice*, Saint-Simon's own brother-in-law, the Duke de Lorges, asked for the hand

[1] Saint-Simon, xvi. 57.

of the daughter of this very same de Mesmes whom Saint-Simon had thus covered with obloquy. The latter writes: "About half-way through the Parliament's exile at Pontoise, I was working one afternoon, alone, with the Duke d'Orléans, when the latter informed me that the First President had asked for his consent to the marriage of his eldest daughter with the Duke de Lorges. My surprise and anger were so great that I rose abruptly and hurled my stool to the other end of the room." [1]

The marriage, however, took place, but Saint-Simon could not bring himself to sign the contract, nor would he see the newly wedded couple, until at length, after much negotiation, he yielded so far as to see the young Duchess de Lorges for a few moments at the house of the Duchess de Lauzun; but "silent tears," sleepless nights, and, finally, the illness of his wife were required to bring this about, and the irascible Duke eventually only "made the harrowing sacrifice at the entreaties of Mme de Saint-Simon." Even then it was but a pretence at a reconciliation.

Just as there were different degrees among the nobility, so also there were definite distinctions among the magistrates. "There were higher and lower magistrates, and the former take vengeance on the latter for the disdain with which the Court treats them and the humiliations they suffer at its hands. But it is no easy matter to say where the higher magistracy ends and the lower begins." [2] Let us endeavour, however, to delimit these social demarcations, which are, certainly, difficult to define, as are, in any country, all petty distinctions which tradition has confirmed, but which purists sometimes repudiate.

On a closer investigation we can distinguish not two, but three, categories. There was the *Grande Robe* or higher magistracy, consisting of members of the Supreme Courts (Parliaments, Court of Exchequer, Court of Accounts); the *Petite Robe*, or lower magistracy, consisting of the procurators, notaries, and registrars; while between the two there was a middle and ill-defined zone filled by the barristers for whom a new definition, the *Moyenne Robe*, had

---

[1] Saint-Simon, xvii. 157.   [2] La Bruyère, *De la ville*.

to be invented, since they refused to belong to the lower and were excluded from the higher. The social hierarchy within the Bar might be established approximately as follows: magistrates, barristers, notaries, procurators (the solicitors of to-day), ushers, clerks, and sergeants.

Saint-Simon is always insisting that "the Parliament belongs to the *tiers-état* or third estate." The members of the Parliament called themselves nobles, which indeed they were; but the nobility of the lawyers was one of "dignity," and inferior, as we have seen, to that of "birth." In reality, it was only a nobility of wealth, as it was based on purchased offices. It is true that the Presidents of the Supreme Courts enjoyed the same right as "gentlemen" to the title of "chevalier" or knight, and that theirs also was an hereditary nobility, while counsellors of these same courts, although their nobility was only personal, transmitted it, together with their office, to their sons and heirs. To be exact, the heirs only enjoyed noble rank if their ancestors had held an office which carried nobility with it. "Just as alchemists declare that gold changes itself thrice before it finally acquires its genuine properties, so also the third generation and its modifications purifies the blood and removes therefrom the last taint of plebeian origin." [1]

This explains the arrogance of the magistrates, and what was called the *morgue de la robe*. The lawyers, "those common folk, formerly sat on the steps of the dais on which the peers and chief barons had their place," but the sons of those humble lawyers had now grown more bold. "They made a dais of the steps, as we see to-day, and from the dais they have advanced themselves to even higher seats," [2] and from these they look down on humbler folk, and at times make even the greatest nobles pay dearly for their disdainful airs. This "arrogance of the Bar" did not only refer to its contempt for the middle-class from which it sprang, but of which it also was the flower, but it also implied the icy reserve and unyielding tenacity with which it opposed the pretensions and insolence of the higher nobility. Let us then see how, when

[1] Loyseau, *Des Offices*, i. 9.   [2] Saint-Simon, x. 369.

placed face to face, the nobility of the Law and the nobility of the sword could join issue, and what language a First President of the Parliament could employ towards even the most exalted personages.

Here is the case of the Marquis de Montataire and his wife at a sitting of the Court over which the First President, de Harlay, presided:

"Husband and wife were both great talkers as well as being reputed to be exceedingly litigious. They attended a sitting of M. de Harlay's court, and, when their turn came, the husband wished to speak, but was interrupted by his wife, who proceeded to state her case. The President listened awhile and then cut her short by asking the husband: 'Sir, is this your wife?' 'Why, yes,' replied Montataire, much astonished at this question. 'I am deeply sorry for you,' said the First President, who thereupon shrugged his shoulders, and turned his back upon them. No one present could refrain from laughing. They went home outraged and indignant, and this insult was all they got out of the First President." [1]

Another day "the Duchess de la Ferté sought an interview with de Harlay, and had to put up with his manners like everybody else. As she left, she complained to her man of business, and called the First President an old monkey. The latter had followed her, but said not a word, and when she noticed this, she feared he had overheard, though she hoped this was not the case. Still he gave no sign and conducted her to her coach. Shortly after her case came on, and was swiftly decided in her favour. She hurried off to the First President and overwhelmed him with thanks. He humbly and modestly disclaimed any credit, bowing to the ground repeatedly. Then, looking her straight in the face, 'Madame,' said he, in a loud voice, before all the room, 'I am only too glad that an old monkey was able to give some pleasure to an old female of the same species,' and then, without another word, handed her out, it being his custom to take leave of people in this fashion, and to escort them from one

[1] Saint-Simon, v. 168.

room to another. The Duchess de la Ferté could have killed him or died of shame herself; she was so embarrassed that she did not know what to say, while he remained wrapped in profound silence and in an attitude of the deepest respect, with his eyes bent on the ground until she had entered her coach." [1]

The magistracy was justified in holding its head high even in the presence of the great nobles. The families of the magistrates were rich, as they had to be in order to purchase offices which were often very expensive. One Maupeou, a *maître de requêtes*, bought the post of Deputy President of Parliament for 750,000 livres and 20,000 livres thrown in. He handed on his office to his son, the future Chancellor, and was able to obtain for the latter the hand of a rich heiress, the only daughter of the Marquis de Roncherolles, who brought him a dowry of over 50,000 livres per annum.

Once in possession of their offices, the magistrates regarded them as their absolute property. In its Remonstrances of 19th January 1756, the Parliament of Normandy pleaded "that it is as unjust to deprive a magistrate of an office which he has acquired, as it is to dispossess him of an estate which he has inherited from his ancestors." Whenever, as often happened in the course of this century, a conflict arose between the Government and the Parliament, the magistrates declared "that it was their duty to cease from their functions and resign their offices, but that this resignation could not be accepted." In fact, the office was the property of its holder, and, in France, property was inviolable. But if the office could not be seized, this did not apply to the magistrate himself, and the King could always exile him or imprison him so as to force him to resign it. The *vénalité des offices*, or 'purchase of office,' therefore, invested the magistrate with a definite status of which he was justly proud, as it rendered him comparatively independent. It is questionable whether this was satisfactory or even justifiable, and much has been written for and against

[1] Saint-Simon, v. 168.

this purchasing of offices. Without in any way venturing to solve so controversial a question, we may, however, note Loyseau's weighty opinion: "If the holder is worthy of his office, there is no reason why he should buy it. On the other hand, if he be unworthy, there is even less reason for selling it to him." [1]

Not only could a judicial office be bought, but it could become hereditary in certain families, and in the course of the eighteenth century a sort of privileged oligarchy came into being, which held a monopoly of the Bench, and the Maupeou family is one of the most notable examples of successive generations all holding high legal positions; in fact, since the preceding century no less than fifty members or connections of this clan were members of the Parliament of Paris alone. Many a magistrate could, in those days, echo Dandin's words to his son: "Wherever you look, be it in my study or in my dressing-room, all those Dandins whose portraits you see were lawyers." [2]

Omer Joly de Fleury, the Advocate-General, is notorious, not only on account of his fierce denunciation of the Encyclopedists and *Emile*, but also from Voltaire's humorous description of him in Parliament: "When we read him we do not discover a Homer, when we see him we do not find good looks, and when he opens his mouth he is no orator." The following details about his nephew are told by Beugnot: "He was the most typical and unpleasant specimen of mediocrity that had ever been seen at the Palais Royal. In these days it is hardly possible to understand how such a man could rise to one of the most important offices in the State, but we shall be able to do so if we recall the conditions existing in 1785. The family of Joly had been lawyers for a long time, and had produced a magistrate in the Procurator-General of that name who was a contemporary, and almost the rival, of d'Aguesseau. Since that time the family had firmly established itself in the Councils and on the *grand banc* of the Parliament. It had contracted very honourable alliances, and, as all the members of the family united their in-

[1] Loyseau, *Du droit des offices*, i.   [2] *Les Plaideurs*, ii. 5.

fluence to transmit their offices in this profession from father to son and from uncle to nephew, ministers were not strong enough to resist their pressure, even when the interests of the State and of the King demanded it. The chief families of the Parliament of Paris formed a kind of oligarchy."[1]

Even outside Parliament the Bar formed a class apart in eighteenth-century society, with its distinctive customs, its legitimate pride, and also that self-confidence which is derived from a corporate spirit allied to that of caste. In his *Confessions du Comte de* ***, Duclos expresses it thus: "Most of the lawyers are obliged to live among their own kind, and their intercourse fans their pride. They never cease inveighing against the people at Court, whom they pretend to despise, although they never stop dinning into your ear the names of those with whom they have the honour of being acquainted. No titled person dies but quite half the Bar appears in mourning, a convention which the barristers fulfil to the smallest detail, whereas it is rare to see a magistrate in mourning for his cousin the solicitor."

The judicial appointments cost large sums to buy, but their emoluments were very small. On de Luynes' authority, the post of President of the Parliament at Douai cost 100,000 livres, whereas the income was but 3000. But there were the perquisites (*épices*) besides, and these were not to be despised. These were formerly "voluntary gifts which the successful litigant presented to the judge out of courtesy, and consisted usually of sugar-plums, sweetmeats, or comfits (*épices*), but which, in the course of time, took the form of money, and what had been an act of politeness and generosity thus became a tax, and a compulsory one at that."[2] Thus magistrates who had paid a large sum for their offices reimbursed themselves at the expense of the litigants, and this act of extortion was euphemistically called "plucking the bird." The poor litigant, moreover, usually had to grease the palm of the judge's porter when he wished for an interview, for does not Petit Jean warn him: "He may knock and he may bow, but he won't enter

[1] Beugnot, *Mémoires*, i. 53.   [2] Loyseau, *Des offices*, i. 8.

my house unless he oils the knocker. No money, no porter, and the door remains shut." There used to be an old saying at the Palais: "*Qui mieux abreuve, mieux preuve*" ("He who waters most makes the best show"). Some magistrates derived as much as 30,000 livres per annum from these *épices*, and one might well say of them as Saint-Simon used to say of the old Councillors of the Grand' Chambre: "They loved their money-bags overmuch."

"The duty of judges is to dispense justice, their profession is to postpone it. Some of them know their duty but practise their profession." La Bruyère the cynical is right, although we should not invariably accept his judgments on the society of his day, because he is inclined to paint it very black, and did not himself occupy in it the position which his talents deserved. In the eighteenth century it was not uncommon that, like his Orante, a litigant carried his case from judge to judge for ten long years and then, five or six years later, was lucky enough to obtain a judgment—appointing yet another tribunal to which he might appeal. There was some reason, under this system, for the complaint that the judges "had made lawsuits immortal," and when at Bordeaux, Pontac, as *Premier Président du Parlement*, displayed four interlaced P's blazoned on his coach, people said it really meant *pauvre plaideur, prenez patience*. It is, therefore, easy to appreciate the old proverb: "A litigant requires three bags—one for money, one for his documents, and one for patience"; and in Duclos' romance, which so faithfully depicts the manners of those days, from which we have already quoted, we may read this curious testimony to both the dilatoriness and expense of lawsuits: "It is usual to obtain the judgment of several tribunals on the same case, so one has to begin young if one wishes to see the end of it. I was extremely sorry for one poor devil who won his case, which related to a field, but this was, unfortunately, not sufficiently large to pay the lawyer who had charge of the matter. His legal expenses could have covered the field with gold, and it is estimated that one square foot of such litigious matter is worth a good deal more than a square foot of land."

Saint-Simon, in his cynical way, attributes the intentional prolongation of lawsuits to "the salaries, the fees, the perquisites, and all the filth of that profitable employment, which all, from the First President to the most humble member of the Parliament, multiply daily, drawing their wages for every hour of their so-called labours." Nevertheless, as we have seen, the fortunes thus made provided handsome dowers which even the sons of Dukes and Peers did not disdain.

A contemporary pamphlet, entitled *Dialogue entre un plaideur et un avocat*, published in 1751, contains this conversation: "Well, sir," says the litigant, "how is the suit of these poor orphans progressing?" The lawyer replies: "Why, their property has only been held as security for eighteen years, and, as yet, but a third of their fortune has been filched away. What are you complaining of?" This being the case, it seems strange that there were so many people who were willing to spend "a third of their fortune" in lawsuits, and it looks to us as if those who, like the author of *Les Plaideurs*, lived in the eighteenth century pursued this folly to excess. They had excuses, however, and the chief one was this: just as the society they lived in was divided into nobles and commoners, so also land was divided into noble property and vulgar property, and as in society the lines of demarcation between the classes were extremely vague, so that it was difficult to assign his exact rank to any given person, it was often very uncertain whether this or that property was "noble"—that is, exempt from all levies, or "rural" or "vulgar," and therefore liable to taxation. Thus one might say that there was not a foot of land which might not be a cause of dispute or the subject of a lawsuit, naturally to the lawyer's benefit. In this we find the chief reason for those suits which dragged their weary course for an average of fifteen and even twenty years, between the communes and private individuals on the one side, and the great nobles on the other. The scales of justice tilted, usually, in favour of the latter. Gui Patin tells the following story (which in the succeeding century might well have had Voltaire as its narrator) to his friend Spon: "Yesterday [4th October 1655] a woman of thirty-two was hanged outside the Fort l'Evêque gate for uttering false coin, while the man who made it was pardoned. It appears that he had good money as well as the counterfeit which he manufactured." But even if they lacked good money the great nobles had the favour of the Court and the protection of the Minister, though La Bruyère assures us that "it was not absolutely impossible for one in high favour to lose his case." [1]

Another criticism to which the magistracy of that time was exposed was that there were too many young and even quite youthful magistrates at the Palais. A First President was no longer a greybeard as he used to be, for he might resemble Mme de Sévigné's "young man of twenty-seven who, thanks to 40,000 francs, has bought himself all the experience required to preside over a Supreme Court." And, again, Servan, the Advocate-General, complains: "It is a shameful spectacle for a wise man to see such childish ignorance and feebleness displayed by one who has to give his decisions with all the authority of an experienced man. To think that he is the arbiter of my fate! If any evil-disposed man were to acc   me, that is the kind of judge before whom I should have to appear!" [2]

An examination was required of all who aspired to legal office, but it was a simple one, and often, as we shall see, a mere farce. "La Baroire called himself Biret, and was the son of a rich merchant of La Rochelle. He married a daughter of M. l'Hoste, brother-in-law of Arnauld, an Intendant. He proceeded to buy himself the post of Counsellor to the Parliament, which cost him eleven thousand crowns, and duly applied for admittance. He was a great fool, but his father-in-law had influence, and he was permitted to take his seat for the latter's sake. People said that it was M. l'Hoste who was being admitted, not his son-in-law. Cumont was examined at the same time, and did very well, so they thought they would let them both pass, the one bringing the other in with

[1] *De quelques usages.* [2] Servan, *Œuvres,* ii. 69.

him. Some one asked Biret whether it was the custom in Paris for wives to be responsible for their husbands. "Yes," he said. "Well, go and fetch yours, so that she may be responsible for you." [1]

Lower in rank than the magistrate was the *Avocat* or barrister, whom Voltaire thus ironically described: "A barrister is a man who has not enough money to buy one of those posts which are prominent in the world's estimation, so he studies the works of Theodosius and Justinian for three years in order to learn the practice of Paris, and then, having been entered on the rolls, he has the right to plead in return for his fees, provided he has a loud voice." [2]

The "loud voices" of that century have not come down to us, and posterity cannot listen to the grandiloquent pleadings of celebrated counsel of that time such as Cochin, Gerbier, Loyseau, de Mauléon, and Élie de Beaumont. Their oratory was florid and rhetorical at the beginning of the century, sentimental in the middle and closing years; but an historian of the manners and morals of the eighteenth century would be more interested in summing up, if that were possible, the more characteristic cases with which they had to deal. We shall come to that later on.

In the earlier years of the century the barristers "still formed a body distinguished for the nobility and independence of their profession, the weight of their words, and their personal worth," [3] and they preserved their "independence of speech" throughout. Delaverdy, the future Controller-General of Finance, had a son who was counsellor to the Parliament while he himself was a barrister. The First President reproached him on one occasion for wanting in respect to a Court which had condescended to admit his son to its bench. "Sir," he replied, "if my son had been man enough to stand on his own feet, I should not have made him sit." [4]

---

[1] Tallemant, ix. 68.
[2] Voltaire, *Dictionnaire philosophique*; "Avocat."
[3] La Bruyère, *De la ville*.
[4] Berryer, *Souvenirs* (1774–1838), i. 56.

Barristers could rise to a position almost equal to that of the magistrates, but their income, as well as their importance, was much diminished by a very vexatious procedure which soon became established at the Palais. This was the abuse known as the *appointements*. In defiance of the Ordinance of 1667, which laid down that all cases should be tried in open court and free of charge, most of them were now dealt with in writing—that is, were *appointées*—so that the judge was able to multiply the documents and fees which this entailed, while dispensing with the barrister altogether. In this way the barristers lost cases which now went to the *Procureurs* (who resembled the solicitors of to-day), and these men were now to be seen lounging in their own coaches, and drawing incomes of 50,000 francs a year. According to Mercier, they always wore black because they inherited from everybody. Often the judge would heap his sarcasm on some barrister in open court, and the latter would cheerfully pocket both the affront—and his fee! "Sir, you are a rogue," would come from the Bench, and "Your Lordship is always pleased to joke" would be the humble reply. But cases had now passed so largely into the hands of the procureurs that barristers were obliged to attend the evening parties of the formers' wives in order to pick up a few for themselves. All legal procedure now began with the procureur's summons. He chose the barrister, and the litigant got little farther than the former's chambers. Respect, however, did not come with gain. "Saints have been barristers, sergeants, even comedians; in fact, they have belonged to all professions however humble, but not even one has been a procureur." [1]

Close on the heels of the procureurs came the formidable and rapacious host of *Greffiers* or registrars, whose office had become hereditary. "It was only after the great plague of 1580 that this new plague in the State made its appearance and the post of registrar became hereditary, and it has been well said that it was the registrars who undermined the State." [2] Next came the

---

[1] Furetière, *Fureteriana*, p. 144.   [2] Loyseau, *Des offices*, ii. 8.

Huissiers, or ushers and sheriff's officers, even more greedy for plunder than all the rest, armed to the teeth against all poor debtors, treating their houses like cities given up to pillage, and seizing their furniture in order to sell it to the highest bidder in the public highway. And lastly, bringing up the rear of this legal army, came the *Bazoche*, a noisy battalion of starving clerks, to whom the wife of the procureur or barrister measured out his daily pittance, and who would even appear in the middle of a party in order to beg for the key of the bread cupboard, which the lady of the house had, very wisely, put in her pocket. This is illustrated by a story, as popular in the seventeenth century, when Furetière introduced it into his *Roman bourgeois*, as in the eighteenth, when Mercier repeats it. It dealt with the miserly wife of a barrister who, while attending a smart afternoon party, was horrified to see her bread cupboard, which could not be opened, enter the room on the back of a street porter, and accompanied by the facetious clerk who was the originator of this disconcerting prank. The clerk's life was, undoubtedly, a hard one. "His day began at six in summer and at seven in winter. His frugal breakfast at nine was over in a few minutes, and he did not dine till two. These young men were allowed a bare hour for recreation, and then went back to work till nine o'clock in the evening. The day ended with supper, which was rarely eatable, but it was now too late for these weary youths to enjoy even a play, as all theatres closed between nine and ten." [1] Here are some verses, ironically entitled "The Happy Day," by one of them, Collin-Harleville, who was afterwards famous as an author, in which he deplores his unhappy fate:

> "Un pauvre clerc du parlement
> Arraché du lit brusquement,
> Comme il dormait profondément,
> Gagne l'Etude tristement;
> Y grifonne un appointement,
> Qu'il ose interrompre un moment
> Pour déjeuner sommairement;

---

[1] Berryer, *Souvenirs*, i. 34.

THE LAWYERS

> En revanche, écrit longuement;
> Dîne à trois heures sobrement,
> Sort au dessert discrètement,
> Reprend la plume promptement
> Jusqu'à dix heures—seulement;
> Lors va souper légèrement;
> Puis au sixième lestement
> Grimpe, et se couche froidement
> Dans un lit fait, Dieu sait comment!
> Dort, et n'est heureux qu'en dormant—
> Ah! pauvre clerc du parlement!" [1]

The clerk had one great festival and privilege known as *La Plantation du Mai*. Every month of May, the clerks marched with flags flying and drums beating to the Forest of Bondy in search of the finest oak they could find. This precious trophy was then decorated with flowers and streamers and carried back in triumph to the Court of the Palais, known as the "May" Court. It was flanked by broad staircases crowded with shops, and up these the lawyers climbed daily with their bags. The clerks used to tell of one who was accosted by a peasant "who was not born yesterday." "Sir," said he, "would you kindly tell me what this fine building is?" "Why, certainly," replied the man of law jokingly; "it is a mill." But the peasant went one better. "Why, of course! I recognise it now, and ought to have realised it sooner when I saw all these donkeys carrying their sacks thither."

Let us, however, penetrate into the Palais itself. Here is the Great Hall or *salle des pas-perdus*. Three or four arches shut off alcoves which are used as libraries, where the latest books may be found. The others, as well as the benches round the wall, belong to the procureurs and the

---

[1] "A poor clerk of the Parliament, torn roughly from his bed, where he was sunk in heavy slumber, mournfully makes his way to the office. There he scribbles in his ledgers, only daring to interrupt his labours for a moment to swallow a hurried breakfast. To make up for this, he begins his toil anew until three, when he dines sparingly, discreetly vanishing before the dessert. He then takes up his pen again until ten—only! A meagre supper, and briskly up six flights to a bed, how cold and uncomfortable God only knows! Then sleep and happiness at last! Ah, who indeed would be a poor clerk of the Parliament!"

barristers, to each of whom one is assigned, so that a client may find him easily among the mob which fills the hall. The procureurs wear robes, the chief clerks are in black coats. The magistrates had long discarded the black coats and high-collared cloaks which, according to the edict of 1684, was the dress prescribed for them when not in their robes. Cloaks were now as rare as the long beards of old, and the magistrates preferred "the grey dress of country wear, with the stock tied round and passed through the buttonhole." They are also less early at their work in the Palais. Formerly they rose before daybreak, and might be seen at work by candlelight as early as five o'clock in the morning. In the eighteenth century a small crowd would collect to transact their legal business at seven in the morning, but they were not thought sufficiently important to be dealt with by the gentlemen in the Great Hall, and were, therefore, heard by what were aptly called "the seven-o'clock barristers." But the High Courts did not sit in public till nine in winter and half-past eight in summer, and rose at eleven.

But what were these eighteenth-century magistrates out of office hours? We ought not to judge them all by the extravagant display and frivolity for which a few were justly censured. It would appear that when they had laid aside their high-collared cloaks, most of them shed also their solemn airs and that "honourable gravity" which Loyseau so insistently urged on the judges of his own day. For instance, Barassy, a member of the Grand Council, and Salaberry, President of the Court of Accounts, were not above disguising themselves as Turks in order to take part in a comedy.

"President de Salaberry and his wife used to spend every summer at Cheverny; my wife's name-day fell on 27th August, and in this year it was suggested that we should have a celebration in which I, for my part, willingly co-operated. A round pavilion with a leafy colonnade was constructed in a thicket between the Castle and the Orangery. Between each column a little green cabinet was contrived, and at the back was built a leafy screen which concealed a theatre. All the actors who were to take part were dressed as Turks or negroes. The idea of the play was that a great prince, hearing that in the realm of France there was a noble and beautiful lady, sent to her his Grand Vizier and his retinue, to amuse and entertain her with a fête. Several people had given us their assistance, and my friend Sedaine had sent me some short scenes. At five o'clock all the musicians, dressed as Turks and headed by M. de Barassy as the Grand Vizier, came to invite the ladies to the fête. The Count and Countess de Gaucourt, the Maréchal de Saint-Hérem, M. and Mme de Cypierre—in fact, all the rank and fashion of the county—were present. All entered the kiosk, Salaberry, as the Keeper of the Seraglio, having welcomed them outside with a song, while I received them inside in my capacity as his deputy, surrounded by mutes and retainers. I invited them to partake of light refreshments; ices were served, and our guests took the floor, and we danced the ordinary dances as well as ballets and a dance of the mutes. As night fell, a rocket and a flare gave a signal, and we all went out on to the lawn, where a splendid display of fireworks was given." [1]

Apart from this Councillor, who, it appears, "had six carriage-horses, two riding-horses, a coachman, a postillion, a groom, a cook, a valet, and a laundryman," and this President, transformed into a Turk, we would do well to consider for a moment those great personages who, by their learning and upright life, shed a lustre on the Parliaments and Bar of old France. Several, like the Presidents de Brosses and Bouhier, of the Parliament of Dijon, and Daguesseau, President of the Parliament of Paris, were men of letters as well. The latter's knowledge was so profound that when a lady was seeking for a tutor, who would have had to be a walking encyclopædia, for her son, Fontenelle told her: "Madame, only the Chancellor Daguesseau is capable of satisfying your requirements," and Saint-Simon says of him: "He had great wit, penetration, knowledge of every kind, the gravity which becomes a magistrate, piety, and simplicity of heart." In his retire-

[1] Cheverny, i. 376.

ment at Fresnes, where he devoted himself entirely to his real inclinations and favourite occupations, such as study, family life, and the education of his children, Daguesseau wrote for his eldest son those serious yet charming *Instructions sur les études propres à former les magistrates*, in which he warns his son against "the corruption of the present century, and its welter of licentiousness." He was the ornament of the Bar during the early part of the century, just as the honest and courageous Malesherbes was its pride during the middle and later years; but the latter's life is known to all, for it is part of history, and every one has read of the noble devotion with which he defended his king. But there is an anecdote about him which is not, perhaps, so widely known, and which, also, throws an interesting light on legal customs and abuses of the time. It deals with the case of Monnerat, and shows us how little personal liberty was safeguarded in the eighteenth century.

On 24th April 1767 a corn merchant of Limoges, named Monnerat, was arrested by the Superintendent of Farms and imprisoned at Fort l'Evêque. He asked to be informed of the reason for his incarceration, and was told that he had passed under the name of Comtois, and had dealt in contraband tobacco. He protested in vain, and, in virtue of a *lettre de cachet* or royal warrant, issued at the request of the Farmers-General, he was thrown into a dungeon at Bicêtre, and a chain weighing fifty pounds was hung round his neck. At the end of six months he was released; immediately proved that he had been the victim of an error, and claimed as his sole damages a sum sufficient to cure him of scurvy, which he had caught in the filthy dungeons of Bicêtre. The Farmers-General refused him any damages in money, so that he had recourse to the High Court, demanding that it should summon them before it. They refused to appear, but, in spite of the Controller-General, Terray, and the Chancellor Maupeou, whom the Farmers-General had succeeded in winning over, the Court strove to obtain justice for Monnerat. Thereupon the King ordered its Presidents to attend him at Compiègne, and sternly forbade them "to proceed

THE LAWYERS

with the case of Monnerat," and as they retired from his presence, Maupeou and Terray, who remained with the King, remarked upon the discomfiture of the old judges, who, looking back, saw "the King and his two ministers laughing uproariously." It was their intention to drive the High Court into open revolt so as to have an excuse for abolishing it. The magistrates, wiser than the Government, confined themselves to remonstrances, which reflect the greatest honour on Malesherbes, who undoubtedly inspired them. After recalling the indignities which the ministers had inflicted on them at Compiègne, the magistrates continued:

"We feel it our duty to demand from Your Majesty that public apology which we feel is our due, but we will not insist on a matter which is only a personal one. The rights of the Bar are very dear to us, but those of Humanity are even dearer, and what brings us, sire, to the steps of your throne, is the wish to acquaint you of the extent to which the principles of humanity and justice have been violated under the vain pretence that only excessive severity can restore your rights." Then follows a description of the appalling treatment suffered by Monnerat: "At the Castle of Bicêtre there are subterranean dungeons, hollowed out in bygone days in order to confine certain notorious criminals, who, after being sentenced to death, only obtained pardon by denouncing their accomplices, and it would seem that they were left to drag out an existence which was worse than death. Complete darkness reigned in these cells, and in order to introduce the bare sufficiency of air, subterranean pillars were erected, which were pierced lengthwise by slanting shafts resembling underground funnels. By this means some communication was established with the outside air without any light being admitted. The wretches who are thus interned in these damp haunts, which inevitably become unsanitary after a prisoner has dwelt in them for some days, are fastened to the wall by a heavy chain and are only supplied with straw, bread, and water. Your Majesty will hardly believe that people have been such barbarians as to immure in this pit of horror, for a whole month, a man who was merely suspected of fraudulent dealing, a man who stoutly maintained that he was innocent and that an error had been made, and against whom there was no shadow of proof. Even if he had been convicted of smuggling, it would be impossible that Your Majesty would order him to be confined in these dreadful dungeons, since there must, of a surety, be some proportion between crime and punishment.

"Formerly *lettres de cachets* or royal warrants were reserved for matters of State, and in those days, sire, justice was bound to respect the secrets of your Government. They were then issued in cases which appeared to warrant their use, such as when the sovereign was moved by the tears of a family fearing dishonour. To-day they are considered necessary whenever any ordinary man fails in his respect for a person of quality, as if these powerful personages did not already enjoy sufficient advantages, and they are also the usual punishment for indiscreet speech, of which there is never any proof save hearsay, which is always a doubtful one, since an informer is himself a suspected witness. But without discussing the various motives which prompt them, it is sufficiently notorious that higher orders intervene in all matters concerning people of low degree, matters which affect neither Your Majesty nor the public weal in any way, and this practice is so generally established that any man of respectable family thinks it beneath his dignity to demand redress for any wrong from the ordinary Courts of Law. These warrants, signed by Your Majesty's own hand, contain the names of people with which Your Majesty could never be acquainted, and they are at the disposal of your ministers and of their secretaries as well, as is evident from the enormous numbers which are issued. They are bestowed upon the governors of the capital and of the provinces, who cannot make use of them save on the reports of their delegates and other subordinates. They are doubtless entrusted to many other hands, as we have lately seen that they are scattered broadcast at the behest of a mere

Farmer-General—we might even say at that of his employees, for it is only servants who could know a man suspected of fraud and point him out. The final issue, sire, is this: No citizen in all your realm can rest assured that his liberty will not be sacrificed to some private grudge, for no man is great enough to be safe from a minister's hatred, and none so insignificant that he may not be worthy of some official's malevolence."

The last sentence was written in Malesherbes' own hand.

In 1750, Malesherbes had been appointed First President of the *Cour des Aides* or High Court, and it might well be said that from this time onwards it became "the refuge of the poor and the oppressed." The expression is Gaillard's, who, at the beginning of the nineteenth century, wrote a life of Malesherbes based on his family papers.

Malesherbes was a worthy chip of that old block, the Chancellor Lamoignon, who refused to be presented to Mme de Pompadour, who never forgave him. He was too old, he said, to be presented to beautiful ladies.[1]

One sentence in the above-quoted Remonstrance should be noted: "The final issue is that no citizen in all your realm can rest assured that his liberty will not be sacrificed to some private grudge," *i.e.* by means of a *lettre de cachet*. A *lettre de cachet* was an order from the King contained in a letter which was closed with his *cachet* or seal and countersigned by a Secretary of State; and with reference to these so frequently mentioned letters, we may quote this impartial testimony of a contemporary, Sénac de Meilhan: "The agents of the Government have sometimes abused this weapon of correction, and petty offences have been expiated by long years of captivity. Jealous husbands, avaricious parents, unnatural fathers—all such have, on false pretences, beguiled ministers into issuing these severe orders, and many examples of this abuse of authority can be found during the reign of Louis xv."

The most illustrious victim of this abuse was Mirabeau. A succession of *lettres de cachet* confined him first in the fort

[1] Gaillard, 26.

of the Île de Ré, then in the Château d'If, next in the Fort de Joux, near Pontarlier, and finally, from 1777 to 1780, in the keep at Vincennes. From this last prison he wrote to his father, the Marquis de Mirabeau, known as "The Friend of Man," a long and touching letter, from which certain passages are worth quoting. It is of value to historians of this century, because many others had the same cause of complaint against parental tyranny, even if they had not the same power of expressing it. Others like Mirabeau, though without having to reproach themselves with much for which he was blameworthy, had been imprisoned, thanks to a *lettre de cachet* obtained by their fathers through the culpable weakness of some intendant, possibly for no other reason than to prevent a marriage which the head of the family thought was beneath the dignity of his house. Mirabeau begins his letter as follows:

"MY FATHER,—Having long debated on the attitude I ought to adopt, I have now come to a decision, and since I am quite fixed and immovable in my determination I am able, and, in fact, it is my duty, to write you this letter, which I have the honour to send you herewith. You have condemned me, my father, to a living death, which, as you well know, is far worse than any death by violence. Is it not worse than the grave to suffer, in complete solitude, every privation and anxiety, and to be separated from all one loves? Death delivers one from all regrets, all desires, all grief, and surely the captivity which I am enduring is a worse punishment than that could be?"

He then dwells on all his transgressions, and admits that he "is blameworthy but not a criminal." He demands to be tried, and makes this appeal to his father's pity:

"I have implored you to consider your own conduct, and I beseech you again to examine your conscience and to reconcile with it the severity of your action. Have you the sole right to proscribe and condemn me? To raise yourself above laws and customs in order to ruin me? You, father, the eloquent and famous champion of property, you dispose of my person on your own authority alone! You, 'the Friend of Man,' you treat your son with a despotism such as this! You who cannot proceed against the liberty, life, or honour of the least of your servants unless seven judges have condemned him, you thus arbitrarily decree my fate! Let my enemies show themselves instead of attacking me in the obscurity of their offices! Are laws of no avail in my country? Is the sovereign no longer their guardian and protector? If justice be honoured, and if the courts are still open to all citizens, surely you can safely put me on my trial? If I be innocent or guilty, cannot the magistrates absolve or condemn me? If it is my father who, urged by some hidden prejudice or violent motive, is bent on my ruin, why does not the Law intervene between him and his son? I am not his slave, nor the slave of any one; I am a citizen.

"I will sum up all I have said, and the inferences I wish to draw. I am worthy of blame, but my punishment is not in proportion to my crime. Father, I cannot, really I cannot, endure this kind of life any more. Let me see the sun, breathe the fresh air, see a human face once again. If only I had the literary resources which have so long been my only solace in my trouble, if only I knew whether my son lives and what he is doing." [1]

We have seen the political rôle which the Parliament tried to play in the eighteenth century, from the day—15th September 1715—on which the Regent restored to them the right of Remonstrance, in order to reward them for setting aside the will of Louis XIV. in his favour By virtue of this right the Parliament tried, during the course of the century, to arrogate to themselves a legislative power which was the prerogative of the King alone, for the King's pleasure was, in fact, the sole fundamental law of the realm. In order to defeat those laws which did not command a majority of their suffrages, the members of the Parliaments adopted a very clever method of circumventing them. They merely claimed "the unfettered right of

[1] Mirabeau, *Œuvres*, vii.

verifying laws," that is to say, as they explained it, the right of defending the King against his ministers, who might deceive him by making him sign laws which were contrary to the already existing statutes of the kingdom. The King, on the other hand, in order to break the resistance of the Parliaments, resorted to expedients which, by their brutality, discredited the Royal authority in the eyes of the nation, while enhancing the prestige of his opponents. Whenever, therefore, the Parliaments refused to register any new law, they were treated to sharp and violent language, delivered by the ministers at the Lits de Justice, or else hurled at the spokesmen of the deputations which they sent to Versailles. The recalcitrant councillors might also find themselves exiled in a body, or else confined to their own houses under a military guard, and in these incessant and far-echoing conflicts the throne lost its prestige and credit more and more. The following story bears witness to the anxiety which they caused the King and the recriminations to which he gave vent:

"One day the King entered in a very excited state. I withdrew, but could hear what was said from my corner. 'What is the matter?' cried Madame [de Pompadour]. 'Oh, these judges and the clergy are always at daggers drawn. They weary me with their quarrels. But I detest the judges most, for my clergy are faithful at heart and attached to me, while the others want to put me in leading-strings.' Here M. de Gontaut entered, but on realising that serious matters were being discussed, he remained silent. The King walked up and down in a very agitated manner, and then exclaimed suddenly: 'The Regent made a great mistake in giving them the right of Remonstrance. They will end by ruining the State.' 'Oh no, sire,' said de Gontaut, 'it is too powerful for wretched little lawyers to wreck it.' 'You don't know,' replied the King, 'what they are doing and thinking. They are a lot of republicans, and there are enough of those already. But things will go on as they are so long as I live.' " [1]

When the members of a Parliament abandoned their

[1] Mme Campan, p. 93.

functions in a body, the administration of justice was suspended throughout the province; the decisions of the tribunals remained unenforced, as all dishonest litigants were able to elude their consequences by merely lodging an appeal; those who had been found guilty did not suffer their penalties; the accused, even if innocent, remained in prison; disorder increased as it went unpunished, and the prisons were filled without ever being emptied. This was the state of affairs which the First President of the Parliament of Normandy, Miromesnil, the only magistrate who had not abandoned his post in 1763, described in a report to the King on the state to which the Parliament's withdrawal had reduced the country.

As we know, the Parliaments excused their refusal to register certain taxes by declaring themselves the defenders of the People's Rights, but the value of this claim has already been examined. We might, however, without going into detail, consider certain facts which give us a clearer view of the position occupied by the members of Parliaments in the society of that day. In the second half of the eighteenth century there was a kind of feudal reaction which took the form, not of claiming new rights, but of pushing the old to greater lengths. For instance, the Lords of the Manor deprived the peasants of certain *droits d'usage*, or the rights of using the forests for gathering their necessary fuel, and the unclaimed land on which they pastured their cattle. From every quarter the peasants protested against these usurpations, and looked to the Parliaments, but these in every case gave their decision in favour of the Lords of the Manor, for the obvious reason that they themselves were nobles and landed proprietors. "It is remarkable that the critical faculty which developed so much in the eighteenth century was never found lacking in the Parliaments when it was a case of trying other people in cases affecting justice, equity, or the common weal, but that it deserted them utterly when they came to deal with matters concerning their own privileges and immunities in questions of taxation. If there is any danger of the high-sounding protestations of the Parliaments deluding us or rousing us to false enthusiasm, it would be well to remember their selfish and pitiless acts as members of a territorial aristocracy. They had virtually lost their old position in the State when they became landed proprietors, and exchanged the lawyer's bonnet for the seignorial helmet, and even if the great nobles continued to excite their envy by their prerogatives, and wound their vanity by their disdain, yet these Parliamentarians themselves formed a nobility of the second class, looking down upon the rest of mankind from their lofty elevation, and ever ready to avoid their obligations and to transfer the burden to the masses." [1]

In its protests against the edicts of 1771, which created the so-called "Maupeou Parliament" and suppressed the judicial offices while indemnifying their holders, the Parliament of Toulouse declared that the rights of property had been shaken to their foundation, yet this same Parliament had carefully refrained from protesting when the Government had violated the most sacred rights of property in the case of the Protestants.[2]

The mass of the people, however, which every day was burdened with some new tax by a monarchy always in need of money, sympathised at heart with those who so vigorously defended their pockets, so that when the Parliaments, after one of those brief spells of exile, the only effect of which was to accentuate the Government's weakness, returned to the scene of their labours, they were greeted on the road with cheers and public rejoicing. When the Parliaments which Maupeou had suppressed re-entered Paris, "the people greeted their return with transports of joy." Louis XVI. re-established them on 12th November 1774 at a Lit de Justice, which Mme Roland describes to Sophia Cannet four days later:

"You have asked me to give you some details of the event which fills all minds at this moment, but you are not so distant from the capital as to be ignorant of all that happened last Saturday. The position of our house (on the Quai de l'Horloge, at the corner of the rue de Harlay)

[1] *Histoire de Languedoc*, xiii. 1212. [2] *Ibid.* xiii. 1214.

enabled us to see the whole show, and to witness the people's delight, which never seemed more general or more sincere. The acclamations which filled the air struck me as being all the more moving because they really expressed the feelings of all classes. The King arrived at the Palais at eight, heard Mass at the Sainte Chapelle, and then proceeded to the Great Hall, where he remained till about two. As he left, his brothers, the two Princes, took leave of him, M. de Provence proceeding to the Cour des Aides, where he reinstated that High Court, and M. de Malesherbes made a speech which, so they say, visibly moved and touched the Prince, while M. d'Artois went to the Louvre to re-establish the Grand Council. M. de Nicolaï, the President *à mortier*, that is, wearing the bonnet of his office, who was so roughly handled by Beaumarchais in his famous *Mémoires*, was greeted with cries of, 'Down with the Mortier!' as he left the Grand Council.

"A prince ascending the throne under such critical circumstances could not avoid this necessary and eagerly desired reinstatement. What has he to fear? The Parliaments are but so many old ruins, still revered, but no longer an effective barrier to the royal authority. They are but a cherished and a powerless idol, which has had to be restored to its worshippers, who are consoled by its presence."

CHAPTER III

THE FINANCIERS

SAINT-SIMON hesitates to "sully the pages of his *Mémoires* with the name of a financier" called Pléneuf. "He was a 'Berthelot,' that is to say, one of the common people who acquire wealth by plundering their fellows and who, from the humblest of farms, rise by their labour and talents to the first place among extortioners and financiers. All these 'Berthelots,' by helping one another, have achieved success, some more, others less, while the one I am alluding to had filled his coffers from many sources, his final and most lucrative position being that of Army Contractor. A grave, ponderous, heavy man in appearance, he was restrained by no scruples."

La Bruyère notes that "if a financier fails to bring off his coup, the courtiers call him a *bourgeois*. If he succeeds, they ask his daughter in marriage." This Pléneuf had "succeeded" wonderfully, whereas the Marquis de Prie, godfather to the Duke d'Anjou, had practically nothing, and being anxious to plan out a career, his thoughts turned to an embassy. Alas—he had not the wherewithal. Now Pléneuf, who was enormously wealthy, had a daughter, and therein lay the Marquis' opportunity. The Marquis had no scruple in deciding to marry beneath him, so, in 1714, Mlle de Pléneuf duly became the Marquise de Prie, and her husband—well, she accompanied him to Italy when he was appointed Ambassador, and contented herself with being "a great success at the Court of Turin, owing to her modest demeanour," and also because "she was handsome, well made, and endowed with an indescribable charm which carries one away," as Saint-Simon says; while d'Argenson, who knew her well, describes her as being

THE FINANCIERS

"a beautiful figure, and even more charming than she is beautiful." This explains his extraordinary and scandalous good fortune during the Ministry of the Duke de Bourbon.[1]

What manner of men were these Farmers-General, such as Pléneuf? "Babouc learned that in Persepolis (Paris) there were forty individuals who leased the Empire of the Persians and paid the monarch a small rent for it."[2] There were, in fact, forty Farmers-General in the middle of the eighteenth century. They leased the farming of all indirect taxes, of which the chief were: *la gabelle* or salt tax, *les aides* or subsidies, the direct taxes being *la taille* or land tax, *la capitation* or capitation tax, and *le vingtième* or twentieth. The latter were collected directly by the tax-collectors, and handed over by them to various receivers, who passed them on to Receivers-General. Finally they flowed into the various treasuries, which were all under the authority of the Controller-General. The Farmers-General, on the other hand, were obliged to supply a capital of sixty millions between them, in order to guarantee the royal revenue. They received a fixed sum in return, on condition that they made themselves responsible for collecting all indirect taxes, and thus became the middlemen or, in a sense, "the buffers" between the taxpayers and the Crown which derived the advantage of throwing the odium attaching to the collection of taxes on to a third party.

At all times the financial officials retained for themselves a large part of the sums raised for the royal treasury, for "just as some wax always sticks to the fingers of those who handle it, so also money remains in the hands of those in charge of the finances—a fact they never forget."[3] The financiers, indeed, called it "plucking the King's goose," although, as we shall see, there were various methods for restoring its plumage. In 1716 it was decided to tax the financiers, whose profits were considered excessive, and indeed the financial situation was so deplorable that an

---
[1] Saint-Simon, xvi. 316, xix. 50; D'Argenson, i. 56.
[2] Voltaire, *Le monde comme il va. Vision de Babouc*, 1756.
[3] Loyseau, *Traité des Ordres*, viii.

honest man, like Saint-Simon, openly advocated bankruptcy in the Council. In order to carry this into effect, a Court of Justice was set up at the Grands Augustins on 14th March 1716, which summoned the Farmers-General before it, summarily disposed of their case, and sentenced them to severe punishments. For instance, "on 6th July, the Court sentenced M. Lenormand to pay compensation to the amount of twenty thousand livres to the arts and crafts corporations for the injustice he had inflicted on them, as well as a sum of a hundred thousand livres to the King. On the 11th, M. Lenormand made public atonement, dressed in a shirt only, with bare feet, and holding a lighted candle in his hand, while placards with the inscription, 'A Robber of the People,' in large letters, were attached to his breast and back. When he reached the market near the pillory the crowd rent the air with cries: 'Thief! Scoundrel! Hang him!' Having thus made his expiation in this garb, he was given his clothes, and when dressed, was conveyed by coach to La Tournelle on his way to the galleys, but here the gaoler tied him to a tree in the middle of the courtyard, as if to a stake, in order to expose him to the vulgar gaze. Crowds flocked to gratify their curiosity, and by paying four sous to the gaoler, were able to take their revenge on Lenormand for the hardships he had caused them and for all his other peculations. He never uttered a word, though some struck him brutally on the head.

" On 16th July, one Gruet was sentenced, as a penalty for peculation and breaking the law, to make expiation in the same way, to be exposed in the pillory on three market-days, and to be sent to the galleys." [1]

No wonder Montesquieu was justified in his 98th *Lettre persane*, when he wrote of these Farmers-General: "They are just now in a terrible plight. A tribunal has been set up called the Court of Justice, because it is going to plunder them of all their goods and chattels."

The taxes were estimated at 160 millions, but only a very small part was destined to replenish the royal coffers, "because these thieves were themselves fleeced by

[1] Buvat, i. 157, 159.

others—the favourites or the mistresses used to traffic in the abatement of these taxes. It is said of a speculator who was taxed at 1,200,000 livres, that he replied to a nobleman who offered to get him relieved from this assessment in return for 300,000 livres down: 'My dear Count, you come too late. I have just concluded a similar arrangement with your wife for half that sum.' M. de Fourquieux, President of the Court of Justice, was given the ironical title of *Garde des Seaux*, or Keeper of the Seals, because he had appropriated for himself out of the plunder of the famous Farmer-General, Bourvalais, the latter's silver *seaux*, or wine coolers, which he had the impudence to display on his table." [1]

In order to fill the coffers of the State, all means seemed justifiable. The coinage was debased, useless and even ridiculous offices were created, for which the vanity of the *bourgeois* had to pay dearly, and which were as promptly abolished, as, for example, in 1716, when the holders had only paid a part of the purchase price. On another occasion as much as possible was borrowed from the Farmers-General, who were themselves, once the crisis was past, handed over to the Courts of Justice, which despoiled them of all they possessed. This iniquitous procedure filled both nobles and magistrates with glee, and they could not show enough scorn for "these financiers." Yet, as Duclos wrote in the middle of the century, "persons of quality have no longer any right to scorn the financial class, since nearly all are, in some way, related to it. If there are any who have not married beneath them in this way, it is only because the wealthy have not troubled sufficiently to search them out. The jokes about the financiers, which are cracked behind their backs, are prompted more by envy of their wealth than by contempt for their persons. To their faces every one overwhelms them with attention, expressions of regard, and consideration. Why, indeed, should the financiers be held in such low esteem? After all, the State requires a revenue, and there must be citizens who can be entrusted with collect-

[1] Mouffle, i. 17.

ing it in return for some advantage to themselves." [1] When speaking of the Farmers-General one is too apt only to recall to mind the saying of the Marquis de Souvré, which was probably more witty than just: "On Fleury declaring that the Farmers-General were the 'supports' of the State, he replied: 'Yes; but in the same way as a rope supports a hanging man.'" [2] It is not our business to whitewash them: but this should be adduced in their favour, that when the Government created a new office, it handed it over to a Farmer-General on the condition of his giving it the profit attached thereto. What did he do? He undertook to sell it, but at his own risk, and indeed it often happened that the new office found no purchaser. Thus the State got its money, while the Farmer-General was left with an unproductive, or even farcical, office on his hands, for which he had been obliged to pay out of his own pocket. They had their uses, therefore, and Babouc perceived that "the wealth of the financiers which had so disgusted him, might yet have excellent effects, for the Emperor (the King of France), if in need of money, could from that source draw more revenue in an hour than he could collect in six months by ordinary means. He saw that these large clouds, swollen with the dew of earth, would repay in rain as much as they had absorbed from it." [3]

We know that one of the principal causes of the fall of the monarchy was the disorder and poverty which reigned in the Treasury, and the State, in order to remedy this condition of affairs and to obtain the supplies necessary for the war and the expenses of the King and his Court, did not hesitate, on occasion, to appear as a defaulter. In February 1770, in order to meet the deficit in the Treasury, then amounting to 63 millions, the Abbé Terray, who was then Controller-General, resorted to the following dishonest expedient. Many people used to invest their savings in bills issued by the Farmers-General, or in others guaranteed by the general revenue. These were short-dated

[1] Duclos, *Considérations*, p. 204. [2] *Mémoires de Richelieu*, v. 180.
[3] Voltaire, *Le monde comme il va.*

investments, similar to our Treasury bonds, enabling the investor to repay a debt or liquidate some proposed purchase by a certain date. On 18th February 1770, two decrees of the Council suspended payment on both. "Instead of laying hands on funds invested in the Farms and in the Public Revenue offices, the State might as well have broken into private houses and forcibly carried off everything which the owners had collected in them, for it was a barefaced robbery, and the more scandalous for being committed in the name of the King, who should have punished it, and by his officers who dispense justice in his name and sent to prison any unhappy scoundrel they found perpetrating a similar offence." [1] By this colossal swindle—and this is not too strong a word—Terray, the Controller-General, failed to meet bills amounting to 200 millions, and when accused of stealing money out of the people's pockets, cheerfully replied: "Where the devil do you want me to take it from?"

At the end of the seventeenth century, La Bruyère had written with severity: "Do not inquire too deeply into a speculator's wealth"; but when he himself investigated the kind of talent which was required for "succeeding" in finance, he was forced to add: "Intelligence of some kind is needed for amassing a fortune, especially a very large one, but it is neither good nor bad, great nor exalted, strong nor refined; in fact, I don't know what its nature is, and wait for some one else to enlighten me." But he could easily have enlightened himself had he lived in the middle of the succeeding century, and he would have realised that finance had ceased to be, as in his day, a kind of lottery, where often chance alone decided "whether one lost or gained one's stake," but had become "an art and a science which had its principles and methods like any other." [2] And La Bruyère might even have softened his terrible indictment of the speculators, if he had seen at their work, or met in society, those whom Duclos on another page describes as follows: "Finance is no longer what it was

---

[1] *Mémoires de l'Abbé Terray*, 1776.
[2] Duclos, *Considérations sur les mœurs*.

formerly. There was a time when a man, whatever he might be, threw himself into the game with the fixed determination to make his fortune, with no other weapons save cupidity and avarice, with no scruples about any meanness in his early dealings, entirely unscrupulous as to the methods he employed, and impervious to remorse when his goal was reached. With such qualities he could not fail to succeed. The *nouveau riche*, while preserving his earlier character, added to it a savage pride, of which his wealth was the measure. He was humble or insolent in proportion to his losses or his gains, and his importance in his own eyes was, like the money he worshipped, subject to increase or decline. The financiers of those days were very reticent, for their mistrust rendered all men suspect, and popular hatred placed yet another barrier between them and society.

"To-day things are very different. Most of those who have entered finance with a competence have received a careful education which, in France, is more in proportion to the means by which it can be acquired than to birth. It is not astonishing, therefore, to find the most charming people among them. Many of them love and cultivate letters, are sought after by the best society, and do not receive in their houses any but such as they may choose. The old prejudices against them exist no longer, for though witticisms are still made about them from force of habit, these are no longer embittered by the indignation which the odious methods of the past drew down upon finance in general. I know that no one has yet spoken of finance favourably, but I, who speak freely of all things as they strike me, I am not afraid to shock those who are prejudiced against it and inveigh against that to which, without knowing it, they possibly owe their very existence.

"Finance is essential to the State, and is a profession whose dignity or degradation depends solely on the way it is pursued."[1]

The Farmers-General did indeed supply many able administrators like Helvétius and Lavoisier, who were

[1] Duclos, *Les Confessions du Comte* ***, p. 266.

honest men to boot, and *l'Espion anglais*, who was severe on the financiers, felt it necessary to add that "the good deeds of Samuel Bernard and M. de Montmartel could not be numbered,"[1] while Fréron tells of a French gentleman who, finding himself penniless in Holland, called upon the mayor and was met with the query: "What are you worth? What is your profession, and what qualifications have you?" "I am a gentleman," was the reply; "those are my credentials." "Oh, very well," said the mayor; "carry them to the bank."[2] As a matter of fact, the nobles offered their titles to the bankers, who accepted them for their daughters in return for ready money.

"I find," says Montesquieu, "that most of those people who amass a large fortune, once they have accumulated it, are filled with despair that they are not of illustrious parentage." But they consoled and "purified" themselves by giving their daughters in marriage to some impoverished nobleman. For instance, the Count d'Evreux, who belonged to the proud house of Bouillon (he was the third son of the Duke of that name and grand-nephew of Turenne), was short of the money essential to keep up his position as a colonel of cavalry, and so "he decided to marry beneath him, and make Mdlle Crosat a princess by the King's favour, her father being a man of mean extraction, who had begun as a financier in a small way, become banker to the clergy, and eventually, after seeking his fortune on the sea and in banks, was at this time rightly regarded as the richest man in Paris. Mme de Bouillon, who came to acquaint us with the news, urgently begged us to visit her large and grotesque family. She gave us a list of its members, and we called upon them all, finding them in the seventh heaven of delight. The wedding at Crosat's expense was magnificent, and he also housed and fed the newly married couple."[3] That was the beginning of the story. Now for the conclusion. The Maréchal de Boufflers was created a peer for his splendid defence of Lille, and appeared to take the oath at the solemn meeting of the Parliament

---

[1] *L'Espion anglais*, i. 259.   [2] *Année litteraire*, vi. 140.
[3] Saint-Simon, v. 163.

held on 19th March 1709. "It was strange that the very day which saw the triumph of the defender of Lille was also that on which the thunderbolt was launched against the man who had refused to aid him, for it was on the night of the Maréchal de Boufflers' admittance to the Parliament that the Count de Toulouse conveyed the King's orders to the Count d'Evreux that his services were no longer required." Saint-Simon says further: "Crosat was enormously rich, and proud in proportion, owing to his daughter's marriage to the Count d'Evreux. He was bitterly to repent it, and reaped nothing but sorrow from it for the rest of his life." [1]

There is no better illustration of this alliance between the nobility and finance, usually lucrative but not always happy as far as the former were concerned, than the rise of the family of that celebrated financier, Samuel Bernard. For his services to the State he was ennobled by Louis XIV. in 1700. He bought his estate of Rieux, which is one of the baronies of the Estates of Languedoc, from a ruined Count, and thus became Bernard de Rieux. He married his daughter to M. de Sagonne, a *maître des requêtes*, and she was much courted in polite society. She died in 1716, and Dangeau wrote in his diary: "She was a woman very popular in the fashionable world." One of Samuel Bernard's sons married a Mlle de la Cosse, of high birth, and another took, as his wife, the daughter of the Marquis de Saint-Chamond. On hearing of this match, the Count de Boulainvilliers, the haughtiest of nobles, said to his daughter: "As you know, I am too proud of our family ever to countenance a suitor of that kind where a daughter of mine is concerned." However, only six months later, M. Bernard, who had married Mlle de Saint-Chamond, became a widower, and he now wedded—as his second wife—this very same Mlle de Boulainvilliers, descended though she was from the very ancient house of Croÿ! Her father had been suddenly converted to finance, realising, no doubt, like Mme de Sévigné, that millions, after all, were as good as a family tree. And Samuel Bernard had a great many. "His table cost him 150,000 livres per annum for dinner alone." [2] On

[1] Saint-Simon, xii. 223. [2] Barbier, ii. 418.

SAMUEL BERNARD
CHEVALIER DE L'ORDRE DE ST. MICHEL, COMPTE DE COUBERT
From an engraving by Pierre Drevet, after Hyacinthe Rigaud

16th August 1733, there was a splendid wedding when his granddaughter, aged twelve and a half, married the Marquis de Mirepoix, of the house of Levis de Ventadour. "Many people," wrote Barbier, "blamed the latter for allying himself with a family of such low origin and so much abused as the Bernards," but then her grandfather presented her with a dowry of 800,000 livres, and all Paris flocked to see the fête which he gave in honour of this "grand marriage." The *Mercure de France* of September 1733 grows lyrical in describing it:

"On the night of Sunday to Monday, the 17th August, Charles Pierre Gaston de Lévis de Lomagne, Hereditary Marshal of Foy, Chevalier, Marquis de Mirepoix, Count de Terrides, etc., married Anne Gabrielle Bernard, daughter of Gabriel Bernard, Count de Rieux, Baron and Lord of la Livinière, Privy Councillor of the King, President of the Parliament and of the second Chambre des Enquêtes, and his wife, the Lady Henriette de Boulainvilliers. On this occasion, M. Bernard, with his customary magnificence, gave an entertainment in his mansion in the rue Notre-Dame des Victoires, which filled all present with astonishment and admiration. It began at seven o'clock in the evening with a concert, in which the best singers and musicians that M. Bernard could procure took part. At seven o'clock the whole mansion was illuminated. About nine, when the concert was over, all the company descended to the ground floor, and, after traversing a whole suite of apartments, assembled in a hall where a sumptuous repast was served. Here the taste and magnificence of the host displayed itself in all its splendour. The hall had been built in the garden, and was 72 feet long by 42 feet broad. In the centre was a horseshoe table 150 feet in circumference. The entry of the guests was heralded by a fanfare of trumpets and drums, and the company there collected included all that was most noble and distinguished in the kingdom. At the conclusion of the martial music, soft melodies were rendered by an orchestra, which was raised on a platform, and played throughout supper, and MM. Charpentier and Danguy, whose skill on the musette and lute respectively is so well known, played together within the space in the centre of the horseshoe table, and provided a most amusing interlude by their inimitable humour. At midnight the company rose from table and proceeded by coach to Saint-Eustache, the bride's parish church. Police on foot filled the space in front of the Bernard mansion, lined the route which the procession was to follow, and were posted in large numbers outside the church. The whole square opposite the latter was illuminated. The High Altar and Choir were superbly decorated by the official City decorator, and were so brilliantly lit with great numbers of candles in chandeliers that it was scarcely possible to believe it was night. But the finest ornament of all, and *the one which should most flatter M. Bernard*, was the crowd, drawn from all classes, which flocked from every quarter of Paris to see this splendid wedding, the choir and nave being crowded with people of the highest rank, although not actually guests, and the rest of the church being packed as on a great feast day. The streets leading to Saint-Eustache were lined for a great distance with strings of coaches."

In order to satisfy the curiosity of its readers to the utmost, the *Mercure* also provided them with a plan of M. Bernard's mansion and the great hall erected for the wedding.

At this date, Samuel Bernard might truly be considered a power in the State. Orry, the Keeper of the Seals, spoke to d'Argenson about him, and the latter noted in his diary for 14th August 1733: "I said to Orry that Bernard was much attached to him, and he replied that he would go through fire on his behalf. Our two chief ministers rely on Bernard more than ever, whether in commercial matters or for loans, and I shall henceforth see more of Bernard than hitherto, as they consult him so frequently on important points." While ministers consulted him, poets sang his praises, and Voltaire saw him in the Elysian Fields among those "whose powerful assistance, immense reputation, and profound wisdom have upheld the State, and whose efforts have enriched them with all the treasures of the world."

It was no wonder that as a result of all this flattery and adulation, Bernard's vanity became prodigious; in fact, "his pride was so extravagant that in a way it endowed him with nobility."[1] One of his daughters became the beautiful Mme Dupin, who, in her sumptuous Hôtel Lambert, only received, as Rousseau, her secretary, notes, "Dukes, Ambassadors, and *cordons bleus*. Her intimate friends were the Princesse de Rohan, the Countess de Forcalquier, Mme de Mirepoix, and Milady Hervey."[2] Her husband, M. Dupin, became Farmer-General, thanks to Samuel Bernard's purse, and we hear of one of those curious gatherings which were such a feature of French society in the eighteenth century in his wife's salon, for Rousseau writes that "M. de Fontenelle, l'Abbé de Saint-Pierre, M. de Bernis, M. de Buffon, and M. de Voltaire frequented her drawing-room and dinner parties." Thus men of letters met and dined with ladies of the very highest rank, and the hostess who collected round her table people drawn from such different classes was the wife of a financier!

The power of these eighteenth-century financiers was based on the fact that they were rich, not in lands, more or less waste, like the nobles, but in what was extremely rare at this time—cash. The brilliant nobleman of the day required a great deal of money to buy the enormously costly clothes in which he flaunted himself at Court, to keep open house for a hundred or two hundred guests, to keep numerous carriages, and kennels with packs of every sort of hound required for all forms of hunting. In order, therefore, to keep up their position, those of his class "who had taken the trouble to be born" married the daughters of those who had taken the trouble to amass wealth. But still they often conceived it to be their duty to cultivate in their own homes that laziness and arrogance which, together with their name, were the only legacies they inherited from their parents. On the other hand, when the rich *bourgeois* wedded noble damsels, they also wedded themselves to the

---

[1] Hénault, *Mémoires*, ch. iv. [2] Rousseau, *Confessions*, ii. 7.

prejudice and pride of the nobility to which they pretended to belong, and despised the "vile *bourgeoisie*" from which they had sprung. But their punishment was not long in coming, for they were themselves despised and even scorned by their own wives, who thought they had done them all too much honour by exchanging a name for their money-bags.

For these same reasons the Bar allied itself to Finance. Lamoignon de Malesherbes, then Councillor to the Parliament and afterwards Director of the Library, son of Lamoignon de Blancmesnil, First President of the *Cour des Aides*, married the daughter of Grimod de la Reynière, a Farmer-General—in other words, "five hundred thousand silver livres in cash, two hundred thousand livres in reversion, and several years of board and lodging. As M. Grimod has four children, this illustrates the wealth of these financiers." [1] The marriage was facilitated by Lamoignon procuring for Grimod's son the reversion of the post of First President of the *Cour des Aides*.

Frequently the nobles and magistrates found wives among the financier class who did them honour by their intelligence and superior education. For instance, Mlle Pléneuf, the future Marquise de Prie, had "great intelligence and was extremely cultivated, being widely read in the best authors." [2] Many of these rich men sent their sons abroad: Frénilly seeing Switzerland, Holland, and England, while Antoine Delahante, son of a Farmer-General, travelled in Switzerland and in the south of France, and Mme de Pompadour herself is an example of the excellent education which was often received in the world of finance. Not only Le Normant de Tournehem, the Farmer-General and friend of Mme Poisson, but M. Poisson himself, the agent of the brothers Pâris, had Mlle Poisson taught singing, dancing, and drawing by the very best masters, and when Mlle Poisson became Mme Le Normant d'Etioles, she welcomed at her castle of Etioles such distinguished men of letters as the President de Rocheret, who read *Pamela* to her, Crébillon, Fontenelle, and Montesquieu,

[1] Barbier, iv. 344.   [2] Saint-Simon, xix. 51.

while Voltaire sang the praises of "the divine Etioles," who later, as Mme de Pompadour, was to dazzle the Court with her brilliant and various talents. The time had passed when a Turcaret, as ignorant as he was ridiculous, loved music "terribly, because a fine voice accompanied by a trumpet induced sweet reveries"; and we may gauge the difference from Marmontel's description of the splendid La Poplinière, the financier in whose house Rousseau produced his opera, *Les Muses galantes*: "His mansion at Passy became the most delightful of residences. He employed the best orchestra known in those days, the musicians living in his house, where they devoted the mornings to practising, with marvellous precision, the symphonies they were to play in the evening. His suppers were graced by the principal actors of the theatres, especially by the dancers and singers of the opera; and when the ear had been charmed by these wonderful voices, a further and agreeable surprise was provided by seeing Lany and her sister, the young Pluvigné, leave the table and dance to the music of the orchestra in the supper-room. All these gifted musicians were Italians, and were received, lodged, and boarded in his house, and each one was a star in himself. Rameau composed his operas there, and on feast days he would play us tunes on the organ of the private chapel with amazing skill. Never did a *bourgeois* live in so princely a style, and even princes enjoyed the pleasures he provided. He had a private theatre in which comedies were performed and acted by people of fashion. These comedies were rather inferior, it is true, but they were in such good taste, and sufficiently well written, that they were applauded, not merely from politeness alone. Their success was further assured, as they were followed by suppers to which were invited the élite of the spectators, the Ambassadors of Europe, the very highest nobility, and the most beautiful women of Paris." [1]

Nor was La Poplinière the only financier who installed a theatre in his house. Lalive de Bellegarde, another Farmer-

---

[1] Marmontel, *Mémoires*, Book IV.

General, and father of Lalive d'Epinay, was the owner of the famous Theatre de la Chevrette, which Rousseau mentions: "In spite of my stupidity and clumsiness, Mme d'Epinay wished me to take part in the entertainments at La Chevrette, a castle near St. Denis, belonging to M. de Bellegarde. There was a theatre there (in 1748) where plays were often performed. They gave me a part, which I studied incessantly for six months on end, and which made me perspire from the beginning to the end of the performance."[1] Mme d'Epinay tells us in her *Mémoires* of the kind of play which was given at this theatre, and in which Rousseau, who was later to figure so frequently in those *Mémoires*, appears for the first time:

"We began with *L'Engagement téméraire*, a new comedy by M. Rousseau, a friend of Francueil, who introduced him to us. The author played a part in his own piece. It is the work of a man of much wit, and possibly, even, of genius. He is not polished in his manners—at least he does not appear so, though he can turn a compliment well enough. He seems ignorant of the ways of society, but his great intelligence is obvious. He is swarthy, and his bright eyes give a certain animation to his expression—but to return to my entertainments, for they are really very delightful. Our audience consists largely of peasants and servants, and the President de Maupeou does not wish his wife to join us. The fact is that she played a part which was a trifle risky, which she had bespoke for herself on hearing the play read, and acted it very freely—possibly too much so." (This was the part of the servant, Lisette, who declared that "husbands, it is true, are the greatest of hypocrites.") Mlle d'Ette, Mme d'Epinay's friend, wrote to M. de Valory in this connection: "The President's little wife is such a madcap and so amusing that you would die of laughing," and indeed the little lady would have little difficulty in playing Lisette, as we can see from the letter she wrote to her great friend, Mlle d'Esclavelles, afterwards Mme d'Epinay: "After my marriage to this little black man, whom, over and over again, I had refused, he never

[1] Rousseau, *Confessions*, ii. 7.

A CONCERT
IN THE HOUSE OF THE COMTESSE DE SAINT-BRISSON
From an engraving by A. J. Duclos, after Augustin de St. Aubin

ceased to be kind and gallant, and tried his best to be amiable, and indeed I was touched by his efforts, for it was not his fault that he was what he was. Nowadays, for a change, one scene follows on the heels of the last." This "little black man," Maupeou, had a low forehead, bushy and very black eyebrows, a pointed nose, and a receding chin, while his complexion was bilious, now yellow, now green, which earned him at Court the nickname of *La Bigarrade*, or "The Lemon." In 1744, being then President, he married Mlle de Roncherolles de Pont Saint-Pierre, a lady of high degree, "who brought him an income of 50,000 livres, a very honourable marriage";[1] but quarrels soon became frequent. Not only did the lady act her parts freely, but she could use her hand freely too. "One day at my toilette," she writes to Mlle d'Esclavelles, "I saw in the glass my President entering my dressing-room. I pretended not to see him, but turned my back and looked out of the window, humming. He approached on tiptoe and kissed me. 'Mercy,' I cried, smacking him hard. 'Oh, sir, is it you! I ask your pardon! I am grieved beyond words.' No wonder Mme de Maupeou played the lively Lisette in *L'Engagement téméraire* so successfully!

We read some pages back of "the good deeds" of a Samuel Bernard and a Montmartel. Let us add the following lines of Saint-Simon to this eulogy of the financiers: "The Abbé de Louvois refused the Bishopric of Clermont on grounds of health, but really because he had long been waiting for the highest posts, and now found himself too old to accept one so inferior. Father Massillon, of the Oratory, so celebrated for his sermons, profited by his refusal, Crosat, the younger, nobly and piously paying his expenses."[2] And when, later, Massillon wished to found, in Auvergne, his asylum of la Châsse for aged and impoverished priests, Crosat, the banker, always generous, subscribed 40,000 crowns towards the foundation.

Why, then, were the Farmers-General so unpopular in

[1] Barbier, *Journal*, iii. 485.   [2] Saint-Simon, xiv. 196.

the eighteenth century? There were two reasons which, above all, irritated the general public against them, one being the "brigades" of collecting agents who acted under them, and were commonly called *gabelous*, from the most detested of all taxes, the *gabelle* or salt tax; the other was the vanity and ridiculous display practised by some of their number, of which the following funeral notice is a good example. It made all Paris laugh, and ran as follows:

"Your presence is requested at the conveyance and interment of the very high and mighty Lady Elisabeth Bontemps, wife of the very high and mighty Sir Nicholas Beaujon, Councillor of State, Secretary to the King and Receiver-General of the Finances of La Rochelle." [1]

As regards their display, we have already seen what Samuel Bernard was capable of accomplishing when he married off one of his daughters. De Frénilly says of his great-uncle, M. de Saint-Waast, administrator-general of the domains and receiver-general of the "twentieth": "I have never found, in any palace, such luxury displayed with more signs of wealth and taste than that which I saw in the great drawing-room of the house he had built on the Tuileries. In his library he kept the famous *Frileuse* which Houdon had made for him," and Forbonnais remarks sagely: "That which is not acquired by toil is spent with ostentation, and ostentation is the delight of common souls." [2] For it was just those who had made their fortunes rapidly who were foremost in displaying their extravagance.

Nor was it in reckless expenditure that the financiers aped the nobility, but also in the indecent haste and levity with which they married and gave in marriage. Here is an example of a marriage which had been hastily arranged, and is thus gaily described by Mme d'Epinay:

"Yesterday morning, being Wednesday, my mother called me to her room and said: 'M. Rinville, the elder, has just proposed to M. de Bellegarde that Mimi should marry one of our distant cousins, who is said to be a very nice fellow, and we are going to dine to-day with Mme de

[1] *L'Espion anglais*, i. 172.   [2] Forbonnais, *Recherches*, ii. 118.

Rinville, when M. d'Houdetot [the intended] will be present, and we shall see how matters stand.'

"On our arrival we saw the whole family ranged in a circle—M. and Mme d'Houdetot, their son, and all imaginable Rinvilles. The Marquise d'Houdetot rose hastily as we entered, and, advancing with open arms, embraced my stepfather [M. de Bellegarde], my mother, Mimi, and me, whom she had never seen. After all this embracing, old M. de Rinville took my stepfather by the hand and ceremoniously presented him to Mme d'Houdetot, who in turn presented him to her son and her husband, and we were all presented and embraced all over again. Mme d'Houdetot then took my stepsister, Mimi, aside, and overwhelmed her with questions and compliments, without pausing for reply, and in two minutes was enchanted with Mimi's manners and intelligence. The two young people were then set down to table next each other, while M. de Rinville and the Marquise d'Houdetot took charge of my father, and my mother, who did not like to leave Mimi, was placed next to her and the Marquis d'Houdetot. At dessert the marriage was already being discussed freely, in spite of it having been impressed upon us not to mention this subject. On returning to the drawing-room we drank our coffee, and when the servants had retired, M. de Rinville suddenly said to my stepfather: 'See here, my friend, we are now a family party, and among friends, as we all are, there is no need for mystery. So let us speak plainly. It is just a question of Yes or No. Does my son please you? Yes or no? And your daughter? Yes or no again. That is the crux of the matter. I look upon your children as mine, and I will only add this: your daughter, my dear colleague, has quite captivated Mme la Marquise' (here he bowed to that lady), 'as I can see, while our young Count is already head over heels in love. Your daughter has but to say whether he is agreeable to her, and if so, let her speak. Come, my goddaughter, give us your views.' My stepsister blushed. They smothered her with flattery, caressed my father, and did all they could to turn our heads and give us no time for reflection. My mother, realising that my stepfather's blind faith in M. de Rinville would induce him to consent to anything, here interrupted the storm of applause and said to Mme de Rinville, in a voice loud enough to be heard above the tumult: 'It seems to me, Madame, that M. de Rinville goes too fast. Matters are not so far advanced that our young people need give their answer yet. What if, anxious to marry, they took a fancy for each other and the business were to fall through.' 'Ah, you are right,' cried M. de Rinville, raising his hands and clapping them. 'What a pleasure it is to meet people who give such good advice' (he was pretending to interpret my mother's thoughts in his own way), 'so let us by all means first discuss the marriage contract, while the young people have a talk together. That was a very timely reminder—very timely indeed. Go, my children; amuse yourselves while we find the means to make you happy as soon as possible.'

"When they had sat down, M. de Rinville announced that the Marquis d'Houdetot would give his son on his marriage an income of eighteen thousand livres per annum from his property in Normandy, and the squadron of cavalry he had bought for him in the previous year. The Marquis, who was leaning on his stick, confirmed this, and the Marquise devoured my stepfather and mother with her eyes. 'As for me,' she cried, 'I don't understand business, but I will give all I can—my diamonds, yes, certainly my diamonds. They are very fine. I don't exactly know how many I have, but, as many as there are, I shall give them to my daughter-in-law absolutely and not to my son.' 'There, my dear colleague,' said M. de Rinville, with emphasis, to M. de Bellegarde, 'that is a truly generous and munificent gift,' and he then inquired whether my stepfather was content with those proposals. The latter expressed himself satisfied, but added that his chief object was his daughter's happiness. Here he was interrupted by the others delivering a eulogy of the young Count, M. de Rinville replying in the same terms on his goddaughter's behalf. M. de Bellegarde then said he would treat his daughter as he had his other children, giving her a dowry of three hundred thousand livres and her share of his property on his death 'We are agreed, then,' said M. de Rinville, rising: 'I would ask you to sign the contract this evening; the banns shall be published on Sunday for the first time: we can get a dispensation for the others, and the wedding shall be on Monday.' "

CHAPTER IV

THE DOCTORS

WE have dealt with the magistrates and the world of finance. We will now see what became of those doctors whom Molière had so scourged and ridiculed in the preceding century, and whom Pascal himself had so roughly treated in the following passage: "If the physicians had not got soutanes and mules they would never have duped the world, which cannot resist so portentous a display," on which Voltaire, who never lets any occasion slip when he can put Pascal in the wrong, comments as follows: "The fact is that the physicians never ceased to be ridiculous, and only acquired general consideration when they left off these trappings of pedantry."

But the eighteenth-century doctor was no longer the pedant of Molière's day. He was "an elegant gentleman, dressed in black silk lined with ermine, powdered and scented like any young magistrate. He lightly turns back his lace cuffs, gracefully feels the pulse of the mistress of the house, gossips a little on theatres and such matters, and then hurries away so quickly that he has to be called back to write his prescription, which he has quite forgotten."[1] We recall the line in Boileau's *Les Embarras de Paris*: "Guénaud on his horse covers me with mud as he rides by"; but Guénaud no longer rode; he lolled in his coach. Mercier cries: "Where are the Guénauds on their mules? Where are MM. Purgon and Diafoirus? Instead of a grave gentleman with severe expression, with stately gait, and weighing his every word with care, one finds an agreeable person, talking of everything but medicine,

[1] *L'Espion anglais*, i. 246.

extending a delicate white hand on which he is careful to display a large diamond." [1]

From the eighteenth century, probably, dates the rise, as also the fortune and prestige, of doctors as the physicians of ladies of fashion.

"The influence which the best-known doctors exercised in France on their society patients, and especially on the ladies at that time, was amazing. The latter displayed reliance and submission towards their medical attendants, and their boundless admiration showed itself in the most delicate attentions. I can only compare it with that which their grandmothers, at the end of the reign of Louis XIV., felt for their spiritual directors; but, in truth, this change in their affections may easily be explained by the fact that the body had by this time supplanted the soul in importance. As in fifteen cases out of twenty they were summoned for a whim rather than from necessity, they obviously had more complaints to listen to than remedies to prescribe. They were obliged to listen with the utmost attention to long accounts of their patients' ills, and, at the same time, not to take them too seriously for fear of instilling real alarm, a sure way of becoming unpopular and being shown the door; whereas if they roughly described the symptoms as pure imagination they would, as infallibly, have wounded their patients' self-esteem and come to be regarded as harsh and unsympathetic. There was an art in reviving the courage of these delicate souls, by prescribing for them, with some semblance of attention, those harmless remedies which calmed their nerves without injuring their health, and in terminating their visit, which had begun under the appearances of deep solicitude, with a light and graceful pleasantry. What a difference between these charming doctors and those of Pascal! When this great thinker said: 'Who wants a physician without a soutane?' he did not foresee so great a change." [2]

But what of the patients? In a great social upheaval, such as a war or revolution, these imaginary or over-

[1] Mercier, ii. 93.　　　　[2] Lévis, p. 238.

sensitive invalids no longer had time to brood over their ailments and feel their pulse. They were cured very quickly, since really they were only suffering from what Béralde wittily called "the doctors' disease." Lévis writes: "While on this subject, I would like to mention the peculiar effects which the Revolution produced on people's health. It seemed inevitable that all those delicate and languishing persons could not survive if deprived of all the comforts and amenities of life. But, on the contrary, those who remained in France bore, without apparent ill-effects, privations of every kind, all manner of trials, and even poverty and imprisonment, while those who found themselves exiled from this country exposed themselves, under strange skies and often in rigorous climates, to the inclement seasons and recovered the use of their legs, which they had long believed they had lost. Never were the virtues of temperance and exercise more clearly demonstrated and their neglect more dearly paid for. The evidence was decisive, for all these folk used to complain of the vapours and of disordered nerves." [1]

Although in the eighteenth century doctors no longer wore the gown and bonnet as in Molière's day, and if it could no longer be said of this elegant gentry that "the beard makes half the physician," yet many of them made themselves conspicuous by their behaviour and their costume. For instance, Dr. Gardanne, whom Mme Roland mentions in her *Mémoires* while reviewing the ranks of her suitors, was a Provençal "who, while munching sugarplums, remarked with a gallantry savouring rather of the schoolroom, that he loved sweetness, to which the young lady, blushing a little and with a simper, timidly replied that men were supposed to be very fond of it, because they were greatly in need of always being treated therewith. The fine doctor appeared quite overcome with laughter at this epigram. . . . A doctor in his full dress is not a very seductive figure in a girl's eyes, and I, for my part, have never in my life imagined Cupid in a wig. Gardanne, with his professional air, his southern accent, and his black and

[1] Lévis, p. 243.

closely set eyebrows, was more likely to allay the fever than to inflame it."[1]

As a rule the physician was a man of the world, frequenting the drawing-rooms and the company of literary men. That fine gentleman, Lorry, was the intimate friend of d'Alembert, the doctor of Mlle de Lespinasse, and he attended Voltaire during his last visit to the Parisians. Sometimes even a doctor, in order to show the extent of his practice, would push his pretensions and love of titles to a point which excited ridicule, as the following anecdote of Chamfort's illustrates: "D'Alembert, who already had a great reputation, was at Mme du Deffand's, where the President Hénault and M. de Pont-de-Veyle were of the company. A doctor named Fournier also called, and, on entering, said to Mme du Deffand: 'Madame, I have the honour to present you my humble duty'; to the President: 'Sir, I have the honour to salute you'; to M. de Pont-de-Veyle: 'Sir, your humble servant'; and to d'Alembert: 'Good morning, sir.'"

But often such civility actually concealed fierce hatreds and undying rivalry between colleagues. *Figulus figulum odit, medicus medicum*, as the Latin proverb has it; and in 1761 all Paris rang with a violent quarrel which broke out in the Medical Faculty itself, between Bordeu and Bouvart, the latter having, in full session, accused the former of having relieved his patient, the Marquis de Pondenas, of his watch and snuff-box. The affair dragged on, becoming wider in its scope and more envenomed from day to day, until the Parliament intervened and proclaimed Bordeu innocent in 1764. But the matter had reached even to the King's ears, for one day, at the Grand Couvert, the Duke de Bouillon exclaimed: "Sire, either Bordeu stole and ought to be hanged, or Bouvart slandered him, and ought to be hanged also."

The doctor of those days had to reckon wit among his accomplishments. He had to make amusing remarks, such as are ascribed to the vindictive Bouvart. At one time the bark of the elm was reputed of great virtue in medicine,

[1] Mme Roland, *Mémoires*, p. 137.

and one of his patients once asked Bouvart whether she ought to take it. "Take it, Madame," said he, "and make haste while the elm recovers." Another patient, who was very rich, once sent his servant to him with a fee which Bouvart considered too small. "Tell your master," he exclaimed, waving it aside, "that I treat the poor for nothing." When his rival, Bordeu, died, he said cruelly: "Really, I would never have thought that he would have died horizontally," meaning he expected him to die vertically, or, in other words, hung from a gallows. But a happier tribute to poor Bordeu went the round of Paris at the same time, and confirmed his reputation as a great physician: "Death was afraid of him and caught him sleeping." [1]

Besides these personal rivalries, there were others between the Faculties of Montpellier and Paris, for the former often supplied physicians to the Court which infuriated the Medical School at Paris, and in Paris itself there was, for many a long day, an epic struggle between surgeons and physicians over alleged encroachments by the former. M. de la Martinière, First Physician to the King, in asking the Council to decide definitely and finally on the extent of their respective functions, declared that a wall of brass would be required to keep surgeons and physicians apart; to which d'Argenson replied: "You are quite right, but when the wall is built, on which side should the sick be placed?" [2]

Although they were honoured and petted in society, the Court seems to have treated them with less consideration. The First Physician had, it is true, the title of Count, and the other doctors of the King's household enjoyed the same privileges as other members, but they were spoken of, and even addressed, by their surnames only. The following shows their position very clearly. In February 1738, the Dauphin was operated on for an abscess in the cheek. So-called consulting physicians and surgeons were summoned to Versailles from Paris. Their duty done, Luynes writes that "these gentlemen had fondly hoped that they

[1] Duc de Lévis, p. 240.   [2] Luynes, ix. 401.

would be given a royal coach in which to return, and expected this as a mark of distinction and bounty on the King's part." But after waiting several days for an answer, the First Lord of the Bedchamber, who was away, decided that even when he was in waiting royal coaches had never been assigned to doctors, and that "people of quality who applied with the greatest eagerness for this honour might well feel aggrieved if the King's coaches were given to doctors and surgeons and to—people of that sort!" These gentlemen were deeply offended by the words "and people of that sort." [1]

A word on the sick and on the diseases peculiarly prevalent in the eighteenth century would not be out of place at this point. We need not dwell on the languishing ladies who had "the vapours," and called in the doctor to diagnose, as Molière says, that "their pulse was misbehaving," but will deal, rather, with the more serious maladies which were then common in Paris. Mme Roland wrote to her friend, Sophia Cannet, on 17th September 1767: "I have no news save that I am suffering from a slight attack of the disease which is rampant in Paris. This is a cold called *la grippe* [influenza]. I have no idea how this name originated, so I can't tell you. This cold causes bad headaches, fever, and nausea, and sends one to bed." Littré knew, or thought he knew, the origin of the word *grippe*. "This infectious catarrh is called *grippe* because it grips or seizes so many people," and he might have quoted, in support of his theory, the following passage from Mercier: "Almost every year, about the middle of November, most people succumb to a catarrh, due to the sudden prevalence of a damp and cold atmosphere, and to fogs which suppress perspiration. Many die of this disease, but the Parisian, who laughs at everything, calls these dangerous colds *la grippe* and *la coquette*; and three days later the scoffer is himself seized and goes to his grave." [2]

With regard to treatment, most eighteenth-century doctors, as Béralde said of those of his day in *Le Malade*

[1] Luynes, ii. 36. [2] Mercier, *Tableau de Paris*, iv. 143.

imaginaire, indulged in "purgatives and bleeding with the greatest promptness." Bleeding, especially, was the great remedy for every ill, and a universal panacea. It was employed for the most varied maladies, and if once was not sufficient, the patient was bled a second time, as illustrated by Molière's 'new doctor,' who bled till he had drained all the blood away.

In Molière's day, Guy Patin wrote: "I have been treating a gentleman of Languedoc these last three weeks for a very severe and dangerous smallpox. He has been bled ten times: *et ante eruptionem, et in ipsa eruptione, et post eruptionem.*" Patin dealt in the same way with all his patients, great and small, young and old, and whatever their ailments might be. Thus, too, did Gil Blas' famous Sangrado, "though it is true that he, in thus treating his patients, killed them off too hastily to please the notary, who complained that that man had deprived him of many a sound will and testament." But Guy Patin was proud of his sanguinary cures: "We cure our patients of eighty and more by bleeding them, and are as successful with children of two and three months. Not a day passes but we bleed several babes as well as septuagenarians, *qui singuli feliciter inde convalescunt.* I have once bled an infant of three days for erysipelas in the throat. He is still alive thirty-five years later." [1] Nor did he spare his own family, for when his son fell ill, he bled him twenty times; nor even himself, since, when suffering from a cold, he performed the operation on himself seven times, and exclaimed, when cured: "I am rid of it, thank God! I now only require some strength," and when this returned to him, he continued as vigorously as before to phlebotomise his patients, and we hear this executioner crying: "Long live Galien's excellent method, and the lovely line of Joachim du Bellay:

"'Oh, excellent, oh, sacred, oh, divine bleeding!'"

Other eighteenth-century doctors were as sanguinary as he. Tronchin wrote in 1762 to the Countess d'Arcussia:

[1] Guy Patin, ii. 419, iii. 418.

"I well remember, about six years ago, being consulted by a patient of one of the largest cities in France, who was in a worse plight than you, about his hundred and thirty-third blood-letting, which, in spite of his doctor's prescription, had been impossible owing to lack of blood. The doctor, however, considered it necessary, but did not see his way to performing the operation, there being no blood left! So he postponed it for a week, in the hope that some more blood might possibly collect in the interval. It was during this respite that the patient consulted me. He was by now shaken by continual spasms and suffered from chronic convulsions. It is now only a year since he has recovered from an ailment for which even the first bleeding was useless, so what would have happened at the hundred and thirty-third? And a poor wretch who steals a loaf of bread is hung!" [1]

Tronchin's protest was justified, but blood continued to flow under the lancet of these crazy phlebotomists, who doubtless believed with Sangrado that "nothing multiplies so much as blood." One physician, however, Marceau, did venture to reckon up their hecatombs in 1754. He thus concludes his Memorandum: "These frequent blood-lettings kill 4000 people annually in Paris and 40,000 in France." [2] But his Memorandum did not assuage the doctors' thirst for blood. The Archbishop of Paris, Mgr de Beaumont, suffered from colic, and his doctor, Cochu, and Moreau, the chief surgeon of the Hôtel Dieu, "deemed it necessary to bleed him thrice." [3] M. de Brissac lost his son, aged fifteen. "Tronchin," writes Luynes, "had forbidden him ever to be bled, because this young man had grown enormously, and he ought not to be weakened further after nature had already taxed his strength so severely. But his fever increased in violence, and M. Tronchin, who was sent for, could not come at the moment, and the ordinary doctor prescribed that he be bled twice. At the second, the patient died." [4] And, as a final example, let us see what the Duchess d'Orleans wrote from Marly on

[1] Tronchin, p. 45.
[2] Delaunay, p. 229.
[3] Hardy, i. 240.
Luynes, xv. 62.

2nd June 1709: "The doctors had bled my cousin, La Trémoille, six times, and so copiously, that at the autopsy no other cause of death was discovered, save that he had not a drop of blood left in his veins."

But the disease which, in the eighteenth century, took the heaviest toll was the smallpox, and the tragic lists of its victims can be read in all the memoirs of the time. On 1st August 1723, Marais wrote: "The smallpox rages in all Paris, and more than 3000 children have died of it." On the 30th, he noted again: "The smallpox is killing every one —the beautiful Mlle Dufranc, aged twenty, the Countess de Boulainvilliers, Mme de Monmort, my neighbour, the Duchess d'Aumont. . . . The Duke d'Aumont, her son, caught it from her and died in four days: so father, mother, daughter-in-law, and son have all been carried off in six months." In the following May died the son of the Prince de Rohan, that Prince de Soubise, who was "the best-looking man at Court." In six days the dread scourge carried off both him and his wife, "who had nursed him."

Montesquieu deplores the fact that so many young people were cut off in the flower of their youth by this fell disease. "This smallpox," he writes to the Duchess d'Aiguillon, on 3rd December 1753, "is a terrible scourge, and adds another death to the one which each one of us has to suffer eventually. The beautiful picture which Homer draws of those who die, and of that youthful harvest which falls under the Scythe of the Reaper, cannot apply to this death."

This malady seemed to attack ladies of quality in particular, and, indeed, fashion required that a wife should shut herself up and isolate herself with her husband as soon as the latter showed the first symptoms of the malady. "The ladies and the world of fashion in general feel deeply the loss of Angenne, who is dead of the smallpox [in 1716]. The Duchess d'Olonne is dead also, having shut herself up, though half-dead with terror, together with her husband, who was hardly worthy of such devotion on her part. She was the daughter, by his first marriage, of Barbezieux [and granddaughter of Louvois]

—young, with a lovely figure, amiable, and full of virtue and devotion to her duties. It is a great pity." [1] According to Voltaire, 20,000 people died of smallpox in Paris in 1723.

As for remedies, there was indeed a preventive in inoculation, but its use was opposed by the fatal prejudice of public opinion. Thus when the Duke d'Orleans had his two children inoculated, the sensation both at Court and in town was immense. "Some days before, the Duchess burst into tears in her husband's presence, when he said to her: 'Madame, although I have made up my mind, if it is so abhorrent to you, and you feel that you cannot consent to this inoculation, well, it shall not be done. They are your children as well as mine.' To which she replied: 'Oh, sir, let them be inoculated and leave me to my tears.' It turned out the greatest success, and when the children had recovered and the Duchess appeared with them at the Opera, she was applauded like a successful new play. M. d'Orleans had taken every precaution, and had brought M. Tronchin, the famous physician and pupil of Boerhaave, from Geneva. He was reputed the greatest authority on inoculation in Europe." [2]

The Orleans family were applauded but not imitated. For instance, Chirac persisted in the error of his ways. "Smallpox," said he, "look to yourself. I will vanquish you by bleeding." In 1763 the Medical Faculty appointed a commission of twelve members to study the question of inoculation, but as it included both "inoculators" and "anti-inoculators," this led to disputes and nearly to blows. D'Alembert wrote in this connection: "Little more was required and this quarrel among the learned doctors would have had such a sanguinary sequel that they would have had to call in the surgeons to their aid." Finally, after five years of deliberations and discussions, the Faculty voted, the result being an equal number on either side, and an official pronouncement was therefore impossible.

Outside the Faculty the opposition was even more persistent, and for this the Chancellor, Pasquier, gives one curious reason. "An English doctor, Horlock, suggested

---

[1] Saint-Simon, xiii. 132.   [2] Collé, ii. 47.

inoculating me. My father accepted on my behalf, but could not get my mother's consent to having my sister inoculated also. Shortly after, my sister caught the smallpox, was very ill, but recovered, though badly pock-marked. This opposition is, therefore, difficult to explain were it not for the fact that at this time, among devout persons, like my mother, many believed that it was deliberately tempting Providence to infect a human being with a disease which, in the course of nature, he might never catch. Many of the clergy supported this view." [1]

We will now, with the help of memoirs, make the acquaintance of some of the more celebrated doctors of the time, as, for instance, the King's First Physician, Boudin, who, Saint-Simon said, "was a *boudin* (black pudding) in figure as well as in name." He was a humorist, as may be gathered from the joke he played on the redoubtable Fagon. A certain Berger defended the following thesis: *An ex tabaci usu frequenti vitæ summa brevior?*—at a sitting at which Fagon presided and Boudin, as Head of the Faculty, was present. Fagon, of course, was the Great King's doctor, "and all the Court bowed before one who had held in his hands not only an old king's life, but also that of an all-powerful woman who was as infirm and even older, and he had therefore risen higher than any minister," but he was also "the tyrant of the medical world, and it was Boudin who tamed him. At last he could make Fagon do as he wished, even to the extent of being admitted to his friend's house at all hours, although he immured himself like a hermit.

"Fagon literally hated tobacco like poison, and Boudin dedicated to him a medical thesis [the thesis of Berger] against its use, but demonstrated it in his presence by smothering himself with snuff, which, in any case, always covered his hands and face." [2]

Saint-Simon tells us that Chirac "was, both in theory and practice, the most learned doctor of his time, and he was admitted by all his colleagues, even by those of great reputation, to be their master, every one treating

[1] Pasquier, *Mémoires*, i. 3. [2] Saint-Simon, *Mémoires*, viii. 165.

him with that respect which students show to their teacher, with the result that his authority was that of a second Æsculapius. But his audacity surpassed belief." Here is an example: "In 1719, the Duchess de Berry, daughter of the Regent, was seriously ill. The doctors despaired of saving her, and could only suggest the elixir of Garus, then coming into fashion. Garus administered it himself, and insisted that no purgative be given to the patient, as in that case his elixir would become a poison. In a few moments the Duchess rallied, and the improvement was maintained until the next day. It is said that Chirac, moved by a rule of medical etiquette which prefers the death of a patient rather than that a quack should secure the honour and glory of curing him, made her take a purgative, with the result that a relapse took place, and she fell into her agony and died. Garus accused Chirac of murder to his face, but the latter turned his back on him with icy disdain and left La Muette where there was no more for him to do." [1] Saint-Simon adds these details: "The Duchess lingered the rest of the day and only died about midnight. Chirac, seeing the agony approaching, walked across the room, and making a mocking bow at the foot of the bed, the curtains being drawn back, wished her a pleasant voyage in insulting terms, and then left for Paris." [2]

The following story of the same Chirac, physician to the Regent and to Dubois, is less objectionable:

"Cardinal Dubois always ate the wing of a chicken every evening. One day, as it was about to be served, a dog ran away with it, and the kitchen staff had to put another on the spit as quickly as possible. At that moment the Cardinal called for his chicken, and the House Steward, foreseeing the storm which would break if the truth be told, quickly decided on a course of action, and determined to keep his master waiting. He therefore coldly intimated that His Eminence had already supped. 'What, supped?' exclaimed the Cardinal. 'Certainly, Eminence; though it is true that you appeared so engrossed in business that you ate but little; still, if you so desire, a second chicken shall

[1] Duclos, *Mémoires secrets*, i. 359.   [2] Saint-Simon, xvi. 284.

be served without delay.' It was just then that Dr. Chirac, who was wont to visit the Cardinal every evening, put in his appearance. The household told him what had occurred and implored his assistance. On seeing him, Dubois cried: 'Here is a strange thing! My servants want to persuade me that I have supped! I have not the slightest recollection of it, and, what is more, I am extremely hungry.' 'So much the better,' said Chirac; 'your labours have exhausted you, and the first morsels of food have only served to stimulate your appetite. You may eat again without any harm, as long as it be but little. Serve His Eminence,' he continued, turning to the footman. 'I will watch him finish his supper.' The chicken was brought, and the Cardinal thought it was an undoubted sign of good health to eat a second supper, with the permission, too, of Chirac, who was the apostle of abstinence. So he ate his chicken with the utmost good humour." [1]

Finally, here is a story of one of the King's physicians. Sénac, who was fonder of intrigue than of war, if the following anecdote is true, had attended and cured Marshal Saxe, and accompanied his patient, who was then convalescent, to the war of 1745. Siege was laid to Tournai, and one day the Marshal drove with Sénac, in his coach, to within range of the guns of that fortress. Alighting, he said to Sénac: "Follow me." "But the shells! I see yonder batteries preparing to fire at our carriage!" cried Sénac. "Oh, well, pull up the windows in that case," said the Marshal impatiently. But his doctor went to ground in the nearest trench. Our present-day doctors have more courage than he.

[1] Duclos, *Mémoires secrets*, ii. 15.

CHAPTER V

THE BOURGEOIS OF PARIS

THE exact position of the middle class was very difficult to define in the eighteenth century, nor is it any easier to define the term *bourgeois*. Officially, the "*bourgeoisie* were those who lived on wealth acquired by their labour in commerce, or any other profession, or on property left them by their fathers." They were, in fact, taken generally, a class which was comfortably off, widely respected, living in towns where they owned their own houses, and, according to Voltaire, enjoying all the amenities of life. "What makes Paris the most flourishing city in the world is not the large number of its magnificent and opulent mansions replete with every luxury, but the vast number of private houses, in which people live in a state of comfort unknown to our ancestors, and at which other nations have not yet arrived. If we compare Paris with London, which is the former's rival as regards area, we find the latter far inferior in splendour, taste, magnificence, in amenities, pleasures, arts, but, above all, in the arts of social life. I do not hesitate to state that there is five times as much silver plate in the houses of the *bourgeoisie* of Paris as in those of London. Your notary, your lawyer, your tailor, is far better lodged, has far better furniture, and is far better waited on than any magistrate in the capital of England. More poultry and game is eaten in Paris in one day, than in a week in London. A thousand times as many candles are burned in the former, for in London, except at Court, candles are unknown. I will not dwell on other capitals. Amsterdam, which, after London, is the most thickly populated, is the home of parsimony; Vienna and Madrid are but poor cities; Rome has fewer inhabitants than Lyons, and I much doubt if it is as rich. In these reflections we have some cause for congratulating ourselves on our good fortune; for if Rome has more beautiful buildings, London more numerous shipping, and Amsterdam greater warehouses, yet we must admit that, in no other city in the world does a larger number of citizens enjoy so much abundance of all good things, so many amenities, and so pleasant an existence." [1]

Here is a curious instance of this abundance which Voltaire mentions, and of the luxury which accompanied it in *bourgeois* houses. On 17th May 1769, one Trudon, son of a rich grocer, married a Mlle Jouanne in the Parish Church of St. Nicholas des Champs. The lady's wedding presents included: a gold watch set with diamonds; a patch-box, also adorned with diamonds; a rock crystal snuff-box mounted in gold; two gold-handled knives, one being for meat and the other for fruit; a diamond ring, 6000 livres, etc. etc. Hardy, to whom we owe these details, noted them in his diary "in order to hand down to posterity this example of the luxury of the *bourgeoisie* in this century." [2]

But in spite of the wealth and display of which he made no secret, the *bourgeois* did not escape the disdain of the great nobles or even of their footmen. The epithet *bourgeois* was used as a term of contempt, just as, formerly, the pages had so insolently hurled this abusive word at poor Françion, the hero of Charles Sorel, in the courtyard of the Louvre. "It is a term of contempt which they give to all who are not of the Court." [3] Similarly the *bourgeois* felt the utmost disdain for the lower classes from which he had risen, but of which he was the flower, and he did not wish to be numbered among the lower orders. For instance, during the festivities held at Paris in 1745, on the occasion of the arrival of the Dauphine, the *bourgeois* Barbier complained bitterly of the sad confusion of classes

---

[1] Voltaire, *Lettre à l'occasion de l'impôt du vingtième*, 1749.
[2] Hardy, i. 142.
[3] *Histoire comique de Françion*, ed. 1858, p. 173.

which he had experienced in the Assembly Rooms. "The success of these Rooms did not come up to expectation. The provost of the Merchant Guilds had intended to supply the public—that is to say, the *bourgeoisie* of Paris—with a resort for dancing and amusements. But this was not to the *bourgeois* taste. On entering, one found the most lamentable confusion on all sides. The rooms were filled only with the dregs of the populace. Tongues, loaves, and the legs of turkeys were flung from the sideboards for any one to catch, and all this caused a veritable riot! A large and excellent orchestra was playing, but no one danced, though sometimes a crowd of blackguards would dance in a ring. The wife of a cobbler or a dressmaker would have felt themselves disgraced if seen dancing in such a place." [1]

In politics, the Paris *bourgeois* was, in the eighteenth century as always, a severe critic, ever ready "to improve the police and reform the State," but, mark you, to reform the latter, not to subvert it. He was a supporter of the Government provided it was not extravagant; for he was even more fond of "his poor money," as the advocate, Barbier, used to say, and though he was a firm upholder of law and order, it grievously annoyed him to see the offices and pensions which were heaped on the great to the detriment of the little. "They gave a pension of 36,000 livres a year to d'Arménonville, the Keeper of the Seals, and another of 20,000 to M. de Morville, his son. That is the way in this country. They curtail the annual income of a hundred poor families, an income which just enables them to live, derived from shares representing loans to the King, and then give 56,000 livres in pensions to people already occupying high positions, which permits these to amass considerable fortunes, and always at the people's expense, merely in order that these great personages may idle and do nothing. Can anything be more senseless?" [2]

Marivaux, in an admirable and all too short paragraph, expresses himself as follows: "The *bourgeois* of Paris is a hybrid animal, resembling the great noble in outward show, and the lower classes in character. Generally speak-

---

[1] Barbier, iv. 19.   [2] Barbier, ii. 16.

ing, you will find him frank and friendly, but you must not try and touch his purse."[1] Barbier, who was always shrewd and prudent, and amicably disposed to authority, wrote: "They say there are more than twenty *lettres de cachet* prepared [for the recalcitrant members of the Parliament]. Such a course is both just and necessary in order to assure the Sovereign's authority. . . . As a rule, it is dangerous for a subject to play with his master, since, if you play too well, he may get annoyed and throw the cards in your face."[2]

Ever on the look out for news, the *bourgeois* read the gazettes, and as a "patriot" followed the armies in their campaigns, applauded their victories, but cheered even more loudly for that beneficent Peace which, when it came, enabled him to draw his interest with more regularity at the Hôtel de Ville. If there was a risk of war, he strongly approved "the Government's intention of gathering a strong army for the approaching campaign." But that certainly did not mean that the rich *bourgeoisie* of Paris were to be enrolled together with the lower classes! On one occasion, Paris was ordered to supply 1800 men between the ages of sixteen and forty for the militia, and here is Barbier's comment: "All those who are obliged to draw lots must report themselves to the Commissioners of their quarter, so that [here Barbier's indignation becomes almost lyrical] the son of a rich merchant who has been brought up with every comfort and received the best education, may find himself on the same list as his father's footman, as servants, workmen, office-boys, cobblers, and even worse, such as street porters, chairmen, even those of his quarter, cabmen, and people of that kind, all of whom are named in the decree. All this is humiliating and hard to endure. I might almost say that it is unbearable! The saddest part is that the sons of merchants who do not pay a large capitation tax, all kinds of booksellers, and others of their kind, and the shop employees have all actually been drawn with the merchant's footmen, and people from all classes of the population like artisans,

[1] Marivaux, *Le Spectateur français*, ii. 17.   [2] Barbier, v. 334, 274.

porters, cabmen, etc. This has greatly wounded their pride, and at the same time they have been not a little pitied by all sensible folk, because they really are the *bourgeois* class, which ought not to be subjected to such a humiliation." [1]

In the eighteenth century the *bourgeoisie* were better educated than the nobility, for, whereas the young nobleman contented himself with visiting the academies in order to learn how to handle the rapier, to ride, and dance the minuet, the *bourgeois* used his wealth for the purpose of systematic studies in the colleges, where the pupils, to an overwhelming extent, were all of the middle class.

Towards the middle of the century, the *bourgeois* was inclined to adopt a moral and sentimental attitude, just as the literature of that time tended to be moralising and "full of sensibility." He honoured and often preached "virtue," partly, no doubt, because he was naturally moral, but partly, also, because there must be sound principles in the State to safeguard the coffers, and this led him to sympathise with the authors of those *contes moraux*, or moral tales, which were so prolific in this century. He revelled in *Pamela, or Virtue Rewarded*, which had such an enormous success, and such a multitude of imitators, and he would weep openly in the theatre, since there was no need to be "ashamed to cry," as in La Bruyère's day. On the contrary, in 1719 Dubos found that "men like crying just as much as laughing when they go to the theatre," and in 1758, Rousseau, who later was to make the fair sex cry in floods, rallied "those weeping ladies in the boxes who are so proud of their tears" in his *Lettre sur les Spectacles*.

Mercier sums up the character of the Parisian of this century in these words: "Taken generally, he is of mild disposition, honest, polite, and easily influenced, but one must not take his levity for weakness; occasionally he quite enjoys being got the better of, but I think I know him well enough to assert that, if he is driven into a corner, his obstinacy will prove invincible. We have only to

[1] Barbier, iii. 425.

remember the 'Ligue' and the 'Fronde.' As long as his grievances are not unbearable, he will merely express his ill-humour in rhymes and jests, and he will not discuss them in public, if, in private, he can ventilate them fully." [1] Such was the *bourgeois*, and we must next consider his good lady, the *bourgeoise* of Paris. Her hood, which was the peculiar badge of her class, distinguished her alike from the ladies of the nobility and the women of the people, but she had also her distinctive moral character as a class. "They are a most respectable class of women, especially those belonging to the lesser *bourgeoisie*, attached to their husbands and children, careful, economical, and splendid housewives; in short, they are an example to all of hard work and common sense." [2] The women of Paris loved the city, and "preferred to be buried at Saint-Sulpice than to live in the country," [3] and the *bourgeois* of Paris throve there so well that he would not leave it. Voltaire laughs at "the voluptuous Parisian who has never travelled farther than Dieppe, whither he goes in order to eat fresh fish"; [4] and the younger Crébillon and Sallé wrote a witty pamphlet entitled, *The Journey from Paris to Saint-Cloud by Sea, and the Return from Saint-Cloud to Paris by Land*, which they dedicated to those stay-at-home Parisians who never would lose sight of the towers of Notre-Dame. They describe how "the Parisian, setting out on this long voyage, packs all his clothes, supplies himself with provisions, and bids a fond farewell to wife and family"; he boards the small ketch which seems to him like a huge vessel; mistakes the ladders of the washerwomen of Chaillot for the minarets of Byzantium, "feels himself far from his own country, and bursts into tears as he thinks of the Rue Trousse-Vache." Once arrived at Saint-Cloud, "he conceives a sublime idea of the earth's size, and realises that Nature, living and smiling, actually extends beyond the gates of Paris." On his homeward journey he sees a stag in the Bois de Boulogne, and this is his first introduction to Natural History.

[1] Mercier, *Tableau de Paris*, i. 68.   [2] *Ibid.* iii. 40.   [3] *Ibid.* ii. 218.
[4] Voltaire, *Dictionnaire philosophique*: "Patrie."

He is a true patriot, and tells one and all that "he is a native-born Parisian, that his mother sells silks at the Barbe d'Or, and that he is cousin to a notary," and when he finally returns to the bosom of his family, he is received with enthusiasm, and with admiration for his courage, so that this ancestor of Tartarin is entertained by all his neighbours as "the bravest and most intrepid of travellers."

In spite of their indolence, the good people of Paris gladly inconvenienced themselves in order to see the King and princes dine or dance in public. Thus on 22nd February 1745, a Monday morning, "the road from Paris to Sceaux was crowded with coaches all going to see the Dauphine [the Infanta of Spain] arrive and sup, and mostly filled with people who have no chance of seeing the fêtes at Versailles. The road from Paris to Versailles was also blocked by a similar stream of vehicles, bearing people on their way to Versailles, where a room might cost 150 livres for the three days. It is all very well talking about poverty, but people always seem to have money for fêtes and pleasures."[1] It was on the occasion of these festivities in honour of the Dauphin's wedding, that Voltaire's *La Princesse de Navarre* was performed, a play which, when set to music by Rousseau, became known as *Les Fêtes de Ramire*. The Duke de Richelieu, as Lord of the Bedchamber, was "the sole dispenser of tickets to all seats," which Barbier thought "very odd," but he adds later: "Happily those who are unable to get places at these private entertainments will have the consolation of seeing all the Court assembled in the State Apartments, and will view the masked ball in greater comfort. They say that this will be very largely attended, and it is this which is drawing such crowds of *bourgeois* from Paris to Versailles." The curious who came to Versailles every Sunday to see the King dine in public "greatly admired his skill in removing the top of his egg with one back-handed stroke of his fork."[2] For this journey to Versailles, the *bourgeois* had recourse to the *carrabas*, a majestic vehicle

[1] Barbier, iv. 15.   [2] Mme Campan, *Mémoires*, p. 16.

drawn by eight horses, but which went somewhat slowly, as it took "six and a half hours to do four short leagues; it carried twenty persons, enclosed in a long wicker cage, who spent an hour wrangling before they could settle in their places, so tightly were they wedged, and when the machine started off, all their heads bumped together." [1] Some got out at Meudon, for the Parisian liked to walk in the country on Sundays. "We often used to go to Meudon," writes Mme Roland; "it was my favourite excursion. On Saturday evening in summer my father would say: 'Well, where shall we go to-morrow if it's fine?' and then, smiling at me: 'To Saint-Cloud, I think. The fountains will be playing, and there will be crowds.' 'Oh, papa,' I cried, 'do let me go to Meudon; I would much prefer that.' At five o'clock on Sunday morning we would all be astir, and a light dress very simply made, with a few flowers and a muslin veil, would betray our intention. We three would then start, and proceeding to the Pont-Royal, which I could see from my windows, we would embark on a small boat. In silence we would then be gently but swiftly carried to the riverside at Bellevue, not far from the glass factory, whose thick black smoke we could see some distance off. From there we used to reach the avenues of Meudon by steep paths." [2]

[1] Mercier, viii. 104. [2] Mme Roland, *Mémoires*, p. 106.

CHAPTER VI

THE POPULACE OF PARIS

"In front of the splendid colonnade of the Louvre, old clothesmen openly display rags and tatters in the square. Grandeur and indigence side by side!" This contrast, which so greatly impressed Mercier, is a picture of what Paris itself was in the eighteenth century, and it was also one which impressed Saint-Preux, that is Rousseau, on his arrival in Paris. "This town," he wrote, "is perhaps the city in the world where fortunes are most unequal and where flaunting wealth and the most appalling poverty dwell together." [1]

As we have passed in review both nobles and *bourgeoisie*, let us see, for a moment, how the populace or lower classes of Paris lived in this eighteenth century. Their lodgings were not very expensive, for a small family could find a dwelling for a hundred francs or so, but it would not be a very grand one. "Where do you live?" "In the Rue Saintonge, at a milkwoman's, in a hole looking on the yard where one can't see clearly even at noon." [2] As for clothes, if one wished to dress cheaply, one went a round of the market. Clothes and shoes were to be found there at low prices, though the shops were so badly lit that one often did not see what one was buying, and frequently found oneself disappointed. "On coming out into the daylight, under the impression that you have bought a black coat, you find you have got a green or violet one, and your suit is all spotted like a leopard." [3]

Those humble folk who got their clothes at the market, and those good women who, on Mondays, frequented the

---
[1] Rousseau, *La Nouvelle Héloïse*, ii. 14.
[2] Rétif de la Bretonne, *La petite éventailliste*.   [3] Mercier, ii. 250.

Place de Grève to buy their dresses and jackets secondhand, were not Parisians in the true sense, for at least two-thirds of the inhabitants were provincials. These people often came to Paris from the depth of the country in order to amass a little money, each one in his trade, and the trades varied according to the provinces. Thus those from Savoy were shoeblacks or carpenters, those from the Limousin were masons, the Lyonnais, chair-carriers, the natives of Normandy, stonecutters and paviors, or else sold thread, while those of Auvergne were all water-carriers, for you had to buy water in Paris: "The public fountains are so few and badly kept, that you have to have recourse to the river. No *bourgeois* house is sufficiently supplied with water. Twenty thousand water-carriers are engaged from morning till night, each carrying two full buckets, from the first to the seventh floors, and even higher. One load of water costs six liards or two sous."[1]

The wigmakers of Paris were famous throughout Europe for their deft fingers and wagging tongues, and were recruited from Provence and Gascony. There were no less than twelve hundred in Paris, employing six thousand assistants, all engaged in shaving, or principally in powdering heads, curling ringlets, and tapering the toupees. Their guild dated its privileges from St. Louis, and it is well known with what energy such corporations defended their rights. The State, moreover, for financial reasons, continued to multiply these bodies, and we shall see how jealously it would, on occasion, defend the privileges, often quaint enough, which it had granted for purposes of revenue. The following is an article which Marmontel sent to the *Mercure*, but which that prudent paper did not dare to print, because the author permitted himself a dig at the Master Fruiterers of Paris:

"Sir,—This day, the 24th August, in the Rue Saint-Honoré, four women, each leading a donkey carrying fruit, chiefly plums, were arrested by four members of the watch and taken before the Commissioner, where they were de-

[1] Mercier, i. 143.

"BELLOWS TO MEND!" Engraved by E. Bouchardon
From "The Cries of Paris."

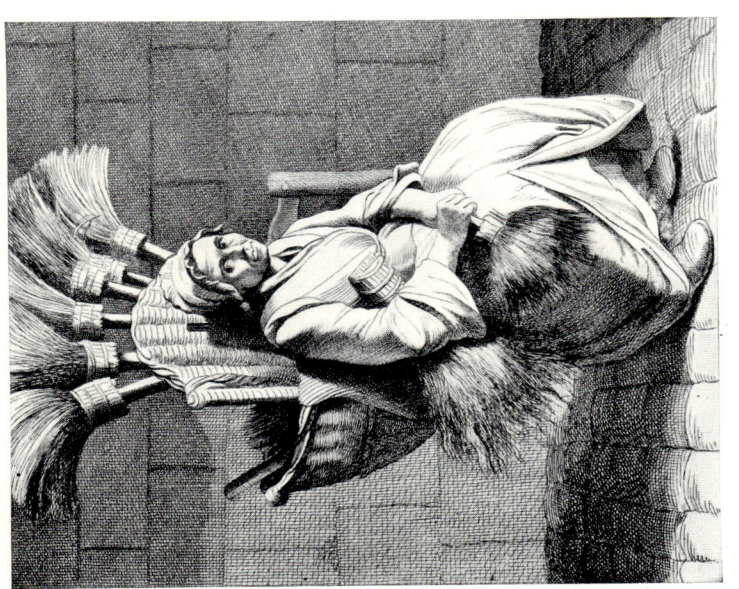

"NEW BROOMS!" Engraved by E. Bouchardon
From "The Cries of Paris."

prived of their plums and carried to the Lieutenant of Police. The latter confiscated the plums and sentenced the women to a fine, the donkeys being held as surety. I myself saw the plums, the donkeys, and the distress of the women. I inquired whether the donkeys had kicked, bitten, or otherwise injured any passer-by, but was assured that the poor beasts were quite peaceable, a statement which, as they were extremely thin, I had no difficulty in believing. So I then asked whether the women had thrown the plums at any one and perhaps put somebody's eye out, but was told that they had been conducting their business in an orderly manner, selling their fruit at two sous the quarter, and very honestly supplying any Savoyard, mason, or cobbler who could afford this succulent addition to his repast of hard dry bread and water from the neighbouring fountain. Finally, I was constrained to inquire whether the fruit was good and fit to eat, suspecting that the medical faculty might have declared that bad fruit was conducive to autumnal fever. But again a poor workman supplied the answer by inducing me to eat one of the plums which he had bought immediately before the wholesale confiscation, and I found it very ripe and excellent. I was cudgelling my brains as to the motive which had led to this great severity towards the plums, the donkeys, and the women, when a gentleman dressed in black and with a round wig, who, I understood, was a sworn member of the Guild of Master Fruiterers of the city of Paris, accosted me and said: 'Sir, these women have broken the law. They stopped to sell their goods, whereas they are only permitted to sell them while walking. They may not collect customers around them, for by so doing they infringe the rights and privileges of the Master Fruiterers, who alone have a licence to sell in a stationary position and at fixed points in all the city of Paris. You will see that this is utterly essential to good order, and that if the donkeys were to stop and poor people enabled to buy at will for two sous what we fruiterers sell for twelve, the resulting disorder would be appalling." [1]

[1] Marmontel, *Mémoires*, ii. 306.

"The quarter round the markets and the Place Maubert no doubt had its customs, possibly even notable ones, but as they are not the customs of the nation, they are not worthy of mention, and they do not figure in novels because they have no place in Society." [1] We think differently now, but the authors of the eighteenth century, novelists as well as others, shared Grimm's opinion on the *canaille*, as even the Lord of Ferney liked to call them, and Rousseau himself, seeking for Emile a wife who would be worthy of him, wrote: "It is difficult to find among the dregs of the people a wife who could make an honest man happy"; [2] and in another passage, after remarking that "fashionable folk disguise themselves," he adds that "the common people show themselves in their true colours and are not pleasing." Their excuse is that they are often hungry.

A Paris workman earned fifty sous a day at the most, and bread was selling at thirteen sous the pound in 1770. Hence the disturbances which were so frequent in this century were always accompanied by the same cry of "Give us bread!" This cry was often heard as the King passed by, for the people had been imbued for centuries with the belief that the King's Government was obliged to provide sustenance for its subjects. During Fleury's ministry the bakers' shops had to be protected by the soldiery to prevent pillage, and rice was distributed to the Parisians; but the well-to-do were shy of being abroad in the streets after seven in the evening, and in the morning the cooks were sent to market under a footman's escort. In March 1753, d'Argenson writes: "A curate of Sainte-Marguerite assures me that over eight hundred people have died of starvation in the Faubourg Saint-Antoine between the 20th February and the 20th March; the poor wretches perished in their garrets of cold and want."[3] Occasionally the Government would act with severity and hang the ringleaders, but that did not provide bread for the remainder. "There have been such violent disturbances over bread in Paris that blood was actually shed and the

---

[1] Baron Grimm, *Correspondance littéraire*, iv. 330.
[2] Rousseau, *Emile*, v. [3] D'Argenson, *Journal*, vii. 426.

Government was obliged to hang three of the most guilty, or of the most unhappy, of the demonstrators. This severity did not allay the excitement, because it did not meet the general want, and hunger can drive men farther than Kings." [1] These bread riots usually started in the Faubourgs Saint-Marceau and Saint-Marcel and in the Place Maubert, "where dwell the poorest, most turbulent, and most undisciplined of the population. Here all private disputes quickly become general, and a woman who is discontented with her husband will plead her cause in the street, accuse him before the tribunal of the populace, gather her neighbours about her, and recite the scandalous catalogue of her man's misdoings. All differences of opinion end in blows, and, of an evening, peace is patched up when one party's face has been well scratched." [2]

If we wish to have some idea of what those brawls were like, we ought to read, not the oft-quoted scene of the cab-driver in Marivaux's *La Vie de Marianne* (a cabman who swears is no new thing), but rather those *Bouquets poissards* of Vadé, so beloved of the populace because it saw itself truly reflected therein: in them, as Boileau would have said, "Parnassus really speaks the language of the market." This was the language of the fishwives or *harengères*, so called, says Le Grand d'Aussy, because, from time immemorial, they dealt in salted herrings. The modern fishwives deal in salted jests, but it is just these which are found in the works of Guillaume Vadé, the inventor of the *genre poissard*, although it would be hardly seemly to quote examples of them here.

The people of the market and the Place Maubert, mostly artisans and workpeople, were wont to frequent Vaugirard and its low haunts on Sundays and Mondays, for the expression to "keep Monday" was already well known to the eighteenth-century workman. On those days also they could enjoy the famous *Courtille*, where reigned the no less celebrated Ramponeau, "who fills the thirsty multitude at three and a half sols the pint, a truly marvellous generosity for an innkeeper. And the people have

---

[1] Duclos, *Œuvres*, iii. 312.   [2] Mercier, i. 250.

not been ungrateful, for they have made his name famous for ever by creating a neologism in his honour which is often used—to wit, the word *ramponer*, which means having a drink at some country pub—and a few more." [1] For more sober people there was the vendor of cordials, carrying a tin urn, with feathers in his cap and wearing a white apron, who might be seen every Sunday on the boulevards and in the Champs Élysées crying, with many a trill: "Come and drink wine of Condrieux, Canary wine," though he really will only sell you liquorice water at a farthing a glass. This was harmless, in all conscience, but it was in this century that spirits began to play havoc among the working class. They could be obtained in the tobacco shops, the chief of which were, naturally, in the densely populated quarter of Saint-Marceau. "Here, in these smoky dens, one might see soldiers, street porters, and idle workmen all crowding round a jug of brandy. Alas, who can number the ills this brandy causes!" [2]

The poor man was driven "to burn his stomach" with brandy because duties had raised the price of wine till it was beyond his means; for the tax authorities "required four sols for a bottle of wine which was only worth three, and the wine he did drink was as adulterated as was most of the *regrats* that were sold to him. This word *regrat* is found in Rousseau, who liked to use technical and popular words, and in his *Confessions* he mentions a *regrat* of salt, which Grimm and Diderot wished Mme d'Epinay, or, rather, her husband, who was a Farmer-General, to give to mother Levasseur. "The salt which is sold to the people at *regrat* for thirteen sous the pound, is not only adulterated at source, but practically half of it is composed of garbage. The Farmers-General forced these *regratiers* to poison the wretched consumers by selling the salt itself to the former for thirteen sous, thereby leaving them no alternative but to recoup themselves by adulterating it. They mix it with water, sand, and every kind of filth." [3]

We often read in the memoirs of this century that in

[1] Mercier, ii. 133.   [2] *Ibid*. ii. 25.   [3] *Ibid*. iii. 190.

certain years there was great want in Paris, and that beggars always abounded. Duclos put them at 30,000, and d'Argenson wrote in June 1749: "One could not stop at a door without being accosted by ten clamorous beggars." In order to get rid of them, the watch would periodically round up these wretches and confine them in the *dépôt*, a kind of prison, where bad food and idleness soon took their toll of them. Many finished their days in the hospitals. "I am going to hospital," said the poor Parisian. "My father died there, and so will I." [1] And he would die swiftly, for in these pestilential places the mortality was appalling. The lamentable state of the hospitals was, in fact, one of the worst features of this time. On every side protests were raised against the horrid practices which were employed in them, for "to see the way in which the sick are treated in hospitals, we might well imagine that mankind had created these gloomy asylums, not to tend the sick, but to hide them away from happy folk whose pleasures would be troubled by the sight of these unfortunates." [2] When, in 1788, Tenon, the great surgeon, wrote a memorandum on the Paris hospitals by the King's command, his description of the Hôtel-Dieu is truly terrifying. He counted no less than 2627 sick in one building, all of whom were lodged promiscuously, and adjoined the mortuary and dissecting-room. Six patients were put in one bed—three at one end and three at the other, so that the feet of the former touched the shoulders and faces of the latter, and *vice versa*. For want of room they could not lie on their backs, but had to sleep on their sides: but did they ever sleep? "Slumber never comes to these creatures of sorrow and suffering," says Tenon, and his words cannot be read without a shudder.

Yet to these haunts came those Sisters of Charity in their humble grey, whose devotion drew even from Voltaire this cry of admiration: "There is not, perhaps, on earth anything to equal the sacrifice of beauty, youth, and often of high birth, which this gentle sex offers gladly in order to solace, in the hospitals, that welter of human

[1] Mercier, iii. 204.   [2] Chamfort, ii. 17.

suffering, the sight of which is so humiliating to human pride and so revolting to our refinement. The nations separated from the Roman faith have but imperfectly copied so noble a charity." [1] It was with the help of these noble sisters that, at the end of the century, Mme Necker was able to open that hospital, the foundation of which does her so much credit. Necker's *Compte Rendu* for 1781 narrates that "in 1778 Mme Necker tried the experiment of a hospital for 120 sick, each with his own bed, tended with the utmost care and cleanliness, accommodated in big, airy rooms, and nursed by Sisters of Charity"; and she was able to show that "a sick person costs rather less than seventeen sous a day," and "that this expense cannot be compared, without astonishment, with that which is incurred in hospitals where the wretched patients lie six in a bed." Having superintended this Charity Hospital—now the Necker Hospital—where, as she says, "she tried to combine the rules of reasonable economy with the laws of a pitying humanity," for ten years, she handed over its administration to the excellent Vicar of Saint-Sulpice, for the hospital had been able to shelter "all the poor sick of Saint-Sulpice and Gros-Caillou." [2]

The poorer classes of Paris displayed two very marked characteristics: they were easily moved and they were curious, as the following anecdote shows: "Two highwaymen were going to be executed. I saw a crowd of people following them, and noticed two features which, I think, only the populace of Paris could display, for they hurried to this spectacle with eager curiosity, while at the same time expressing the greatest pity for these wretches. I even saw a weeping woman running as hard as she could so as not to miss a detail of an execution, the very thought of which filled her eyes with tears." [3]

---

[1] Voltaire, *Essai sur les mœurs*, ch. cxxxix.
[2] *Nouveaux Mélanges extraits des Manuscrits de Mme Necker*, ii. 301.
[3] *Ibid.* ii. 301.

BOOK III.—THE PROVINCES

CHAPTER I

PROVINCIAL LIFE IN THE EIGHTEENTH CENTURY

"*Elle avait de beaux yeux pour des yeux de province.*" In these words the impudent Valère, in Gresset's *Le Méchant*, dismisses the youthful Chloë, whom he loved before he became a Parisian, but whom in her provincial surroundings he came to despise, having discovered that "one lives only in Paris; elsewhere one vegetates." But this young fool's sentiment has been expressed by wiser contemporaries in terms scarcely less impertinent. For instance, Duclos writes: "What a difference, nay, what a contrast, is there between the Capital and the Provinces! As much as between one nation and another. Those who live a hundred leagues from the Capital are a century behind in thought and action, and when a man returns to Paris after a long absence, people find him quite rusty, as the saying is." [1]

Yet many a man who had left the provinces lived to regret his error, and even Valère "could not be happy without his Chloë." But, however that may be, one could live very happily away from Paris, with or without Chloë, for there are many lovely districts in France, and in them were towns which, as we shall see, were just beginning to grow and to beautify themselves. As for the provincials, in spite of their oddities and often absurd ways, and in many of them these were highly developed, as we shall see, yet when one came to know them, one was fain to admit that

[1] Duclos, *Considérations sur les mœurs*, ch. i.

"they were good folk"—as was the conclusion Gresset came to in his comedy.

Let us see, then, how people lived in the provinces during the eighteenth century; into what classes provincial society was divided; how the towns were built and administered, and what were the customs and habits of the inhabitants. This is not very easy for reasons too numerous to give, but the chief one, and it should be noted, for it reflects so exactly the spirit of the age which we are now considering, is given us by Mallet du Pan: "The Parisians and the writers (that is the rub) do not bother at all about the provinces, and in listening to them one might well imagine that the Government did not extend outside the gates of Paris" [1]—in other words, authorities on this subject are extremely rare.

The chief personage in the province was the Governor. When the "illustrious" Governor makes his state entry into the capital of his province, the magistrates proceed to his mansion in a body. He takes his seat in the Parliament in an arm-chair decorated with *fleur-de-lis*, and the First President administers the oath. After that he is seen no more, unless perhaps occasionally, for he much prefers to reside in Paris than in the "exile" of his province, where he is usually replaced by a *Commandant-en-chef*, or Chief Constable. Thus during the whole of this century up to the Revolution, the Condés were, father and son, Governors of Burgundy, but they never visited their province except to preside at the opening of the Estates, and to listen to compliments and odes in their honour; after which they hurriedly returned, either to Paris and their magnificent mansion, the Palais Bourbon, or else to their Castle of Chantilly, where they hunted like kings, and were surrounded by a court of artists and men of letters. During twenty years, the Maréchal de Villars only resided three months in his district of Provence! In 1776 a decree divided the thirty-nine governments into two classes: the first consisted of eighteen, and these were to be bestowed on princes and maréchals of France, while the others were

[1] Mallet du Pan, *Mémoires*, i. 134.

to be given to lieutenant-generals of the King's armies. But, prince or lieutenant-general, the Governor was everywhere replaced by the Intendant. The former lived at Court, and the inhabitants of his province knew him not, save, perhaps, when now and then some more ambitious provincial came to Paris and asked for his good offices with the King or the ministers.

The Intendants, whom we have mentioned above, are, therefore, of far greater importance from our point of view. D'Argenson explains their position very well in the following passage. Law, the financier, said to him one day: "I would never have believed, sir, all that I have learned since I took charge of the finances. Do you realise that this kingdom of France is governed by thirty Intendants? You have no parliaments, no committees, no Estates, no Governors, and I would almost add, no King—no ministers, merely thirty *maîtres des requêtes* who are sent to the provinces, and on whom the happiness or misfortune, the plenty or the poverty, of these provinces solely depends."[1]

In those days, France was divided into thirty-two, not thirty, administrative districts, each under an Intendant or his deputy. We find both good and bad Intendants, though, as we shall see by the work they did, the good far outnumbered the bad. It was the custom in the eighteenth century for an Intendant to remain long in one post—for ten, twenty, even forty years—and occasionally the office passed from father to son, as in the case of Amelot in Burgundy, Saint-Priest in Languedoc, and the Gallois de La Tour in Provence. He thus became attached to his district, where he had friends and often property of his own; he defended the interests of those he governed at headquarters, and, in short, had ceased to be, as he had been in the seventeenth century, exclusively the King's representative. He was now also the representative of the province, and this was the chief reason for the general respect in which he was held and the high position he occupied in the life of the town. Many of these Intendants sprang from wealthy families among the legal or financial

[1] D'Argenson, *Mémoires*, i. 43.

classes, dwelt in fine mansions, had a large staff of servants, and a great number of carriages for their progresses, while their wives held their receptions and were considered as "little Queens."

Good Intendants were, as we have said, numerous, and many were justly celebrated—such as Turgot in the Limousin and du Cluzel in the government of Tours. Their power for good was great, because, in their progresses, which were frequent, they were able to appreciate the requirements of their people and to learn their habits. Assisted by their deputies, who were very necessary to them owing to the difficulty of communications, they did their best to ensure the safety of the road. This was no light task, for on the main roads robbers were very daring, and the mounted police entrusted with the duty of keeping them secure were insufficient, and were badly paid. For instance, "on 30th April 1721, the Lyons coach, passing through the Bourbonnais and close to the forest of Empoigne and the hamlet of Saulieu, was held up by six mounted men, who, having roughly handled the postillion, who tried to beat them off, made all the passengers alight, robbed them of all the contents of their pockets, watches, snuff-boxes, and ready money, even undoing the belt of one, in which he had sewn up twelve thousand livres in *louis d'or*, made them lie face downward so that they could not lift their heads, and then, while four of the robbers stood over them, pistol in hand, threatening to shoot if their victims dared to move, the other two proceeded to ransack the coach itself. Altogether they got away with two hundred thousand crowns in gold, silver, clothing, and merchandise, and, having completed their work, the coach was allowed to proceed." [1]

Buvat also tells us that "on the same day, the Angers courier and his postillion were killed, three and a half leagues from Chartres, by four highwaymen who had lain in ambush." [2]

---

[1] Buvat, ii. 242.
[2] The coaches took five days from Lyons to Paris. There were two kinds in use between Bordeaux and Paris: the *Carrosse*, which took a

Up to the seventeenth century, trade, which was everywhere impeded owing to the lack of proper roads, was carried on with the help of mules. From this century onwards, carts replaced mules, but they told heavily on the old roads which the adjacent landlords were supposed to keep in repair, each one his own stretch, though this was a duty which they rarely carried out. This was where the Intendants intervened. They it was who, in the eighteenth century, endowed France with her magnificent network of roads in the face of the abuse of an ignorant and reactionary population, and the protests of most of the Parliaments. Take Trudaine, Intendant of Auvergne, who, in his mountainous country, opened up wide carriage roads, well planted with trees, and who, in 1743, was "given the charge of keeping up all bridges and roads." In 1750 he established a special department of works to deal with them, and henceforth the Engineer became a personage in the society of the day, and wore a grey uniform embroidered with gold and silver. At the end of the century, André Chénier, in his "Hymn to France" (1790), pays a tribute to both the Trudaines (the son, Trudaine de Montigny, succeeded to his father's office) and lauds:

"Ces vastes chemins, en tous lieux départis,
  Ou l'étranger à l'aise, achevant son voyage,
  Pense au nom des Trudaines et bénit leur ouvrage." [1]

---

week, and cost 72 livres a head, and 2 sols a pound for luggage, and the *Messageries*, which carried and fed their passengers for 34 crowns. The mails were carried by the *Ordinaire*, a kind of char-à-banc with padlocks, which left Paris for Bordeaux twice a week. (Grellet-Dumazeau, *La Société bordelaise sous Louis xv. et le salon de Mme du Plessy*, 1897.) Mme du Deffand took two days from Paris to Forges, which is 28 leagues distant. (Letter to the President Hénault, 2nd July 1742.)

The incident which forms the plot of the celebrated drama *The Lyons Mail* (when Lesurques was mistaken for Dubosc and sentenced to death) took place on 28th April 1796, at Lieusaint, not far from Paris.

[1] "Those great roads which run over all the country, on which the stranger, travelling at his ease, remembers the name of the Trudaines, blessing their handiwork."

Owing to its frequent floods the Rhine was always a menace and even an actual danger to the communes on its banks, and on occasion it had even inundated the streets of Strasbourg. "To the Intendants of Alsace, in the eighteenth century, belongs the honour of beginning the great struggle with the river, which continues to this day. It was they who, in order to put an end to its repeated incursions, undertook, as one of them wrote in 1750,[1] to construct, not only barriers of fascines, but also dikes, and even to dam whole tributaries of the river."

Thanks to these engineers, who were also architects, and to the encouragement of the Intendants, the towns began to cleanse and even adorn themselves; but progress was slow, for, as we have seen, the Intendant's labours were often brought to a standstill by the inertia and even ill-will of the inhabitants. We can see how difficult but how necessary the work of sanitation was, from this passage in Arthur Young: "Clermont is built and paved with lava. Much of it forms one of the worst built, dirtiest, and most stinking places I have met with. There are many streets that can for blackness, dirt, and ill-scents only be represented by narrow channels cut in a night dunghill. The contention of nauseous savours with which the air is impregnated when brisk mountain gales do not ventilate these excrementitious lanes, made me envy the nerves of the good people, who, for what I know, may be happy in them." [2] This dirt and the consequent infection caused, or aggravated, the epidemics which so frequently and disastrously visited the towns in the eighteenth century, as witness this petition which, in 1783, the Town Council of Saint-Quentin sent to the Council of State: "The insanitary condition of our streets is such that the air is poisoned thereby, and this is the chief cause of the sickness which prevails here. The petitioners have done their utmost to remedy the evil, but they have met unexpected difficulties on the part of their fellow-citizens, and are, as yet, still unable to overcome them." Naturally cemeteries

[1] Rod. Reuss, *L'Alsace* . . ., i. 12.   [2] Young, i. 280.

JEAN CHARLES PHILIBERT TRUDAINE
(INTENDANT OF AUVERGNE)
From an engraving by Louis Carmontelle

abounded within the towns, every parish, every convent, every hospital having its own, and these were often very badly situated. In 1784 the Mayor of Josselin in Brittany states that "the cemeteries of Notre-Dame and Saint-Martin are badly situated, the one being in the centre of the town, close to the manorial bakehouse, and the worms from the corpses fall into a well sunk by a wall of the cemetery"; and one of the most terrible epidemics of the century was the outbreak of plague at Marseilles, which is so harrowingly described by most of the chroniclers of this period.

In order to combat these appalling scourges, the first step was to introduce some sanitation in the towns, and this was one of the beneficent labours of the Intendants, and it is rightly said, that in this century, the towns first take a place in French civilisation. Under Louis XIV., Versailles absorbed everything, and was, as Dupaty expressed it, "the mountain" which prevented the King seeing his provincial towns; and it would not be too much to say that, in the eighteenth century, the King of France had no conception of France, for Louis XV. only saw those provinces he passed through, when, in time of war, he joined his armies in the field; and Louis XVI. never stirred from Versailles at all. If then, in the reign of Louis XV., the towns grew in wealth and beauty, it was entirely due to the enlightened rule of Intendants like Tourny in Guyenne, who entirely transformed the city of Bordeaux. In many towns of Burgundy the ancient ramparts, with their towers and bastions, became avenues planted with lime and chestnut trees. Streets were enlarged and houses adorned with balconies of wrought-iron. Numerous stately mansions were erected, and, in the country, fine castles surrounded by parks and gardens took the place of the remaining fortresses of olden days. The lighting was also improved in most towns. No longer did the citizens go abroad at night with lanterns, and the nobles with torches borne by their footmen. Lanterns were hung in the streets, the cemeteries removed outside the towns. Streets were widened and paved, so that people could now dance in comfort, whether it be the *bourrée* in Auvergne, the *branle* in Poitou, or the *farandole* in Provence.

Let us next make ourselves acquainted with the inhabitants of these streets and houses, and, as far as we can, see the life they lived. In a large city the magistrates were the most important personages. The provincial nobility, crippled with debts, and utterly impoverished, had sold their estates, and it was the lawyers who bought them in nearly every case. They now dwelt in their castles, where they would spend their vacations, and when they returned to town for the Law Terms, they lived in fine mansions and drove in splendid carriages. The First President, the Intendant, and the Chief Constable were the three chief personages in the town, and it was in the drawing-rooms of the three ladies, their respective wives, that local society was wont to assemble, while in the smaller towns it was an honour to be invited to the parties of the Bailiff's or the Sheriff's lady. In towns boasting a Parliament, such as Toulouse, the beginning of the legal year, which took place in winter on the morrow of St. Martin's Day, was always celebrated. At dawn the great bell of the Palais or Law Courts rang a peal: the magistrates in their red robes heard a Red Mass (of the Holy Ghost), also called the "Mass of Bows," owing to the deep bow which each magistrate made as he passed the altar. Pascal said of these gentlemen: "See their red robes, their ermines in which they wrap themselves like furry cats, the palaces where they sit in judgment, the *fleurs-de-lis*, and mark how essential all this pomp is to them!" At solemn sessions, called 'Sessions of the Red Robe,' the First President and his colleagues appeared wearing their gold-fringed caps, their ermined capes, and their mantles lined with miniver.

Throughout France the members of the Parliaments had developed a great *esprit de corps*. "At the end of the eighteenth century it was notorious that no one could dream of obtaining a post in the Courts with the hope of becoming counsellor in a Parliament without having first obtained the corporation's assent. The Parliaments, by secret ordinances which, however, were never inscribed in the Minutes but were, nevertheless, in force and acted upon, decreed that henceforth they would admit no counsellor who was not of noble birth or the son of a counsellor. In the seventeenth century the Parliament of Provence decreed that the sons and grandsons of farmers should be excluded for ever.

On the other hand, however, many magistrates were exceedingly generous, and often assisted the poorer classes, as in 1737 and 1739, which were very hard years in Normandy, and when famine, bringing other evils with it, was widespread; then we see the presidents and counsellors of the Parliament joining with the clergy in opening funds for the poor, and subscribing largely themselves. The First President, Pontcarré, was well known for his generosity, and d'Aguesseau writes him the following delightful letter: "The King has been informed of the very effective zeal and great wisdom with which the Parliament of Rouen has provided for the sustenance of the poor of that great city during the evil times which have so sorely tried it. You have not been content merely to take the necessary steps to cope with such great evils, but the Parliament has gone further in showing an example which has been followed by all the corporations of the said town. If your modesty has withheld from me much of the good work done on this occasion, I can, however, assure you that I am not ignorant of it. I cannot tell you, as well as the whole Parliament, how deeply the King is pleased with their conduct, and, above all, with yours. I send you this testimonial with the very greatest pleasure."[1]

Next in this social hierarchy come the *bourgeoisie*, whom, as we have seen, it is so difficult to define. Loyseau says that "the term *bourgeois* applies only to the inhabitants of a town," but it does "not include all the inhabitants of the town, for nobles living in towns do not call themselves *bourgeois*. The common people of the lower classes also have not the right to arrogate this term to themselves, nor can they aspire to civic honours or to a voice in the Assemblies, for these are the distinctive privileges of the *bour*-

---

[1] Floquet, vi. 408.

geoisie." The citizens who, excluding the nobility and the lower classes, form this *bourgeoisie* consist, in the first place, of merchants, though, later, procurators and barristers infused a legal leaven. But it was rare to remain in the *bourgeoisie* after three generations, for when one of them grew rich he would buy some office for his son, having, as ever, a passion for office. In 1750, Tocqueville counted 109 persons in a small provincial town, all occupied in dispensing justice, while no less than 126 were busy carrying out the sentences of the former.[1]

Here is a glimpse of the interior of a rich *bourgeois* house, that of Adrien Delahante, who, at Crespy in Valois, had accumulated the offices of notary, registrar, etc. etc. "His house consisted of a ground floor, first floor, and attic. On the ground floor was the kitchen, called the *salle basse* (one remembers the *salle basse* in 'Tartuffe'), the study, and a small closet or workroom at the end of a small yard. The first floor consisted of *la chambre haute*, a passage with a guest-room, and three servants' rooms at the end. In the yard were a shed, a bakehouse, a stable, a chicken-run, and a pigeon-house, though in reality the house really consisted of two rooms, the *salle basse*, and the *chambre haute*. The former was used for ordinary everyday life, the latter for special occasions and the entertainment of distinguished visitors." [2] It is, therefore, as a mark of respect that Boileau's host in *Le Repas ridicule* entertains him in the *chambre haute*.

"There is one thing which no one has yet seen on this earth, and, in all probability, never will see, and that is a small town which is not split up into cliques, and where the ever-smouldering quarrel over precedence may not be stirred into flame at any moment, even in church, by the collection, the incensing, the consecrated bread, processions or funerals, and where gossip, lies, and slander are unknown, and the Bailiffs, the President, the Sheriffs, and the Counsellors may be seen chatting together amicably." [3] This passage of La Bruyère's would be borne out in almost

---

[1] *Ancien régime*, p. 164. [2] Delahante, i. 78.
[3] La Bruyère, *De la société et de la conversation.*

every detail if we had the courage to study the list of all the trifling and paltry quarrels which, all the year round, set the various corporations at loggerheads and agitated the entire town; but we might try to give ourselves some idea of this unceasing strife. The Parliaments, say, fell foul of the Intendant, whom, as in Languedoc, they would persist in calling by the opprobrious title of a "retired commissioner." Moreover, being very jealous of the respect due to them, the members of the Parliaments were often at odds with the barristers, who were themselves extremely touchy, and who, if they thought themselves hurt, would refuse to plead in the Courts, and here was enough material for a pretty feud. The following anecdote gives us some idea of the disdain, amounting to horror, which the nobility felt for the *bourgeoisie*: "When the first insurrection broke out in Paris, the Bishop of Autun, a deputy to the States-General, heard that Mme de Brionne was on the point of flight. He went to her immediately and asked: 'Why this sudden resolution, madame?' to which she replied: 'I do not wish to be a witness, still less a victim, of scenes which would terrify me.' 'But surely,' persisted the Bishop, 'you need not leave France entirely?' 'Well, where do you suggest I should go?' 'I don't suggest you should stay in Paris, as you are frightened, nor that you should retire to one of your country places, but would advise you to go and spend a short time in some small provincial town where you will be unknown. Live there quietly and without ostentation, and no one will discover you.' Cried Mme de Brionne: 'Really, M. de Périgord— to a small provincial town! I will play the peasant as long as you wish, but a *bourgeoise*—NEVER!' There spoke a Rohan, the widow of a prince of the house of Lorraine."[1]

The *bourgeois*, for his part, disliked the country squire quite as cordially; but what irritated his class against the nobility more than all else, was not so much the traditional claims put forward by the real "gentleman," but the arrogance displayed by the new nobility—

[1] Beugnot, i. 134.

"these gentlemen of the second-class"—as Mme de Staël calls them—"whose patents were made out overnight, and possibly, even, by the venal connivance of the King's secretaries. The nation would willingly have submitted to the predominance of the old historic families, and I do not exaggerate when I say that there are only two hundred such in France. But the hundred thousand nobles and the hundred thousand clergy who all wished to enjoy the same privileges as a Montmorency, a Grammont, or a Crillon, caused general rebellion; for the merchants, the men of letters, the small landed proprietors, and even the capitalists, could not understand wherein lay the superiority of a nobility which had acquired it by many bows and scrapes and much money, and which, after a mere twenty-five years, carried with it a seat in the chamber of nobles, not to mention privileges to which even the most honourable members of the Third Estate could not aspire." After recalling how in England the House of Lords is not closed to men who have rendered distinguished service whether in commerce or the Law, and that the representative character of this House is a witness to the benefit which the commonwealth derives from their admission, Mme de Staël continues: "But what advantage did the French derive from these Vicomtes de la Garonne and these Marquises de la Loire, who not only avoided paying their share of the State's taxes, but whom the King himself did not receive at Court because proofs extending over four centuries would have to have been adduced before they could be admitted there, and they had only been nobles these twenty-five years? The conceit of this class could only be exercised among its inferiors, and these were twenty-four million people." [1]

The *bourgeoisie* passed on, with interest, the disdain which the nobles showed them, to the *menu peuple*, the lower classes. The working class was, as far as they were concerned, non-existent, though the *bourgeois*, like Arnolphe, liked to be addressed in style as Monsieur de

[1] Mme de Staël, *Considérations sur la Revolution française*, Part I., ch. xiv.

la Souche. Chrysalde's tirade against the peasant called Gros-Pierre, in the first act of *L'Ecole des femmes*, is well known:

> "Qui n'ayant pour tout bien qu'un seul quartier de terre,
> Y fit tout à l'entour faire un fossé bourbeux,
> Et de Monsieur de l'Isle en prit le nom pompeux." [1]

Such Gros-Pierres swarmed in the eighteenth century, when so many *bourgeois* became landed proprietors, and it should be remembered that the *de*, which to-day is called "the particle of nobility," was in those days by no means a sign of the aristocracy, though a rich *bourgeois* who "lived nobly"—that is, one who did not practise any trade or profession—was only too glad to adopt it. In contracts, the title of *noble homme* was given to rich *bourgeois*, while the lesser *bourgeois* or merchant had to be content with that of *honorable homme*.

Cournot, the philosopher, who was born at Dôle, tells, in the reminiscences of his childhood, how strict in county society was the demarcation between the various ranks: "Nothing was more marked than the hierarchy of rank in *bourgeois* society. The wife of the procurator or notary was called 'Mademoiselle,' the wife of the Councillor was 'Madame,' without any opposition, and often the wife of the barrister, or *gradué*, as he was also called, received the same title. The same shades differentiated the doctor from the surgeon and from the apothecary. The one was admitted to *bourgeois* circles, the other only knocked at the door. Saint-Simon has told us how minutely the different ranks were distinguished among the nobility, but what will be soon forgotten is that the middle or *bourgeois* class, so scornful of the great, sifted itself no less carefully, and with an even greater minuteness, which to us seems quite as ridiculous, considering the meanness of the individuals and the vulgarity of the details." [2]

---

[1] "Whose sole possession being a few yards of land, he surrounded them with a muddy ditch, and thus adopted the high-sounding name of Monsieur de l'Isle."

[2] Cournot, *Souvenirs*, p. 12.

To sum up, we might say that except at the two extremes, such as the princes who had no class above them, and the beggars who had no one below them, every class in society revenged itself on the class below for the scorn shown to it by the class above, thus presenting a very pretty cascade of rancour and snobbery running down the whole social scale.

But after he was ennobled by the acquisition of some office or other, then the *bourgeois* held his head very high: "The new noble," says Aurelly in Beaumarchais' *Les Deux amis* (1770), "is so full of his dignity that he feels he is compromising it if he bows to a commoner." "Yes," replies Mèlac; "the narrower the gulf between men, the more careful are they to expatiate upon it."

The lawyers looked askance at the merchants, especially if they were merely traders. Nobles engaged only in wholesale trade, though it was very difficult to say where one ended and the other began. A royal decree tried to fix the limits in 1701: "It is Our Will and Pleasure that Our nobles may freely trade wholesale, both within and without Our Realm, and that this shall not be held to be derogatory to their nobility. Such persons shall be reputed, and held to be, wholesale merchants and traders who trade in warehouses, selling their merchandise in bales, cases, or whole pieces, and do not sell in open shops, and have no display or signs in their houses or at their gates."

Luynes gives an amusing example of this ridiculous attitude toward trade. M. Le Leu, who had the honour to be King's Procurator for Forests and Domains, wished to marry his daughter to M. Marsolier, a rich silk merchant, but made it a condition that Mme Marsolier should never enter her husband's shop. "She even avoided passing through the Rue Saint-Honoré, though that did not stop people calling her the Duchess de Velours (velvet)." [1] After all, her father's position was merely that of Procurator, and, as Voltaire says, "we may pardon pride in a Cicero, a Cæsar, or a Scipio, but when, in the depths of some provincial town, a man who may have bought some petty

[1] Luynes, xi. 383.

office takes it into his head to become haughty, he merely becomes a laughing-stock." [1] The *bourgeoisie* looked coldly on the Religious Orders, not from reasons of vanity, but for others affecting their purse, since these Orders escaped the duty of *l'ustensile* (the billeting of soldiers), which fell upon the middle classes.

Voltaire justly ridicules the contempt which the nobility always displayed towards trade and traders, in the following passage: "Any one who wishes may be a Marquis in France, and a man arriving in Paris from the country, who has money to spend and a name ending in *ac* or *ille*, is entitled to say: 'A man like myself, a man of my standing,' and to treat a merchant with supreme contempt. The latter hears his profession ridiculed so often that he would be a fool to be ashamed at it; but I really do not know which is the most useful citizen in a State—a well-powdered gentleman who knows exactly at what hour the King rises or retires, and gives himself great airs when playing the flunkey in a minister's anteroom, or a merchant who, from his office, gives orders to Surat or Cairo, enriches his country, and contributes to the happiness of the world." [2]

In 1751, Duclos, who so faithfully describes the habits and customs of his day, pays homage to the *commerçants*, which is in itself a sign of the times. "They are admirable men and necessary to the State, inasmuch as they do not acquire riches for themselves save by creating prosperity and stimulating honourable industries: their wealth is the reward of the services they render. They are not met with in society as frequently as financiers, because they are occupied by their business, which does not allow them to waste time—of which they know the value—in frivolous amusements, a taste for which goes hand in hand with indolence. All professional prejudices are not equally false in value, and the estimation in which merchants hold their trade is a just one. They undertake no enterprise and derive no benefit which the public does not share with them, and

[1] Voltaire, *Dictionnaire philosophique*, "Orgueil."
[2] *Lettres philosophique*, Lettre x.

there is every reason why they should take a pride in their profession. The merchants are the chief agents of national prosperity." [1]

Finally, we must glance at the artisan or labouring class, whose lot in most provinces was a hard one. In Brittany, for example, many were literally dying of starvation, and in 1777, de Loudéac, the Procurator of Customs, wrote: "Some of these wretches who are cotton-spinners are so destitute that they have nothing with which to clothe themselves. There actually are families who, in order to enable others to attend Mass on Sundays and feast days in their turn, are obliged to strip themselves, in order to cover their neighbour's nakedness, and then remain in their hovels huddled under straw." When one of those frequent epidemics swept the province, little wonder that the parish was decimated.

The country folk were conservative by nature. "The people of Normandy are accustomed to revere their customs as they do the Gospel, and a change of religion could be introduced in Normandy with greater ease than a change in the legal code." [2] In some cities the night watchman still walked the streets, ringing his bell at midnight, and at one o'clock crying: "Good people asleep, wake; remember your own last day and pray for the dead."

The provinces were bound to be conservative owing to their distance from the capital, the difficulties of communication, and the rarity or, rather, complete absence of facilities for travel. "It would be curious to compare the activity which reigns in intellectual as well as in business circles to-day with the torpor and inertia which I saw in days gone by. The only paper was the *Gazette de France*, which appeared twice a week, and was the only intellectual stimulus we had; and as for business, one solitary coach a week linked the provincial towns with Paris, and that was not always full. I can remember when a slightly better rag, called the *Courrier d'Avignon*, made its first

---

[1] Duclos, *Considérations*, ix.
[2] D'Aguesseau, *Lettres inédites*, ii. 225.

appearance in our province, and we felt as if we had come into a fortune."[1] Arthur Young, in his "Diary," often refers to this stupor in which the country districts were sunk. He notes, on arriving at Château Thierry on 14th July 1789: At "a period so interesting to France, and indeed to all Europe, I wished to see a newspaper. I asked for a coffee-house—not one in the town! Here are two parishes and some thousands of inhabitants, and not a newspaper to be seen by a traveller, even in a moment when all ought to be anxiety. What stupidity, poverty, and want of circulation! I have been to-day on one of their greatest roads within thirty miles of Paris, yet I have not seen one diligence. . . . At Moulins there was a coffee-house where I found near twenty tables set for company, but as to a newspaper, I might as well have demanded an elephant." And this in August 1789, at the moment when the fate of the King and of France was trembling in the balance!

With regard to the amusements of these provincials, the country towns were the haunts of strolling players and quacks, and mummers were allowed by the municipal authorities to set up their theatres in the open, provided they gave one performance for the benefit of the local poor. They performed opera as well as tragedies and comedies. But tight-rope walkers and vagrant musicians were more common, especially showmen of marionettes, who willingly "performed Ovid's Metamorphoses with the aid of divers engines." Nor must the vendors of elixirs be forgotten, who sold remedies efficacious for every ill, as, for instance, "the Swiss tonic, composed of plants which fortify the stomach and aid the digestion." The public was permitted to indulge in such amusements as would "tend to the recreation of honest people," such as bowls and tennis; while, on the other hand, all games of chance such as faro, trente et quarante, and others were usually prohibited, and players of them were liable to be arrested by the watch. But these games were played, by permission, in the *académies* or gaming-houses.

[1] Montlosier, *Mémoires*, i. 161.

Fairs, however, were the great recreation of the provincials, each town having its own, full of amusement and numerous entertainments. The most famous of them was the Fair of Beaucaire, which, though shorn of much of its ancient splendour, was still much frequented. This is Frénilly's description of what he saw there: "All its tiny streets were roofed by large sheets hanging from the third stories of the houses, which gave the town the appearance of being shaded by a huge parasol. In the streets below, two rows of shops, which were lit up for part of the night, offered for sale merchandise from all the quarters of the globe. Here a Persian could buy Wedgwood cups, and an Englishman wine from Shiraz. Between the town and the Rhone stretched an enormous common, known as the Champ des Aulx, or Field of Garlic, because, during the Fair, the supplies of this bulb, which were to feed the whole of Southern France, were stacked here. A little farther south, on the opposite bank of the Rhone, lay Tarascon with its wooden bridge and famous Tarasque, the procession taking place during the Fair of Beaucaire." [1] In this connection we should note the procession of King René at Aix, which was in some respects unique. Marmontel, who had been invited to be present by the Duke de Villars, Governor of the Province, was deprived of seeing this entertainment owing to bad weather. But he "saw some samples, such as a drunken street-porter representing the Queen of Sheba, another King Solomon, and three others the Three Magi, all covered with mud up to their ears. I could not help admiring the serious demeanour of the Provençals at this spectacle, and took care to imitate it, though I was often hard put to it not to laugh. I noticed, among other things, one of these personages carrying a white rag at the end of a pole, while three other rascals followed him and simulated drunken antics every time the first man lowered his pole. I asked the meaning of this mystery, and the gentleman I was talking to replied: 'Do you not see that they are the Three Wise Men, who are being led by the Star, and who

[1] Frénilly, *Souvenirs*, p. 95.

go astray every time the Star disappears from their view?' I did not even smile. Nothing is a greater check to laughter than the fear of being stoned." [1]

But we must turn to the pages of Crommelin, superintendent of the bonded tobacco warehouse at Autun, for a description of the higher provincial society in the eighteenth century.

"Our one occupation was to divert ourselves, our one care to vary our amusements. Thus every day saw a succession of dinner-parties, suppers, concerts, balls, card-parties, excursions, and entertainments of all kinds. In the mornings, after coffee or chocolate, every one attended to his business, clerks wending their way to their offices, lawyers to the Court, while the gentlemen of leisure congregated in the Place du Champ. When the dinner-hour approached, one might be dining either with the Governor, who entertained often and well at his mansion in the Rue de l'Arquebuse, or with M. d'Autun, whose apartments were magnificent, the plate splendid, and the table of the best, or else at the Donjon with the Collegiate Chapter, or with the Jesuits, who gave their guests keepsakes, or with the Friars, if it was their feast day; in fact, one dined at one place or another, with or without special reason, but in every case with the sole idea of amusing oneself and others. The afternoon was spent in excursions to the Marble Gate, the Temple of Janus, or to the Parpas road, and at this hour the public recitations took place at the College, or else some musical or dramatic performance might be going on. The ladies went out in coaches, escorted by gentlemen on horseback, and on their return from this outing they would pay a few calls, indulge in archery, or play a few sets of tennis. Then came supper, and one might be asked to stay and spend the evening at some comedy, and on the morrow there might be a newly arrived dromedary to look at, or else the puppet shows, a pantomime, animated tableaux, tight-rope walkers, or some display of optical illusions. If none of these were available, one walked a little on the Terrace, or remained at home. The

---

[1] Marmontel, *Mémoires*, p. 219.

game of reversi was very popular, or we might play at piquet even, or brelan, nain jaune, or lansquenet "[1]

In those days of long ago parents educated their children very strictly, nor were they less respected, nor, I may add, less loved, for we have since learned from bitter experience that spoiled children turn out far from grateful—a sad truth which Balzac illustrated in his masterpiece, *Le Père Goriot*. But in the eighteenth century if a child was said "to fear its parents," it meant the child loved them. A contemporary writer tells us that "the word *craindre*, to fear, means *aimer*, to love, and is thus used in this country when speaking of God or parents." The country was the Tonnerrois, and the writer Rétif de la Bretonne, who, in addition to his licentious novels, wrote a serious and truthful book in 1779, entitled *La vie de mon pere*. This father was called Edmond, and his again was named Pierre, who must have been a terrible parent, as the following anecdote shows. The scene was at Nitry, near Tonnerre, in a labourer's cottage. "In this country it was the custom, as it still is, to despoil any girls who were found to be attractive, and the young lads would seize all they could, such as their bouquets, their rings, and their needlecases. One Sunday after the High Mass, Edmond, on coming out of church, saw a rival snatching Catherine's bouquet, and was seized with jealousy. He approached this charming girl, and, offering her his own buttonhole, said: 'Here are roses which will suit you more than they do me.' 'Let us at least share them,' said she, and as it was composed of roses red and white, she kept the white ones. Hardly had Edmond shyly withdrawn, when a new rival ventured to seize the flowers he had just given her, but Catherine, who had parted with the first without demur, struggled to keep possession of the second bouquet. 'I suppose it is because Edmond gave it you,' said the disappointed boy; but his words were overheard by the terrible Pierre, Edmond's father, who was surprised that his son, who was still so young, dared to lift his eyes to a girl without his permission. He said nothing at dinner, but carefully made inquiry, and

[1] Crommelin, *Mémoires de la Société éduenne*, New Series, vol. vi.

a gossip informed him that since Edmond's return from Noyers he had spoken three times to Catherine Gautherin. So on the next day, as they were going ploughing, and Edmond, in his shirt, was already mounted on Bressan, his father came up and said: 'Give me your whip.' 'Here it is, father,' said the boy, handing it over, and three lashes, applied with all the force of the strongest man of his day, tore the shirt in three places and soaked it in blood. Edmond only moaned, and his father gave him back his whip with the words, 'Remember it.' He then went in without another word. But the father regretted his severity. As Edmond was busy digging in the garden that evening, he saw his father leaning against a tree, one hand to his forehead and wiping away tears with the other. He had never seen his father cry before, and was amazed. The world must be coming to an end if his father wept! His father approached him and, taking his spade, said: 'That is enough work for to-day, my son. Go and rest; I will finish this job.' Never before had his father uttered the words 'my son.' "[1] Excessive and even brutal severity did not by any means exclude affection.

Even children of good family were educated with considerable strictness, and Talleyrand describes his early upbringing as follows: "My grandmother was lady-in-waiting to the Queen, and had five children. Their early education, as was the case with all who were closely connected with the Court, had been much neglected, or was at any rate very rudimentary, and latterly only consisted in teaching them what were called 'the customs of polite society.' In fact, too much care for such matters would have been regarded as pedantic, though excessive tenderness would have been looked upon as something new, and therefore ridiculous. At this time (the middle of the eighteenth century) children were the heirs of the family name and arms, and enough provision was thought to have been made for them by preparing them for preferment in rank or honours, in arranging their marriages and improving their chances in life. It was not fashionable for

[1] Rétif de la Bretonne, *La vie de mon père*, Part I., Book I.

parents to show affection for their children, and it certainly was not the custom when I was young. I was left several years in a faubourg of Paris, and was still living there at the age of four, when the woman with whom I had been boarded out let me fall off a cupboard, and I dislocated my foot. She did not report it for several months, and I have been a cripple ever since. This accident influenced all my life, as it convinced my parents that I could not become a soldier, at least without great disadvantage to any career in that profession, and so induced them to look for another. This course seemed to them to be the best suited for furthering the family fortunes. For in great houses it was 'The Family' which was loved far more than individual members, especially the younger ones, whom nobody as yet knew." [1]

Let us, however, return with Marmontel to the *bourgeois* of the province, or rather to the smaller *bourgeoisie*. We have read in some of the extracts from his *Mémoires* how happily, and merrily even, people could live, at little cost, in the depths of the provinces in this century, so we will allow him to describe that life still more in detail. His home was at Bort, a small town of the Limousin, which is to-day the country town of the Corrèze, and thither his thoughts would fly when, in old age, he wrote his *Mémoires*, seeing himself again as a child on the little farm of Saint-Thomas on the banks of the Dordogne, "where I used to read my Vergil in the shade of the flowering trees, among the beehives. Here I was taught to read in a Convent, where the Religious were friends of my mother, and from thence went on to a school kept by a priest who devoted himself from inclination, and without any fee, to the instruction of children. The Abbé Vaissière, for that was his name, having fulfilled his duties in church, devoted all the rest of his time to reading and to our lessons. He would walk a little in fine weather or, for exercise, play a game of pall-mall, but these were his only amusements.

"I was the eldest of a large number of children, and my father, although he was rather strict, was the best of

[1] Talleyrand, *Mémoires*, i. 7.

parents, hiding his affection under a rough and severe exterior, and he loved and venerated my mother. His only reproach to her was her weakness for me; but it had some excuse, for I was the only one of her children whom she had nursed herself. Her mother did not love me less, and I can still see the little old lady with her delightful ways, her sweet and merry laughter, who, as housekeeper, presided over the household and afforded all of us an example of true filial tenderness; for her mother and mother-in-law were still alive, and she looked after them with the greatest care. I am going back rather far in talking of these great-grandparents, but I remember they were still alive at the age of eighty, drinking their little glass of wine by the hearth, and remembering the good old days, of which they told us many a wonderful story.

"There were also my grandmother's three sisters, and my mother's sister—that aunt who is still with me—and my father found himself alone among all these women, with a whole swarm of children around him, and with but little wealth. But we managed all the same. Good order, economy, work, a little business, but above all frugality, helped us to live in comfort. Our little garden provided nearly all the vegetables required, while our orchard gave us fruit in plenty, and our quinces and apples and pears, together with our honey-cakes made with the honey of our own bees, provided the most sumptuous repasts in winter, both for us children and for the old ladies. The flock of Saint-Thomas' fold dressed itself in its own wool, and this applied to children and women alike, my aunts spinning it, as they also did the hemp which provided our linen. When, of an evening, by the light of a lamp fed with oil from our own nut trees, the youth of the neighbourhood used to gather round and help us comb out the beautiful hemp, it was a delightful picture indeed." [1]

The most striking characteristics of provincial life were, therefore, hard work and prosperity among the upper *bourgeoisie*, and content and comfort among the lesser, while in almost every case we find, during this

[1] Marmontel, *Mémoires*, i.

eighteenth century, integrity and family affection, and all those other virtues which flourish around the domestic hearth, but which are all too often described as if they had been wholly and generally corrupted. In short, the great social event of France during this century was the rise of the *bourgeoisie*, and nothing was more justified than Sieyès' answer, on the very eve of the Revolution, to the question as to what the Third Estate was—"Everything"; and Bouillé declares that "the Third Estate had gathered all the respect, the wealth, and the real power which the clergy and nobility had lost. France had founded colonies in America, had established maritime trade, and created industries. The immense riches which had flowed into the country had fallen only into the hands of the middle classes, since the prejudices of the nobles excluded them from all trading, and prevented them from engaging in any of the mechanical or liberal arts. The towns had grown enormously; some, like Lyons, Nantes, Bordeaux, and Marseilles, had equalled in importance and outstripped in wealth the capitals of many neighbouring states. Nearly all small towns had become more or less commercial, and were inhabited by small *bourgeois*, who were richer and more industrious than the nobility. These had received an education which was more essential to them than to the gentry, of whom many obtained the highest posts in the State without any merit or ability on their part, while the majority were destined to fritter away their existence in the lower commissioned ranks of the Army. In Paris, no less than in the big cities, the *bourgeoisie* was far superior in wealth, ability, and personal merit." [1]

Bouillé has mentioned Nantes, and this town is also described by Buffon, who visited it in 1738, in a letter to his friend, the President de Ruffez: "The inhabitants are all merchants, who are looked down upon in our country, but I am bound to confess that I find their way of living eminently sensible. They do not make any fuss about preferring a seat in a stage-coach at one pistole a head to a coach and six, and would rather enjoy the plenty of a

[1] Bouillé, *Mémoires*, ch. iii.

bourgeois than the poverty of a noble. Everything here shows signs of wealth produced by trade. . . . Pride and beggary go hand in hand, true offspring of that scorn with which trading is regarded."

Some lines of Lavergne may well conclude this chapter, since they sum up admirably the progress which the *bourgeoisie* had made and the high place they had won for themselves in French eighteenth-century society. "In order to have some idea of the true state of society (this was, of course, before the Revolution), we must realise that the preponderant class was not the nobility nor the clergy, but one more rich and enlightened than either, namely, the Third Estate, which included the lawyers, the writers, the landed proprietors, the municipal officials of the towns, the judges of the County Courts, and all the wealthy merchants. The events of 1789 did not establish its power, they merely revealed it. But it was this class which, just because it was the most influential and the most numerous, was later to provide most of the victims of the Revolution." [1]

We must add, in conclusion, that this influence was a right and proper one. A foreigner, Green, writes in his *History of the English People*: "The French *bourgeoisie* [in the eighteenth century] was the most alert and most intelligent of all the middle classes in Europe."

[1] Lavergne, *Assemblées provinciales*, p. xiii.

CHAPTER II

THE HIGHER CLERGY

In the eighteenth century the Episcopate became, to a large extent, a preserve of the nobles; so much so, indeed, that in 1789 the hundred and thirty Bishops of France only included one commoner in their ranks. Moreover, just as among the upper middle-class there were parliamentary or legal families, so also it was possible to point to episcopal families like the Rohans, La Rochefoucaulds, and Choiseuls among the nobility, and these Gentlemen-Bishops acquired both honours and wealth. As regards the former, certain sees such as Rheims and Beauvais carried with them a peerage of France; others the Presidency of the Provincial Estates; the Archbishop of Narbonne, for instance, presiding over the Estates of Languedoc, and the Archbishop of Aix over the General Assembly of the local communities, since the Estates of Provence had been suspended by Richelieu in 1639. Their wealth, although this was often exaggerated, was very considerable, and was calculated by the Abbé Expilly to produce an annual income of 170 millions. The main sources from which these eighteenth-century Archbishops and Bishops drew their income were as follows: In the first place, they enjoyed *la mense épiscopale* or diocesan revenues, derived from landed property and feudal rights, amounting in the see of Strasbourg alone to 400,000 livres. Next came the Abbeys which had been granted to them, as, for instance, in the case of de Boisjelin, Archbishop of Aix, who held the Abbey of Saint-Gilles, which was worth 14,000 livres; Saint-Maixent, 14,000 livres; and Chaalis, 50,000 livres; but it must be remembered that these revenues were often burdened with annuities which were wrested from the King's bounty—annuities which cost the King nothing, and which were multiplied in the course of the century. Some sees were far from rich (that of Digne being only worth 7000 livres), and these were the poor or "degraded" bishoprics. All this is well known, but here are a few facts which are, perhaps, of some interest to an historian of social manners and customs.

If we read the Royal Almanack for 1789 we may well be amazed at the age of the Bishops, for the majority were appointed between the ages of thirty and forty; in fact, it had become the custom not to nominate Bishops over forty years of age. Once appointed, they did not remain long, certainly not long enough, in the same see, especially if it was one of the "stopgap bishoprics," though there are notable exceptions. Belsunce, for instance, refused to quit Marseilles for Bordeaux, and Fleury congratulated him in the King's name, "for the great example of disinterestedness he had given," and the people of Marseilles manifested their joy at retaining their Bishop, while the civic authorities came in state to thank him.

In this century the Church was the great refuge for younger sons or such as were unsuccessful elsewhere. *Une vocation de cadet*, or younger son's vocation, often only implied a sickly body or an infirm mind. The Abbé de Clérembault, son of the Maréchal, who enjoyed the revenues of four abbeys, was a "very ugly hunchback,"[1] while another, the Abbé de Vaudrun, son of the Lieutenant-General killed at Altenheim, "was a dwarf, with all a dwarf's ugliness and enormous head, and one of his shrivelled little legs was a foot shorter than the other." Yet he took Orders, and nearly became a bishop! In reading these lines of Saint-Simon one is reminded of Bourdaloue's fine sermon, in which he animadverts on the duties of parents in relation to the vocations of their sons: "It may be that the eldest son has not been favoured by nature at his birth, or, perhaps, may lack some of those qualities which are necessary for upholding the honour of his house,

[1] Saint-Simon, x. 246.

and so, without a thought of the intentions which God may have with regard to him, people endeavour, as it were, to humble the boy and degrade him to the status of a younger son, preferring the latter before him, and, in order to extort his consent, they resort to every artifice and violence, and mingle caresses with threats." Just as in the days of Bourdaloue, in the eighteenth century everything was sacrificed to the honour and "glory" of the family. As Chateaubriand said later: "My father was completely swayed by one passion, and one only, and that was his name and position," but this passion, entailing so many compulsory or lukewarm vocations, was a great evil for the Church, and the story of the Abbé de Mailly was a striking example. His mother, the Countess de Mailly, "known as 'the Snipe,' owing to her long nose, had literally hounded him into Orders, and then left him to starve for years at Saint-Victor. He had been sent there, while still a boy, with another brother, who was more pious and tractable, who donned the habit, became Prior, and finally Bishop of Lavaur. The Abbé de Mailly had even less inclination to become a monk than he had to be a priest, but his mother forced him even by torture until he at length yielded. We may imagine what sort of a priest he made, and what learning he imbibed. But he was a good man, and made a virtue of necessity. He received a small abbey, a post as almoner to the King, and then another abbey even more paltry. His ambition was boundless, and he was very up to date and exceedingly careful not to raise any obstacle, but rather to smooth his path in every direction. He led a very boring existence for many years in this degraded position, envying, as he often told me, even the soldiers on guard, but he dreamed of a Cardinal's hat, and paid assiduous court at Saint-Germains in order to pave his way to a nomination. At last he was appointed Archbishop of Arles,"[1] and died a Cardinal in 1721.

A great eighteenth-century Bishop, Massillon, expressed his indignation with parents "who force their children into the Church merely in the family interest." He

[1] Saint-Simon, iv. 298.

says: "Has nature made the heart of a younger son more pure or more inclined to fulfil those sacred and sublime duties of the priesthood than those of his brothers? ... And so, my brethren, in order not to divide your goods, you sacrifice your children and the fruit of your loins;" and he goes on to denounce those who only aspire to the service of the altar for the sake of honours and wealth. "A sacred calling which we did not expect, strips us in an instant of all worldly dross and bears one into the holy place, when, lo! the death of an elder brother changes all our views, hurls us back into the world we have left, and our vocation for the altar dwindles as new earthly hopes spring up in our hearts. Barbarous and inhuman parents count it as nothing to sacrifice all their other sons and thrust them into the abyss in order to raise one of their sons to a position above that of his ancestors, and thus make him the idol of their vanity. My God! how terrible for these unnatural parents will be the presence of their unhappy victims on the Day of Judgment! and may the horror of their fate appeal to Your Justice to avenge their blood on the authors of their being and of their eternal misfortune!"[1]

Mme de Sévigné mentions that "when Le Tellier was appointed Archbishop of Rheims, Mme de Coulanges said to him, laughing: 'What folly to go to Rheims! you will be bored to tears. Stay here and we will go for walks together.' This remark, made to an Archbishop, made us laugh, and we did not consider it very canonical." But, as we shall see in this century, neither Archbishops nor Bishops needed much persuasion "to stay here," that is, in Paris. Ratabon, Bishop of Ypres, never left Paris, declaring "that there was such a miasma in his Cathedral that he fainted every time he set foot in it."[2] Saint-Simon wrote this at the beginning of the century, but as time passes we find even fewer of those pious prelates of whom it might be said, as Saint-Simon did of the Bishop of Saint-Pons: "He was rendered truly illustrious by his virtues as a Bishop as well as by an unbroken residence of over

---

[1] Massillon, *Sermon "On Vocations."*   [2] Saint-Simon, x. 5.

forty years in his diocese." It should be noted that lengthy residence was already considered "illustrious" when Saint-Simon wrote these lines in 1713, but it was a reputation which Bishops sought less and less, until towards the end of the century, Mercier could write: "Boredom drives them from their sees, which they look upon as exile, and nearly all of them flock to Paris where they can enjoy their wealth and take their place at Court, where they enjoy a freedom which their diocese denies them, since there a sense of duty would compel them to practise irksome hospitality. Ambition, which is always nourished by what it has already secured, drives them to Court and into the offices of Ministers." [1]

Still those who, all too rarely, remained with their flock did not lack their reward. Cardinal de Janson had been the King's Grand Almoner, but "he preferred his diocese to all the favours and distinctions showered on him at Court, and he was held in great respect by his people being especially adored by the poor." [2] This hardly applied to Cosnac, Archbishop of Aix, who had been rarely seen in his diocese, and whose funeral oration was delivered by one of his flock: "By God's mercy he had the honour of dying in his episcopal residence, in which he had resided but three years during an episcopate of twenty years and some months. His doctor, who was on intimate terms with him, had often warned him that, owing to his annual visits to the Court, he might die in a tavern like any libertine. The last rites which were rendered to the Archbishop at his funeral were the same as had been observed when his predecessor was carried to his grave amidst the tears and regrets of the people." [3]

If, in the eighteenth century, a Bishop received a Royal command to remain in his episcopal city, it was called "being exiled" to his diocese, "as if," remarked the pious Bishop of Amiens, Mgr Lamotte, "a bishop could be exiled in the midst of his flock." Those Bishops who, as

---

[1] Mercier, i. 270.   [2] Saint-Simon, x. 12.
[3] Haitze, *Histoire de la Ville d'Aix*, vi. 486.

great nobles, spent their lives in Paris or at Court, left the duties of administering their sees to a suffragan Bishop, "a kind of consecrated and mitred valet," as Saint-Simon calls him. Many, indeed, once they had been appointed, gladly dallied in Paris before proceeding to take possession of their new diocese, as in the case of the Cardinal de Polignac, who was Archbishop of Auch for fifteen years without setting foot in his bishopric, and who actually died, in 1741, without having ever seen his flock!

When in residence, and in order to mitigate the dullness of their existence, some Bishops surrounded themselves with Vicars-General chosen from their own class, who formed their intimate circle. Grimaldi, Bishop of Mans, had a large number about him, and the Chancellor Pasquier describes them as being "younger sons, who, having no prospects, only embraced the ecclesiastical profession in order to pave their way to better things, and the Bishop, who had been their friend at the Seminary of Saint-Sulpice in the past, had promised that he would summon them to his side whenever he obtained a mitre. He kept his promise, and a crowd of Vicars-General descended upon Mans, and soon made a very different place of the episcopal residence from what it had been hitherto. They went into society and cultivated assiduously those whose friendship might be useful. The Bishop regarded this bustle with an indulgent eye, his own visitations being rare, though he would sojourn long in the various country houses when he found pleasant company."[1]

Some prelates displayed a vanity which was hardly in keeping with the teaching of the Gospels. "On the anniversary of the late King's death, the Bishops who were present at Saint-Denis decided that they wanted cushions, and, strange to relate, it was only the Cardinal de Polignac who prevented this, whereupon their Lordships had the audacity to go and complain to the Regent."[2] We might contrast with this the humility of M. de Machault, Bishop of Amiens. At the King's coronation the Bishop of Amiens acted as subdeacon. Machault was the only one of

[1] Pasquier, *Mémoires*, i. 8.   [2] Saint-Simon, xiv. 116.

all the Bishops who attended the coronation of Louis XIV., who wore a cassock of violet cloth. The King asked him why he did not wear one of silk as the others did. "It is a privilege of my See" was the reply. Truly a fine privilege, for it was that of a truly Christian humility! But the majority of the Bishops in this age were more likely to agree with one of their number, Le Tellier, who once remarked that it was "difficult to be an honest man if one did not have an income of a hundred thousand livres."

Dufort de Cheverny, in his *Mémoires*, gives us an example of the luxurious life led by some of these Bishops. He is speaking of de Thémines, Bishop of Blois.

"Having travelled much, he determined to model his episcopal residence on a Roman palace, and everything in it was as splendid as it was extraordinary. He had pictures but no mirrors, his furniture was simple, though each piece was the choicest of its kind. Having a marvellous taste in books, he collected two libraries, one of 60,000 volumes on every possible subject, and another of 12,000 of the most beautiful and rarest editions of all countries. He kept the most magnificent state whenever the great nobles of the Court passed that way." [1]

The Bishops who kept such state and delighted in displaying their wealth were probably few, but those who did made such a stir that they brought their order into a discredit which, as we shall see, was undeserved, for "the good Bishops" were then, as always, in a great majority.

As we have seen, many Bishops surrounded themselves with a large number of Vicars-General who composed their household, and they preferred to live with these young nobles, newly hatched from the Sorbonne and aspiring to the episcopate, than with the humble clergy of their dioceses, whom they treated with scant courtesy on the rare occasions that they deigned to receive them. Dufort narrates of M. de Thémines that "he would give them but scant attention, sometimes even dismissing

[1] Dufort de Cheverny, i. 429.

them as soon as they put their heads through his door, and he never asked them to dinner."

"If a Persian or an Indian were to visit Paris it would require six months to explain to him what the 'Commendatory Abbots' were, so many of whom idled about Paris." [1] To hold *in commendam* implied that a secular ecclesiastic had been substituted for a regular abbot to enjoy the honours and revenues attached to the latter's title. These commendatory titles ought only to have been conferred on ordained priests, but they were often bestowed on secular clerics whose only ecclesiastical qualification was the tonsure which they had received at the age of seven, and since then had taken no further Orders. Abbeys were actually conferred *in commendam* upon infants in their cradles.

Of the younger sons, whom necessity rather than inclination drove into the Church, few became priests except with a view to a mitre, but the vast majority who could not aspire to anything but a simple benefice, were content with the tonsure, and the title of Commendatory Abbot, and it was the latter who, living entirely in the world and at Court, were so much talked about in the eighteenth century. They were to be met everywhere—where they ought not to have been. Mercier, who, as usual, paints them in an unfavourable light, says: "Paris is full of Abbots, mere tonsured clerks who serve neither Church nor State, who live in complete indolence and who never do a useful or worthy action. An Abbot of this kind is found in many houses, where he is styled 'friend,' and is but a footman out of livery. He is Madame's humble slave, assists at her toilet, does the housekeeping and looks after Monsieur's worldly affairs. He acts as tutor to the children, and, in the greater houses, is treated much as the other servants. While his duties last, he does, perhaps, enjoy some consideration, but when these are over, he is given a small pension or a benefice of some kind, and is then dismissed. One may also see a large number of little

---

[1] Montesquieu, *Pensées diverses*.

creatures who call themselves Abbots, but wear neither bands nor skull-cap and appear, instead, in a little coat in the Prussian style, with gold buttons, impertinent curls, and effeminate manners." [1]

The following story describes one of these Commendatory Abbots, who, as Montesquieu has said, "idled about Paris"; but this one idled about on all the highways of Europe, for he was for ever travelling, and always in the best of tempers. This was the very agreeable and very frivolous Chevalier de Boufflers, Abbot *in commendam* of Belchamp and Longueville. Here is Grimm's description of him: "M. l'Abbé de Boufflers was well known from his early youth, owing to his intelligence, his talents, and his many follies. Many were the improper and even frankly impious songs, such as the 'Tale of the Queen of Golconda,' which he composed at Saint-Sulpice when he was studying with an eye to a bishopric, but a thorough examination of conscience no doubt persuaded him that this vocation was really not in his line. But as it was a question of keeping an income of 40,000 livres derived from benefices which King Stanislaus, from friendship towards our little ecclesiastic, had given him in early youth, he exchanged his collar for the cross of a Knight of Malta, an exchange which did not prevent him from retaining his benefices. And thus the Abbé de Boufflers became the Chevalier de Boufflers, and the latter lost none of the charm or the folly of the Abbé, though he caused less notorious scandal."

Duclos also, in an amusing anecdote, depicts the pride of one abbess to whom another gives a lesson in Christian humility: "The Abbess of Maubuisson, daughter of the Elector Palatine, Frederick v., and granddaughter of James I. of England, whose birth was only the least of her merits, asked Mme de Chaulnes, Abbess of Poissy, to attend the benediction of an Abbess which was to take place at Maubuisson. The latter replied that she could not come unless Mme de Maubuisson promised to place her on her right hand, and Mme de Maubuisson's answer was: "Tell Mme de Poissy she need have no fears. Since I became a

[1] Mercier, i. 267.

"WHAT DOES THE ABBÉ SAY?"
From an engraving by Nicholas de Launay, after J. M. Moreau le Jeune

religious I no longer distinguish my right from my left hand except in making the sign of the Cross." [1]

While speaking of the luxury in which the Bishops of this century lived, we must not forget that they were bound to entertain largely, and that their position obliged them to offer hospitality to persons of note, who could not be received without some state and considerable expense. On one occasion Richelieu, the Governor of Languedoc, whose magnificence we have already mentioned, proceeded to Toulouse on business. He naturally stayed at the Archbishop's house, and remained a week, not alone, but accompanied by a large and extravagant retinue. That week must have cost the Archbishop a very considerable sum. On the other hand, many Bishops led a simple life amid sumptuous surroundings. At the beginning of the century, Fénelon's table at Cambrai groaned under good things which were served on silver plate by numerous footmen in splendid liveries, but the Abbé Ledieu relates that on the evening when he visited Cambrai, Fénelon "ate very little—a few spoonfuls of egg and milk, and he looked extremely thin." M. de Thémines, Bishop of Blois, of whom we have already spoken, "entertained magnificently when he had to, and received the Maréchals of France, princes, and other great folk, but, when he was alone, the enormous episcopal palace was only lit by a candle. The porter would escort you to the Bishop, and the Bishop would take you back to the porter." [2]

We know that towards the end of the eighteenth century some Bishops were accused in the *Lettres secrètes*, an anonymous pamphlet published from 1781 to 1783, of having succumbed to "the disease of being Statesmen," and people maliciously distinguished between those who "administered provinces" and those who "administered the sacraments." Talleyrand says: "The French clergy consisted of men of whom some were genuinely pious, others distinguished as administrators, and others again who were merely worldly, and, like the Archbishop of Narbonne (Dillon), delighted to put off the attributes of

[1] Duclos, iii. 463. [2] Dufort, i. 430.

their office and live as great nobles." The Archbishop of Narbonne could well afford to do this, for he drew an annual income of 300,000 livres as President of the Estates of Languedoc without having to render any account for them. But he was a remarkable administrator, and as President of the Estates he constructed roads and encouraged trade and industry, so that he well deserved Bachaumont's fine eulogy: "His administration will be a memorable epoch in the annals of Languedoc. The draining of swamps and the opening up of canals which will benefit both agriculture and commerce, all these works will preserve his memory among his grateful people, who showed their appreciation in so marked a fashion during his recent tour in the mountains of Cevennes, Gévaudan, Velay, and Vivarais, undertaken with a view to studying with his own eyes the condition, requirements, and resources of these various districts." [1]

This century also produced Bishops who were great builders, of whom Du Plessis d'Argentré, Bishop of Limoges, is a good example. He rebuilt the Episcopal Palace which can still be admired in our day, and, during the years from 1766 to 1787, spent 1,100,000 livres on this work alone, so that the rest of his life he had to contend with his creditors. Prelates who, like him, fell heavily into debt were not uncommon, but they usually treated it in the grand manner, like Dillon, Archbishop of Narbonne, whose "extravagance soon gravely embarrassed his finances. Louis XVI., who, as a lover of order, preached economy and the settling of debts from morn till night, heard rumours of this. He therefore remarked to the Archbishop one day: 'People say that your Grace is very heavily in debt.' 'Sire,' replied the prelate, 'I will inquire from my steward and shall then have the honour of submitting a statement to your Majesty.'" [2]

But the most criminally extravagant of all these eighteenth-century prelates was the Cardinal de Rohan. "The extravagance of the Cardinal-Bishop of Strasbourg

---

[1] Bachaumont, *Mémoires secrets*, 16th October 1760.
[2] Beugnot, *Mémoires*, i. 135.

is still remembered in Alsace. He would spend several months at his Castle of Saverne, entertaining as many as two hundred guests at a time. The freedom of action which he had inaugurated in this house had degenerated into such licence that many of his guests had their meals served in their rooms, and never appeared in the drawing-room, and some even spent several days there without seeing their host." [1]

Next we should cast a glance at the Hunting Bishops. If Mme Campan can be believed, this same Cardinal de Rohan, when Ambassador in Vienna, "one Corpus Christi, accompanied by his whole Embassy staff, all dressed in green and gold-laced uniforms, actually broke through a procession which blocked their way as they were going to hunt with Prince Paar." [2] Mgr Dillon indulged his passion for hunting in truly princely style. "His chief fault was an unbridled passion for the chase, and Louis xv. once reproached him with this at his levee. Mgr Dillon was then only Bishop of Evreux, but his horses and hounds had already scandalised all Normandy. 'You hunt a great deal, as I know,' said the King, 'but how can you forbid your clergy to hunt when you yourself set them such an example?' 'Sire,' was the reply, 'in my clergy it is their own fault, in me it is the fault of my ancestors.' " [3]

Bernis, on the other hand, was wiser than Dillon, and gave up the chase from the day he became Archbishop of Albi. Of him the Infant of Parma wrote in 1764: "I am filled with wonder that the sight of snipe and partridges does not cause you more regret." [4]

The philosopher Bishops must also be mentioned, though they were very rare in this century. Chamfort's epigram is well known: "A mere priest must believe a little, or he will be looked upon as a hypocrite, but he must not be too sincere in his beliefs or people will call him intolerant. A Vicar-General may permit himself a smile when religion is attacked, a Bishop may laugh, and a Cardinal may give his cordial assent." But it would be utterly wrong

---

[1] De Levis, *Mémoires*, p. 158. [2] Mme Campan, i. 69.
[3] Beugnot, *Mémoires*, i. 135. [4] Bernis, i. 54.

to suppose that in the Church of the eighteenth century scepticism increased as the prelate rose in dignity. Some, affected, perhaps, by the spirit of the age, were undoubtedly anything but models of piety. "Cardinal de Loménie was so indifferent to the means he employed for furthering his own interests, that he inclined to modern philosophy in order to gain the favour of its chief exponents. Voltaire's correspondence bears this out, and it was so widely known, that people used to quote the King's reply when the Archbishopric of Paris was sought on the Cardinal's behalf. "No," said the King, with an annoyance which did him credit, "the Archbishop of Paris must, at least, believe in God." [1]

Having seen the worst side, let us hasten to add that the Episcopate of the eighteenth century must not be judged by the Dubois, Rohans, or Loménies de Brienne, who compromised and sometimes even disgraced it. First of all let us consider the great number of Bishops, who, very naturally, were held up as models of charity and of devotion to the poor and unfortunate. A few characteristic anecdotes will suffice to support a truth which, doubtless, needs but little proof. For instance, when M. de la Ferronaye, of Saint-Brieuc, jumped into the water and saved a drowning child, his only reply to the congratulations of Louis xv.'s courtiers was: "A La Ferronaye goes into water as he would go into fire." Bachaumont says of Mgr d'Apchon, of Auch: "People have been so amazed at an act of charity and civic devotion on the part of a Bishop that they refused to believe it until they had definite proof. It now appears certain that on 30th March the Archbishop of Auch hurried to his episcopal city where a fire was consuming practically a whole quarter of the town. Seeing a mother and child vainly awaiting rescue in the midst of the flames, he offered first 800 and finally 1200 livres to any one who would make the attempt, but it was so dangerous that no one dared. At last, carried away by a zeal which was truly apostolic, he himself rushed into the flames and succeeded in saving both. He has since

[1] De Levis, *Souvenirs*, p. 103.

given the woman an annuity of 800 livres, which is to be continued to the child. This Archbishop is Mgr d'Apchon."[1]

In speaking of the terrible plague in Marseilles in 1720, Barbier says: "The Bishop nursed the sick with truly amazing devotion." This Bishop was Mgr de Belsunce, and a contemporary pays further tribute to his devotion. "He regarded his office as chief shepherd of his flock merely as an additional reason for devoting himself to the welfare of his people. He might be seen like Aaron, the High Priest of old, walking the streets and squares, literally 'among the living and the dead.' His palace was surrounded by corpses and he was scarcely able to leave it without having to tread on them. 'I have had great difficulty,' he writes to the Archbishop of Arles, 'in removing 150 corpses already half putrified and gnawed by dogs which lay around my house, and were already infecting it.' In fact, the good priests who used to accompany him were almost all struck down, as were his own servants."[2]

We have had occasion to mention Bishops who lived in luxury, who hardly ever resided in their sees and neglected their flocks. But there were many others of a very different type. Here is one whom Bernis praised for his "simple manners"; one whom his diocese called "the Father of the Poor," who spent his life penetrating even up into the mountains in order to visit his priests and his people. His name was Massillon. On his appointment as Bishop of Clermont he announced his arrival in the following terms: "It is right that the sheep should know their shepherd and hear his voice, but it is as essential that the shepherd should know both his sheep and the pastors set over them to guide them." With that he set off and began his first Visitation which was to last eight years. He made another which lasted seven, and his biographer tells us that, at the age of seventy-five, he began a third, which he was not permitted to finish, a fact he announced to his diocese in these humble and affectionate words: "This will be the last time that we shall have the consolation of visiting your churches. The Divine patience has

[1] Bachaumont, *Mémoires*, 31st May 1781.   [2] Papon, iv. 663.

already extended our episcopate too long and has deferred to give you, in our stead, a shepherd more worthy of it—one who will repair our faults and co-operate more faithfully than we have done with the designs of Divine Providence on your behalf. As we await the end of our pastorship—and it cannot now be long delayed—we never cease to hold you in all-fatherly affection, and our infirmities will never weaken the tender love with which we have always enfolded our people. We would be more than happy if our solicitude has been as much for your good as it has been real and sincere on our part." [1]

And we may stand at the death-bed of yet another "good bishop." "On 8th April 1738 died M. de Croissy, Bishop of Montpellier, who had fought against the Bull *Unigenitus* and ultramontane doctrines for twenty-one years. Although seriously ill and seventy-one years of age, he insisted, in spite of his doctor's orders, in observing the Lent of 1738 with all the strictness enjoined by ecclesiastical discipline. On Palm Sunday he still had sufficient strength, though suffering greatly, to pronounce the blessing in his Cathedral, and to walk in the procession in full pontificals, bearing his palm in his hand. But on Good Friday he received the Last Sacrament, and ordering the people to be let into his bedroom, he made his confession before a weeping crowd. But his own weakness and the tears of those surrounding him caused his voice to fail him. He died on Tuesday in Easter week in the forty-second year of his episcopate. A large sum of ready money was found in his cash-box, which he had put aside so that he should not be a burden on any one, in the event of his threatened deposition by a Council, which had hung over him for ten years, one day becoming a reality. All this money he left by his will to the General Hospital at Montpellier." [2]

We have only been able to devote a short space to this subject, and we can hardly have gained any intimate knowledge of the French Episcopate of the eighteenth century, but we would be rash to venture to judge it as a whole.

[1] Attaix, p. 51.   [2] Roschach, *Histoire de Languedoc*, xiii. 1055.

Still, we would not be far wrong if we admit that, while there undoubtedly were bad shepherds, the stir they caused had no relation to their numbers, and that Sénac de Meilhan was right when he declared that "the clergy of France was probably more worthy of respect than any in Europe. A very large number of its prelates gave alms abundantly and were distinguished for the piety and purity of their lives." [1]

[1] Sénac de Meilhan, *Du gouvernement*, p. 54.

CHAPTER III

THE COUNTRY GENTRY

"It has not been my desire to make my fortune through Court interest, and I have endeavoured, instead, to build it up by developing my property and accepting all from the hands of the gods and from them alone." These were proud words that Montesquieu wrote, and there were very few among the nobles of the eighteenth century who were as wise as he. Many deserted their ancestral acres from various motives, and Boulainvillers is right when he says in his *Essais sur la noblesse de France*, 1732: "It was love of luxury which ruined the nobility, because it attracted them to Court"; and this is confirmed by the artless and curious *Livre de raison*, which was compiled by Pierre César de Cadenet de Charleval, and continued by his son and grandson during the years 1728 to 1763. The extracts which are given here reveal in detail the disastrous progress of a noble Provençal family along the road of extravagance and luxury.

"Our little property had grown, little by little, owing to unremitting economy, though it must be admitted that luxurious living was then less common than it is now; for my uncles have told me that my great-grandfather never wore anything but woollen clothes and coarse linen, with straps to his shoes. Wigs were unknown, as were all those accessories on which we now spend more money than was required, in those days, for the ordinary household expenditure. But even so it was not difficult to increase one's capital.

"The lady of the house looked after her servants herself, and saw that they started work at the proper time, for then that was the custom; but if one tried to act in a similar manner in these days, one would merely be laughed at. I can still remember the dining-room in winter with its flagstones, its two big walnut chests in the windows, its big olive-wood cupboard, and a bed with linen sheets and stamped leather hangings. It was my uncle who turned it into a sideboard as it now is, and it has cost me between 600 to 700 livres.

"The first who broke away from all this was my grandfather, who wanted to go to Paris; and there he spent 14,000 livres in a year, which caused my father to say that the pair of spectacles which grandfather brought back as a present for him had cost him 14,000 livres. We already had a carriage and four white horses in the stable, but my grandfather came home with a great liking for riding horses, being a fine big man and a great horseman, and thenceforward he kept a great many. He also brought back with him a footman, and my father used to say that he never dared ask him for a drink, as he was so much better dressed than he himself was. Thus luxury developed by degrees: we no longer set aside savings to add to our capital, and it is difficult enough to make both ends meet in these days with what is left." [1]

La Bruyère had written, in the previous century, that "if a noble lives at home in the country, he lives a free life, but without outside support, whereas if he lives at Court, he has powerful protectors, but is a slave." [2] Already in his day many noblemen preferred the gilded slavery of the Court to a freedom attended, as they considered, by loneliness and boredom, especially as they no longer enjoyed that absolute and all but unbridled independence which they had formerly abused, until Richelieu razed their castles. Now they had to bow their proud heads before the Intendants, whom they feared even more than they hated, and who made their residence in the province unbearable, since they themselves were no longer masters there. Saint-Simon, who never ceased to abuse the Intendants with all his invective and sarcasm, writes of them

[1] Baudrillart, *Histoire de luxe*, iv. 308. [2] De la Cour.

as follows, in his *Parallèle des trois Bourbons*: "They usurp authority over so many matters that nothing is left to the gentry or to the landed proprietors, and all who can abandon their estates and the countryside flock to live in Paris, or at Court, whence they can look upon their lowly estate and fortune, and endeavour to obtain such consideration and such powerful interests as will enable them to cope with the Intendants." But the Intendants were difficult to cope with, if we believe the impassioned author of *Les Soupirs de la France esclave*. He writes as follows: "At the present moment an order of the Court, drawn up by the Intendant and delivered by a footman, makes a whole Province tremble. They call themselves Intendants of Justice, Police, and Finance, and this is certainly the case, since they control everything and exercise complete jurisdiction. They can be seen holding court in their own houses, where they judge the suits of individuals, and hear the complaints and grievances of every comer. It is true that they have restrained the excesses which wicked nobles used to commit—and this is most estimable—but under the pretext of restraining them they also expose them to every kind of vexation. The greatest nobles of the Province have to bow before them, and the Intendants summon them by means of a lackey. When the Intendant passes through a district, the local squire ruins himself in giving him a magnificent reception, and in spite of all the meanness to which he may have to stoop, a gentleman will not escape being bullied like the most wretched of mankind if he fails even a hairbreadth in his duty." They took good care not to fail, and for a very good reason, since, though they were not liable to the land tax, the nobles were not exempt from the capitation tax, nor from the twentieth or tenth, and they had, therefore, every reason for being on good terms with the Intendants, who alone had the power to reduce their taxes. Indeed, a Marquis de Sédaige could write to the Intendant of Auvergne: "It is my most heartfelt desire to wait upon you," and M. de Sartiges wrote to the same man: "I am deeply grieved, sir, that you have left this district so soon after my arrival. I would have been charmed to wait upon you. But as soon as I get to the country this will be my first duty." [1]

In the eighteenth century the country gentry did not like to reside in town, and gladly remained in the seclusion of their castles. The reason is not far to seek: "Those gentlemen of Auvergne who, at the Revolution, were neither on military service nor employed at Court, were accustomed to reside within their castles all the year round. Very few lived in the towns, and they avoided especially such towns as Clermont and Riom, where there were so many offices carrying nobility with them. Since most of them had little money, they dreaded to be humiliated by the wealth of the *bourgeoisie*, by the pretensions to which their privileges gave rise, and by the conceit which their offices fostered." [2] These country gentry not only had "but little money," but were quite often poor, and some, as we shall see, were very poor indeed. But let us first cast a glance at these gentlemen of old by conjuring up, with the aid of the author of the *Mémoires d'Outre-Tombe*, that solitary and gloomy Castle of Combourg and the nobles who now and again would visit it:

"On my return from Brest, the Castle of Combourg was inhabited by my father, my mother, my sister, and myself. The whole staff consisted of a cook, a housemaid, two footmen, and a coachman, while the stables sheltered one hunter and two old mares. These twelve living creatures were completely engulfed by a manor which could have housed a hundred knights with their ladies and squires, their pages and chargers and all King Dagobert's hounds, with ease. From year's end to year's end no stranger came to the Castle, save one or two gentlemen, the Marquis de Montlouet and the Count de Goyon-Beaufort, who begged our hospitality on their way to lay a claim before the Parliament. They arrived in winter on horseback, each carrying a suitcase on his pillion. My father, who was

[1] Jalenques, *La Noblesse de Province*.
[2] Le Grand d'Aussy, *Voyages*, iii. 267.

always very ceremonious, received them bareheaded on the steps in the wind and rain.

"On entering, the gentlemen talked of the wars in Hanover, of their family affairs, and of their lawsuit. In the evening they were conducted to the North Tower, where the state bedroom, known as 'Queen Christina's,' had been prepared for them, with its great bed, seven foot square, with curtains of green gauze and crimson silk, and supported by four gilt cupids. The next morning, when I came down to the Great Hall and looked out through the window upon a flooded or frostbound countryside, I could only see two or three travellers riding along the deserted avenue by the pond, and these proved to be our guests on their way to Rennes." [1]

They might, indeed, go to Rennes every two years to attend the meeting of the Estates, which usually lasted six weeks. That these were well spent is apparent from Mme de Sévigné's charming letter of the 5th August 1671, describing the meeting of the Estates of Brittany: "Good cheer is here carried to excess, for they bring in joints roasted whole, and the doorways have to be heightened in order to admit the pyramids of fruit. There are fifteen or twenty tables at which play is continual: balls never cease, comedies are performed three times a week, and altogether it is a brave show. . . . I had all but forgotten the three or four hundred pipes of wine which are drunk." The Breton gentlemen of the eighteenth century had lost neither the appetite nor the thirst of their ancestors, and the meetings of the Estates continued to be as merry in the time of Chateaubriand as of old. "When the Estates met in Brittany it was a great time of entertainments and balls. One dined with the Commandant, with the President of the Nobility, with the President of the Clergy; in fact, one dined—and drank!—with every one, at long tables, where sat the du Guesclins, who were farmers, with their great iron swords, and the Duguay-Trouins, who were sailors with their cutlasses. All these gentlemen who attended the Estates in person resembled

[1] *Mémoires d'Outre-Tombe*, i. 129.

THE SQUIRE AND HIS TENANT FARMER
From an engraving by J. L. Delignon, after J. M. Moreau le Jeune

a Diet of Poland, but a Poland on foot not on horseback, a Diet of Scythians not of Sarmatians. The smart gentlemen from Paris who accompany the King's officers used to say that we yokels used to line our pockets with tin in order to carry home the Commandant's chicken fricassee to our wives. These jokes were paid for dearly. A Count de Sabran was lately left on the pavement for some ill-natured jest. This descendant of the Troubadours and of the Kings of Provence, as tall as a Swiss, was killed by a little hare-hunting Morbihan squire about as tall as a Laplander. But this Ker could show as proud an ancestry as his adversary; for if Saint Elzéar of Sabran was near relation to Saint Louis, Saint Corentin, great-uncle to our noble Ker, was Bishop of Quimper in the reign of King Grallon II., *three hundred years* B.C.!" [1]

The country gentleman lived on his manor or *gentilhommière*, which was usually enclosed either by a plain wall or else by a more imposing one with a tower at each of its four corners. On entering, one found oneself in a large courtyard facing the house, on either side of which and built against its walls were the barn, the stables, the winepresses, and the bakery. Behind the house lay the privy garden. Within the house, one room was considered "the chief part of the dwelling," this being the kitchen, which had been for a very long time the centre of every home: here the squire's meals were served, and here he interviewed his servants. Here also, in their high-backed chairs beneath the great overhanging chimney-piece, he and his wife would pass the long winter evenings surrounded by their servants. Next to the kitchen was *la salle*, usually on the ground-floor and often called *la salle basse* for that reason, and this was reserved for the squire and his family. On the first floor, but only in the more exalted families, was the *salle haute*, used for receptions and entertainments. The furniture was very scanty. A room was usually only supplied with two firedogs on the hearth, a pair of candlesticks on the chimney-piece, a stool, one or two coffers or trunks,

[1] *Mémoires d'Outre-Tombe*, i. 244.

and a bed. There was, however, one expensive luxury which a gentleman found it difficult to dispense with. He considered it due to his position to maintain a large staff of servants, and in order to pay them he would borrow and incur debts which were frequently increased by perpetual lawsuits over his rights with the peasantry and the communes. One fine day the sheriff's officer knocks at his door. He may thrash the officer, but in the end he has to pay. Little by little, owing to lack of funds, his property is neglected, the castle which he can no longer afford to repair gradually becomes uninhabitable; at length he decides to leave, and soon, as the Marquis de Mirabeau expresses it: "The owls take possession of the keep and the snails of the garden." Then comes a new race, the lawyers, astute *bourgeois*, who, after having involved the squires in ruinous lawsuits, buy up their estates for a song, and, through them, become ennobled.

Undoubtedly the gentleman who in war shed his blood for his King, who at all times had a great pride in his position, together with a great disdain of money, was morally superior to the avaricious *bourgeois* and crafty lawyer who, by their sharp practices, enriched themselves by despoiling him. But the gentleman—and this cannot be gainsaid—was, in most instances, ruined through his own fault, for he did not work nor supervise those who worked for him on his own lands; he was robbed by his servants and by his steward, and, partly because he could not pay those who served him, and partly through his own stupid carelessness, he let things slide, knowing, all the while, that he was being plundered. Many a noble might well have written in his will, as did a facetious *maître des requêtes*: "I leave my steward nothing, as he has been eighteen years in my service."

"Most of the large estates belonged to the great nobles, who were more engaged in spending money and seeking applause than in putting by a competency for their children, and these estates, which were stinted of every penny possible, were naturally bound to deteriorate and diminish in value. Thus the people as a whole suffered in two ways;

for the sources of production within the State were continually being diminished, and the Sovereign, whose interest lay in supporting the great houses, was obliged to throw the burden of his liberality upon his people." [1] In this way the provincial nobles impoverished not only themselves, but the State itself. And now we come to the tragic consequences which this maladministration of their properties brought on the gentry.

In 1756 the Abbé Coyer in his *Noblesse commerçante* paints the appalling but true picture of these country squires, "who see daily the houses of their ancestors falling in ruins about them, yet are unable to stay the process. Let us traverse these manorial lands which cannot maintain their lords, see these farms empty of cattle, the fields badly cultivated or not cultivated at all, the rotting harvests about to be seized by a creditor; this castle which is but a burden to its owners; a father and a mother who are only united in their misery. Of what avail are these tokens of honour which poverty degrades, these arms rusted by time; this family pew in the parish church on which an alms-box for the squire's benefit should be fixed; these prayers, in which the family are mentioned by name, but which the vicar, if he dared, would turn into charitable appeals to the faithful; this hunting which only affords pleasure to the well-to-do and which only becomes a business to those who are not; this right of justice which is disgraced by misfortune and cannot be exercised—of what use are all these?"

This is the indignant language of an author who, while speaking, as we shall see, the strictest truth, wished to make the nobility ashamed of their sloth and to drive them into trade which might save them from ruin. But there is also a note of mockery; for during the whole of this century, jests, more or less subtle, and puns, more or less cruel, were hurled at the poor country gentry—those "hare-catchers," those "Marquesses of Carabas." In derision they were often called *hobereaux*, the name given to the smallest of all birds of prey, the falcon, which was used for hunting

[1] Forbonnais, *Recherches* . . ., 1758, ii. 68.

larks. "In some of our provinces the name of *hobereau* is given to the small gentry who tyrannise over their peasants, and more especially to the hare-hunting gentlemen who hunt on their neighbour's land, without permission, and who hunt less for their own pleasure than for profit." [1]

Here is a description of one of these poor *hobereaux*, at whose expense an author amuses himself at Falaise:

"M. d'Argiville was one of those gentlemen who are dreaded by the game of their district owing to their guns, by the peasants owing to their chicanery, and by the parish priest owing to their relations with the Bishop's Vicar who, from time to time, is gratified by receiving a hare or a partridge. He belonged half to the town and half to the country. His lady was stout, with a florid complexion, and as proud as a village dame who has never seen any one more exalted than the local procurator-fiscal; her sole occupation was that of multiplying the population which inhabited her yard, and of making her barn and granary pay. Nevertheless, she gave the title of Baron, Knight, and Abbé to three urchins, who, from their dress, might be mistaken for those who looked after the sheep and pigs rather than her offspring. On our arrival, we tried at the gate to find some one who would tell us where the Château of Argiville might be. An uncouth ploughboy, who acted alternately as the squire's coachman, huntsman, and cook, explained to us with much wealth of language that we were at our destination. So our coach rolled in, across a vast expanse of dungheaps on which a large number of hens, geese, and pigs were playing the first scene of our comedy.

"M. le Baron, the eldest son, having exchanged his wooden clogs for shoes, came out to welcome us as far as he knew how, and bade us enter a kennel honoured by the name of hall, and seat ourselves on chairs the use of which had been almost forgotten. At this point Mme d'Argiville arrived from the mill, and shortly afterwards her husband appeared with a large hare on his back. Supper was then served. On an extremely doubtful pewter dish were placed

[1] Buffon, *Histoire naturelle*, "Oiseaux," ii. 44.

two pullets, chosen from among the thinnest in the yard, while, between them, lay half of an old roast hare, all larded with great chunks of fat, which was as yellow in colour as its smell was penetrating. In a large dish was another stewed hare, which exhaled mingled odours of the garlic and turnips with which it was seasoned. Supper over, we were taken to see the squire feed his cows, a performance for which he put on a brown linen hat, a patched cloth smock, and enveloped himself up to his knees in twisted straw leggings to protect him from the cold and wet." [1]

Many of these needy gentry endeavoured to conceal their poverty, and strove to preserve their exquisite manners amid all their misery. If they had but one old henchman left, they would furbish him out in some wretched cast-off clothing which would be called livery, and employ him either as coachman or as cook as occasion required. This was the case with "a certain gentleman who had lost all his fine property and had neither castle nor tower, dovecot nor warren, but still owned some houses, a field or two, and a few meadows. But he was not less noble for all that, and kept up all his fine manners. His lady had no maid, and had to dress herself, but they had a most admirable servant who cooked and worked in the garden, served at table, groomed the horses, and was dressed in a livery which was far too short, and an old pair of the squire's boots when he was sent to the town to have my lady's cap done up at the milliner's." [2]

Whereas most of them ruined themselves by their interminable quarrels with their neighbours, whether noble or peasant, these lawsuits drained their resources but slowly, while gambling reduced them to beggary at one fell swoop. In Normandy many a lordling gambled away both income and property at the card-table, such as, for instance, a certain Baroness de Saint-S . . ., who, in a neighbour's castle, lost not only all the money she had with her, but even the coach and horses which had brought her over.

[1] *Les Aventures provinciales*, "Le Voyage de Falaise," 1707.
[2] Gautier, *Les Caractères et les mœurs de ce siècle*, 1789.

Her husband sent to fetch her in a farm-cart drawn by oxen, with two small trusses of straw—one for the driver and one for her.[1] In the country round Orleans the gentry was quite as poor, and here originated the rhyme:

> "C'est un gentilhomme de Beauce
> Qui se tient au lit quand on refait ses chausses."[2]

Some of those who were reduced to beggary tried to save themselves by means of that classic remedy, a rich marriage. "On the eve of the Revolution," writes the Marquis de Bouillé, "some families whose reputation had survived, endeavoured to preserve, or rather to repair, the loss of the family fortunes by allying themselves to plebeian families. The rest of this ancient nobility languished in poverty and resembled those ancestral oaks which time and weather have reduced to a mere skeleton."[3] The Archbishop of Sens wrote in 1709 to the Controller-General: "If any gentlemen remain in the villages of my diocese, they are quite unable to assist the poor, and would themselves, in fact, if they dared, gladly beg the charity of others."[4]

But they did "dare," for necessity compelled them, and they would write urgent and pitiable petitions to the Controller-General who dispensed the Royal favours, imploring "the Royal bounty," if not for themselves, then for their children, since many had large families. For instance, M. de la Baronais wrote: "Though the future of my eleven sons preys on my mind, the fate of my daughters distracts me. I have eight, of whom two are nuns; but think of it, sir, I have six left at home—one of forty, one of twenty-nine, and the others aged twenty and eighteen. What can I do? If I could even be certain that on my death they would have the hundred pistoles which I have been granted these last years, that would at least keep them from starvation!"

M. de Couladère, who lived near Montauban, pleads

---

[1] Bernier, 152.
[2] "A gentleman of Beauce lies abed when they darn his hose."
[3] *Mémoires*, chap. iii.   [4] Boislisle, iii. 144.

in the same strain: "You will forgive me, sir, if I take the liberty of laying our sad case before you, for I and mine are now reduced to extremity. My family consists of a brother, a sister almost as old as myself—and I am sixty-six—four boys, two daughters, and a daughter-in-law. Last year hailstorms destroyed the entire harvest of our small property near Couladère, and again this year our harvest has been ruined by last winter's frosts. Our position is now so hopeless that I venture to approach you with the humble request that you would look into our case. Not a pistole that I can raise on even the best of my property but must be laid by in order to prevent starvation, and I can provide nothing for the service of the King to whom all belongs. We may well be numbered among the poor, for we are on the point of going a-begging, and you will understand that we cannot work for our daily bread without staining our honour. I fear we shall fast often enough on bread and water, but I know not whether that be any merit. It is pitiful that people of gentle birth like ourselves should be reduced to such great straits, and now our baker refuses to supply us with bread, as he sees that our harvest is ruined." [1]

These appeals for assistance were possibly, in some cases, exaggerated, but for all that, the distress among the country gentry was widespread, and in some cases truly lamentable, as can be proved by official documents. In 1725, for instance, an inquiry was set on foot by order of the King, to report throughout the realm on the *facultés*, or revenues, of all nobles who were exempt from the land tax. It was desirable to ascertain the amount which these exemptions cost the non-noble landowners, since they alone were obliged to pay this tax. The Intendant of Auvergne submitted to the Controller-General, Dodun, a list of all the revenues enjoyed by every noble in his district, of whom there were 520 in Auvergne. Of these only eighteen had an income of over 8000 livres a year! while 203 had from 1000 to 8000 livres; 300 had less than 1000 livres, and 98 of these were "poor and obliged by their

[1] De Vaissière, p. 343.

distress to labour in the fields themselves, while one, with six children, is reduced to begging!"

But even in such straits as these the nobles retained their pride, and there was no greater affront which a gentleman could suffer, even if his worldly goods consisted only of his cloak and sword, than to be mistaken in society for some honest *bourgeois* who had committed the error of acquiring wealth by his own hard work. "What can be more ridiculous," says Rousseau, "than for a great noble who has lost his all to display in his poverty all the prejudices of his birth?" [1] And Beugnot provides a good instance of this stubborn pride. The scene is laid at the residence of the Duke de Penthièvre, a very estimable gentleman, a son of the Count of Toulouse, who was himself the son of Louis XIV. and Mme de Maintenon.

"On presenting oneself in the morning at Châteauvilain, one craved the honour of an audience from one of the Prince's gentlemen, and it would be granted for the same day after Mass. The Prince welcomed all who were presented to him with the same charming affability. The nobles were asked to dine with him, and others were entertained by his First Gentleman. M. du Hausier and M. de Florian were in waiting alternately, and both were models of courtesy. After dinner the First Gentleman would suggest the alternatives of taking coffee with him or with the Prince, and one naturally chose the latter. Proceeding to the drawing-room, one would find all the distinguished company which had dined with the Prince assembled there, and these would salute the new arrivals with a civility not devoid of condescension, in spite of the fact that some were very badly dressed, and others did not appear to be extraordinarily aristocratic. Yet, for fear of being mistaken for any of the non-noble, all had girded on their old swords and their hunting-knives, these ornaments being permitted at the Court of Châteauvilain." [2]

Many even went so far as to consider that the name was everything, and that the antiquity of their titles outweighed even the greatest services rendered to King and

[1] Emile, i. 3.   [2] Beugnot, i. 77.

State. In his *Considérations sur l'esprit et les mœurs*, Sénac de Meilhan portrays some of these preposterous figures under the name of Adramont. He is a fictitious personage, but the author must have met the type often enough, and as he often disguises real people by means of a pseudonym, Adramont may well have been an acquaintance of his. "The family of Adramont have inhabited their little castle and their ancestors have married the daughters of nobles for four hundred years. But not one of the family has ever risen above the rank of captain, made his mark in history, distinguished himself in the Church or in politics, nor has their name, though well enough known near their castle, even been heard of in the rest of France. Adramont unceasingly boasts of his ancient lineage, and dwells with satisfaction on the recent origin of certain families whose great services and high office have rendered them illustrious. He may often be heard to speak of 'a man of my rank, a man like myself,' and wishing to give mortal offence to a man whose ancestors had occupied some of the foremost positions in the magistracy, he used to repeat: 'Bear in mind that I, at any rate, have never had a Chancellor in my family.'"

Voltaire, when he was Historiographer of France, obtained the post of gentleman-in-waiting to the King on 22nd December 1746. The family of Arouet came from Poitou and had all been merchants, father and son, for many years. When the news spread in Poitou that one of this plebeian family was entering the ranks of the nobility, a lordling of the country, the Chevalier de l'Huillière, expressed his indignation in a curious letter, which not only displays the arrogance of these *hobereaux*, but also the lamentable ignorance which could exist in this enlightened age:

"I have been informed, my dear uncle, that the King, basely advised by evil-minded persons, has gratified with the title of Gentleman-in-Waiting a certain person called Arouet, from St. Lou, whose mother was a Domar, and who has taken the name of Voltaire. The King will surely not offer such an affront to the nobility as to dispense him from establishing his lineage, but he will have to look for it among his mother's relations, for on his father's side he belongs to the plebeian class. Such a step would be a dishonour to all gentlemen of family and coat armour, who have been nobles from father to son from time immemorial." [1]

We may pardon and even smile at the harmless vanity of these Artabans, but it is less easy to excuse the harshness with which the provincial nobility defended, and we might add, the zest with which they extended, their manorial rights. We know that the "feudal" prerogatives had increased at the end of the old régime, and that Feudalism seemed to enjoy a new lease of life. It was, as it were, the revenge which the Lords of the Manor took, when they saw the nobility gradually invaded by nobodies, like the Arouets, merely by the purchase of office, and the middle classes ousting them from their long-established position in the political life of the nation. They revenged themselves by tyrannising over the peasants in the provinces.

In 1788 the Intendant of Brittany, Bertrand de Molleville, wrote to Necker that "the feudal régime is growing ever more rigorous," this, in his opinion, explaining the hostility of the peasants towards the nobility and great landed proprietors. These feudal rights could not have been extended without the connivance of the officers of justice, who depended entirely upon their overlords. We shall refer later to these singular manorial justices when we come to speak of the peasantry.

Under the old régime we know that the nobles had the monopoly of all hunting rights, and the peasantry was forbidden to possess arms; in fact, they were driven to poaching. But an even worse result was that large packs of wolves attacked not only the flocks, but people as well, this occurring in certain parts of Brittany. Every kind of game, the sacred game of the manorial forests, devastated

[1] Desnoiresterres, *Voltaire* . . ., iii. 121.

the fields, and often the owners had to spend the nights on their land so as to protect them from wild boars and other marauders. "In the Forest of Paimpont the tenants of the barony of Gaël were obliged to assist in driving off wolves and other wild beasts when so required, under pain of a fine." The noblemen had no scruples about hunting over sown land and through vineyards before vintage time, in spite of all the decrees which prohibited this. "If," said the people of Plélan in Brittany, "we find them in our fields and try to stop them hunting, they reply: 'If you wish to be killed, you have only to say the word.'"[1] In other districts the people complained that "the gentry, in order to avoid the ordinary roads, actually cut down the hedges which enclose the fields." It is true, though it is no excuse for such abuses, that many of them had no other occupation but hunting and fishing.

One of the most curious, as it was the most intolerable, of abuses to which, under the old régime, the chase gave rise, was the amazing latitude given to those officers who were placed at the head of the *capitaineries*—that is to say, those whose duty it was to preserve the game in the royal forests. "M. de Montmorin, Captain of Fontainebleau, draws immense sums from his position, and behaves like a veritable brigand. He extends his captaincy over neighbouring properties, and sells the right of hunting over them. The inhabitants of over a hundred villages no longer sow their fields, since their crops and corn are eaten by hinds, stags, and other game. They have only a few vines, which they protect for six months in the year by posting pickets and guards with drums and rattles to keep off these rapacious beasts."[2]

The habits of the provincial nobles, especially in the mountain districts, were boorish and often savage. They had no restraint over their temper, and often came to blows over the merest trifles. Mme d'Epinay writes of her uncle: "He has a lawsuit with a neighbouring gentleman over a bit of shooting which is not as large as my room,

---

[1] Sée, *Classes rurales*, p. 496.   [2] D'Argenson, vii. 387.

but he insists that only there can he find red-legged partridges." During the case, M. de Preux, the uncle in question, met his adversary on the debatable ground, quarrelled, shot at him but missed, and was himself killed by the other. But the gentlemen who were known as "the bad men" were the real terror of the countryside. Here is a memorandum of 1767 by the sub-delegate of Falaise, on a certain François d'Argouges, Lord of la Coulonche: "He tyrannises over and ruins his people. He is so despotic that even the King's officers dare not go there in order to collect the taxes, as he threatens to seize them and imprison them in his Castle. In fact, instances of this sort have occurred." He was known as "The Devil of la Coulonche." When the parish priest of Saint-Maurice received from his footmen the insolent and illegal order to present this devil in human form with holy water, he replied: "Alas, go and tell your Master that I have not the power to exorcise."[1] That his vassals eventually revenged themselves will surprise no one. In 1789 the Castle of Coulonche was destroyed, its title-deeds burned, and the lord's steward only saved his skin by jumping into a pond.

We may remember in *Mauprat*, George Sand's novel, how the Mauprats were cut-throats and brigands. At the beginning of the novel the clerk comes to make an inventory of the family furniture. One of the Mauprats strangles him between the stable door and the wall, and the clerk dies a few minutes later. George Sand adds a footnote: "The Lord of Pleumartin has left such memories in that country, that no one will say that the story of *Mauprat* is exaggerated. The pen refuses to write the horrible obscenities and the refinements of torture which sullied the life of this madman, and perpetuated the traditions of feudal brigandage in Berry up to the last days of the old Monarchy. His Castle was besieged, and, after an obstinate resistance, he was taken and hung. Many people still living, and by no means advanced in

[1] Bernier, p. 144.

age, remember him." George Sand had gathered from hearsay all the legendary tales which were related in Poitou and the neighbouring districts about this fearful Marquis de Pleumartin, which she then published in *Mauprat* in 1846. In this novel, the Château de la Roche-Mauprat resembles that of Rocheposey, which belonged to the Marquis. Historical researches made on the spot have yielded the following information about this infamous personage:

Ysoré, Lord of Pleumartin and La Rocheposey, "lived in a kind of fortress which dominated the Anglin. He terrified his tenants to such an extent that one of those whom he had ruined, the Sieur Cortal, finding himself without hope or resources, fled into the neighbouring forest, and being there secretly fed by his relations, remained in hiding until his persecutor's arrest. A descendant of this Cortal still lives in the person of M. Fradin de Vouneuil-sous-Biard, who told me these facts and had heard the stories of Ysoré's cruelties from his earliest childhood."[1] D'Argenson tells us about Ysoré that "he had no band under his orders, but he undoubtedly kept a large number of servile retainers, who were only too ready to comply with his whims, and had sold themselves without scruple to his passions; for these services he paid high wages. All manner of cruel jests, many of them ridiculous and some most unpleasant, were told of him in Poitou, and the two following may be given. He groomed and looked after his horses himself, and one day a peasant maliciously directed to him a stranger who wanted his horse shod. The Marquis consented, but only asked in return that the stranger would point him out the man to whom he owed the job. 'He is not far away,' said the latter; 'why, look! there he is walking in the square,' and with that he went on his way. The Marquis immediately had the peasant seized, his shoes torn off, and then, heating an iron till it was red hot, he nailed it to the man's foot.[2] Another day three monks on their travels stopped at his Castle. Ysoré welcomed them and congratu-

[1] Carré, *Revue du dix-huitième siècle*, ii. 1.
[2] D'Argenson, *Mémoires de la Société archéologique de Touraine*, vii.

lated them on their jovial appearance. He gave them a very good room, but locked the door, and, as he thought them too fat, next morning only offered them a small piece of bread, which appeared hanging by a thread from the ceiling.

"At length his arrest was decreed, and a detachment of the mounted police under the orders of M. de la Salle was sent to invest the castle. It was said in Poitou that the latter had been the friend and boon companion of Ysoré in the days before he had turned outlaw. After the usual demand for surrender, M. de la Salle approached the castle to offer terms, only to be shot dead by the Marquis, who recognised him. But the castle was taken by storm, and Ysoré hid himself in a secret cell built in a chimney. They looked for him in vain, but at last questioned a young negro, who never left his master. The negro refused to speak from fear of his master's vengeance. At last he indicated the chimney with a gesture; a fire was immediately lit, and rather than be suffocated and roasted, the Marquis surrendered.

"He was imprisoned first at Poitiers, then in the Conciergerie of the Parliament of Paris, and finally sentenced to death on 2nd September 1756. The sentence was not carried out, 'and he probably remained for a little while in the Conciergerie, and then died there.'"

Fortunately the Ysorés of the eighteenth century were rare, and having described the plundering and criminal *hobereaux*, we can now turn to the "good lords of the Manor." Here is an example of one of them. The winter of 1709 was long remembered for its bitter cold and famine; but we read in the annals of the Harcourt family for that year: "*Monday, 3rd June.*—The distribution of soup began at eleven in the morning, on the stroke of the little clock in the tower, and this was continued daily." Besides this there was always a regular meal for the poor, arranged by the Duke and the parish priest, consisting of: "Rye bread, barley bread, and bread made of grey peas, stewed white peas, and tripe." We have a curious confirmation of this charity of the Harcourts, for in 1760 the Chevalier de

Mirabeau, who was travelling in Normandy, was received at the Castle of Harcourt, and wrote of his host to his brother, the Marquis de Mirabeau and father of the orator, in the following terms: "*25th September* 1760.—I am at Harcourt, and am full of admiration for the real goodness and true greatness of my host. I cannot tell you of the pleasure I experienced when, on feast days, I saw the people everywhere about the Castle, and all the good little peasants and their good little wives assembled to look at their kind master, almost pulling out his watch to see the fob, all with an air of the closest relationship but without any undue familiarity. Nor does this simplicity detract from a seemly dignity, for it is a fine large house. A large staff of well-trained and polite servants, and a large number of honest and pleasant people pass their lives here, and there is the very best of food and wine that one could wish; hunting and shooting of every kind, etc. The good Duke does not let his vassals go to law. He hears their complaints himself, judges them, and settles them with the most admirable patience. In short, he is one of those rare men who are distinguished by their goodness, mildness, charity, and real good nature." [1]

The Marquis de la Rochejaquelin describes in his *Mémoires* the friendly relations which existed between the lords and the peasants in Brittany during the eighteenth century:

"The mutual relations of the lords of the manor and the peasants were unlike those existing in the rest of France, for there was a kind of bond between them which was probably unknown elsewhere. The owners of the Bocage did not farm their lands there to any great extent, but shared the produce with the farmers who cultivated them, so that they had daily interests in common, and connections were based on mutual confidence and good faith. As the estates were much divided and even the smallest property was split into twenty-five or thirty farms, the lord was in continual communication with the peasants who lived round his Castle. He treated them like a father,

[1] Loménie, *Les Mirabeau*, i. 27.

visiting them in their farms, talking with them about their daily life and their cattle, and sharing their accidents and misfortunes, which necessarily affected him also. He was present at the weddings of their children and drank wine with the other guests. On Sundays there was dancing in the court of the Castle, in which the ladies joined. When a boar or wolf hunt had been arranged, the parish priest warned the people of it in his sermon, and each man took his gun and went joyfully to his appointed post, and the huntsmen stationed the guns, who obeyed all orders to the letter. And they went to battle in the same way and with the same docility." [1]

Before concluding this chapter we might take one or two figures from the pages of Frénilly, which may serve as specimens of the Poitevin gentry in the middle of the eighteenth century.

Let us first take the Intendant of Poitou, M. de Nanteuil. He was the chief personage of the province and set the fashion. But M. de Nanteuil did not set a good one, for he left his work to his delegates, and his only tables were backgammon tables, and the players his only guests. So we will leave him at his game.

The Bishop, M. de Beaupoil de St. Aulaire, was a little old man, with a frigid and dry demeanour, who held receptions at which etiquette was enforced with magnificent severity, and gave formal dinner parties to forty guests at a time.

Among the nobility we find the Marquise de Nieuil, wife of a naval commander. She was very witty, and very deaf, though she pretended not to be, and read the movement of people's lips, so that one could talk with her a long time without noticing her affliction. Her elegant mansion was a model to all others. Her mother, the Marquise des Francs, aged seventy, was majestically enthroned at the end of the drawing-room, near the fireplace, and was flanked by two contemporaries, Mme d'Aventon and Mme Vittré, who, as they sat by the hearth, might have been taken, the former for her cat, so soft spoken and wheedling

[1] Rochejaquelin, *Mémoires*, p. 34.

was she, and the latter for her dog, being impudent, snappish, and garrulous.

The President, Irland de Bazôges, was only thirty-five, full of importance and jealous of his position in the province. His little wife was ugly, but always good-humoured, even when gambling, for they gambled often and high at Poitiers. For instance, at Mme de Vigier's, who was so polite and so "venerable," one only found turkeys, those excellent Poitevin turkeys!—stuffed with truffles, and card tables.

Finally, let us present the Marquise d'Aloigny de Rochefort, one of those fine names which were so numerous in Poitou. She was small and hump-backed, had a biting wit, and no small idea of herself. Her husband had himself painted standing at the foot of her bed, and she, in like manner, at the foot of his. She had a very plain daughter who had all her mother's wit and malice, and they passed their days in annoying each other, as when the daughter told every one her age in the presence of the mother, who was extremely anxious to conceal hers.

But we must mention one more noble figure as the most perfect example of this old provincial nobility—a great lady of a bygone age, much respected by all the country round, and, as we shall see, richly deserving it. This was the grandmother of M. de Talleyrand-Périgord, who thus describes her in his *Mémoires*:

"Several gentlemen of ancient lineage formed, as it were, a court about my grandmother; but this court had none of the servility of the thirteenth century, but exhibited a deference combined with intelligence and refinement. M. de Benac, M. de Verteuil, M. d'Absac, M. de Gourville, M. de Chauveron, and M. de Chamillard delighted in accompanying her to Mass on Sundays, each one performing some duty on which their very politeness shed distinction. On their return from Mass they assembled in a large room in the Castle, called the Medicine Room. In the anteroom all the sick who had come to seek my grandmother's assistance had been collected. We passed through them, and Mlle Saunier, who was the oldest of her maids, brought them in one by one, my grandmother being seated in a velvet arm-chair with a black lacquer table before her. Being her grandson, I stood close to her. Two Sisters of Charity would then question each of the sick as regards their wounds or infirmities, and prescribe the remedy most suitable to each case, and my grandmother would then indicate the place where it would be found. One of the gentlemen who had accompanied her to Mass would then go and find it, while another brought a drawerful of linen. I would take a piece, and my grandmother herself would then cut off what she required in the way of bandages or compresses. The sick person also took away some herbs for making a broth, some wine, some medicinal drugs, as well as other little things, of which the most appreciated were the kind and benevolent words of the gracious lady who had interested herself in his or her sufferings."[1]

[1] Talleyrand, *Mémoires*, i. 10.

CHAPTER IV

THE VILLAGE

In 1739 d'Argenson wrote in his *Journal*: "During this last year the general distress throughout the kingdom has grown to unprecedented dimensions. People are dying like flies from poverty and eating grass. The situation is worst in Touraine and Upper Poitou, but it is rapidly approaching Versailles. Famine has caused three risings in the country, at Ruffec, Caen, and Chinon, and women carrying bread have been murdered on the King's highway. The other day the Duke d'Orléans brought a piece of bread made of fern meal with him to the Council, and at the opening of the discussion he laid it on the table before the King with the words: 'This, Sire, is the kind of bread your subjects are eating to-day.'"

This is indeed a gloomy picture, but we must not forget that d'Argenson was himself a disappointed man, and thought that everything was hastening to ruin when he himself was not in office. His picture is true in the main, but it is not altogether complete; when speaking of the peasants in the eighteenth century we must be careful not only of the exaggerations inevitable in all biased historians, but also of overmuch generalisation. In the first place the condition of the peasantry varied according to the localities in which they lived, some provinces being naturally richer than others; in some the assessment of the taxes which weighed upon them was less severe than in others; and finally we must distribute our final judgment on the prosperity or otherwise of the French countryside over a considerable number of years which would include both good and bad harvests. D'Argenson was writing in

1739, and the years 1739 and 1740 were, throughout France, a period of terrible famine and appalling distress, this being especially the case in Touraine, where lay his estate of des Ormes, where he could hear the complaints and witness the rising of the peasants with his own ears and eyes. In 1739, too, Massillon wrote to Cardinal Fleury that very moving letter from the depths of Auvergne which is now justly celebrated for the great courage and apostolic zeal displayed by the writer:

"It is notorious, your Eminence, that Auvergne, a province with no trade and practically no outlets, is the one which, when compared with all the other provinces of the Kingdom, is most heavily burdened with subsidies. The Council is well aware of the fact. They amount to six millions, a sum which the King would not draw from all the lands of Auvergne if he were their sole owner.

"The people of our countryside are living in dreadful misery, and have neither beds nor furniture. For half the year most of them lack even the barley or oat bread which is their only food, and which they have to withhold from themselves and from their children in order to pay the taxes. Besides this poverty, which is now the general and normal state of the country districts, our miserable people have been overwhelmed by hailstorms and bad harvests. Last winter, especially, was so dreadful, that we only escaped famine and wholesale mortality, which indeed seemed inevitable, owing to the warm-hearted and extraordinary charity displayed by people of all classes; and we thus avoided the worst. The fields were deserted and our towns could scarcely accommodate the countless multitudes of these unhappy people who flocked there in search of bread.

"But I would beg your Eminence not to regard the liberty I am taking as merely an excess of episcopal zeal. Beyond all that I owe you already, I owe you the Truth even more. Far from exaggerating, I do assure you that I have weighed my words most carefully in order not to distress you."

Yet if we consider the countryside in the second half of this century we do find, at any rate in some of the provinces, a definite, even if very slight, improvement. It is an undoubted fact, as many authors state, "that material progress becomes evident after the second quarter of the century, and is more obvious from 1750 onwards, after the conclusion of the Seven Years War." [1]

In 1787, Arthur Young found himself in Béarn, and he sets down his impressions as follows: "A succession of many well-built, tight, and comfortable farming cottages, built of stone and covered with tiles, each having its little garden enclosed by clipt thorn hedges, with plenty of peach and other fruit trees . . . an air of neatness, warmth, and comfort breathes over the whole. It is visible in their new-built houses and stables; in their little gardens." And when the writer leaves Pau, the city of Henry IV., he concludes this delightful description of Béarn with the sentence: "Each peasant has 'the fowl in the pot.' " [2] But—and this shows that the progress which has been happily noted above was not general even at the end of the century—Young had been so astonished to find so high a standard of comfort among the French peasantry, that he had begun his description with these significant words: "As I took the road to Moneins I came upon a scene which was so new to me in France that I could hardly believe my own eyes."

Walpole, another Englishman, was also agreeably surprised by the condition of the peasants in the second half of the eighteenth century, and adds his testimony to the above in these words: "I find this country grown prodigiously wealthy since I was last here, twenty-four years ago. [He is writing in 1765.] Boulogne has become a lively and comfortable town with a lot of new houses. Even the smallest village has a prosperous air about it, and the wooden clogs have vanished." [3] But Boulogne was favoured by the English in this century because it lay on the road to Paris, and since as many English came over to France as French crossed to England, both would drop not a few

---

[1] Ardascheff, p. 90.   [2] Arthur Young, *Journal*, i. 72.
[3] Baillon, *Walpole*, p. 17.

gold pieces in coming and going, and thereby enrich the port and its surrounding country. Nor did this escape Walpole, for he writes, as far as English travellers were concerned: "The crumbs which drop from the post-chaises which carry these crowds of English to Paris must have contributed largely to the prosperity of this province." But, had Walpole's post-chaise penetrated farther into other districts, and especially to those out-of-the-way villages far from the high roads, it would have passed those bands of beggars which swarmed during this century, and were the scourge of every village, and Walpole would have witnessed at this time the terrible havoc wrought by the abnormal frosts of 1760 or 1767—the ruined harvests, the ravaged vineyards, the sickness and death, the hordes of starving peasants which roamed the countryside, living on ferns and setting the farms on fire in order that they might steal the stampeding cattle. In 1769 an official report tells us: "They are obliged to resort to the vilest and most revolting nourishment, even searching the styes in order to rob the pigs of their food; others tear up plants and roots from the earth, and eat what they would have never dreamed was eatable; others again live on carrion." [1]

In quoting these extracts, which are so dissimilar and so directly opposed to one another, we must emphasise the fact that we cannot ourselves judge, nor accept the judgments of others, as regards the condition of the peasantry, because any definite or general conclusions which one may arrive at about one province or one epoch of time may be as definitely contradicted by another chronicler in his description of the same province in another year. But one solid fact does emerge from all the mass of memoirs, letters, and documents bearing on this time, and that is that the lot of the peasant in the eighteenth century was certainly far from enviable. In some parts, doubtless, the peasant had become a smallholder, and in Brittany this class was a large one, although more often than not it was very poor.

In 1772, the Abbé Malle, the Vicar of La Chapelle-

Rapport des Alcades, dans Kleinclausz, Histoire de Bourgogne, p. 252.

Jeanson in Brittany, wrote to the Intendant that fever and dysentery had made their appearance in his parish. "Meat would be of great value, but bread is essential unless the poor people are to die of starvation, which I greatly fear they will. Misery, poverty, and famine seem to have reached their height, especially in my parish, which lacks all assistance, for there are but five or six persons who can give any alms, and that only at their doors. In my parish there are 2200 souls, of whom at least 1800 beg for bread which they cannot find, and most of them live on the boiled stalks of cabbage, or, failing that, on grass. I cannot, without tears, dwell on my utter helplessness to succour them. If by heads of families you mean those who own property of any value, whether great or small, I can count about 150, of whom three-quarters own little plots of land large enough to work in a single day, but these are in as miserable a condition as the bigger farmers. If you apply the name 'proprietors' to those who have means of their own, there are about 36, of whom 30 own small holdings, but they are so wretched that it does not prevent many of them from begging bread and fading away. This is the state of my parish, and I ought to know, for I have visited it every year for the last twenty-two years."[1]

Every property which was not in noble hands was divided equally among the heirs, and was thus eventually completely split up, and this progressive parcelling of estates was, as we know, one of the characteristics of agriculture in the eighteenth century. In Brittany a property would consist often enough of a small house, with its little garden and some patch of pasture or tillable ground. And it must be added, that if, by God's grace, the persons of the peasants were now free, their lands remained in serfdom, and in a hopeless state, since the rent exacted by the overlord, and to which they were still liable, often amounted to half the profits. The peasants grew discouraged and deliberately neglected their land, because, as they said, they knew only too well "that where they

[1] Dupuy, p. 297.

sowed, the overlord would reap," and that saying was common enough in most parts of France.

Arthur Young visited Brittany in September 1788, and the following passage in his *Journal* has great interest for us, since it deals with Combourg, a place we know well already. "The country has a savage aspect: husbandry not much further advanced, at least in skill, than among the Hurons, which appears incredible amidst enclosures; the people almost as wild as their country, and their town of Combourg one of the most brutal, filthy places that can be seen: mud houses, no windows, and a pavement so broken as to impede all passengers, but ease none—yet here is a château, and inhabited. Who is this M. de Chateaubriand, the owner that has nerves strung for a residence amidst such filth and poverty?" [1]

The M. de Chateaubriand was none other than the future author of *La Génie du Christianisme*, and not his father, as it is said in *Les Mémoires d'Outre-Tombe*, for the latter had died in 1786, and in this very year, 1788, Chateaubriand was himself in Brittany, where, in order to qualify for the Order of Malta, he was about to receive the tonsure from the Bishop of St. Malo. Moreover, 1788 was the year in which the Estates of Brittany met together, and of the assembly which he has so vividly described. If Chateaubriand was able to "stand" the misery and filth which so shocked Young, it was because his eyes and his sense of smell had accustomed themselves to them from early childhood, and because many other towns and villages were quite as bad as Combourg in these respects, such as Montauban, for instance, which Young describes in much the same terms a few pages farther on.

Thanks, however, to Intendants who were both intelligent and patriotic (for patriotism, though regarded as totally lacking in the eighteenth century, did show itself in the form of ardour for the public weal), such as Turgot, land was cleared, farm settlements were established, with the King's valuable assistance, and new methods of agriculture were introduced and encouraged, and by the end of

[1] Young, i. 146.

the century France was, in consequence, better cultivated and more productive than ever before. It was also owing to the pressure which the Intendants exerted on Ministers that the taxes were reduced in favour of the poorer farmers. Unfortunately the only method of lightening the crushing load which had weighed upon the peasants for centuries would have been a more equitable redistribution of these taxes, but the old system which spared the rich and fell most heavily on those least capable of paying remained in force. In the middle of the century, Forbonnais wrote: "If justice were fairly administered, it would enrage the rich, but it would prevent the poor from paying so much more heavily, in proportion, for their property, the safety of their goods and chattels, and the security of their families." Let us, therefore, review shortly those taxes which most heavily burdened the countryside and were regarded with the greatest detestation.

The first was the *Taille* or land tax, which fell wholly on the peasantry. On the first Sunday of October, the parishioners were summoned by the church bell to assemble after Mass and elect the Collectors. If the parish did not pay its full quota, these Collectors were obliged to make up the difference on pain of imprisonment. Naturally the post was not sought after! Boisguillebert in his *Détail de la France* gives a remarkable account of what the assessment and the collection of the *taille* really meant in eighteenth-century France. The assessment was first made by parishes: "When the round sum laid down by the Council for any one district is known, every one waits upon the Intendants in order to secure favourable terms for their parishes, regardless of whether these are able to pay more or less than their share. It is, therefore, no unusual thing for a parish of 100 hearths and comprising 1500 acres to pay a great deal less than a parish half its size." Next, the assessment is made of individuals. "The elected Collectors, in their turn, hold their court in order to distribute the tax among their fellow-parishioners. But this is done in such a manner that, in the belief that poverty excuses everything, the first step is to take vengeance on those by whom they fear they may themselves be injured on similar occasions, and this spirit of revenge often prevails unto the third generation; thereafter they look to the interests of their own relations and friends, rich or poor." The rich, especially, were conciliated, their very wealth preventing them from being imposed upon, whereas the poor did not dare to bring actions which they were sure to lose, for it was worth no one's while to oppose the big men—*les coqs*—of the village. In Voltaire's *Droit du Seigneur*, when the bailiff reminds Mathurin that he has promised to marry Colette, the latter replies:

"Oh bien! je dépromets.
Je veux pour moi m'arranger désormais:
Car je suis *riche* et *coq de mon village*." [1]

When the assessment had been completed, there followed the collection, which Boisguillebert thus describes: "As this is one of the most disagreeable duties imaginable, the Collectors are unwilling to perform it except in company, so that where there are seven, you may see seven walking up and down the streets instead of relieving each other, and as the *taille* cannot be collected in one year, the collectors for this year will plunder one side, while those of last year will be busy on the other, and these bands form a kind of army which wastes a whole year lounging about the place and collecting little but a thousand curses and insults, and all because as soon as the assessment has been made, it is the interest of those who have been taxed, and who can rely on no protection, to conceal all signs of wealth, and this involves a complete cessation of trade and all commercial transactions."

In Touraine, for instance, "my parish priest told me that eight families who, before my departure, were living by their own labour, now begged their bread. And now, horrible to relate, the *taille* is exacted with more than military severity, for the collectors, aided by the tax-collector's officers and locksmiths, break open doors, and

[1] "I take back my promise, for I wish henceforth to live my own life. I am rich and the 'cock' of my village."

THE PROFESSIONAL LETTER WRITER
From an engraving after Jean Jacques de Boissieu

seizing the furniture sell it for about a quarter of its real value." [1]

Next to the *taille* come the *Aides* or subsidies, and Rousseau gives an account of the collectors of this tax and of their misdeeds in his *Confessions*: "One day, on my journey to Lyons in 1732, I went out of my way in order to explore some country which looked to me quite delightful, and finding on close inspection that it was even more charming, I penetrated ever farther until I was quite lost. After many hours of aimless walking, I felt quite exhausted from hunger and thirst, so I stopped at a peasant's house, which, although not very tempting, was the only one I could see. I thought it would be as in Geneva or Switzerland, where all more or less well-to-do inhabitants are in a position to offer hospitality. I asked the farmer to give me a dinner, for which I was prepared to pay, but he only put before me some skim milk and some coarse barley bread, saying that was all he had. So I drank the milk with pleasure and ate the bread, husks and all, but it was not very fortifying to a man worn out with fatigue. The farmer observed me closely, and being convinced by my appetite that my story was true, said that he realised I was an honest young man who would not betray him, and immediately opened a trap-door next to his kitchen, down which he dived, reappearing with a loaf of good wheaten bread, a most appetising if much dwindled ham, and with what rejoiced my heart more than all the rest, a bottle of wine. To these he added a most succulent omelette, and I dined as surely no other wanderer ever dined before. But when it came to paying, all his old anxiety and fear revived; he refused my money, which he said he did not want, with extraordinary vehemence, and I could not for the life of me imagine what terrified him so. At last, with shaking limbs, he uttered the terrible words *commis* (tax-collectors) and *rats de cave*. He told me he had to hide his wine on account of the subsidies, and his bread on account of the *taille*, and that he would be a lost man if any one began to doubt that he was not dying of hunger." [2]

[1] D'Argenson, vii. 55.   [2] i. 4.

This passage is confirmed by a parish priest: "The tax collectors who collected the subsidies (*rats de cave*) come and measure your barrel; know exactly how much liquor is consumed at such and such a fair; how much spirit was consumed at such a first Mass; in fact, they are so feared that people dare not give even a glass of wine in charity to some poor wretch [like Rousseau!] for fear of having to pay the duty on *trop du*,"[1] the *trop du* being anything over and above the amount fixed for one's personal consumption.

La Bruyère also has an often-quoted and much-discussed passage on the peasantry: "One sees certain wild animals, male and female, all about the country, black, livid, scorched by the sun, bound to the earth which they scrape with invincible obstinacy. They seem to have an articulate voice, and, when they rise, display human faces —they are, in fact, human beings. At night they withdraw to their dens, where they feed on black bread, water, and roots. They spare other men the labour of sowing, tilling, and reaping, and therefore deserve that they should not lack the bread which they themselves have sown." This picture is purposely painted in the darkest colours in order to impress the reader, but it is not quite imaginary and is confirmed, in part, by official reports and eighteenth-century documents in provincial archives. In 1742 the sub-delegate of Falaise writes to the Intendant: "A large number of parishes pay very little, but there are others which are hopelessly over-assessed, or, rather, crushed, and where the inhabitants are dying of want. These people are naked as worms, black as negroes, and sustain themselves on the most miserable nourishment."[2]

La Bruyère writes: "At night they withdraw to their dens," and, according to the memoirs of the time, this was all the home which the peasantry of Lower Normandy could claim as their own.

From Briouze to Avranches, and from Vire to Domfront, the dwelling of the peasant was merely a low and confined hut, half-buried in the ground, and sometimes built of roughly hewn ashlar, but where this was unobtainable

[1] Bernier, p. 167. [2] *Ibid.* p. 55.

the walls were made of loam with a brick foundation. The hut was usually about twelve feet square, deprived of light and air, and damp because it was underground; though lacking both floor and ceiling, it served as eating-room and common bedroom. The beds, which had no curtains and no partitions, touch one another, so that "the nightcaps often get mixed in them, and the household utensils roll about among them." He is indeed fortunate if "the other domestic buildings are scattered over his plot and the pig does not grunt, the cows low, and the sheep bleat under the same roof as the family, only separated from them by a screen made of straw or a partition of badly joined planks."[1]

Le Grand d'Aussy, who lived in Auvergne in 1788, has left this vivid and picturesque narrative of how the Auvergnats lived in winter: "The scarcity and consequent high price of firewood in the mountain districts caused great trouble among the peasantry there during winter. They therefore did without fires by living among their cattle. Usually the dwelling was divided into three parts—the stable on the right, the barn on the left, and the house in the middle—all joined together and with only one door. When the cold season begins the whole family leaves the house and enters the stable, which thus becomes their winter residence. These stables are built in the shape of a rectangle, with a loft above in which the hay and other dry fodder for the cattle is stored, with two unglazed attics which admit the air, and two doors, one opening to the outer air and one into the house. But in order to make these stables warmer and to make the loft larger, they are built very low. The animals are stalled to right and left, and the beds of the family are set up at the end where it is warmest, and in order to reach them you have to pass between the two ranks of animals. These beds are really boxes made of fir-wood, fixed to the ground and filled with straw. Beside this, the poorer folk have but one blanket, while the more well-to-do add a kind of mattress or a large sack full of oats. These sacks are called 'field mattresses,' because it is in the fields that the oats which form the bundle grow.

[1] Bernier, p. 50.

Only the rich have feather-beds—a luxury which is much envied. Thus a girl who, on her marriage, brings a dowry will insist on a clause in the marriage-contract that her husband must provide her with a feather and not with a 'field' mattress.

"The life which the family lead is a strange one. They rise at eight or nine. The father and the boys, and farmhands, if there be any, then feed the cattle, while the wife and daughters run into the house and, having lit a fire of brushwood, make soup. They then dine, as quickly as possible so as not to freeze, and then all run back to the warm shelter of the stable. At five o'clock in the evening they have some more soup, and then retire again till next day's dinner. All household duties devolve upon the women. They milk the cows and make butter and cheese, and they therefore rise earlier and go to bed later than the menfolk. If snow has fallen and blocked the path to the pump, one of them is told off to sweep a fresh one. She has to go to and fro, often up to the waist in snow, before she has scraped a road for her companions. A man would consider himself disgraced if he were to fetch water himself, and he would certainly become the laughing-stock of the village. These mountain rustics have all the profound scorn and despotic disdain for women which is peculiar to all savage or semi-barbarian races, and regard them as slaves who exist to perform the functions which they themselves consider vile and degrading. Their sole occupation is to talk of their cattle, or occasionally, if their business requires it, to thresh their corn and visit the neighbouring markets. Beyond that, their life is that of a savage, sunk in profound sloth and inactivity.

"It is, however, very rare for a family to spend the winter alone and isolated in their stables. Usually several households join forces, and if one of them owns a stable which is larger and warmer than the others, they will congregate in that one during the day. In the mornings, when the soup has been eaten, every one makes his way thither, and all sit round on benches, and I need hardly say how they spend their time. They gossip, laugh, inveigh against the taxes, tell tales about the young girls of the neighbourhood, and speak evil of their parish priest, their overlord —in short, of every one who is not present. At five o'clock they prepare to eat their soup, then still gossip awhile, and finally all go home to their respective beds." [1]

Let us next turn to the *Gabelle*, the salt tax—the peasant's nightmare—and its cursed collectors, the *gabelous*, who spied on him ceaselessly and tortured him with their inquisitions: Has he taken 7 lb. of salt, at twelve and fifteen sols the pound, from the salt depot, as many times as he has mouths to feed in his house? Has he specified whether the salt was for his cooking or his salt-cellar, or whether it was to salt his bacon or his butter? If not, fines and confiscation followed, and the poor wretch's furniture would be sold if he happened to have bought cheaper salt from the pedlar instead of from the official source.

In this connection we might quote some amusing verses by Voltaire, written in 1775, and entitled "Les Finances." We must, however, bear in mind that, although the author of the *Dictionnaire philosophique* began as a pamphleteer, he, of all eighteenth-century authors, has left us the most exact details of the habits, customs, and conditions of the people—in short, of the society of his day. Here we have an honest *bourgeois* of Paris who, "devoured," as Voltaire himself had been, by the exactions of Terray, the Controller-General, had retired to Champagne and his vineyard. One day, as he was arranging his cellar, he is visited by a stranger, whom he takes for the squire owing to his brilliant escort *habillés en guerriers*—dressed as warriors. He offers him the best of his vintage, and then humbly inquires whom he has the honour of entertaining:

"Je suis, dit l'inconnu, dans les fermes nouvelles
Le royal inspecteur des *aides* et *gabelles*.
—Ah! pardon, monseigneur! Quoi, vous *aidez* le roi?
Oui, l'ami—Je révère un si sublime emploi,
Le mot d'aides s'entend: *gabelle* m'embarrasse.
D'où vient ce mot?—D'un Juif appelé Gabelus.

---

[1] Le Grand d'Aussy, *Voyage d'Auvergne* (1788), p. 281.

—Ah, d'un Juif! je le crois.—Selon les nobles 'us'
De ce peuple divin, dont je chéris la race,
Je viens prendre chez vous les *droits* qui me sont dus.
J'ai fait quelques progrès, par mon expérience,
Dans l'art *de travailler un royaume en finance*.
Je fais loyalement deux parts de votre bien:
La première est au roi qui n'en retire rien:
La seconde est pour moi. Voici votre Mémoire:
Tant pour les brocs de vin qu'ici nous avons bus;
Tant pour ceux qu'aux marchands vous n'avez point vendus,
Et pour ceux qu'avec vous nous comptons encore boire,
Tant pour le sel marin, duquel nous présumons
Que vous deviez garnir vos savoureux jambons.
Vous ne l'avez point pris, et vous deviez le prendre.
Je ne suis point méchant et j'ai l'âme assez tendre
Composons, s'il vous plaît. Payez dans ce moment
Deux mille écus tournois par accomodement." [1]

Voltaire adds in a note that "a man who has so many pigs should use so much salt for pickling them, and if they die he must still take the same amount, or else he is fined and his furniture sold."

The exactions and vexation of the *gabelous* were such that contraband trade was largely indulged in to circumvent them, and the *faux-saulniers*, or smugglers of salt, increased enormously in numbers in spite of the threat of fines and even of the galleys. In the district of Tours alone the Farmers-General kept a staff of not less than 1906 persons, both on horse and foot, in order to cope with them.[2]

[1] "I," said the unknown—"I am the Royal Director of the *Aides* and *Gabelle* for the new farms." "Your pardon, my lord! So you aid the King?" "Why, yes, my friend." "I reverence such employment, but I heard the word *aides* and the *gabelle* frightens me! Whence comes this word?" "From Gabelus, a Jew." "From a Jew! I can well believe it!" "Anyway, like those noble people whose race I so admire, I have now come to claim my rights from you; and, in fact, my own experience has taught me much of the art of travelling the Kingdom on behalf of the Finances. Thus I loyally divide your goods into two halves: one for the King who won't derive any benefit from it, the second for myself. So here is your account. So much for the wine we have drunk here, so much for all you have not sold to the merchants, and so much for what we still hope to drink with you. So much for the salt with which we presume you have flavoured your succulent hams. Why, you won't take it? Believe me, you must. I am not a brute, and have a tender heart, but, pray, let us settle. You must instantly pay the sum of two thousand crowns by agreement."

[2] Dumas, p. 76.

In the famous *Compte Rendu au Roi* of January 1781, in which Necker lays bare the social consequences of the *gabelle*, there is a passage which it is well worth quoting, as it is of importance for the social historian: "A universal outcry has been raised against this tax," and he goes on to explain why "in certain parts of the realm it is regarded with horror." Salt is carried from a free district into one that is taxed, and this naturally means enormous profits. But in order to suppress this illicit trade the police has had to be armed. "Thousands of men, ever attracted by the lure of easy gain, are continually joining in a trade which is illegal; agriculture is abandoned for a career which promises large and speedy returns; even children take to it in their early years and under their parents' eyes, and thus grow up oblivious of their duties. In this way, by the mere operation of a fiscal combination, a generation of lawless men is bred."

The Right of the Chase has already been mentioned. It ruined the peasantry. Chamfort writes: "The flatterers of princes have said that the chase is an image of war, and indeed the peasants, whose fields it devastates, must think that they resemble one another closely enough." Mercier is justly indignant about the Court of Woods and Forests, which condemns to the galleys all poor wretches who, as he puts it, have committed *perdricide* and *lièvricide*. "If the hare eats his cabbages, the pigeon destroys his crops, or the carp swims in the river which waters his field, he must not touch them, and he must allow himself to be devoured by hare and pigeon alike." [1]

Some lords, as in Brittany, exacted dues for smoke, which had to be paid by those who made fires and smoke. As all those who had *feu et lieu* were liable, Pasquier writes that this gave rise to the expression *sans feu ni lieu*: "We described a man as being *sans feu ni lieu* when we wished to describe one who had no settled domicile." [2]

There were, however, some wealthy districts, so let us, in Le Grand d'Aussy's company, take part in one of

---

[1] Mercier, ii. 34.   [2] Pasquier, *Recherches de la France*, viii. 48.

those joyous vintages in the country of Champagne: "Men and women, each with their baskets on their arms, arrive at the foot of the hill together; here they halt and form a line. The chief of the band then chants a joyous song, all the rest joining in the chorus. They then go up and spread over the vineyard and begin their work, which goes on without cessation, save for occasional bursts of song from one or other of the vintagers, and the jokes which are made at the expense of the passers-by. In the evening, as soon as supper is over, the festivity begins anew. Round dances are indulged in and ribald songs are sung which, as they are appropriate to the occasion, are known as vintage songs. Soon the gaiety becomes general. Hosts, guests, friends, servants, all are dancing together, and so ends a day of toil which might almost be called a holiday. This is what I witnessed in a district of Champagne." [1]

Thus, in a good year, the peasant is contented and has his good time, but he is never certain—and this is the sadness of his lot—whether in the coming year he will have sufficient to eat, and it would seem that we must agree with d'Argenson when he wrote these grave words: "I would lay it down that a kingdom such as this, which is reduced to such a pitch that the harvest, whether good or bad, is the factor which decides happiness or misery, is itself condemned to perpetual misery." [2]

The years of famine were, in fact, numerous—"those years," as Montesquieu says with emotion, "which were sad enough for the poor, but sadder still for the rich in a Christian people." Famine was followed by disease, and the epidemics were often terrible. Du Cluzel, Intendant of Tours, wrote to d'Ormesson on 12th April 1783: "When the inclemency of the seasons and their inconstancy, and when the air, full of harmful vapours, affect bodies already worn out with toil and want, death reaps a mighty harvest." [3]

The two most important personages in the village were the Bailiff, who was generally detested because he represented the Lord of the Manor, and held, in his name,

[1] iii. 59. [2] ii. 149. [3] Dumas, *Généralité de Tours*, 368.

the so-called Manorial Courts to which we shall refer farther on, and the Parish Priest who, on the other hand, was generally revered and loved, because he belonged to the people, because he was poor, and also because the country folk of the eighteenth century were still deeply religious. The church was, indeed, the centre of village life, and "its communal house." "With its tower whence the bells pealed merrily, both day and night, on the great feasts, its altars, its relics of the saints, with its feasts which were the only holidays of the countryside, its brotherhoods, which comprised the whole population, the church set the lead to the whole village."[1] We ought to add that the parish priest would have been more popular still if he had always had enough to live upon, but he was reduced to the barest necessaries of life by those greedy tithe owners, the bishops, and chapters, and was ever at law with his flock with regard to this tithe, of which he only kept a third, and which was levied on produce as well as on flocks. "It were desirable," so the parochial archives tell us, "to suppress the tithes, for their suppression would bring about an edifying peace between priest and people, and there would be no more of those lawsuits which are, alas, so common." As, in many cases, the parish priest was unable to live on the slender stipend which the Bishop left him, he made what he could by raising the "casual" fees on baptisms, marriages, and funerals. The stipends, which varied in different districts, scarcely ever exceeded 700 livres, and more often fell as low as 300, which was not a "living wage," and this explains the complaints of the Lower Clergy which were heard on every side. We find the following protest in *Les Soupirs de la France esclave*: "None are so wretched and so oppressed as the Lower Clergy. While the Bishop plays the great nobleman and spends scandalous sums on hounds, horses, furniture, servants, food, and carriages, the parish priest has not the wherewithal to buy himself a new cassock. The burden of collecting the tithe falls on him, but the Prelates, not he, pocket it. The Bishops treat their priests

[1] Attaix, p. 39.

not as honest footmen but as stable-boys." That the pamphleteer has not exaggerated the poverty of the clergy is confirmed by the following passage drawn from the memoirs of a village priest—and we could quote many more of the same kind: "It is no unusual thing to meet parish priests who have neither *victum* nor *vestitum*, and who have to beg a bowl of soup here and a stew there."

But the parishioners had not only to pay "casual" fees to their priests. Bishops and Abbots, who owned the tithes, seemed to have forgotten that they had been instituted to pay for the seemly performance of Divine worship, and the parishioners were thus obliged to pay out of their own pockets for the upkeep of the presbytery unless some good priest undertook to repair and decorate his church out of his own slender resources. This was done by that Breton priest, Monier, Vicar of Soudan, whose scrupulous piety is reflected in his *Journal*, from which we may quote these moving and candid lines: "In building the bakehouse this year with money which I could have spent more usefully for the good of my soul in giving it to the poor, I have studied the comfort of my successors more than my own. I do therefore most earnestly beg them to remember me in their Masses and in their almsgiving, that I may obtain mercy. Moreover in this year (1746) I have also, at my own expense, had a step made for the High Altar and bought a crucifix of ivory mounted on ebony which cost me as much as 15 livres. *Laus Uni Deo!*"[1] Who, therefore, would dispute this fine tribute to our parish priests from the pen of a foreigner: "The parish priests of France formed one of the most respected classes in society. On his return to London, Dr. Burney said: 'I know no men who are such a credit to Humanity as the parish priests of Paris. Even if their incomes were in most cases insufficient, yet their zeal, their habits, and their piety shed a lustre on these citizens, who deserved a better fate.'"[2]

The "zeal" of the country clergy is well exemplified in the following lines, written by a parishioner: "The

---

[1] *Annales de Bretagne*, 1899–1900.   [2] Sénac, *Du gouvernement*, p. 56.

presbytery at Y—— is always open, and the priest is ever accessible. This good man has to travel six leagues to his episcopal city, and when he arrives, His Lordship's servants regard him as too early a visitor, and he is left to freeze in an anteroom. After his audience with my Lord, he returns at once, and before he has time to go to bed, or even to rest a little, his parishioners clamour for him to visit some person who has been seized with indigestion. But he never murmurs." [1]

It was the parish priest's duty to announce all new legislation to his flock, and this he did either from the pulpit or by nailing the notices to the church door. But it was questionable whether the peasant could read them. He might possibly be able to, if there was a school in the village, but this was by no means a general rule. It will suffice if, in dealing with this vexed question of primary education in pre-Revolution days, we quote the conclusion of the learned work compiled by the Abbé Allain: "We can state definitely that primary instruction existed in our country before 1789, and that thousands of primary schools, unequally distributed though they were, provided an elementary education for the children of the lower classes." But they certainly were "unequally distributed." In Burgundy, for instance, "many" parishes had their own school; in the diocese of Angers only "half" of them, and these schools were pious foundations, obviously religious in character, and a kind of "continuation" schools for instruction in the Catechism. The Cevennes and the Vivarais were less fortunate, and in 1783 the Council of State noted that "most of the sheriff's officers and officials cannot sign their names on the deeds which the barristers and notaries have drawn up," [2] and it is well known that in 1789 large numbers of electors were unable to write their names on the parish rolls.

The *régents*, or schoolmasters, were usually chosen by a general meeting of the parish summoned by the parish priest. "But where did they come from? This was one of the shortcomings in the organisation of primary education

---

[1] G ***, *Caractères*, p. 154.   [2] *Histoire de Languedoc*, xiii. 1320.

before the Revolution. They came from anywhere and were a little of everything," [1] and they had to do a good many things for very little money. Thus, in Normandy a schoolmaster received "3 or 4 sols a month for every pupil" and an annual stipend which, in some parishes, was such a modest one that he never got it! In the Archives of Calvados there is a quaint copy of the appointment of such an instructor. "The peasant inhabitants of the parish assembled together with a view to appointing a *custos* (this was the chief duty) to look after the clock, ring the *Angelus* night and morning, peal the bells on feast days and Sundays, assist at the singing of Divine Office, serve Mass, decorate the altars, scour the candlesticks, and take charge of the school (this was an afterthought) throughout the year, except during the month of August." [2]

In spite of the Church and the constabulary, bands of beggars, vagabonds, and robbers were still to be met with in the countryside, and they would often terrorise the population. They knew well that the authorities were powerless to cope with them, and, as we shall see, were usually inclined to ignore them. In connection with this state of insecurity and the terror which often prevailed in country districts, we must say a word about the Monster which spread panic throughout the Gévaudan, and became a legend throughout the kingdom for many a long day. The story is often met with in contemporary memoirs.

In 1764 the Gévaudan was ravaged by carnivorous beasts which destroyed the flocks and struck terror into the population. From 1764 to 1767 no less than fifty-one persons were devoured. The terrified imagination of the inhabitants attributed this slaughter to a Monster, and this soon drew the attention of all France, becoming notorious under the name of "The Beast of the Gévaudan." "The papers," writes the Duke de Croÿ, "were full all the winter (1765) of the ferocious Beast of the Gévaudan which had killed over sixty people and against which over

[1] Allain, p. 127.   [2] Bernier, p. 162.

twenty thousand men had been mobilised in vain. The English, thereupon, invented the pleasing jest that the Beast, after defeating one of our armies, attacked an old crone's kitten, which promptly killed it with its claws, and that, when opened, the Beast was found to be full of guns and standards belonging to the French it had slain." [1] Eventually repeated drives established the fact that they were dealing with packs of wolves, and these were dealt with by poison.

Here is a picture of country life compiled from contemporary memoirs. "Occasionally the villages are visited by pedlars, the sons of farmers and smallholders who were too poor to support them. These carry the most varied objects in their baskets: such as knives, scissors, needles and thread, ties and handkerchiefs. Their arrival at a farmhouse is always welcome, and once past the watchdog they will enter with a humble 'Good-day, Master. Good-day, Mistress. Do you require any haberdashery to-day?' and then they place their basket on the chest, distributing a few trifles among the children, thereby giving all the family great pleasure. The pedlar's knowledge of human nature is rewarded by a place at the foot of the table and a lodging in the stable, while next morning the farmer's wife will not let him depart without exchanging homespun and rabbit-skins for some of his wares." [2]

We need not dwell long on the habits and character of the peasant. He was much the same in the eighteenth century as he is in France to-day, working hard and for long hours, economical, reserved, something of a coward, very devout and even superstitious, as when he invokes St. Loup on behalf of his sheep and St. Clair to preserve his sight, helping his neighbour when he can do so without opening his purse, and respectful to the powers that be, for he remembers the old proverb: "Cunning wins more than force." But when he is driven too far and finds himself wronged, he will strike in his turn, and in his rage will spare nothing and nobody, as is shown in the many peasant

[1] Croÿ, *Mémoires*, ii. 192.   [2] Bernier, p. 72.

risings which famine and the exactions of the tax-collector caused in this century. His outstanding characteristic, however, was, and is, his affection for the land, his land, on whose conquest he had lavished such labour, care, and cunning, and which he had striven ever to enlarge. Let us see how in Normandy a peasant, step by step and stage by stage, worked himself up, first to being an *honeste homme*, then a *sieur*, and finally *coq de sa paroisse*.

"The peasant is always reckoning, always calculating, always reasoning with an eye to his own interests. He is reticent about his affairs, his trade, and his journeys, except in so far that he may one day, after a glass or two, be heard to declare that the Government is a bad one, the harvest poor, that he finds it hard to live, and is now losing as much as he once hoped to gain. But his money increases for all that."

Thanks to his labours and economy he at last becomes a farmer, but he goes on working. "He works from morn to night, and does not even sleep at night. Instead he lights a big lantern and goes to visit his stables, and when he does go back to bed he has nightmares in which the wolf is in the sheepfolds and the stoat in his chicken-run. He talks about his poverty all the year round, and redoubles his excuses whenever an obstinate borrower comes and asks him for a small loan. He has sworn his most solemn oath, time and time again, that he has not got a farthing with which to pay the collector, but that very evening, after vespers, he goes and walks round a little field which is for sale, decides that he can do with it and bids a certain sum for it through a stranger. Then drawing a big bag, with many a groan, from the depths of a chest, he carries it, with more groans, to a notary and pays the vendor in cash."

But he soon begins to realise that farming does not sufficiently repay his labour, since half his profits go to his master, and so, by means of an advance he now becomes a tenant, paying his master a definite sum, but otherwise independent. At the same time he rises one step higher in the social hierarchy, but still plays the part of a humble—and needy—individual.

"He is still modestly dressed in his long jacket, and keeps his hair short, and we see him gently ambling to town to carry to his master two fat capons and a part of the rent due. On arrival he taps lightly, bows low to the footman and the serving-maid, prostrates himself before Monsieur, slowly draws the money from his capacious pocket, talks of the bad harvest, of last year's hailstorm, of the wolf who has eaten one of his lambs, of caterpillars, moles, and field-mice, pleads for a short respite in paying the remainder, and when this is granted, once more commends himself to his good master's mercy and patience."

Some years pass, and the owner either dies or else finds himself in want of money. The property is up for sale, but who in the parish is sufficiently moneyed to buy it? Listen to the sly story-teller: "My heart is wrung with sorrow, for I have just met the most unhappy of mortals. It was not an owner whose taxes have been increased nor an unemployed labourer. No, it was a poor farmer who had bought carts, oxen, and horses, and who had all but ruined himself in buying a small property as well, a property which his children will never make pay. And the wretched man's misery is not yet at an end, nor will it ever be! For he will go naked and starve all his life in order to buy yet another small property, which will enable his children to live in comfort and be idle, dress fashionably, and efface the recollection of their good father's mean extraction." [1]

Before we close this chapter we must say a word about the Manorial Courts, which have already been mentioned several times, and which still existed in many places, to the great despair of the peasantry who were subject to them. In 1749 Barbier expressed the wish in his *Journal* "that all Manorial Courts whose officers were peasants, might be suppressed, as the countryfolk are ruined by the costs of all these judicial proceedings, but this will never happen, because all the great Lords are jealous of exercising their judicial prerogatives." [2] He was quite right, and on the eve of the Revolution there were still about 80,000

---

[1] L'Abbé G ***, *Caractères* (Bernier), p. 178.   [2] Barbier, iv. 372.

Manorial Courts in existence. The Royal Justices dealt with the *bourgeois* in the towns, and the Manorial Justices with the countryfolk; but what justice could the latter expect from these village judges, bailiffs, procurators, and clerks, all of whom were dependent on the overlord, who could dismiss them at will, and usually treated them just as if they were his servants? When a gentleman brought an action against the peasants connected with taxes or some trifling matter, before judges of that kind, it was not likely that they would give a judgment against him! The proverb said: "A Lord of straw will devour his steel vassal," and, in his *Seigneur du Village*, Voltaire makes his bailiff exclaim:

> "Car je suis le magister ici,
> Je suis baillif, je suis notaire aussi" (i. 1).[1]

Indeed, it often happened that a bailiff in one Court was procurator in another, notary in a third, surveyor in a fourth, and so on. The clerk in *Le Mariage de Figaro* "used to eat with two sets of teeth," and was called Double-Main, but some of them seemed to have three and even four paws, so many claws did they display in snatching the innocent peasant's halfpence, and they well knew how to educate him in trickery. Loyseau thus describes these Manorial Courts, or "village extortions," as he calls them: "In order to bolster up a bad case it is necessary to make the judge, the clerk, and the procurators drunk in the village tavern, for the tavern is usually the High Court where the documents are drawn up and the cases settled in favour of the party who pays the bill. And when these extortioners and blood-suckers get a rich client into their hands, they are adepts at prolonging the legal processes, and contrive to hang up the case as long as his money lasts.

> " 'Non missura cutem nisi plena cruoris hirudo.'

"Unhappily, the Manorial Courts were not capable of maintaining order and security in the countryside, for even in the places where they did exist, they had become ridiculous, since the Lords of the Manor were so impoverished

---

[1] "Here I am, judge and bailiff, and notary all in one."

that they had the means neither to pay the costs of criminal proceedings, nor to repair the ruined prisons of their castles, and the brigands laughed at the judges and the constabulary, robbed travellers at their own sweet will, and attacked and pillaged isolated houses, of which there were so large a number. The gibbets, which still stood at the entrance to the villages as a sign of the prerogatives of the Lords of Manor, still extant but no longer exercised, now failed to inspire them with any fear. These gibbets were made of stone with a cross-bar on the top from which the condemned in days gone by were hung. They were silent witnesses of the lord's judicial powers, and the higher his dignity, the more numerous were the pillars. A mere lord had three, a baron four, a count six, and so on. But people had not been hung for a long time now, and in some districts evil-doers were not even arrested, and we shall see the reason for this.

"In 1766 a Commission of Three Councillors of the Parliament of Toulouse was appointed to inquire into the abuses in the administration of criminal cases in the Vivarais and the Gévaudan. Their report is appalling. Wherever the Commission sat, it called all the judicial officials of the district before it, and collected all the available statistical details, which were as curious as they were terrible. Here are some of them. Most of the Manorial Courts retained the officials prescribed by the ordinances—judge, procurator, and clerk—but as often as not these had neither tribunal, nor prison, nor register. The judges testified that they did not dare to take action for fear of their lives, and this may well explain the report which the Commissioners drew up. It included murders of all kinds and with all known weapons such as swords, knives, bayonets, and axes, and even by kicks; robbery under arms both on the King's highway and in private houses, people who had been drowned, domestic tragedies, inheritances forestalled by murder, and so on. This was an example of judicial impotence in the mountainous regions of Languedoc of such imposing people as an Archbishop of Vienne, an Abbot of Aiguebelle, a Prince de Soubise, a Duke d'Uzès, a Count de Voguë, and many another Justiciar whose authority was as empty as his name was high-sounding."[1]

Let us, however, conclude our survey on a happier note, with a cheerful anecdote which illustrates the well-known shrewdness of the French peasant, who does not allow himself to be laughed at even at a princely table:

"The mayor of the small village of Talans in Burgundy enjoyed, *ex officio*, the right to a seat in the Estates of the Province, and this gave him the privilege of eating at the Prince's table when he came down to open them. At this time the mayor was a little man to look at, but not lacking in wit, besides being extremely pleased with his prerogatives. The young pages who waited at table thought they could amuse themselves at his expense, so as soon as one had filled his plate, another, who stood behind him, immediately removed it and gave him a clean one. This little joke, which condemned him to fast while all around him were enjoying a sumptuous repast, soon began to annoy him. As he was being served with the wing of a pheasant, his plate was snatched away, whereupon he aimed a hard blow with the handle of his knife at the fingers of the little rascal, who quickly withdrew them out of reach. The Prince, who was young, and had been much amused at this jest, although he had pretended not to see what was going on, said to him: 'Why, what is this, sir? You strike my pages?'

" 'Oh no, my lord, I am only teaching them to read. They are mixing up their L's (*ailes*) with their O's (*os*)!' The Prince laughed heartily at this joke and ordered the pages to stop teasing him."[2]

[1] *Extraits de l'Histoire de Languedoc*, xiii. 1198.   [2] Dugast, ii. 294.

CHAPTER V

THE ARMY

THE Army under the old régime consisted of Regular troops in which enlistment was voluntary, and of the Militia which was compulsorily recruited.

Let us take the former first. The Captain, assisted by his recruiting officers, formed his company, and filled up the vacancies in it, but the recruiting officers were often obliged to resort to violence. Thus, in country districts, they would carry off young men from the fields, drag them to inns, and, after filling them with wine, force them to put a cross, in lieu of signature, to an enlistment form. Some of these so-called volunteers would protest when sober, and occasionally they would get their involuntary enlistment cancelled. For instance, the Prince de Montbarey, a Minister, wrote to du Cluzel, Intendant of Tours: "As four witnesses have testified that one Mossand was so drunk that the man who took him to the recruiting office was obliged to hold him up, and since such an enlistment is contrary to regulations, I beg you to annul the same." This was dated 25th May 1777.

In Paris, recruiting was practised on the Pont-Neuf in the following manner: "The recruiting officers and crimps, or 'sellers of human flesh,' as they were called, gathered at the Pont-Neuf, so as to collect men for their colonels, who then sold them to the King. Formerly they had dens in which they beat and otherwise ill-treated young men whom they had surprised by force or under orders, so as to compel them to enlist. This monstrous abuse has been stopped, but they are still allowed to use any tricks or frauds to enrol the poor. Indeed, they employ strange means. Some own taverns where they make those who love wine overmuch drunk, while on the eve of Shrove Tuesday and Martinmas they parade the streets carrying long rods from which dangle turkeys, chickens, quails, and leverets with which they attract the hungry. Their wretched dupes, who are gazing vacantly at the Samaritaine and its bell tower, and have never eaten a square meal in their lives, are tempted to fill their stomach for once, and so barter their liberty for one day's pleasure. A bag of money is rattled in their ears with the cry: 'Who wants this?' and in this way an army of heroes is collected which is to be the glory of the Sovereign and the State. These heroes cost thirty livres a head at the Pont-Neuf, but if they are fine specimens they get a little more. The sons of artisans enlist, to the great grief of their parents, and the latter sometimes buy them out, paying a hundred crowns for a man who has cost but ten. This money goes into the pockets of the colonel and the recruiting officers.

"These recruiting officers go swaggering about, their swords at their side, loudly calling on all young men who pass, tapping them on the shoulder, taking them by the arm, and urging them to come along with them in a voice which they try to make as cajoling as possible. The young man thus accosted turns aside with lowered eyes, blushing cheeks, and an air of timidity and modesty, which attracts one's notice on the first occasion that one is witness to one of these strange scenes.

"The officers have their recruiting offices near by, each one surmounted by an emblazoned flag, which is their standard. It is here that those who willingly enlist come to sign the form provided. One of these offices displayed the following verse from Voltaire:

'Le premier qui fut roi fut un soldat heureux,'

but the recruiting officer could hardly have appreciated either the force or the inference of the line he quoted."

As regards the Militia, its members were drawn by lot, and each battalion was recruited from one district. Every man over sixteen (after 1765 this was raised to eighteen) and under forty was eligible for a service which was the terror of the countryside, on whom it weighed most heavily, since, in the eighteenth century, the towns only contained a quarter of the total population of France, and in the towns it was not difficult for many to elude this "lottery of misfortune." All nobles, without exception, were exempt, even the ennobled and all such as "lived nobly"—that is to say, those whose fathers had held a privileged office for twenty years. Also all students were exempt, provided that their fathers did not follow any trade. Paris, too, was, under normal circumstances, exempt. "To sum up, then, all *bourgeois* living on their incomes, all merchants, artisans, and farmers in easy circumstances, members of the legal profession, public functionaries, and those belonging to the liberal professions, literary men, in fact, who all more or less constituted the aristocracy of the working class—all these were exempt from service in the Militia. The privileged classes were not only exempt themselves, but they were able to exempt their servants. So it was practically only the manual and casual labourers, the working class both of the town and country, and the smaller shopkeepers, artisans, and farmers, as well as the humbler employés, who remained subject to this burden." [1]

So as to avoid drawing "a black ticket," the peasant became a footman, or else, as married men were exempt, he would marry the first girl that came along. Many parish registers record that "enrolment precipitates marriages which are often ill-assorted and premature." Turgot, in a letter written from the Limousin on 8th January 1773 to the Minister, de Monteynard, describes the drawing of lots: "Every time the lots are drawn, great disorder prevails throughout the country districts, and a kind of civil war rages among the peasants; for some take refuge in the forests and are then pursued by their neighbours, who, fully armed, hunt down the fugitives in order to recapture them, so as to avoid, themselves, the fate which

[1] Gebelin, *Milices provinciales*, p. 91.

the former have tried to evade. Murders and criminal cases increase by leaps and bounds, and the result is that parishes are depopulated and agriculture neglected. When the battalions are to be assembled, the village authorities have to send in their conscripts under guard of the constabulary and, as often as not, in chains."

In his *Folies amoureuses* Regnard makes the impudent Crispin say:

> "Ce n'est pas aujourd'hui que je vois des combats:
> J'ai même déserté deux fois dans la milice."

Unhappily there were all too many Crispins in the Militia and even in the Regular Army, for desertion was the scourge of the armies under the old régime. D'Argenson writes in 1752: "It is reckoned that more than 30,000 men have been put to death for desertion since the Peace of 1748." [1]

In the Seven Years War desertion caused greater loss than the enemy's fire. But it must be remembered that the army was recruited from the dregs of the towns, among whom the recruiting officers enlisted their men for the Regular Army; the Militia, as we have seen, could only enrol by force, as in the case of border districts when the recruits were unable to cross the frontiers. And it must be added that a military career was not only dreaded, but, except in the case of the nobility, it was considered almost degrading. Up to the time of the Revolution one could read on many public buildings or garden walls the following amazing notice: "No dogs, servants, or *soldiers* allowed." [2]

In the present day the army is the nation in arms, and the flower of the nation is the flower of the army, as it has demonstrated, not only by its deeds but by its losses, which, alas, are irreparable. But in those days the nation and the army were entirely distinct, and we may read what the Count de St. Germain, a War Minister who was famous for his drastic reforms, has to say on this subject: "It would undoubtedly be desirable if we could create an army of dependable and specially selected men of the best type,

---

[1] D'Argenson, vii. 366.   [2] Monteil, *Histoire des Français*, v. 321.

but in order to make an army we must not destroy the nation; it would be destruction to a nation if it were deprived of its best elements. As things are, the army must inevitably consist of the scum of the people and of all those for whom society has no use. We must therefore rely on military discipline to purify and mould the mass of corruption and turn it into something useful." [1]

In times of peace, when the regiments were on the move —and they made an annual progress—their march spelt ruin to the country they traversed. All military stores were conveyed by waggons supplied by those who were liable to statute labour, and this, as the Aldermen of Angers reported, was a heavy burden on the labourers, "rendered even more intolerable from the ill-treatment to which they are subjected by the soldiers, who are naturally inclined to cruelty owing to their much-abused privilege of impunity." [2]

But winter quarters were even more dreaded. The towns did not like garrisons because, as there were no barracks, the soldiers were nearly always billeted on the inhabitants—that is to say, on those humble folk who could not plead exemption either as holding an ecclesiastical or a legal office. The host was bound to supply the soldier billeted on him with a place at the fireside, a candle, one sou a day, and a bed, "according to his means." But two or three soldiers would sleep in the same bed, and were thus deprived, often enough, of the sleep they required. Hence sickness arose; but the soldier was little better off in hospital.

The Marquis de Poyanne, a Lieutenant-General, writes to du Cluzel, Intendant of Tours, on 24th September 1775: "Yesterday I visited the hospital at Saumur, where I found twenty-one carabineers and no possibility of further accommodation. You are so kind-hearted that you would be distressed if you could see these poor fellows crowded into two wretched rooms, where the beds touch, and the only air obtainable is admitted by one small window, with the result that the infection is so great that it is impossible to withstand it. Moreover, when one enters the rooms in the

[1] St. Germain, *Mémoires*, p. 178.   [2] Dumas, *Généralité de Tours*.

morning, when the window has been shut all night, it is impossible to remain in them; in fact, the Mother Superior declared before her whole community that her term of duty being about to end, she would rather be sent to prison than take charge of these two rooms." [1]

It was much the same everywhere, Saumur being no exception. So wretched were the military hospitals in the eighteenth century that we might safely say that they killed far more soldiers than any war.

Having now seen what a soldier's life was like, let us consider the officers. The higher ranks in the army were apportioned between the nobles of the Court and the country gentry; but they were very unequally divided, for, as St. Germain says, "the former immediately receive the higher commands as their right, while the latter, owing to the handicap of birth and poverty, are condemned to spend all their lives in the lower grades." The extent of this favouritism is shown by the fact that in 1789, out of 11 Marshals, 5 were Dukes, 1 a Prince, and 1 a Count. Out of 196 Lieutenant-Generals, all were nobles excepting 9 who had no title. Even among the Colonels we find the same exclusive and aristocratic tendency, for at the head of 109 regiments of infantry were 9 Princes, 5 Dukes, 25 Marquises, 40 Counts, 12 Viscounts, 7 Barons, 5 Knights, and only 6 commoners.[2]

These gentlemen, who merely passed from the idleness of the Court to that of the camp, were often very young. For instance, in 1743, the Duke de Fronsac, son of the Duke de Richelieu, became Colonel of the Septimanie Regiment at the age of seven, the Marshals de Noailles and de Castries at sixteen. The inevitable ignorance and incurable frivolity of these "colonels in bibs," as they were called, were largely responsible for the disastrous campaigns of the Seven Years War. The Abbé Coyer, in his *Bagatelles morales*, describes these little fops: "The capital alone supplies the Generals, and the greatest care is taken as regards their education. The young man who is

---

[1] Dumas, *Généralité de Tours*, p. 129.
[2] Duruy, *L'armée royale en 1789*, p. 83.

THE ARMY

ear-marked for a command must have the best tailor, the best perfumer, the most splendid carriage, and the most expensive liveries in the town, and he must gamble much, dance often, and frequently be seen at the theatre." And then he was ready—to fight!

Moreover, these officers lived in the army as they had lived at Court, accompanied by their carriages and cooks. "A rich officer," said the Maréchal de Saxe, "requires an expensive and splendid outfit when setting out on a campaign. He must have a *berline*, a *vis-à-vis*, a coach and a coupé, five mules with gorgeous trappings, a crowd of footmen and grooms all in splendid liveries. The Generals often entertain 200 guests at dinner, and young officers frequent their tables as they would an inn, reserving their places by turning their plate upside down." [1]

It was not, therefore, enough to be noble; wealth was essential for an officer. "In time of war an officer's pay is so small that it is impossible for him to keep up appearances or to exist, if he has not an income of at least 600 livres from his family." [2] And when peace was made, the officers became *réformés*—that is to say, they were sent home with a pension of a few hundred livres and the cross of St. Louis.

The King granted a month's pay to every officer in order to pay his journey home. Barbier tells us of a lieutenant who had but thirty-three livres with which to get to his home, which lay in a very remote part of the country, and having only his regimentals, he took to selling cheese in the town where his regiment was quartered. "When reproached by his former brother-officers and reprimanded by the Commandant of the town, he replied, quite simply, that he was not doing anything dishonourable, preferring this little business to begging for alms on the way, and that he had no desire nor inclination to steal. As soon as he had collected enough for his journey, he would start for his home."

The malcontents amused themselves by quoting the

---

[1] *Esprit des Lois de la Tactique*, p. 23.
[2] De Saxe, *Traité des Légions*.

case of M. de Maller, a lieutenant and Knight of St. Louis, who at sixty only had a pension of 300 livres, which was still further reduced by taxation, and who, in order to live, put his cross of St. Louis in his pocket, and threshed corn in a barn. And then there was another officer, who had retired, and did not hide his cross, but displayed it as a good advertisement. He was the man whom Sterne met at Versailles upon his Sentimental Journey, and found selling his little cakes: "He told me shortly that he had spent his youth in the army and gained his company and his cross, but as he had been retired after the late war, and had obtained no employment in the present one, he found himself friendless and penniless in the world save only for his cross."

This poor cross of St. Louis, once so sought after, was now so prodigally bestowed and generally ridiculed, that it was considered almost as disgraceful to display it as to be without it.

Just as we have seen bishops absent themselves from their dioceses to the great detriment of religion, so also officers often abandoned their regiments to the great prejudice of discipline. In February 1756, d'Argenson writes: "The King, while hunting in the Forest of St. Germain, met the Orléans Regiment, which was marching to Normandy, and discovered it had neither officers nor flags, drums nor arms! All of these were with the transport, and the officers were in Paris! The King scolded a great deal," but he did nothing!

Military historians of the time sadly bear witness to the relaxation of discipline and the hatred of the service, both of which they ascribe, in great measure, to the continual changes of ministers under Louis xv. and the so-called reforms which were set on foot at each ministerial reshuffle: "It was especially during the Maréchal de Belle-Isle's and the Duke de Choiseul's tenure of office that new regulations were so multiplied that discipline relaxed and the soldier began to loathe a service in which he was for ever learning what he was later obliged to forget. Drill, uniforms, disciplinary regulations, punishments, the scale of promotion, even the names of the various duties—all these were altered with each new Ministry. This ceaseless changing of personnel and of principles continued under Louis XVI., and contributed largely to the alienation of the troops from the Crown." [1]

In connection with these frequent changes of ministers it was said that the porter of the Controller-General, whose post, unlike that of his master, was a permanency, had seen seven ministers (and that was a lot even for those days) succeed one another at the office in less than nine years, and du Gast narrates the following anecdote, which bears on this subject: "I do not remember whether it was M. de Laverdy or M. de Silhouette to whom the Duchess d'Orléans, à Conti by birth, and notorious for her mordant wit, sent her congratulations on the morrow of his appointment as Controller-General. But as they changed so often, she said to the gentleman who was to bear her message: 'You had better inquire of the porter whether he is still in office.'" [2]

But what was worse was that the King not only declined to reprimand, as it was his duty to do, those officers who, in peace time, amused themselves in Paris, but even went to the unheard-of extreme in welcoming with all graciousness a commander-in-chief who had abandoned his soldiers in the midst of a campaign.

It was just after the battle of Rosbach, and on 5th May 1758 we read in de Luynes' *Journal*: "It is about a fortnight or three weeks since M. de Fronsac returned from the army. M. de Richelieu, his father, was furious, and ordered him to return immediately. However, he gave way, and allowed his son to go to the country provided that he did not show himself. But M. de Fronsac did not obey this order in every detail, and, in spite of this, he eventually obtained permission to appear here at Court. It was generally believed that the King would not speak to him so as to show his displeasure, but quite the contrary occurred. The King received him very graciously, and said: 'I am delighted to see you. You will sup with me this evening.'

[1] Sénac de Meilhan, *Du Gouvernement*, p. 106.   [2] Du Gast, i. 16.

This is assuredly a great mark of kindness, but the master should surely sometimes use severity, especially when it is a question of re-establishing discipline which has been badly shaken." This amazing passage requires no comment, but we can understand what prompted Bernis to write to Choiseul, after the defeat of Soubise: "One does not wage war without generals nor with ill-disciplined troops."

Bad discipline and discontent had spread among the officers also, and in 1759 the Maréchal de Broglie wrote in his report: "Every one of our officers has as much courage and more talent and intelligence than any officer in the enemy's ranks, but they have one vital fault: there are few, even among the subalterns, who do not draw up plans of campaign and censure their generals, while practically all regard their rank as wholly beneath them." [1]

As for the generals, they were either incapable or else torn with jealousy of each other, and the resulting confusion is only too plainly written in the pages of history. In 1747, after the battle of Lawfeld, all Paris raged at the criminal mistakes which were generally attributed to the commander: "It is said in Paris that this action was fought contrary to the advice of the Maréchal de Saxe, who was of the opinion that the enemy would be forced to come out of their position. But M. d'Argenson, Minister of War, being jealous of M. de Saxe, persuaded the King to attack the enemy in his trenches, counting on a reverse which would discredit the Maréchal. It is certainly true that there are intrigues and cabals against him among many of the generals." [2]

Later, in connection with the Convention of Closter-Seven in 1757, Duclos, in his *Mémoires secrets sur le règne de Louis* XV., severely criticises the conduct of the French generals: "The Maréchal de Richelieu concluded the famous Convention of Closter-Seven. It must be borne in mind that neither he nor the Duke of Cumberland had been authorised to do so by their respective sovereigns, and the course of events soon reduced this convention to its true value, and rendered its terms illusory. It was the gravest

[1] De Broglie, *Le Secret du Roi*, i. 343.   [2] Barbier, iv. 259.

mistake committed during this war, and was the source of all our misfortunes. The Courts of Vienna and Sweden both condemned it. We ought to have done the same and recalled the Maréchal, who would not have been thought any less of by the English, and sent out a real general in his place. The Count de Maillebois, who served under him, tacitly obeyed all his chief's orders, and took care not to oppose an error which would naturally result in his general's disgrace and his own promotion. This is the way in which our officers behaved to each other in the course of this war. All of them showed themselves to be incapable as well as bad citizens."

Finally,—and we must refer to this—we come to the two great disasters—the surrender of Minden, "the infamy of Minden," as the Count de Gisors called it, and the defeat of Rosbach, that disgrace which wrung all French hearts. Let us see what the Count de Clermont, overwhelmed with grief, wrote on the subject of Minden. His letter, dated 20th and finished on the 24th March 1758, in the camp of Paderborn, was addressed to the Maréchal de Belle-Isle: "Not an officer does his duty. . . . I do not think you have ever heard of a surrender similar to this. It seems as if the besieged asked to be made prisoners of war! On the other hand, you will find many clauses personally advantageous to the officers and others of the garrison; much attention to all the transport, and corresponding neglect for all that would be honourable to the King's troops. What I condemn with all my strength is that the officers wished to return to France. They ought to share the fate of their men, but everything reveals lack of discipline, loathing of the King's service, and selfishness." [1]

And so we come to Rosbach and the Pompadour's wretched protégé, Soubise. Again the Count de Gisors writes to Belle-Isle: "It is essential that you replace our friend Soubise. . . . I will confess, dear father, that I was deeply hurt at the outset when, with regard to this command, I saw you give your vote for a man who had neither the gifts nor the experience. The troops have never had

[1] Rousset, *Gisors*, p. 407.

any confidence in him, and those who have now fallen, owing to his orders, are indignantly regarded as victims sacrificed to favouritism. If this same favouritism keeps him in his place after the defeat he has just suffered, a place for which he has been shown unfit, then you can hope for nothing from those under his command, and the whole army will revolt." [1]

As the Revolution came ever nearer, the French nobility instinctively drew back before the rising flood which was so soon to engulf them, and brought out of the dim past those almost forgotten titles and faded social distinctions with which they hoped to stem the menacing rise of the *bourgeoisie*. This feudal reaction, which was common to the Magistracy, the Church, and the Army alike, is well illustrated by the following passages which have been extracted from three different sources:

With regard to the Magistracy, Augeard writes in his *Mémoires* that "it is forbidden to admit to the High Courts any one who cannot show two degrees of nobility."

As for the Church, it obtained "a legal decision which could not, however, be embodied in an edict, by which, henceforth, all Church property, from the poorest priory to the richest abbey, should be regarded as the appanage of the nobility." Mme Campan, who wrote these lines, did, however, obtain a priory for the parish priest of some friends of hers, and was severely taken to task by the Abbé de Vermont, Marie Antoinette's former tutor, "who had much to do with ecclesiastical patronage." He declared "that the property of the Church should henceforth be solely devoted to the support of the poor nobility, this being in the interest of the State, and that a priest who sprang from the working class and was happy in his parish ought to remain in it." [2]

At this time the Lords of the Manor had their lists of rights and privileges overhauled at the expense of their parish, and with the help of paid clerks called "commissioners of manorial rights" (*commissaires à terrier*). During the summer of 1783, Beugnot tells us that he "had

[1] Rousset, *Gisors*, p. 318. [2] Campan. *Mémoires*, i. 237.

to draw up a memorandum of a very important lawsuit between several Communes of the Duchy of Nevers and the Duke de Nivernais. This nobleman's lawyers insist with amazing hardiness on enforcing feudal rights which, to say the least, are doubtful." [1]

Finally, as far as the Army was concerned, the military nobility had never reconciled itself to seeing the sons of tradesmen obtaining commissions which they regarded as being, by right, their own preserve. They therefore heartily supported the reaction which had set in, apparently successfully, among the magistracy and the clergy, and this was expressed in the notorious and fatal ordinance of 1781, due to the Count de Ségur, then Minister of War, or, as his son insists, to the Committee of Inspectors-General of the Army.

This ordinance decreed that henceforth all candidates for commissions should be obliged to submit proof of four degrees of nobility, and this proof could only be certified by Chérin, the Court genealogist. Ségur, the younger, speaks of the ordinance of 1781 as follows: "Every one in France thinks that my father, by means of this ordinance, excluded the Third Estate from military service, by insisting that all who aspired to commissions must show proof of nobility." In this connection, he clears his father's memory, but that does not concern us as much as the effect which it had on public opinion. "This ordinance was generally held by the wisest men of all classes to be a measure, not only ill-timed, improper, and wholly opposed to the spirit of the age, but also as one of the most decisive causes of that universal discontent which prepared the way for the Revolution in men's minds." [2]

From that moment every man who was not of noble birth was obliged to forgo a military career unless he was content with the inglorious life of a soldier of fortune, although it was admitted that both Fabert and Catinat under Louis XIV. and Chevert under Louis XV. would, all three, have been excluded if the proof of nobility had

[1] Beugnot, i. 22.   [2] Ségur, *Mémoires*, i. 277.

then been insisted on as it was now. The pride of the *bourgeoisie* was mortally offended by this reactionary measure, the more so as, even if the upper middle class, as we have seen, accepted its social inferiority where the so-called great nobles were concerned, they emphatically refused to admit it in the case of the ordinary nobility, because "marriages and ennoblement had brought these two classes together, and placed their relations on an equal footing." [1]

Moreover, it was a most unfavourable moment to choose, and Talleyrand judges this very retrograde step very severely: "All lucrative professions having been barred to the poorer nobility, it was thought that they should be given some compensation. But this measure, which patently substituted birth for personal merit in a profession which must obviously be based on merit, outraged public opinion and all reason. In order to indemnify the nobles for having lost the advantages which the middle class already regarded as constituting a humiliating prejudice in their own case, the latter were offered this further affront and injustice. The soldier, already indignant at the introduction of a disciplinary measure which was as new to him as it was strange—for corporal punishment had always been regarded in France as an outrage—was now definitely alienated. It seemed almost as if it had been decided not to rely on our brave soldiers when the greatest danger was threatening, and when it did come, they were, in very deed, found wanting." [2]

We have now quoted extracts from contemporary memoirs showing many errors and shortcomings in the organisation of the army as well as in the conduct of the generals in the field. But these memoirs also contain many a glorious page, for the armies of France were not always unsuccessful in war, and the French soldier was still without fear and without reproach when he was well led, and many commanders gave an example of courage and calm contempt of death on many a field.

We all know the famous invitation of the Count

[1] Montlosier, i. 198.   [2] *Mémoires*, i. 119.

d'Anterroche to the English at the battle of Fontenoy: "Fire first, gentlemen; we are French and we do the honours here," a politeness which frankly sounds ridiculous on a battlefield; but, thank God, there are many other stories of French bravery in this eighteenth century which will bear quotation. This one, for instance, dealing with the manner in which the Marquis de Brienne, Colonel of the Artois, displayed his devotion to King and Country at the engagement of Exiles in 1747. He had lost an arm, but returning to the line he cried: "I have another left with which to serve my King," and fell mortally wounded.[1] It was at this tragic engagement at Exiles, where the French had to attack the Piedmontese in their solid entrenchments of wood and stone, that Belle-Isle, the Commander-in-Chief, himself strove, in his despair, to tear down the palisades. "Wounded in both hands, he still tried to wrench out the stakes with his teeth, until he fell dead on the field. He had often been heard to say that a general should not survive his defeat, and he proved his conviction to the hilt."[2]

Swagger, when supported by great courage, is not unbecoming in a young officer. In 1744, the Prince de Conti was marching against Piedmont, but in order to advance it was necessary to clear the enemy's fortifications, including the fortress of Montalban, which lay among great rocks forming an almost continuous line of ramparts, and practically inaccessible. However, a young officer, M. de Crussol, attacked them, but slipped as he tried to climb up, for they were very steep. He at once made another attempt in the face of heavy fire. On hearing those around exclaiming that the bullets were raining among them, as indeed they were, he exclaimed: "If there were no rifle-fire who would want to climb this?"

Modesty enhances the value of courage, but the price of courage cannot be expressed in terms of money. "Bréhan, Colonel of the Picardy Regiment, contributed so much to the victory of Hastenbeck, that the Court, which hitherto had ignored his services, sent him a warrant conferring

[1] Voltaire, *Précis du Siècle de Louis XV.*, ch. xxiii.   [2] *Ibid.*

upon him an annuity of two thousand livres. Bréhan replied that he had never desired any pecuniary reward, and begged the King to divide this sum among certain officers in his regiment who were badly in need of it. He was asked to give the names of those who had distinguished themselves, and his answer, which I have read, was in these terms: 'No one distinguished himself more than another, but all fought bravely and are ready to fight again. I am therefore obliged to send a list in order of seniority.' "[1]

We have already quoted from the letters of the young Count de Gisors, whom the army loved because of his bravery, his uprightness, and his noble character. "He was a young man with a brilliant future, with great knowledge both of political and military affairs, capable not only of taking broad views but also of attending to every detail, as polished as he was brave, the darling alike of Court and Army." This was Voltaire's eulogy.[2] When he lay on his death-bed, after receiving a mortal wound at the battle of Crefeld on 25th June 1758, he wrote his last letter to the Maréchal de Belle-Isle with a firm hand: "My very dear father, I am writing this before they bleed me, and beg of you not to be anxious about my wound. At any rate, I did not receive it before I had broken the ranks of the Hanoverian infantry with my carabineers." But the bullet had broken his left hip-bone and penetrated the stomach; the surgeons could not find it, and on the 26th June the young Count de Gisors breathed his last. The Maréchal de Belle-Isle was then seventy-four, and this was his only son, of whom it would have been true to say, "*Tu Marcellus eris.*" There was reason enough for this blow to shatter him, but let us see what de Luynes writes of the old man:

"M. de Belle-Isle is the best of men, as good a patriot as he is tender a father. Yesterday the King did him the honour of visiting him and embraced him, saying he hoped he would never desert him. Such marks of royal favour seemed to persuade M. de Belle-Isle to forget his age, his lungs, which had long been affected by an old wound, and the heavy burden of continuous labour, disagreeable

[1] Duclos, *Mémoires secrets*.   [2] *Siècle de Louis XV.*, ch. xxiii.

enough in present circumstances but, from its very nature, daily reminding him of his loss. His courage is beyond praise and his devotion boundless. Since he first heard of his son's dangerous wound, he attended three Councils of State, speaking at each one for an hour or an hour and a quarter with a composure, a force, a clearness, and an accuracy which were beyond belief. At the present moment he is as much immersed in his arduous and, under the circumstances, very necessary work as ever he was, and though he occasionally bursts into fits of weeping, he immediately resumes as calmly as before." [1]

The wars of Louis xv. brought the country much sorrow and mourning, but though the army tasted defeat all too often, it had its days of glory and its hours of gaiety as well. Voltaire, with his delicate touch, gives us this comfort when he dwells on the ever-youthful gaiety of the French, which is often one of the finest forms of courage. He had just published his *Lettres philosophiques*, which had been burnt by the Common Hangman at the foot of the Grand Staircase in accordance with custom. The police were looking for him, and, on the advice of a friend, he hastened to "absent himself." At this time there was a rumour of a duel in the Army of the Rhine, the protagonists being the Prince de Lixin and M. de Richelieu, and the latter was said to have been mortally wounded. Voltaire, who, as we know, was very intimate with him, heard only the call of friendship and hurried to the army, whence he wrote on 1st July 1734 from beneath the walls of Philipsburg to the Countess de Neuville: "The armies are face to face, and a sanguinary battle is expected at any moment. The French are between Philipsburg, the Rhine, and the Germans. The troops show great eagerness and swear they will beat Prince Eugène. They do not fear him, but, rightly, are entrenching themselves as strongly as possible. They have parapets, a ditch, pits, and then another ditch—a new system which seems excellent and very well designed to make the enemy break their necks when they attack our

[1] Luynes, *Mémoires*, xvi. 489.

lines." The French army took Philipsburg on the 18th July, thus justifying the prophetic and very charming verses which Voltaire had addressed to M―― on the 3rd, and which he had proudly dated "in the camp of Philipsburg." These are the verses:

> "C'est ici qu'on dort sans lit
> Et qu'on prend son repas par terre.
> Je vois et j'entends l'atmosphère
> Qui s'embrase et qui retentit
> De cent décharges de tonnerre;
> Et dans ces horreurs de la guerre
> Le Français chante, boit et rit.
> Bellone va réduire en cendres
> Les courtines de Philipsbourg
> Par cinquante mille Alexandres
> Payés à quatre sous par jour.
> Je les vois, prodiguant leur vie,
> Chercher ces combats meurtriers,
> Couverts de fange et de lauriers,
> Et pleins d'honneur et de folie.
> Je vois briller au milieu d'eux
> Ce fantôme nommé la Gloire,
> A l'œil superbe, au front poudreux,
> Portant au cou cravate noire,
> Ayant sa trompette en sa main,
> Sonnant la charge et la victoire,
> Et chantant quelques avis à boire
> Dont ils répètent le refrain." [1]

The most glorious day for the arms of France was that of Fontenoy. Voltaire, in his dual rôle of poet and historiographer, bursts first into epic verse, and then describes this famous victory "with every detail and mentioning

[1] "Here we sleep without beds and eat on the ground, and in the air, which flames and trembles, I hear the thunder of a hundred guns. Amidst these horrors of war the Frenchman sings and drinks and laughs. Fifty thousand Alexanders, whose pay is four sous a day, will, at Bellona's behest, reduce the forts of Philipsburg to ashes. I see them daily risking their life gaily, and seeking these bloody combats eagerly, covered with mud and laurels, and full of honour and folly. And in their midst I see the phantom shade that goes by the name of Glory, with flashing eye and dust-stained visage, a black kerchief round its neck, and a trumpet in its hand, sounding first the charge or a pæan of victory, or singing some drinking song of which all join in the chorus."

over sixty names." But although these three hundred lines were written in the "heroic style" they were rather boring, and we prefer the few hurried lines which he wrote, straight from his heart, to the Count d'Argenson, Minister of War, on the 13th May 1745 at 11 p.m.—that is, on the third day after the battle: "Oh, what a glorious subject for your historian! It is three hundred years since the Kings of France have achieved anything to compare with this. I am intoxicated with delight. Good-night, my lord."

D'Argenson replied to this note with a letter in a strain of nobility, animation, and a humanity that is typically French, and with this we may fittingly close the chapter on the French army of the eighteenth century, which, in spite of all hostile criticism, comprised brave soldiers as well as commanders fit to lead them—not least, though, alas, it was none too often, the King himself:

"MY DEAR HISTORIAN,—You must have heard the news on which you so warmly congratulate me on Wednesday evening. A messenger left the battlefield on Tuesday at half-past two with dispatches, and I understand that he arrived at Versailles at five on Wednesday afternoon. It was indeed a very moving sight to see the King and Dauphin writing on a drum, surrounded by the corpses of victors and vanquished alike, by the dying and by prisoners. I am now sending you a few details of the day.

"I had the honour of meeting the King on Sunday, close to the battlefield. I arrived from Paris at Head-quarters, which were at Chin, and hearing that the King was out walking, I asked for a horse and joined His Majesty near a spot whence the enemy's lines were plainly visible, and from him I learned for the first time what the present state of affairs is. . . . I have never seen a man so pleased with this enterprise as was the King. We discussed the question which you have answered in four lines, Who was the last of our Sovereigns to win the great battle? I can assure you that courage did not impair his judgment, nor his judgment cloud his memory. Eventually we retired to sleep on our straw, but never was a night so cheerful, and the wit was as sparkling as at a ball. We snatched what sleep we could, but orderlies, aides-de-camp, and soldiers of the Grassin Regiment were ever coming and going. The King sang a song which has many verses, and is extremely amusing. The Dauphin behaved in battle as if he was at a hare-hunt, and almost exclaimed: "Why! I thought it was!" A cannon-ball struck the mud and covered a man near the King with dirt, at which both he and the Dauphin laughed heartily. One of my brother's grooms was wounded in the head by a musket-ball, although he was in the rear of his company. To state the facts clearly, accurately, and without flattery, this victory must be ascribed to the King's decision and firmness. You will know the accounts and details of that awful hour when we all but witnessed a repetition of Dettingen, and the humiliation of our brave lads before the constancy of those English whose rolling fire was so hellish that, I must admit, it stupefied even the most detached spectator. We almost despaired of the State. Some of our generals who have more courage in their hearts than in their heads urged prudence; orders were sent as far as Lille, the King's Guard was doubled, and all the transport packed up. But the King laughed at all this, and proceeded from the left flank to the centre, where he ordered up the corps in reserve, and the brave Lowendhal, but they were not required. A hidden corps, which had also been held in reserve, charged. It was the same cavalry which had already attacked in vain, together with the King's Guards, the carabineers, all that was left of the French Guards, and the Irish, who were especially irresistible when it meant attacking the English and Hanoverians. Your friend, M. de Richelieu, is a very Bayard. It was he who advised and carried out this manœuvre, advancing on the enemy as if the troops were going a-hunting or a-foraging, with weapons lowered and arms braced, officers, servants, cavalry, infantry, all in a rush together. This French onslaught, which is so much talked about, carried all before it, and in ten minutes this unexpected thrust had won the battle. The English battalions turned tail, and lost fourteen thousand killed. It is true that this awful butchery is due to our artillery. Never have so many or such heavy guns been used in battle as at Fontenoy, for there were no less than a hundred. It seems that our enemies were quite outmatched by our Douai guns and our cavalry and musketeers. There is one story about the final charge which I must tell you. The Dauphin, quite carried away, automatically drew his sword and was absolutely determined to take part in the charge, but they begged him to refrain. I must tell you that. I noticed how easy it was to become accustomed to and to ignore the naked bodies, the dying, and the wounded who littered the battlefield. I confess that my heart failed me, and I was obliged to take to my smelling-salts, but I carefully observed our youthful heroes and found them so indifferent in this respect that I fear that in the course of a long life the taste for slaughter may well increase.

"It was indeed a glorious triumph! Cries of 'Long live the King' filled the air, hats were waved on bayonets, the King congratulated his soldiers, visited the trenches, the villages, and the redoubts which were intact, and everything breathed joy, glory, and emotion. But all around was human blood and human flesh." [1]

[1] D'Argenson, iv. 460.

BOOK IV.—PUBLIC OPINION IN THE EIGHTEENTH CENTURY

CHAPTER I

PUBLIC OPINION: A NEW FORCE

IN the previous chapters we have studied individually the various classes which made up French society in the eighteenth century. We must now make the acquaintance of a personage who, although invisible, was all-powerful in this society, and was certainly not dumb—in short, "Le Roi On," as Necker calls public opinion in the manuscripts published by his daughter: "A King without visible attributes, pomp, or throne, but one at whose voice all tremble and obey; a King peculiar in this, that he is Master in small matters as in great;" [1] and this King without a throne limited the absolute power of that other Monarch whose throne was at Versailles; in other words, as Montesquieu put it: "The King cannot do all he is able to do." [2]

Public opinion first assumed a definite shape in France at the beginning of the eighteenth century, thanks to the licence which prevailed in men's minds and morals, and of which the Regent himself was a typical example—thanks also to the scandalous trafficking to which, as we have seen, even the greatest families of France stooped in this age. All this instigated and encouraged in the public mind a tendency which soon crystallised into one of the chief characteristics of eighteenth-century society, and is called "Irreverence."

It had scarce been born when it grew bolder and gradu-

[1] xv. 257.   [2] *Pensées et Fragments inédits.*

ally made itself not only listened to but feared, so that by the end of the century its effect had become so great and its influence so powerful that even Necker, in an article published in 1784, was constrained to pay homage to this new and sovereign power in the following words: "The spirit of society and the love of consideration and applause have set up in France a tribunal before which all men who focus attention upon themselves are forced to appear. There 'Public Opinion' is enthroned, and from its lofty seat bestows its prizes and its crowns, and makes or mars a man's reputation. Foreigners have, for various reasons, great difficulty in forming a true opinion of the authority which public opinion exercises in France, and have difficulty in understanding that it is an invisible power which, though without wealth, without weapons, and without an army, dictates alike to town and Court, and even in the palace of Kings."

In the preceding century no one issued orders in "the palace of Kings" but the King himself. No one at Versailles had the courage to criticise the acts of the Sovereign or his ministers, and was only permitted to praise and celebrate them in prose or verse, and Paris, as the saying went, merely "aped the Court." But now Paris no longer copied Versailles; Paris thought for itself, and was, in fact, the only place where one did think, write, and talk, while the Court, for all its habitual boasting and its scorn of Paris, was careful enough to inquire sedulously and to display anxiety as to what Paris thought and said of the Government. This is what Mercier writes on the subject: "The Court is most attentive to what the Parisians or 'frogs,' as they are called, may be saying. Even the princes ask one another: 'What are the frogs saying?' And if the frogs clap when they appear in public, at a play, or on the road to Ste Geneviève, they are well pleased. Sometimes they are punished by being received in silence, but in any case they can judge from the people's behaviour what the latter think of them, since the enthusiasm or indifference of the public is clearly marked. It is said that they are very sensitive to the reception given them by the capital, because they are vaguely aware that in the crowd there is found both intelligence and wit, and not a few men who are able to appreciate them and their actions at their true value. These latter, moreover, though it is not quite known how or why, influence the judgment of the populace." [1]

The Government respected the judgment of the people of Paris, because it was well aware that these wielded a weapon which was greatly feared at that time, namely, Ridicule; and it was Voltaire, himself the most faithful interpreter of this century, who said that Ridicule kills in France.

The Count de Ségur writes in his *Mémoires*: "As Power had become absolute, Ridicule was our only weapon, and it is a more powerful one than most people suppose. In other countries people do not merely bow beneath the ministerial yoke, they creep to it with servility, and keep a shameful silence. But in France, on the contrary, even if our actions were fettered, no one had ever been able to chain our intellect and gag our mouths; so that while the Government had full liberty in the sphere of action, we knew how to capture the sphere of public opinion, a power so great and so well supported by all that is honourable, that it was often an effective counterpoise in checking the progress of arbitrary rule." [2]

Public opinion certainly did dictate the choice, and then imposed its favourites upon those who, at that time, wielded the executive power. "In his last days, M——, realising the growing influence of public opinion in the appointment and choice of ministers, spoke to M. de L—— on behalf of a man whom he wished to help, saying: 'Manipulate public opinion on his behalf.'" [3]

But it went even farther, for not only did it "help" its favourites to high office, but it also turned out those whom it considered unworthy. During the campaign of 1742, in Bohemia, a French army lay surrounded in Egra, and Maillebois was ordered to go forward and endeavour to relieve it and cover its retreat. But when he was several days' march from Egra, he turned back and left his task

[1] Mercier, i. 58.   [2] Ségur, i. 209.   [3] Chamfort, ii. 192.

unattempted. "The murmurs were loud in Paris. The nation, naturally alarmed, had desired the war, but it soon found cause to blame the means adopted for its prosecution. At this moment all eyes were on Bohemia, and every one hoped that our brave troops, among whom nearly every one of us had friends or relations, would escape. Naturally Maillebois' shameful manœuvre caused general indignation, and (this is the illuminating fact) the public was only appeased by his recall and disgrace, the Maréchal de Broglie being appointed in his place." [1]

In 1748 the Peace of Aix-la-Chapelle was proclaimed in the streets of Paris, but Paris, much as it had desired the end of the war, was far from being satisfied with it, and public discontent was epitomised in a current saying. Barbier writes: "To-day being Ash Wednesday, the 12th February, peace was proclaimed. Those who had assembled at the various places noted that when the heralds had finished reading the proclamation, one of the men-at-arms cried, 'Long live the King,' as was customary, but this cry was not echoed by the crowd. On the other hand, it is said that in the market the fishwives, when they quarrel, say: 'You are as silly as the Peace'—a phrase which in this witty age is the most pregnant criticism of the Peace."

We know that the Duke de Choiseul was exiled for opposing Mme Dubarry's influence, "but," writes Ségur, "public opinion consoled him. It deserted the palace of the monarch, and formed a court in the castle of the disgraced minister"; [2] and Mme de Staël, in her *Considérations sur la Révolution française*, when describing how, on that winter's evening in 1787, Lenoir, the Commissioner of Police, brought Necker, her father, the *lettre de cachet* which exiled him forty leagues from Paris, adds: "All Paris flocked to visit M. Necker during the twenty-four hours which were granted him to make the necessary preparations for his journey," and ends with the words: "Public opinion transformed his disgrace into a triumph."

We shall see how this same opinion avenged the authors who were persecuted at this time, and how amply

[1] Mouffle, ii. 113.   [2] Ségur, *Mémoires*, i. 18.

it compensated them for the penalties decreed against their works. "In June 1762, *Emile* was sold for 18 livres, but after it had been publicly banned, its price rose to 2 louis."[1] This was the reason why obscure authors ardently desired that their books might obtain "the honours of the bonfire." Others only achieved fame on the day when the gates of the Bastille closed behind them. Chamfort describes how one very impecunious author, who had written a book against the Government, used to say: "Good gracious! the Bastille has not called for me yet, and I have got to pay my quarterly bills in a day or two!" The *Espion anglais* wrote on the subject of the Bastille: "Very few French authors have not frequented this prison at some time or another, and, alas, this is the only title to fame of which many of them can boast."[2] But let us see what one of its most distinguished prisoners, the Abbé Morellet, has to tell us about the profits he hoped to derive from his captivity as soon as he was released:

"I must confess, in order to temper the too flattering opinion which people may have of me and my courage, that I was wonderfully sustained by one thought: I used to see my cell illuminated by literary fame, and realised that, once having been an object of persecution, I should be sure of renown. The men of letters whom I had avenged, and Philosophy whose martyr I was, would begin to spread my reputation abroad. The people of fashion who loved satire would welcome me more warmly than before. My road opened out before me, and I would be able to travel it with all the greater profit. These six months in the Bastille would be an excellent advertisement, and would undoubtedly make my fortune."[3]

But although we have seen from the instances given above something of the growing power of this opinion in the eighteenth century, we must now consider how it was able to show itself, to spread, and finally to consolidate its Empire under an absolute monarch. There was no press, for it can hardly be said that the papers of the day, which in any case were few, could speak freely, so public

---

[1] Barbier, viii. 45.   [2] iii. 41.   [3] Morellet, *Mémoires*, i. 94.

opinion was obliged to seek expression in the most varied and, as the following anecdote shows, often in the most unexpected ways:

"On the 19th January 1717 a masked woman attracted general attention by her proficiency in the dance and the singularity of her dress, which resembled that of a professional beggar, she being attired in horrible rags and tatters, all torn and filthy. This excited the curiosity of the Duke d'Orléans and the Duke de Bourbon, both of whom were present, and they approached her to observe her more closely. The former, who scented a mystery under this strange garb, kept on asking her in a whisper who she might be. The mask, after various prevarications which she indulged in so as to stimulate the Regent's curiosity to know who she was, and what her ragged costume might represent, at last satisfied him with the words: 'I am the Mistress of the Realm.' The Regent at once retired, for he understood quite well that these words were an allusion to the general distress which was rife throughout the Kingdom, causing a shortage of money, an excessive rise in the cost of living, and the stagnation of trade." [1]

Chamfort described the government of France as a monarchy limited by popular songs, and it was in these songs that public opinion chiefly expressed itself during the eighteenth century. A general is defeated, and at once becomes the subject of a song. A tax is thought too heavy, and immediately a song lightens the burden. "The nation," said Montesquieu, "consoles itself for losing a battle by making up songs about the general." [2] Its excuse was that the army was not, as it is to-day, the nation in arms. Paris, as we have seen, was disgusted with Soubise, and he was at once attacked in scurrilous songs throughout the town. One described him as seeking for his army, which he had presumably lost, with a lantern in his hand, and crying, when at last he thought he had found it:

"Ah! Ventrebleu! qu-est ce donc que cela?
Je me trompais: c'est l'armée ennemie!"

---

[1] Buvat, i. 242. [2] *Esprit des Lois*, ix. 7.

PUBLIC OPINION : A NEW FORCE

Public opinion also expressed itself in the theatre in the form of hissing or clapping, as the case might be, whenever a line could be construed into an allusion to any recent event, or political personage who might be unpopular or otherwise; and allusions were not difficult to find. On Necker's fall "there was a great disturbance at the Comédie française on Sunday. They were playing *Henry iv.'s Hunting Party*, and the pit and gallery applied the part of Sully to M. de Necker, and recalled the actor who was playing this character again and again. The Guard had the greatest difficulty in checking this demonstration."

Even more curious interpreters of public opinion were the market women, or *Harengères* (fishwives), as they were called, whose position was almost an official one, since custom in those days took the place of a constitution, so much so that whenever Paris was much excited at any great event, these women proceeded to Versailles and were admitted. Luynes records one of their visits to the Queen on the 10th October 1751: "Mme Renard, whose *harangues* were famous among the *Harengères*, was their mouthpiece. The custom was for the Queen to come as far as the door of her room, which was thrown open, and listen to the speech delivered by the spokeswoman of the *Harengères*, who remained in the Audience Chamber."

As may be imagined, these good ladies had frequent complaints to make. For instance, when the Duke d'Orléans was recalled from the army during the Seven Years War, at Mme de Pompadour's instigation, a consolation awaited him on his return to France: "On his arrival, the Duke was complimented by the market women of his quarter, who presented him with laurel wreaths and professed their great devotion to his family. It is said that the Court is deeply mortified by this event."

The public was kept informed of events both at home and abroad by news-sheets and newsvendors. The former were occasionally inspired and sometimes suppressed, but in the latter case they continued to be circulated secretly. The newsvendors were to be found wherever it was fashionable to forgather, such as at the Pont-Neuf, the "heart of Paris," as Mercier called it, this being the fashionable rendezvous at the beginning of the century, and from this was coined the phrase "the news of the Pont-Neuf." Subsequently they frequented the Luxembourg Gardens, and at the end of the century, the Palais Royal. Here there was a particular tree round which these purveyors of news would gather, which thus acquired a certain celebrity. "The other day, at the Tree of Cracow in the Palais Royal, an irresponsible person cried: 'M. de Richelieu has brought about the exile of M. de Maurepas. I expect that as soon as he has made up his mind he will exile the King himself.'"[1]

Marais, who, like his master Bayle, calls these news-vendors "the expositors of all the rumours of the town," thought that they "exceeded their proper sphere and annoyed the public by their tittle-tattle." This tittle-tattle was particularly directed against the English, whom they annihilated verbally, and many "ceaselessly repeated beneath the trees of the Luxembourg, and entirely on the strength of the *Gazette de Hollande,* that France must conquer England and attack London." Mercier tells of "a good burgess of Paris who hated the English and derived great pleasure from going to the Luxembourg and listening to an Abbé, as anglophobe as himself, who "delighted him with his vehement oratory and always repeated the formula: "We must raise 30,000 men, we must embark 30,000 men, it will cost us 30,000 men to take London." The burgess died, and in his will was found the following clause: "To the Abbé of 30,000 men I leave 1200 livres per annum. I don't know his real name, but he is a good citizen and has assured me in the Luxembourg that the English, a savage people who have dethroned their sovereigns, ought to be exterminated." And Mercier assures us that the legacy of the patriotic burgess was duly handed over to the no less patriotic Abbé.[2]

The cafés were the chief places where news was circulated, where witticisms were coined, and the satires and lampoons of the day composed. "It has been prohibited in

[1] D'Argenson, v. 450.   [2] Mercier, ii. 159.

all cafés of Paris to mention Prince Edward [who had been arrested at the Opera and removed to Vincennes] because people took the liberty of blaming the King for what had occurred." [1]

We all know that it was at the Tavern of the Mouton Blanc that those four friends, Boileau, La Fontaine, Racine, and Molière, forgathered in order to amuse themselves at the expense of Chapelain and his *Pucelle*. But later in the eighteenth century the cafés superseded the cabarets or taverns, which were now left to the townspeople. As early as the publication of the *Lettres persanes* in 1721 the cafés had begun to be fashionable: "Coffee is very popular in Paris, and there are a large number of houses where the public may drink it. In some news is distributed, while in others people play chess, and in one of them they prepare the coffee in such a way that people who drink it are greatly exhilarated by it. At any rate, everybody on leaving it believes that he is four times as brilliant as when he entered." [2] This café which so enlivened people was doubtless the Café Procope, which was founded by a Sicilian named Procope at the end of the seventeenth century in the Rue Fossés-Saint-Germain, opposite the theatre of the Comédie française. "Owing to its situation it has attracted many dramatic authors and men of letters, and is becoming the most celebrated café in Paris." [3] There were three other very noted literary cafés in the eighteenth century: the Widow Laurent, in the Rue Dauphine, Gradot's, on the Quai de l'École, and La Régence, famous for its chess players, among whom Diderot and Rousseau might occasionally be found. As early as the second half of the century, Collé mentions with regret that the business of these cafés was falling off, and that the wits and men of letters had deserted them. That was because the latter had found something better: they now frequented the salons.

[1] Barbier, iv. 335. [2] 36th *Lettre persane*. [3] Dulaure, vii. 81.

CHAPTER II

THE SALONS

THE Salons of the eighteenth century are well known, and historians of French Literature have frequently described them when analysing their influence on the writers of the time. We, for our part, must look at them more from a social angle, and we may begin by noting a very important social development that occurred during this century. For the first time, two different classes of men—the great nobles, who hitherto had scorned and ignored the men of letters and artists—now met on neutral ground and became intimately acquainted. Owing to this intercourse, the writers and scholars shed much of their pedantry and bookishness, while the gentlemen of fashion rubbed off their prejudices against science and learning. This great service to both classes was rendered by the salons of the eighteenth century, the first being that of the Marquise de Lambert. "This lady collected in her house a very select company of literary and fashionable people. The former brought to it knowledge and learning, while the latter contributed that breeding and urbanity which even merit must acquire if it wishes to win affection and gain esteem. The men of fashion left her house more enlightened, and the men of letters went away more agreeable than when they entered it."[1]

Talleyrand jokingly quotes M. de Chastellux's remark: "I don't know him, but he must have wit, I suppose, since he visits Mme Geoffrin."[2] Talleyrand's mockery was not justified, for those who frequented Mme Geoffrin's house, or some equally famous salon where people were judged accord-

[1] D'Alembert, *Éloge de Saint Aulaire*.   [2] *Mémoires*, i. 48.

AN ASSEMBLY IN A SALON

From an engraving by François Dequevaullier, after Nicholas Lawreince

ing to their worth, were acknowledged to be men of intelligence and wit. D'Argenson said of Mme de Lambert, whose receptions had inaugurated the century: "Her house shed honour upon all who were admitted to it," and, since the Court had now become a stranger to all intellectual movements, it was in her drawing-room at the Hôtel de Nevers (now the Bibliothèque Nationale) that reputations were first made, and not at Versailles as of yore. Moreover, we might add, in this connection, that in the middle of this century ladies of fashion began to attend those meetings of the Académie française at which new members were admitted. On the 31st March 1756, when Séguier was admitted, "there was a prodigious crowd in order to hear his speech and that of the Director, M. de Nivernois; and, what was an unusual sight at the Academy, ladies like Mme de Villars, Mme d'Egmont, and others sat below, behind the Academicians." [1]

Still confining ourselves wholly to the social side, we might remark that Mme de Lambert, like Mme de Rambouillet in the preceding century, was a Marquise, and Mme de Tencin, who also had a famous salon, was, likewise, a very great lady. But here, in the middle of a century, was a mere *bourgeoise*, Mme Geoffrin, who, succeeding, as was said, to Mme de Tencin's place, actually entertained in her salon in the Rue St. Honoré the highest in the land and the most famous artists and men of letters! Walpole said of her that she was a "marvel of good sense," and good sense was the chief of the qualities displayed by the *bourgeoisie*. And Walpole added that in spite of her birth and the ridiculous prejudices of the nobility on this point, she succeeded in holding what was nothing less than a court, and on receiving every attention, and, what is more, she kept it up. This curious contrast between Mme Geoffrin's "birth" and her "court" is noted in lively fashion by Diderot. "A little girl in a flat mob-cap of dainty muslin went regularly to Mass: she was as pretty as an angel and clasped the most delightful hands in all the world before the altar. But a powerful man observed her, fell in love

[1] Luynes, xvi. 1.

and married her, and now she is rich and honoured, and surrounded by all that are of any consequence, whether in the capital or at Court, in letters, art, or science, and a King [of Poland] is glad to welcome her in his home and call her 'Mother.' " This description is true. M. Geoffrin, who had made a fortune as Administrator of the Glass Works at St. Gobain, did indeed meet the little Thérèse Rodet, daughter of one of the Dauphin's Grooms of the Wardrobe, at the Church of St. Roch, where she was wont to go to Mass daily. She was fourteen, and M. Geoffrin was a widower who would never see forty-eight again, a disparity of age which caused his own daughter, Mme de la Ferté-Imbault, to remark that "the union hardly seemed a suitable one." It did, however, enable Mme Geoffrin to establish her "kingdom" in the Rue St. Honoré. Her drawing-room became the great meeting-place of the eighteenth century, and Sainte-Beuve was right in describing her as: "The chief minister of the society of her time." How true this was can be judged from the following verses addressed to her by the Abbé Delille:

> "Il m'en souvient, j'ai vu l'Europe entière
> D'un triple cercle entourant son fauteuil,
> Guetter un mot, épier un coup d'œil. . . .
> Sans son avec nul n'était à la mode:
> Les enfants du Midi, les habitants du Nord,
>   Le rang, la faveur, la naissance,
> Pour être accrédités dans les cercles de France
> Venaient dans son salon prendre leur passe-port
> Et recevoir leur lettre de créance." [1]

Sénac de Meilhan wrote that in "the last century people used the expression *un honnête homme* to mean what we now call *un homme de bonne compagnie*." [2] How many of these *hommes de bonne compagnie* were there who, in the

[1] *La Conversation*, Chant iii.: "I well remember seeing all Europe standing three deep around her chair, waiting for a word or a glance. Without her approval nothing was fashionable. To her salon came all those, whether from North or South, who were distinguished by rank and birth and wealth, for here alone could they obtain the passport and credentials which opened to them the doors of French society."

[2] *Considérations*, p. 312.

eighteenth century, frequented these celebrated salons? It is very difficult to say. Voltaire states there were "two or three thousand delightful people of refined tastes, who were good company, and in time infected the rest." This may possibly have been "the cream of good society," but it was most certainly not the bulk of those who at this time interested themselves in intellectual matters, for on the 15th July 1768, Voltaire himself writes to Walpole: "We have over thirty thousand people in Paris who take an interest in Art: Athens had no more than ten thousand."

But putting figures aside, let us endeavour to trace the interesting development in the relations between mere men of fashion and literary society which took place between the seventeenth and eighteenth centuries. In the former La Bruyère wrote: "To appreciate merit, and, when once it is discovered, to give it its due, will require two great and outstanding efforts of which most of the great are wholly incapable." But in the eighteenth century the great ones of the earth and the ladies of fashion had no difficulty in "appreciating merit," since public opinion helped them to discover it. Indeed, many of them sought it out, and in order to attach it to themselves, exerted themselves "to give it its due."

The dissimilarity between the two ages is clearly seen in the contrast between the subordinate position held by La Bruyère in the household of the Condés, where, without daring to complain, he had to endure the irritable temper of the Prince and the brutalities of the Duke, and that occupied by Rousseau at Montmorency, where he was the recipient of a thousand kindnesses, and attentions of all sorts, from his host and hostess, the Maréchal de Luxemburg and his lady. Here the parts were reversed, for in the latter case it was the man of letters who had the temper and who had to be courted. For instance, whenever there was a big dinner at the Castle, it was to Rousseau that the hostess gave the place of honour at her side, and, to such length did this go, that when Rousseau sent his *Emile* to be printed, it was Mme de Luxemburg who visited the printer; and when Rousseau believed the latter had betrayed him, it was she who ran all over Paris for him and took the trouble to reassure and calm him—she being a Villeroy by birth, a Duchess and the wife of a Marshal of France to boot, while he was the son of a Genevese watchmaker! But the watchmaker's son had written *La Nouvelle Héloïse*, and that sufficed to make him the friend of a Duchess de Luxemburg and a Countess de Boufflers, and enabled him to rely not only on the protection, but on the friendship of a Prince de Conti, one of those Princes of the Blood, whom in the preceding century La Bruyère had felt himself obliged to call, partly out of flattery, partly from motives of prudence, "the children of the gods." It was precisely these great nobles whom Duclos now recommended to the men of letters as their natural protectors. He explains this very ingeniously: "The people at Court are the very ones to whom letters owe most, and if I had to give advice to a man who has nothing but his wits to rely on, I would say to him: 'If you seek only social connections, make them at Court; for those are the most agreeable and the least embarrassing. Plots, intrigue, and chicanery, and what are called base actions, are only resorted to by those who are rivals in ambition. Now the courtiers would not dream of stooping to injure those who cannot cross them, and often gain glory by obliging them, since they like to attach to themselves a man of merit whose gratitude may redound to their credit. The greater a man is, the more careful is he not to emphasise a social gulf; enlightened self-esteem is not far removed from modesty in the effects it produces. A man of letters who is worthy of esteem will not indulge in any offensive display, but he may be exposed to it from people whose only claim to superiority is their own impertinence and who believe that such display is the best means of proving it."[1]

But poets no longer bowed their heads before insolent and foppish nobles like the fine gentleman whom Chamfort mentions, who tried to impress his superiority of rank upon a man of letters, and to whom the latter replied: "My Lord Duke, I am quite aware of all that I ought to

[1] *Considérations*, p. 238.

know; but I also know that it is easier for people to be above me than to be equal to me." Collé in his *Journal* for June 1750 gives a good example of the growing pride of the literary confraternity: "Lesage had promised the Duchess de Bouillon to read his *Turcaret* to her before it was produced, and it was expected that he would do so before dinner. But he was detained by some business or other and arrived too late. The Duchess received him with an air of impatience and not a little haughtiness, and told him sharply that she had lost an hour by waiting for him. 'Very well, Madame,' said Lesage coldly, 'I will save you two hours to make up for it,' and, making her a bow, he left the room. In spite of all efforts, and though he was implored to stay, he refused to return, and neither would he dine nor read his play." This scene took place at the beginning of the century, for *Turcaret* was first performed in 1709, but at the close of it no great lady, even if she were a Duchess, as in this case, would have dared to receive a distinguished author in such a manner, though he kept her waiting for ever so long, because by this time genius counted as much as a title, and a great author was treated with as much consideration as a great noble. It was the age in which Talleyrand wrote in his *Mémoires*: "Delille dined at the house of Mme de Polignac to meet the Queen; the Abbé de Balivière played at cards with the Count d'Artois, and Chamfort was to be seen arm in arm with M. de Vaudreuil."

This spirit of equality, which tended to efface all social distinctions, greatly assisted in fostering among all classes that "most agreeable life" which Talleyrand affirms was only experienced by those who had lived at the end of the eighteenth century, and of which the Count de Ségur has also left this curious description: "Inequality lingered on in theory and was emphasised by laws, privileges, and rights, but, in reality, it diminished daily. The institutions were monarchical, but the habits had become republican. All posts and offices were still the sole prerogative of certain classes, but outside official circles, a spirit of equality began to pervade the whole of society. Literary fame occasionally even outshone the most ancient titles, and a homage which entirely effaced this inferiority was not merely paid to men of genius, but one might often see men of letters who were second or even third rate welcomed and entertained with a distinction which was by no means accorded to the provincial nobility.

"The Court alone preserved its customary superiority, but as the courtiers of France had become the slaves of fashion more than the slaves of the prince, they thought it modish to waive their rank and to pay court to Marmontel, d'Alembert, and Raynal, hoping, thereby, to raise themselves in popular estimation. This spirit of equality constituted the charm of Parisian society at that time and attracted a host of strangers from all countries. Nowhere else, except possibly in England, were the joys of privacy known, and people could not imagine a society in which pride on one hand and constraint on the other did not have a place, and in which conversation could be carried on without a mask and without restriction.

"Whereas in other countries the distinctions of caste remained fixed and inviolable, every one consorting with his peers, and all interchange, whether of opinion or interests, between the various classes of an enlightened population was non-existent, in France, on the other hand, the opposite had taken place. The frequent intercourse among the various strata of society, the mutual intimacies, the reciprocal regard, and the exchange of views which had now become so general, all increased the wealth of our civilisation, and, through the new relations thus inaugurated, the nobility acquired that knowledge and information of which it had hitherto been deprived. At the same time the 'intelligentsia' among the lower classes learned to value that delicate taste and rare tact as well as the elegant graces and airy but charming manners which are only found among polished courtiers."[1]

We cannot discuss here the far-reaching and complex question of the influence which the great literary productions of the age exercised on the public mind, for that

[1] *Mémoires*, i. 79.

belongs to the history of Literature; but we must not forget that the authors of the eighteenth century did gradually come to guide public opinion. In this connection it would not be amiss to quote these lines of Malesherbes' inaugural address at the Academy in 1775: "In an enlightened age when each citizen may speak to the whole nation by means of the printing-press, those who have the gift of teaching and moving the multitude, in other words, the men of letters, are to the scattered public what the orators of Rome and Athens were to the assembled people."

At first sight it seems strange that these eighteenth-century writers, or "the philosophers," as they were called, apparently did nothing but ridicule the prejudices and criticise "the abuses" on which the society of their day was based, and which were the very foundations of that privileged class which so warmly welcomed these philosophers and their subversive ideas; and it is equally curious that these great gentlemen should be so blind and so—disinterested. But the fact was that the great works of that epoch carried them away, not only by their novelty, but by the genius of their authors, and the Count de Ségur writes: "We were disposed to follow with enthusiasm the philosophical doctrines professed by witty and daring writers. Voltaire seduced our intellects, Rousseau touched our hearts."

But it is undoubtedly true that they allowed themselves to be "seduced and touched" willingly enough, because in their heart of hearts they were convinced that this novel literature would change nothing whatever in the society in which they lived nor affect the privileged position they occupied. "This little campaign gave us pleasure, though the enemy was undermining our rank and our privileges beneath our very feet; we only saw the outward show and did not suspect the hidden offensive. We thought it but a warfare of pen and word, which to us appeared quite devoid of danger to the superior existence which we enjoyed, and [this is the most illuminating revelation] which a possession of many centuries had deluded us into believing unassailable!"[1] In this last sentence lies the explanation of the unexpected liberalism displayed by the younger generation of the nobility. Mme de Staël, who knew the old society so well, sheds more light on Ségur's frank confession, and explains with her usual lucidity why the upper classes thought it practically a duty to compound with public opinion, whose part in the social life of this century we have tried to estimate:

"Philosophy, that is to say, the appreciation of values by the light of reason and not from force of habit, had made such strides in Europe that the privileged classes—kings, nobles, and priests—were the first to offer excuses for those much-abused advantages which they enjoyed. They never doubted but that they would retain them; but they feigned indifference to them, while the more cunning flattered themselves that they had lulled public opinion into respecting what they themselves affected to despise."[2] These curious concessions which the privileged class thought itself compelled to make to public opinion, show us the extent to which the latter influenced minds at the end of the century, and at this time Chamfort proclaims it "the Queen of Society." It was this opinion which made literary reputations in the salons, created Academicians, and bestowed on, or withdrew from, men of the world that precious "consideration" which Necker thus defines as: "That strange distinction, utterly independent of the prince's favour, and which public opinion alone bestows. This consideration was never so sought after as in the reigns of Louis xv. and Louis xvi., since public opinion was powerful and the monarchs weak. Society had a tribunal which was more feared than the prince's authority, and courtiers, ministers even, would have risked incurring the Royal displeasure rather than expose themselves to a chilly welcome in the most distinguished salons of Paris."[3]

[1] Ségur, *Mémoires*, i. 39.
[2] *Considérations sur la Révolution française.*
[3] *Œuvres*, xv. 220.

CHAPTER III

FRENCH MANNERS

Towards the end of the eighteenth century there was one lady in Paris who set the fashion, taught the young, and reminded all of the manners which were essential in polite society. This was Mme de Luxemburg, the wife of the Marshal and the friend of Rousseau. The Duke de Lévis says of her: "She was the supreme arbiter of decorum, good manners, and those forms which are the basis of true politeness. Her sway over the youth of both sexes was absolute; she restrained the thoughtlessness of the young ladies and obliged them to indulge in general [sic] flirtations, forced the young people to preserve discretion and use consideration, and, above all, fed the sacred fire of French Manners. It was in her house that the tradition of those polished and easy manners which all Europe flocked to see in Paris, and tried in vain to imitate, was preserved intact. No Roman censor was ever more careful of the morals of the Republic than was Mme de Luxemburg of the seemliness of society during the last years that preceded the Revolution." [1]

The Revolution destroyed a great deal. In our present-day democratic society, which knows nothing of the laws of etiquette or the infinite variations of bygone politeness, it is difficult to form an exact idea of that code of decorum and gallantry, which was as essential as it was intricate, and which was wholly unwritten; thus we can only form an opinion upon the memories of a perfect education, as was that of Mme de Luxemburg herself, and that which she gave to her own granddaughter, the Duchess de Lauzun. Besenval himself, who is so severe on the former in his *Mémoires,* and doubtless calumniated her, is obliged

---

[1] *Souvenirs,* p. 54.

to pay a well-deserved tribute to "the way in which she brought up the Duchess de Lauzun, for it cannot be denied that this lady is a masterpiece of education and the most perfect woman one has ever met." [1]

Necker has left us a very finished picture of a salon and the duel between the self-esteem of its frequenters and the delicate attentions and subtle distinctions practised by the lady of the house in welcoming her visitors, each one being graded according to his rank or merit. "It was Public Opinion, that is, the opinion which governed polite society, which alone regulated the various shades of difference applicable to all these diverse ranks whether of birth or talent. There was a system which governed them, but it was an unwritten one, and had, in consequence, become so subtle and so delicate that it could almost be called an understood law, and this definition is all the more true because if a person did not actually claim a right, yet closer observation would reveal that he is thinking of the place which is his due, and although the various ranks appear confused on the surface, there is no gradation even of the faintest which is not indicated by some different shade. The greatest skill of the hostess, which doubtless is her greatest pleasure if she be also a great lady, is to make it apparent to all that she understands all these subtle and distinctive shades; but she must do so with great tact in order to give no one a cause for complaint.

"A great lady when holding her court always has a special place by a corner of the fireplace, and her arm-chair must be of a particular kind, but not so ornate as to give the impression that she has changed her usual customs for the occasion. A tapestry frame which can be brought forward and pushed aside with equal ease is usually in front of her, and her hands rest on a piece of embroidery which always seems just begun but shows no definite pattern, on which she stitches away with apparent carelessness. This work dispenses the lady of the house from rising whenever a guest enters. There are, of course, exceptions to this rule, but they are very rare, and such honour

[1] Besenval, i. 149.

is only paid to Princes of the Blood, foreign ladies of the highest rank, generals who have just won a battle, or a popular minister, always provided, in the last case, that he is sufficiently well thought of to leave no doubt that this homage is only rendered to his merit and not to the post he occupies.

"A special welcome, but one only prompted by kindness, is given to those whose position in society is still uncertain, and whom it is desired to reassure; but if they mistake it, a question uttered with a detached air, but containing an unmistakable sting, soon shows them that they have been overbold. The greatest skill is required when people are of about the same status as yourself, or who are not sufficiently removed therefrom to realise that they are beneath you in the social scale, especially at the moment when a word or a gesture on your part might too openly betray your true opinion. Taste and tact are the two guiding stars which aid a great lady in playing her part as a hostess, and it is the latter which prevents her making an error in all those very subtle distinctions which she may wish to make among her guests, who may include ladies of rank, ladies of quality, ladies of the Court, ladies of title, and ladies bearing historic names." We must here break in on Necker's narrative to note that in this ascending gradation he puts ladies of quality *after* ladies of rank, and both Littré and Hatzfeld are wrong when they confuse the two in their respective Dictionaries. In his *La Justesse de la langue française, ou les différentes significations des mots qui passent pour synonymes*, written in 1718, the Abbé Girard has clearly explained the difference: "Rank belongs to the order of the 'Bourgeoisie,' quality to that of the Nobility." As early as 1674, Father Bouhours had stated in his *Remarques nouvelles sur la langue française* that: "A man, and therefore also a woman, of quality means in our language something more than a man of rank."

Necker continues: "It is easy enough for a German genealogist to count the quarterings required for admittance to a 'Chapter,' but to grasp instantly every imperceptible difference and to proportion to it one's time, one's gestures, and one's manner, that is quite another undertaking. It requires all our French dexterity and a great knowledge of the world to carry it through successfully. Moreover, the pride of the people with whom one has to deal daily is extremely delicate, and the least mistake in the consideration due to it is immediately seized upon." [1]

M. Delahante has found among his family archives a curious eighteenth-century book bearing the following title: "*The Dancing Master*: 'A work of great service not only to young people who desire to learn how to dance well, but also to educated and polite people, providing them with the rules required for walking, saluting, and making bows in all kinds of company.' " One chapter is entitled: "How to take off your Hat and replace it," and is illustrated with plates showing the different occasions on which this difficult operation is performed. It must have been quick work, for the author says: "I presume that there be no interval, and that the space between be so imperceptible that I have condensed the one action into three movements in order to demonstrate more clearly each of these separate attitudes, namely, raising one's arm at one's side and bending the elbow—raising the hand to one's head and taking hold of the hat, and, lastly, raising it above one's head and dropping the arm to the side." [2]

Even greater difficulties were encountered on entering a salon, and this act could only be performed with credit after many lessons and rehearsals:

"The entry of a young man into society required serious study and was, after philosophy and the humanities, the final course of his education. It was by no means an inferior science to know how to enter a drawing-room in which some thirty ladies and gentlemen were sitting in a circle round the fire, with both assurance and grace; to penetrate this circle and to make a slight inclination as you walked round it; to make your way to your hostess, and to retire with dignity and without ruffling your fine clothes, for you were dressed in lace, and your hair was dressed in thirty-six curls, all powdered; you were carrying

[1] *Œuvres*, xv. 260.   [2] Delahante, i. 15.

"LES PRECAUTIONS"
From an engraving by Pietro Martini, after J. M. Moreau le Jeune

your hat under your arm, your sword reached to your heels, and you were armed with a huge muff, the smallest being two and a half feet wide! I took a month's course of instruction from the celebrated Petit [the dancing-master], at twelve francs a lesson, in order to qualify in this part of my education, and no actor can ever have been as nervous as I was when I made my first appearance on the social stage." [1]

In a society where the manner of bowing, entering a drawing-room, and behaving at table was considered of such prodigious importance, we can well understand that the manner of expressing oneself was of even greater. An awkward phrase, a vulgar expression, or an unlucky word sufficed to disqualify a man, whereas a felicitous phrase and even a mere exclamation uttered at the right moment and conveying far more than it seemed, consolidated the reputation of a wit. Let us see what happened to Talleyrand, for he was fortunate enough to make this hit.

"A cold manner and an obvious reserve had persuaded some people that I did not lack brains. Mme de Gramont, who disliked people whose reputations she had not made herself, thought to turn me to some profit by trying to embarrass me. I was supping for the first time at Auteuil, with Mme de Boufflers, and was seated at the very end of the table, and hardly spoke at all with my neighbour. Suddenly Mme de Gramont called my name in a loud and strident tone, and asked me what had struck me so much on entering the room into which I followed her, that I had cried, 'Ah! ah!' 'Your Grace misunderstood me,' I replied. 'I did not say, Ah! ah! I cried, Oh! oh!' This miserable answer caused a laugh, and I relapsed into silence and continued my supper. Yet on leaving the table several persons approached me, and in the next few days I received various invitations which enabled me to become acquainted with those persons whom I most desired to meet." [2]

In the preceding century the reputation of being a good

---

[1] Frénilly, v.   [2] Talleyrand, *Mémoires*, i. 43.

conversationalist was bestowed on those who could tell a story well, and "the Abbé de Fleury, afterwards Cardinal, could tell a story admirably, a quality which was common enough under Louis XIV., but is now no longer fashionable." [1] This was because stories were most amusing when accompanied by much detail, but this prolonged them, and in the eighteenth century people did not care for long stories which held the attention for too protracted a period and interrupted conversation. Montesquieu defines conversation in the later age as being usually "a gay dialogue in which each listens but little, yet speaks and replies in a rapid, prompt, and vivacious manner," [2] so that whosoever wished to hold the cards in a conversation and acquire the reputation of a good talker must be a clever man, possessed of a ready repartee, and those quick shafts of wit which seemed to be unpremeditated, and which could sting without wounding. "I shoot arrows," said Piron's Métromanie, alluding to his conversation. Once a guest of Mme Geoffrin's had embarked on a long story, and his hostess, in order to stop him, begged him to carve a chicken. Seeing that he was taking a small knife out of his pocket, she remarked: "Sir, you require large knives and short stories in order to succeed in this country." On occasions only the beginning of a story was sufficient, as when, for instance, at a certain dinner party every guest was requested to tell a story about robbers. Voltaire, when his turn came, began: "There was once upon a time a Farmer-General—I have forgotten the rest, gentlemen." He was not required to finish it.

The eighteenth century was, as we know, the age when "wit reigned in the streets" no less than in the salons, when letters and pamphlets poured from Ferney in an unending stream intended either to scourge or amuse the people of Paris, and Paris occasionally replied in a woman's hand. Here is an amusing example. We know that the Great Catherine, Empress of All the Russias, was Voltaire's friend and the patron of the Philosophers. Her husband

[1] Bernis, *Mémoires*, i. 44.   [2] *Pensées et fragments inédits*, ii. 302.

had just been strangled in prison, and she could say, like Agrippina, "A thousand rumours abound to my shame." This is what Voltaire wrote to Mme du Deffand on 18th May 1767 on the subject of these infamous reports: "Speaking of reputations, there is one woman who is building up a very great one. This is the Semiramis of the North who, in order to establish toleration and liberty of conscience, has sent 50,000 men to Poland. It is a unique step in History, and, I assure you, will have enormous consequences. I pride myself on being able to tell you that I am in her good books, and am her very true knight against all comers. I know very well that she is accused of some trumpery business in connection with her husband, but that is a family matter which concerns me not at all. Moreover, it isn't a bad thing to commit an error which one afterwards has to repair, for one's efforts compel the public to esteem and admire one, and her miserable husband would certainly never have performed any of those great deeds which my Catherine does daily."

On the 26th May, Mme du Deffand replied to these quips in a letter which reveals to us how, in the eighteenth century, a woman of the world was also a woman of wit.

"Never resist, dear sir, any desire you may have of writing to me. You cannot imagine the benefit I derive from your letters, especially from the last, which had the admirable effect of dispelling the vapours which had possessed me. No ill-humour can withstand the eulogy of your Northern Semiramis. 'The trumpery business in connection with her husband which is no concern of yours, as you do not wish to meddle in a purely family matter,' would make even the deceased laugh; but does poor little Ninyas travel with his lady mother? I would rather she entrusted him to your care, preferring your instruction to her good example. I admire her zeal for toleration, and she is not content with establishing it in her own dominions, but she sends fifty thousand missionaries, armed from head to foot, to preach it to her neighbours! That is eloquence indeed!"

What were the subjects talked about in the salons?

Everything, for La Fontaine says: "Every topic is an essential subject for discussion in true conversation." But conversation naturally turned upon those subjects which were fashionable at the moment, and Bernis distinguishes three intellectual currents in thirty years which naturally gave rise to three different topics of conversation in the salons: "When I first entered society in 1735, Wit was the fashion. Each coterie had its own little god, and academies sprang up at Court and in Paris, while men of letters ceased to work in their studies and enjoyed their hour of good fortune. All women thought they were witty; books increased in huge numbers and became frankly frivolous, and conversations became dissertations. Next, however, about the middle of the century—and this was the age of the Encyclopedists—came Science, and everybody kept a geometrician where he formerly had kept a page. To-day it is Politics and the Principles of Government which have supplanted both Science and Wit, and ambassadors have elbowed physicians and poets off the stage. Now everything is the fashion in Paris."[1] As the Revolution approached nearer and nearer, so politics and the government became the all-absorbing topics in the fashionable salons, and the ladies were full of information on affairs of State and details of administration. "I remember," says Talleyrand, "that it was at a ball that Mme de Staël taught M. de Surgers what the 'Empire of the West' was. Mme de Blot gave her opinion about all the officers of the French Navy, and Mme de Simiane thought that Virginian tobacco should not be taxed. 'If I were King,' said M. de Poix, 'I should do so and so.' "[2]

Saint-Preux—in other words, Rousseau—criticises the "jargon of society" when he writes of the salons of Paris in this century; but he is fain to admit that "conversation flows easily and naturally, is neither dull nor frivolous, full of knowledge without being pedantic, gay but not noisy, polished without affectation, gallant and not merely insipid, playful but not ambiguous. Everything is dis-

[1] *Mémoires*, i. 96.   [2] *Mémoires*, 62.

cussed in order that every one may be able to say something, but no subject is plumbed to its depth for fear of becoming tedious. It is brought up quite by the way and rapidly disposed of, but precision gives an elegance to conversation in that every one gives his opinion in as few words as possible. No one attacks another's point of view with warmth, and the latter does not defend it with any obstinacy. People indulge in discussion in order to enlighten themselves, but stop before it can degenerate into a dispute." [1]

One of Rousseau's compatriots, a Bernese gentleman called Béat de Muralt, had already paid a twofold homage to French good manners and gallantry in terms which are so delicate and complimentary that we cannot do better than quote them as a fitting close to our reflections on the salons of the eighteenth century.

"Politeness forms an essential part of French conversation and manners. They are not content with having discarded everything that may offend, shock, or wound, but their aim is to attract people and to gain the esteem of others by their politeness. In this they succeed, and indeed triumphantly, for they have brought it to such a pitch of perfection that cultivated people can derive from it all the pleasures of superb acting. It moves them to kindness towards those who are of no account, and to subject themselves gracefully to that which has no real value. This doubles their politeness, for it is extended to all their conduct as well as to all their conversation, and adorns their least action no less than their most insignificant gesture. A Frenchman gives you his hand politely, and as politely withdraws it; he gives it to a lady crossing a room, and hastens to support her as if the crossing was difficult or even dangerous. He will swiftly stoop to pick up a glove or a handkerchief which has been dropped, with as great haste as if he were snatching it from the fire, and thereby gives the appearance of doing something more than merely picking up a glove or a handkerchief." [2]

This politeness, though charming, is perhaps somewhat

[1] *Nouvelle Héloïse*, Part II., xiv.   [2] *Lettres*, p. 150.

cold and mechanical, and gives an impression of dexterity and practice. But there is in France another form of politeness, more sincere and more delicate than this, which springs from the heart. This also did not escape Muralt: "I will next deal with the gallantry of the French, which is something more than mere good manners, and is, rather, good manners brought to the highest pitch of perfection. By gallantry they mean the art of pleasing others and of embellishing, under all circumstances, the pleasure they accord. They do this wonderfully well, and know exactly how to enhance, by their very manner, the smallest services which they may render. When you have experienced their kindnesses, and compare them with what others may do on your behalf, you will always find, in the latter, something lacking, and you will find it difficult not to regret France. French gallantry is the outcome, not only of goodness of heart, but also of that minute attention to detail in which the French excel; we see that goodness of heart is not only precious in itself, but that it gives a value to other qualities which, without it, are worthless. It dignifies all that it comes in contact with."

This kindness of heart which is inseparable from the true politeness of a Frenchman is praised by Voltaire in one of those quatrains in which, like Pibrac, he described how one ought to behave in society:

"La politesse est à l'esprit
Ce que la grâce est au visage.
De la bonté du cœur elle est la douce image,
Et c'est la bonté qu'on cherit." [1]

Here is a delightful and touching instance of what we have called the politeness of the heart. The Duchess d'Orléans, the Regent's widow, at the age of seventy-one lay on her death-bed. The Archbishop of Paris, M. de Beaumont, came to see her and recited the prayers for the dying. "She made all the responses with great devotion, being fully conscious, and then said to the Archbishop: 'I am deeply

[1] "Politeness is to the mind what beauty is to the face. It is the sweet image of a good heart, and it is this goodness which we cherish " (*Stances ou quatrains*, p. 38).

grateful for all your Grace's kindness. I shall not last long, but I know your health is bad. Take care of it and stay with me no longer.'" [1]

We have not concealed from our readers that during the eighteenth century the habits of certain classes were far from exemplary, but when we have noted and regretted this moral slackness we would do well to recall Duclos' just reflection: "The French are the only people whose morals may deteriorate without corrupting their heart or lowering their courage. A character such as that of Alcibiades is no rare thing in France. Morals and imagination may grow worse, but the innate frankness and natural kindliness of the French will never be contaminated." [2]

This natural kindliness also receives a tribute from Rousseau. Speaking once more through the mouth of his Saint-Preux, he writes to Julie from Paris: "I assure you, from the bottom of my heart, that I honour the French as the only people who truly love mankind and are kindly by nature." [3] The word *bienfaisance*, or kindliness, appears in the Academy's official Dictionary for the first time in 1762, and it was the Abbé de Saint-Pierre who had made it fashionable:

> "Certain législateur, dont la plume féconde
> Fit tant de vains projets pour le bien de ce monde,
> Et qui depuis trente ans écrit pour des ingrats,
> Vient de créer un mot qui manque à Vaugelas.
> Ce mot est 'Bienfaisance': Il me plaît, il rassemble,
> Si le cœur en est cru, bien des vertus ensemble." [4]

There is yet another word which should be mentioned in connection with eighteenth-century society, and that is the word "Humanity." Mercier, so often the chronicler of public opinion, has only described the feeling of the whole

---

[1] Luynes, ix. 315. [2] *Considérations*, p. 23.
[3] *Nouvelle Héloïse*, Part II., p. xix.
[4] Voltaire, *Discours sur l'homme*, VIIe Discours: "A legislator whose fertile pen has drawn up so many fruitless schemes for the welfare of mankind, and who has written these thirty years for people who do not read him, has just coined a word which was wanting in Vaugelas. This word is 'kindliness,' and I confess it gives me pleasure, for when it springs from the heart it includes many virtues."

age when he wrote: "The greatest crime in our day is a hard heart. The word 'Humanity' is the most beautiful in the French language." Voltaire is right in declaring that French "is of all languages the one which most delicately expresses all the subjects on which educated people converse," and, as it is spoken more or less everywhere, he might have added that it helped all Europe to preserve that ideal of society which he considered one of life's choicest pleasures.

Such was society in the eighteenth century. Like all else it had its faults and its merits, and perhaps one fault above all others, although that was of a quality which is typically French, namely, that it revelled, as has been often said, in doing frivolous things seriously, and serious things gaily. Undoubtedly this society loved luxury and pleasure overmuch; but, on the other hand, it did not know that extravagant passion for ease and comfort which often incites people to vexatious compromise and petty acts of cowardice. It did not possess, nor indeed did it desire, political liberty; but its obedience to the King was not servile, for it venerated and loved him—as long as he deserved the title of the Well-Beloved which its affection had bestowed on him.

I do not think I have glossed over any of the faults which these eighteenth-century men and women displayed, and I have ever kept in mind what the greatest intellect of his time impressed upon every one, namely: "To be sincere at all times, especially about your own country. Every citizen is obliged to die for his country, but no one is obliged to lie about it." [1] I therefore hold that, all in all, the century which we have just impartially studied, has a claim to a very high place in the History of Civilisation. No one, I think, will contradict me, when I say that never before had there been in France, nor was there in contemporary Europe, nor, we may even say, has there ever been in the world since, a society so polished, so intelligent, and so delightful as French Society of the Eighteenth Century.

[1] *Pensées et fragments inédits*, ii. 300.

LIST OF PRINCIPAL AUTHORS CITED

ALLAIN (l'abbé).—*L'Instruction primaire en France avant la Révolution.* 1881.

ARDASCHEFF.—*Les Intendants de province sous Louis XVI.*, 2 vol. 1909.

D'ARGENSON (le Marquis).—*Journal et Mémoires inédits* (éd. par Rathery), 8 vol. 1859.

—— *Considérations sur le gouvernement ancien et présent de la France.* 1764.

D'ARNETH et GEFFROY.—*Correspondance secrète entre Marie-Thérèse et le Comte de Mercy-Argenteau*, 3 vol. 1875.

AUBERTIN.—*L'Esprit public au XVIIIe siècle*, 2e éd. 1873.

AUGEARD.—*Mémoires secrets.* éd. 1866.

BABEAU.—*Le Village sous l'ancien régime.* 1882.

—— *La Ville sous l'ancien régime.* 1884.

—— *La Vie rurale de l'ancienne France.* 1885.

—— *Les Bourgeois d'autrefois.* 1886.

—— *La Province sous l'ancien régime*, 2 vol. 1894.

BACHAUMONT.—*Mémoires secrets tirés des registres de Mme Doublet* (1762–1787), 36 vol.

BARBIER.—*Chronique de la Régence et du règne de Louis XV.* (ou *Journal de Barbier*), (1718–1763), 8 vol. 1866.

BASTARD D'ESTANG.—*Les Parlements de France*, 2 vol. 1857.

BATAILLARD.—*Mœurs judiciaires de l'ancienne France.* 1878.

BAUDRILLART.—*Histoire du luxe privé et public, depuis l'antiquité jusqu'à nos jours*, 1878–1881, 4 vol., t. iv.

BERNIER (l'abbé).—*Essai sur le Tiers-État rural en Basse-Normandie au XVIIIe siècle.* 1891.

DE BERNIS.—*Mémoires et lettres*, 2 vol. 1878.

M. BERRYER, doyen des avocats de Paris.—*Souvenirs, de 1774 à 1838*, 2 vol. 1839.

BERTIN.—*Les Mariages dans l'ancienne société française.* 1879.

DE BESENVAL.—*Mémoires* (éd. Berville et Barrière). 1821.

BEUGNOT (Comte).—*Mémoires*, 2 vol. 1866.
BOIGNE (Comtesse DE).—*Mémoires*, 4 vol. 1907.
BOUILLÉ (Marquis DE).—*Mémoires sur la Révolution française, depuis son origine jusqu'à la mort de Louis XVI.* (éd. Berville et Barrière). 1821.
BOULAINVILLIERS.—*État de la France*, 3 vol. in fol. 1727.
G. BRICE.—*Description de la ville de Paris et de tout ce qu'elle contient de plus remarquable*, 4 vol. 1752.
BRISSOT.—*Mémoires* (éd. Perroud), 2 vol. 1910.
—— *Correspondance et papiers* (id.). 1912.
BROC.—*La France sous l'ancien régime*, 2 vol. 1889.
BROGLIE (Duc DE).—*Le Secret du Roi. Correspondance secrète de Louis XV. avec ses agents diplomatiques* (1752–1774), 2 vol. 1882.
BROGLIE (Emmanuel DE).—*Fénelon à Cambrai*. 1882.
BUVAT.—*Journal de ce qui s'est passé de plus remarquable pendant la régence de feu M. le duc d'Orléans, depuis le 2 septembre 1715 jusqu'à la mort de cet illustre prince, qui arriva le 2 décembre 1723* (éd. Campardon), 2 vol. 1865.
CAMPAN (Mme).—*Mémoires sur la vie privée de Marie-Antoinette* (éd. Barrière), 3 vol. 1822.
CAMPARDON.—*Mme de Pompadour et la Cour de Louis XV. au milieu du XVIIIᵉ siècle*. 1867.
CARRE (Henri).—*La Noblesse de France et l'opinion publique au XVIIIᵉ siècle*. 1920.
CHATEAUBRIAND.—*Mémoires d'Outre-Tombe* (éd. Biré), 6 vol. 1898–1901.
CHOISEUL (Duc DE).—*Mémoires*, réimprimés par Calmettes, 1905.
COLLÉ.—*Journal et Mémoires*, 4 vol. 1868.
COMBIER.—*Les Justices Seigneuriales en Vermandois*. 1899.
COURNOT, A.—*Souvenirs* (1760–1860), in 8°. 1913.
COYER (l'abbé).—*La Noblesse commerçante*. 1756.
—— *Développement et défense du système de la Noblesse commerçante*. 1757.
CRADOCK (Mme DE).—*Journal inédit* (1783–1786), traduit de l'anglais. 1911.
CROŸ (Duc DE).—*Journal inédit*, 4 vol. 1906.
DEBERRE.—*La Vie littéraire à Dijon au XVIIIᵉ siècle*. 1902.
DEFFAND (Mme DU).—*Correspondance inédite*, publiée par le Marquis de Sainte-Aulaire. 1859.

Deffand (Mme du).—*Correspondance complète*, publiée par de Lescure. 1865.
Delahante.—*Une famille de finances au XVIIIe siècle*. 1881.
Delaunay.—*Le Monde médical parisien au XVIIIe siècle*. 1906.
Duclos.—*Les Confessions du Comte ***.* 1742.
—— *Considérations sur les mœurs de ce siècle*. 1751.
—— *Essai sur les Ponts et Chaussées, la Voirie et les Corvées*. 1759.
—— *Mémoires secrets sur les règnes de Louis XIV. et de Louis XV.* (Collection des Mémoires relatifs à l'histoire de France, éd. par Petitot et Monmerqué), t. 76 et 77.
—— *Mémoires sur sa vie, écrits par lui-même* (Œuvres complètes, éd. par Auger, 1806).
Dufort (Comte de Cheverny).—*Mémoires*, 2 vol. 1906.
Dugast de Bois-Saint-Just.—*Paris, Versailles et les provinces au XVIIIe siècle*, 2e édit., 2 vol. 1809.
Dupont.—*La Condition des paysans dans la sénéchaussée de Rennes au XVIIIe siècle* (Annales de Bretagne, 1900).
Duruy (Albert).—*L'armée royale en 1789*. 1888.
Dussieux.—*Le Château de Versailles. Histoire et description*, 2 vol. 1882.
d'Epinay (Mme).—*Mémoires* (éd. Boiteau), 2 vol. Sans date.
Estrée (d').—*Le Maréchal de Richelieu, d'après les Mémoires contemporains et des documents inédits*. 1917.
Expilly.—*Dictionnaire historique et politique des Gaules et de la France* (1762–1770), 6 vol. in-fol.
Favart.—*Mémoires et Correspondance*, 3 vol. 1809.
Flammermont.—*Correspondances des agents diplomatiques étrangers en France* (Nouvelles archives des Missions scientifiques et littéraires), t. viii. 1896.
Floquet.—*Histoire du Parlement de Normandie*, 7 vol. 1840–1849.
Fontenay (de).—*La Société d'Autun au milieu du XVIIIe siècle* (Mémoires de la Société éduenne, t. vi. 1877).
Forbonnais.—*Recherches et Considérations sur les finances de France*, 1758.
Frénilly (Baron de).—*Souvenirs*, publiés par Chuquet, 1908.
Gaillard—*Vie ou Éloge historique de M. de Malesherbes, d'après les Mémoires du temps et les papiers de famille*, 1805.
G *,** curé en Basse-Bretagne (Gautier, curé de La Lande-de-Gul).—*Les Caractères et les Mœurs de ce siècle*. 1789.
Galiani.—*Correspondance* (éd. par Perey et Maugras), 2 vol. 1881.

GARAT.—*Mémoires historiques sur la vie de M. Suard, sur ses écrits et sur le XVIIIe siècle*, 2 vol. 1820.
GEBELIN.—*Histoire des milices provinciales.* 1881.
GEFFROY.—*Gustave III. et la Cour de France.* 1867.
GIFFARD.—*Les Justices seigneuriales en Bretagne aux XVIIe et XVIIIe siècles.* 1903.
GLEICHEN (Baron DE).—*Souvenirs.* 1868.
GRELLET-DUMAZEAU.—*La Société bordelaise sous Louis XV. et le Salon de Mme Du Plessy.* 1897.
GUSTAVE III. (Lettres de) *à la Comtesse de Boufflers, de 1771 à 1791* (publiées par Vidié). 1903.
GUY-PATIN.—*Lettres* (éd. par Réveillé-Parise), 2 vol. 1846.
HARDY.—*Mes loisirs* (éd. Tourneux et Vitrac), t. i. (1764–1773).
HARTMANN (Lieutenant-Colonel).—*Les Officiers de l'armée royale à la veille de la Révolution* (Revue historique). 1909.
HAUSSET (Mme DU).—*Mémoires* (Collection des Mémoires relatifs à la Révolution française), t. ii. 1824.
HÉNAULT (Le président).—*Mémoires* publiés par le baron du Vigan. 1854.
HIPPEAU.—*Le Gouvernement de Normandie au XVIIe et au XVIIIe siècle*, 9 vol. 1863–1870.
JALENQUES.—*La Noblesse de la province d'Auvergne au XVIIIe siècle* (Bulletin historique et scientifique de l'Auvergne publié par l'Académie de Clermont). 1911 et 1912.
Journal d'un curé de campagne (1712–1715), publié par Dupuy et Charvot dans les Annales de Bretagne, t. v.
JULLIAN.—*Histoire de Bordeaux.* 1895.
KLEINCLAUSZ.—*Histoire de Bourgogne*, 1909.
KOVALEWSKI.—*La France économique et sociale à la veille de la Révolution*, t. i.: Les Campagnes, 1909.
LAVERGNE (DE).—*Les Assemblées provinciales sous Louis XVI.* 1864.
LE GRAND D'HAUSSY.—*Histoire de la vie privée des Français depuis l'origine de la Nation*, 3 vol. 1782.
—— *Voyage d'Auvergne.* 1788.
LETACONNOUX.—*Le Régime de la corvée en Bretagne au XVIIIe siècle* (Extrait des Annales de Bretagne). 1905.
LÉVIS (Duc DE).—*Souvenirs et portraits.* 1813.
LOMÉNIE (DE).—*La Comtesse de Rochefort. Études sur les mœurs en France au XVIIIe siècle.* 1878.
—— *Les Mirabeau*, 5 vol. (1878–1891).

LIST OF PRINCIPAL AUTHORS CITED

LOYSEAU.—*Les œuvres de maistre Loyseau, avocat au Parlement,* in fol. 1701.

LUYNES (Duc DE).—*Mémoires sur la cour de Louis XV.,* éd. Dussieux, 17 vol. 1860–1865.

MARIVAUX.—*Le Spectateur français,* 2 vol. 1761.

MASSILLON.—*Lettre au Cardinal Fleury* (Œuvres complètes, 1822, t. xiv.).

MATHIEU (l'abbé).—*L'ancien Régime dans les provinces de Lorraine et de Barrois.* 1879.

MÉRIC.—*Le clergé sous l'ancien Régime.* 1822.

MIRABEAU.—*Des lettres de cachet et des prisons d'État* (Œuvres, 1835, t. vii.).

MIRABEAU (le Marquis DE).—*L'Ami des hommes ou Traité de la population* (éd. de 1883).

MONTESQUIEU.—*Lettres persanes.* 1721.

—— *L'Éspirit des Lois.* 1748.

—— *Pensées et fragments inédits,* publiés par le baron de Montesquieu. 1899–1901.

—— *Correspondance,* publiée par Gebelin. 1914.

—— *Voyages,* publiés par Albert de Montesquieu, 2 vol. 1894–1896.

MONTLOSIER (DE).—*Mémoires sur la Révolution française,* 1830, t. i.

MORELLET (l'abbé).—*Mémoires sur le XVIIIe siècle et la Révolution,* 2 vol. 1821.

(MOUFFLE D'ANGERVILLE).—*Vie privée de Louis XV.,* 4 vol. 1783.

MURALT (BÉAT DE).—*Lettres sur les Anglais et les Français* (1725), éd. par Eug. Ritter, 1897.

NECKER.—*Fragments sur la Société et sur le Bonheur des Sots* (Œuvres, 1821, t. xv.).

—— *Compte Rendu,* t. ii.

—— *Mémoire sur les administrations provinciales,* t. iii.

NOLHAC (DE).—*Louis XV. et Marie Leczinska.* 1902.

—— *Louis XV. et Mme de Pompadour,* 1904.

—— *La Décoration de Versailles au XVIIIe siècle* (Gazette des Beaux-Arts, 1895, 1898).

OBERKIRCH (Baronne D').—*Mémoires sur la cour de Louis XVI. et la Société française avant 1789.*

ORLÉANS (Duchesse D'), princesse palatine, mère du Régent. *Correspond.* trad. par Jœglé, 2 vol. 1880.

PASQUIER (le chancelier).—*Mémoires.* 1894.

348 LIST OF PRINCIPAL AUTHORS CITED

(Pidansat de Mairobert).—*L'Espion anglais. Correspondance secrète entre Milord All'Eye et Milord All'Ear*, 4 vol. 1779.
Rétif de la Bretonne.—*La vie de mon père*, 1779 (nouv. édit. de H. d'Alméras). 1910.
Rod. Reuss.—*L'Alsace au XVIIe siècle*, 2 vol. 1897.
Richelieu.—*Mémoires du maréchal de Richelieu*, 9 vol. 1790–1792 (doivent être corrigés par l'ouvrage suivant).
―― *Mémoires authentiques du maréchal de Richelieu*, publiés par A. de Boislisle, 1918 (Société de l'Histoire de France).
Rochejaquelein (Marquise de La).—*Mémoires écrits par elle-même et rédigés par M. de Barante*. 1823.
Roland (Mme).—*Mémoires* (éd. Barrière). 1855.
―― *Lettres* (éd. Perroud). 1900–1901.
C. Rousset.—*Le Comte de Gisors*. 1868.
Saint-Simon (Duc de).—*Mémoires* (éd. Chéruel et Régnier), 22 vol. 1873–1886.
―― *Écrits inédits publ. pour Faugère*, 8 vol. 1880 et suiv.
Ségur (Comte de).—*Mémoires ou Souvenirs et Anecdotes*, 3 vol. 1826.
Sénac de Meilhan.—*Considérations sur l'esprit et les mœurs*, Londres, 1787.
―― *Du gouvernement, des mœurs et des conditions en France avant la Révolution*. 1814.
Servan.—*Discours sur l'administration de la Justice criminelle*, 1766 (Œuvres de Servan, 1825, t. ii.).
Sicard.—*L'Ancien clergé de France*, 2 vol. 1893–1894.
Staël (Mme de).—*Considérations sur les principaux événements de la Révolution française*. 1823.
Stryenski.—*La Mère des trois derniers Bourbons: Marie-Josèphe de Saxe à la cour de Louis XV*. 1902.
Talleyrand.—*Mémoires*, publ. par le Duc de Broglie (1891–1892), 5 vol., t. i.
Thirion.—*La Vie privée des financiers au XVIIIe siècle*. 1895.
Tocqueville.—*L'Ancien Régime et la Révolution*, éd. 1857.
Turgot.—*Œuvres* (Edition Daire), 2 vol. 1844.
Vigée-Lebrun (Mme).—*Souvenirs*, 3 vol. 1837.
Villars (Maréchal de).—*Mémoires* (Société de l'Histoire de France), 5 vol., t. iv.
Voltaire.—*Œuvres*, éd. Moland (1877–1882), 50 vol.

INDEX

Abbots, 233, 234.
Abduction, cases of, 61.
Absolutism, 51.
Académie française, 323.
Agriculture, improvements in, 270, 271.
Amphibies, defined, 53.
Amusements, 113, 114, 117; of lawyers, 140, 141; of Paris populace, 197 ff.; provincial, 217 ff.
Anglophobia, 320.
Appointements, 137.
Architecture, domestic, 108, 109, 247.
Army, the, 291–311; recruits for, 189; lack of discipline in, 300 ff.; songs, 318.
Art exhibitions, 114.
Authors, avenged by public opinion, 316, 317; and the Salons, 322; improved status of, 326, 327.
Automatic flute-player, the, 114.

"Bad men," the, 258.
Bailiff, status of, 280.
Balls, 111, 112.
Bar, the, and Finance, 164.
Barrister, status of, 136, 137.
Bastille, the, 77.
Bazoche, 138.
Beaucaire, fair of, 218.
Beggars, 199, 268, 284.
Belle-Isle, Mme de, 91.
Bernard, Samuel, "success" of, 159 ff.

Berry, Duchesse de, 56.
"Billingsgate," 73.
Bishops, 231, 232; as statesmen, 235, 241; greed of, 282.
Blood-letting, 178.
Bouillon, M. de, 43.
Boulevards, popularity of, 161, 117.
Bourdaloue, le père, on marriage, 65; on gambling, 86.
Bourgeoisie, 122, 152; and noble brides, 163; of Paris, 185–192; and the religious orders, 215; influence of, 225; and the army, 303; and the Salons, 323 ff.
Bourse, the, 105.
Bread, riots (1770), 196, 197; supply of, 106, 107; lack of, 265.
Brigandage, 257, 259, 284.
Brittany, hunting rights in, 256.
Builders, 236.

Café au lait, 107.
Cafés instituted, 320, 321.
Canals, 236.
Caraccioli, Marquis D., 53, 120.
Carrabas, 191.
Carrosse, 204.
Carthusians, the, 75.
Cash, power of, 163.
Castropignano, Mme de, 28.
Cavagnole, La, explained, 19.
Chamousset, Mme de, 103.
Champlost, First Valet, 12.

INDEX

Chief Constable, 202.
Choiseul, Duc de, 73.
Christian VII. of Denmark, 4.
Church, the centre of village life, 281.
Classes of society, 187, 313, 322. *And see* "Clergy."
Clergy, Higher, 226 ff.; and army commissions, 303; Lower, general conditions of, 281, 282; duties of, 283.
Clermont, Count de, 46.
"Climbers" in society, 123, 152, 231.
Coaches, 204, 205.
Coinage, debased, 155.
Commendatory Abbots, 233.
Comus, the quack, 117.
Conversation, art of, 336 ff.
Cordon bleu, 54.
Courage, 304, 305.
Court, the, 1–47; festivals, 54; ball, 58; "the nation's grave," 57; comments on, by Voltaire, 65; rivalry at, 66; Piron's comments on, 66; and battle of Rosbach, 68, 69; under Louis XV., 70, 71; "the glass of fashion," 77, 85; gambling at, 86; seamy side of, 86 ff.; in seventeenth century, 97; amusements of, 112; and the Bar, 132; of the Palais, 139; and doctors, 176, 177; and the bishops, 230; and public opinion, 314.
Courtier, the "perfect," defined, 70; typical, 78; and financier, 152.
Croissy, M. de, 240.

Damiens, R. F., 10, 38, 39.
Darboulin, 11.
Dauphin, the, 20, 22, 23, 24, 176, 191.
Debts, amusing stories of, 60, 83, 236.

Diseases of eighteenth century, 177, 280.
Doctors of medicine, 172–184.
Dress, 112, 113; of magistrates, 140; of procureurs, 140; of *bourgeoisie*, 190.
Drunkenness, 76, 83, 198.
Dubarry, Mme, 81.
Du Cluzel, Intendant, 204.
Du Deffand, Mme, 14, 15.

Education, 158, 164, 188, 189, 221, 222, 283, 284.
Elisabeth, Mme, 20.
Espion anglais, 159.
Estates, 202, 246, 270.
Etiquette, 26 ff.; importance of, 43, 44, 45, 67, 68, 79, 124, 175; medical, 183; of the Salons, 332, 333.
Executions, public, 200.
Experience purchased for cash, 135.

Faculties of Medicine, 176.
Fairs, Paris, 114, 115; provincial, 218.
Family, respect due to, 222, 228.
Famine, 265, 280.
Farmers-General, 153, 154, 167, 168, 198.
Fashion, changes its quarters, 104; its effect on doctors, 173.
Fénelon, François de, 235.
Festivities, 191, 246.
Finance, success in, 157.
Financiers, the, 152–171; 203, 204.
Fireworks, 114, 141.
Fleury, Cardinal de, 6, 18.
Fontainebleau, 66.
Food, 110; in Paris, 105.
Fortunes, how amassed, 157; how repaired, 159 ff., 168 ff., 252.

INDEX

France, influenced by Paris, 95.
French, the, characteristics of, 89, 304, 305, 340, 342.
Frivolity, 68.
Fronsac, Duke de. *See* Richelieu, Duke de.
Frosts, great, 268.
Fruit-sellers, 194, 195.

Gabelle, 277–279.
Gallantry, defined, 340.
Gambling, 58, 60, 61, 68, 85, 86, 217, 251.
Game preserves, 257.
Garde des Seaux, 155.
Garus, elixir of, 183.
Gentleman, defined, 122.
Gentry, country, 242–264.
Geoffrin, Mme, 98, 322 ff.
Gesvres, Duke de, 43, 85.
Gisors, Count de, 91, 306.
Gluttony, 74, 75, 111.
"Good society," 325.
Governments, classes of, 203.
Governors, provincial, 202.
Grande Poste, 103.
Greffiers, 137.
Grippe, 177.

Harengères, 197, 319.
Helvétius, 158.
Henriette, Mme, 20.
Highway robbery, 204.
Hobereaux, 249, 250, 255.
Hospitals, 199, 200; military, 295, 296.
Households, constitution of, 56, 245.
Huissiers, 138.
Humour, instances of, 4 ff., 74, 247.
Hunting, 8, 39–41; Piron's comments on, 66; bishops, 237; rights, 256, 257.

Ignorance, prevailing, 71, 72.
Illiteracy, 283.

Industry, promotion of, 215.
Influenza, 177.
Inheritance, customs, 269.
Inoculation, 181, 182.
Intendants, 203, 205, 206, 243, 244, 270.
"Irreverence," 313.

Janson, Cardinal de, 230.
"Justice," 134, 135; and People's Rights, 149.

Kindliness, 340, 341.
King and Parliament, 147, 148.

Landowners, 242 ff.
Lavoisier, Antoine, 158.
Lawyers, the, 122–151; their quarters, 104, 105; their status in Paris, 185; become Intendants, 203, 204; and traders, 214.
Lenormand, M. de, the case of, 154.
Lettres de cachet, 144, 145, 146.
Liberty of the subject, 143–145.
Libraries, 139.
Literature, direct influence of, 328 ff.
Litigation, 133, 134, 251, 288–290.
Longchamps, 118, 119.
Louis XIII., nobility under, 51.
Louis XIV., 45; and the Treasury, 57; and Paris, 97; coronation of, 232.
Louis XV., characteristics of, 1 ff.; attempted assassination of, 10, 38, 39; courage of, 13; and the Treasury, 57; the Court under, 70 ff.; and gambling, 86; on the lawyers, 148; and military service, 298, 299; his wars, 307 ff.

Louis XVI., 24; and hunting, 39–41; his gluttony, 75; reinstates Parliaments, 150.
Louise, Mme (Mme Dernière), 18, 20, 21.
Louvre, the, 105.
Luxury, instances of, 58, 59; increase of, 185 ff., 235; effects of, 242.

Machault, J. B. de, 10.
Mackau, Mme de, 27.
Magistrates, 123 ff.
Mahon, siege of, 83.
Malesherbes, C. G. de L. de, 142 ff.
Manners, 331–342; good and bad compared, 74.
Manor, Lords of the, 260, 261, 262.
Manor-house, described, 247.
Manorial Courts, 281, 287.
Marie-Josèphe, dauphiness, 42.
Marie Leczinska, 13 ff., 28; her household, 37, 56, 111.
Marriages, "arranged," 62–64; of affection, 90; "into the Law," 123; in financial circles, 159 ff., 168 ff., 252; to avoid army service, 293.
Marseilles, 207, 239.
Masks, 112.
Massillon, J. B., 239–240.
"Maupeou Parliament" (1771), 150.
Maurepas, J. F. P., dismissed, 10, 11.
"May" Court, 139.
Meals, 106, 109, 110.
Middle class. See *Bourgeoisie*.
Militia, 291, 292.
Mirabeau, H. G. R., Count de, 145–147.
Mirabeau, V. R., Marquis de, 146.
Miromesnil, Hue de, 149.
Monday, holiday, 197.
Music, 19, 59, 66, 116, 161 ff.

"Nerves" cured, 174.
Newspapers, 317, 319.
Newsvendors, 319, 320.
Nobility, the, 48–94; removes to Faubourg Saint-Germain, 104; antipathy for the lawyers, 122 ff. ; second class, 150; contempt of the financiers, 155; marry into financial circles, 163; despise the *bourgeoisie*, 186; and traders, 215; and the Bishops, 226; impoverished, 248, 249, 257; and peasants' hostility, 256, 257; fine types of, 263, 264; and the army, 292; and feudal reaction, 302; and army commissions, 303; and the Salons, 322, 323.
Nouveau riche, the, characteristics of, 158.

Offices, sale of, 49, 56, 128, 131, 132, 156.
Omelette, the famous, 56.
Opera, 106; balls, 111.
Order of Malta, 49.
Outrequin, water-contractor, 116.

Palais Royal, 115, 139.
Paris, disliked by Louis XIV. and Louis XV., 24; under Louis XV., 95–121; literary taste in, 98; seamy side of, 99 ff.; fashion, 104; "life" of the city, 104, 105, 113 ff., bread supply, 107; the sights, 114, 115; watering, 116; praised by Caraccioli, 120; Voltaire's farewell to, 121; its *bourgeoisie*, 185 ff.; the populace, 193–200; water-supply, 194; "apes" the Court, 314; the heart of, 320; compared with Athens, 325.

INDEX 353

Parliaments, exiled, 68; rôle of, 147 ff.; "in ruins," 151.
Peasants, oppressed, 149; and the nobility, 256, 265 ff.; varying conditions of, 267, 268, 269; dwellings of, 274, 275, 276; ruined by the chase, 279; characteristics of, 285 ff.
Pedlars, 285.
Pensions, 57.
Perquisites claimed by nobles, 52, 53.
Persepolis (Paris), 153.
Petite poste, 103.
Philosophers, the, 237, 329, 330.
Piron, Alexis, 66.
Plague, at Marseilles, 207, 239.
"Plucking the bird," 132.
"Plucking the goose," 153.
Police, mounted, 204.
Politeness, 339, 340.
Politics, 338.
Pompadour, Mme de, 10 ff., 80, 145, 164, 165.
Pont-Neuf, 104, 193, 291, 319, 320.
Population of France, 97.
Potato, use of, 110, 111.
Precedence, in the Salons, 333.
Press, the. *See* Newspapers.
Prisoners, treatment of, 142 ff.
Procureurs, 137.
Property, rights of, 159; of peasants, 269.
Protestants, the, 150.
Provinces, nobles' distinction in, 49; life in the, 201–225; terror of the, 258.
Public opinion, 313–321; under Louis xv. and Louis xvi., 330.
Public spirit, the growth of, 270.
Puns, 73, 74.

Quacks, medical, 117, 217.
Quentin, the barber, 31.

Rameau, J. P., 165.
Rank, by "purchase," 49.
Rastignac, L. J. de C. de, 75.
Recruits, age of, 293.
Regent, the, 1, 69, 111, 112.
Régents, 283, 284.
Registrars, 137.
Regratiers, 198.
Remedies, medical, 177 ff.
Remonstrance, right of, 147, 148.
Revenue, raised by financiers, 155; diocesan, 226.
Revolution, approach of, 302, 338; influence of, on manners, 331.
Rhine floods, 206.
Richelieu, Duke de, 76 ff.; compared with Voltaire, 84.
Richelieu, Duke de, the younger, 80.
Ridicule, power of, 315.
Rights of the subject, 149.
Roads, dangers of, 204; repairs, 205, 236.
Rodet, Thérèse. *See* Geoffrin, Mme.
Rosbach, battle of, 68, 299, 301.
Rousseau, Jean Jacques, 163.
Royal Order of the Holy Ghost, the, 54 ff.
Rural exodus, the, 96 ff.

Salons, the, 322–330; influence upon manners, 332; how to enter, 334.
Salt tax, the, 168.
Samaritaine, La, 105.
Sanitation, 26, 206, 207.
Saxe, Marshal de, 15, 82.
Sedan-chairs, 99, 100.
Serfdom, 269, 270.
Seven Years War, the, 294.
Sisters of Charity, 199, 200, 264.
Sixième, Mme, death of, 18.
Smallpox, 16, 178, 180.

23

Smoke dues, 279.
Smugglers, 278.
Snuff, prohibited, 111.
Soldiers, billeting of, 295.
Songs, army, use of, 318.
Sophie, Mme, 18, 20.
Soubise, Prince de, 56, 68.
Squire, household of, 247, 248.
Statute labour, 295.
Street lighting, 103.
Street signs, 102.
Surgeons, their rivalry with physicians, 176.

Tabouret, 54.
Taille, 271 ff.
Taverns, superseded, 321.
Taxes, 149, 150, 153, 244, 253, 265, 271–273, 277–279.
Teinturiers, 46, 79.
Tenon, J. R., 199.
Terray, Abbé, Controller-General, 156, 157.
Theatre, the, 113, 140, 141, 165, 166, 189, 319.
Thémire. *See* Marie Leczinska.
Third Estate, defined, 224.
Titles, sale of, 159; for doctors, 176.
Tobacco, 111.
Toulon, Count de, 91.
Touraine, famine in, 265, 266.
Towns, provincial, 201, 206, 224, 245.

Trade, 194, 205, 224, 249.
Traffic in streets, 101.
Treasury, the, 52, 156.
Trudaine, D. C., 205.
Trudaine de Montigny, J. C. P., 205.
Turgot, Baron, 204, 270.

Vaucanson, J. de, 114.
Vaugirard, P. R. M., 197.
Ventadour, Mme de, 2, 52.
Verneuil, Mme de, 27 ff.
Versailles, Court at, 24 ff.; State ball described, 44; poverty at, 57, 58, 66, 68, 191, 314, 323.
Vicars-General, 231.
Victoire, Mme, 18.
Village life, 265–290.
Villeneuve, Mme de, 69, 70.
Villeroy, Marshal de, 2–3.
Vintimille, Mme de, 12.
Voltaire, compared with Richelieu, 83, 84.

Water-supply of Paris, 194.
Waxworks show, 117.
Wealth, power of, 163.
Wedding festivals, 161, 162.
"Whitings," 105.
Wigmakers, 194.
Wigs, 242.
Wolves, 257, 284, 285.
Women, contempt for, 276.